**Inside
a scie**   **years**

Inside Psychology: a science over 50 years

Edited by

Pat Rabbitt (Emeritus Professor, University of Manchester, UK)

Senior Research Associate, Department of Experimental Psychology, University of Oxford, UK
and
Senior Research Fellow, Department of Psychology, University of Western Australia, Perth, WA

OXFORD
UNIVERSITY PRESS

OXFORD
UNIVERSITY PRESS

Great Clarendon Street, Oxford OX2 6DP

Oxford University Press is a department of the University of Oxford.
It furthers the University's objective of excellence in research, scholarship,
and education by publishing worldwide in

Oxford New York

Auckland Cape Town Dar es Salaam Hong Kong Karachi
Kuala Lumpur Madrid Melbourne Mexico City Nairobi
New Delhi Shanghai Taipei Toronto

With offices in

Argentina Austria Brazil Chile Czech Republic France Greece
Guatemala Hungary Italy Japan Poland Portugal Singapore
South Korea Switzerland Thailand Turkey Ukraine Vietnam

Oxford is a registered trade mark of Oxford University Press
in the UK and in certain other countries

Published in the United States
by Oxford University Press Inc., New York

British Library Cataloguing in Publication Data

Data available

Library of Congress Cataloguing in Publication Data
Inside psychology : a science over 50 years / edited by Patrick Rabbitt.
   p. cm.
  ISBN 978–0–19–922876–8
  1. Psychology. I. Rabbitt, Patrick.
  BF121.I55 2008
  150.9′045—dc22

                                                                2008036479

Typeset by Cepha Imaging Private Ltd., Bangalore, India
Printed and bound in the
United Kingdom
by Biddles Ltd, King's Lynn, Norfolk.

ISBN 978–0–19–922876–8

10 9 8 7 6 5 4 3 2 1

To our friends and colleagues. Closely overlapping sets.

Contents

Contributors

Professor Alan Allport
Department of Experimental
Psychology,
University of Oxford,
Oxford, UK

Professor Alan Baddeley
Department of Psychology,
University of York,
York, UK

Professor Robert Boakes
School of Psychology,
University of Sydney,
Sydney, Australia

Professor Vicki Bruce
College of Humanities and Social
Science,
University of Edinburgh,
Edinburgh, UK

Professor Max Coltheart
Department of Psychology,
Division of Linguistics and
Psychology,
Macquarie University,
Sydney, Australia

Professor Fergus Craik
Rotman Research Institute,
Baycrest Centre for Geriatric Care,
University of Toronto,
Toronto, Canada

Professor Anne Cutler
Nijmegen Institute for Cognition
and Information,
Nijmegen, The Netherlands

Professor Michael Gazzaniga
Sage Center for the Study of Mind,
University of California,
Santa Barbara, California, USA

Professor Richard Gregory
Department of Experimental
Psychology,
University of Bristol,
Bristol, UK

Professor Miles Hewstone
Department of Experimental
Psychology,
University of Oxford,
Oxford, UK

Professor Glyn Humphreys
Birmingham University Imaging
Centre,
School of Psychology,
University of Birmingham,
Birmingham, UK

Professor Phil Johnson-Laird
Department of Psychology,
Princeton University,
Princeton, New Jersey, USA

Dr Donald Laming
Department of Experimental
Psychology,
University of Cambridge,
Cambridge, UK

Professor Andrew Mayes
School of Psychological Sciences,
University of Manchester,
Manchester, UK

Professor Michael Posner
Department of Psychology,
University of Oregon,
Eugene, Oregon, USA

Professor Pat Rabbitt
Department of Experimental
Psychology,
University of Oxford,
Oxford, UK
Department of Psychology,
University of Western Australia
Perth, Australia

Emeritus Professor Jim Reason
Department of Psychology,
University of Manchester,
Manchester, UK

Emeritus Professor John Ross
Department of Psychology,
University of Western Australia,
Crawley, Australia

Professor Andries Sanders
Den Haag, The Netherlands

Professor Wolfgang Stroebe
Department of Social and
Organizational Psychology,
Utrecht University,
Utrecht, The Netherlands

Professor John Wearden
Department of Psychology,
University of Keele,
Keele, UK

Professor Lawrence Weiskrantz
Department of Experimental
Psychology,
University of Oxford,
Oxford, UK

Professor Mark Williams
Department of Psychiatry,
University of Oxford, Warneford
Hospital,
Oxford, UK

Introduction

Pat Rabbitt

Historians of psychology seem infatuated by macho metaphors of 'revolution' or 'conquest' in which theories are 'overthrown' or 'destroyed'. Even more momentously, 'paradigms' can apparently undergo 'tectonic shifts'. The placid and witty accounts given by contributors to this book of their work in our science between 1950 and 2008 evoke more pleasant metaphors of evolution, assimilation, adaptation, and collegiality rather than conflict. After all, our subject is only a body of ideas that gifted individuals discuss in quiet and comfortable rooms, often with a good deal of laughter. An introduction to contributors' accounts can add little except brief historical notes to provide context, and even this is feasible only for the (to us!) alarmingly distant 1950s and 1960s, before our subject became the immense conglomeration of disparate bodies of information that it now is. We are all poignantly aware that our small stories, even when taken together, do not constitute a history of psychology in our time. We are few, and do not claim to be representative. If this attempt to redress this problem results in only an annotated list of distinguished names and achievements, with some contentious speculations about the influences that have driven progress in our field, it will at least acknowledge that there was a great deal going on and that our personal contributions were only a small part of it.

It is a defensible provocation to argue that by the late 1950s the navigational chart for Psychology in the remainder of the twentieth century had already been drawn up and that we lacked only the necessary methodologies to achieve foreseen destinations. S-R connectionism was still entrenched in undergraduate curricula, particularly in the USA, but it had begun to disappear from research agendas since McCulloch and Pitts (1943) began discussions of quite different ways in which information may be represented at the level of neurones. Just before the decade, Donald Hebb's (1949) *Organisation of Behaviour* opened lines of speculation about neural networks that still inspire twenty-first century connectionist models and, by its end, Hubel and Weisel (1959, 1962), guided by the obvious necessity to investigate coding of information in neurone networks, made surprising discoveries that altered theories of perception. Computational modelling that might also build upon

Hebb's speculations was further in the future. The possibility that cybernetic control theory might be used in descriptions of behaviour had been discussed by Hick and Bates (1949). Psychologists had seen the opportunities offered by Shannon (1948) and Shannon and Weaver's (1949) model for information theory that, for the first time, suggested ways to quantify levels of difficulties of choices and short-term memory load irrespective of the kinds of stimulus perceived and retained. These new ideas were eagerly exploited throughout the 1950s (Attneave 1954, 1955, 1959; Hake and Garner, 1951; Hake and Hyman 1953; Hick 1952; Hyman 1953; Miller 1958) and, in particular, at the first London symposium on information processing. Small computers to run conveniently the necessary experiments became available only twenty years later. The publication of Goldstein's *The Organism* (1939) had long ago set an agenda for lesion studies in clinical neuropsychology that was very rapidly extended in human clinical studies and in animal studies between 1950 and 1980. The long and radiant careers of Brenda Milner, colleague of Donald Hebb, and then of Hebb's student Doreen Kimura, of Larry Weiskrantz and his distinguished ex-students and colleagues Alan Cowey, David Gaffan, Charlie Gross, and many others, are markers of this progress. The further step, which brought about what some of our contributors term the 'biological revolution', awaited improvements in techniques of surgery and cell recording and, at length, methodologies allowing non-invasive neuroanatomy and real-time *in vivo* investigations by magnetic resonance imaging (MRI), function MRI, and transcranial magnetic stimulation (TMS). The main methodological problems of analysing longitudinal data had already been realized by 1960, but the bleak reality of their uncomfortable implications had tacitly to be ignored until statistical solutions became available forty years later. From this point of view, the right questions to ask are not how we got ourselves from the intellectual framework of the 1950s into that of first decade of the twenty-first century, but for what technological and methodological vehicles we had to queue, why some of our rides took so long to arrive, and what other forms of transportation we may have missed. The speculations of the 1950s got the broad directions right, but new technologies provided the surprises.

A sharp distinction between speculation and implementation over-emphasizes the separation between hypotheses and methodologies. For example, the development of information-processing technology altered our science in two distinct ways: it provided new frameworks, languages, and metaphors that helped us to reformulate hypotheses and so to frame questions that would not otherwise have occurred to us. During the 1950s, teachers of undergraduate courses made the point that, while the metaphors of telephone circuits and solenoid-driven switching devices such as 'relays' and 'uniselectors' were congenial to S-R connectionist models, novel insights from Turing machines, feedback loops, and amplification offered quite new possibilities for description of ways in which the brain might attend, select, process, and represent information. The new devices from which these metaphors were drawn also allowed us to explore and expand them by providing equipment to test them. A neglected aspect of this interdependency is that many of us regard experiments not so much as interrogations to winkle fragments of 'truth' from a sly and evasive universe but, rather, as an external chessboard needed to work through the implications of speculative moves when internal computation peters out. A new piece of equipment that allows a novel experimental manipulation also implicitly suggests, for the first time, fresh and profitable suppositions: 'What if we asked people to do this instead of that ... and if they do that instead of this, what would this tell us about the ways their brains must work?'. Some questions occur only when the means to ask them become available.

It is a comfortable fantasy that science exists in an abstract Platonic space, in a parallel and separate universe uncorrupted by the vicious muddle and turbulence of world events. During the second half of the nineteenth century, psychology, like all sciences, was transformed by the sociocultural and economic precursors, demands, and consequences of World War II. During the nineteenth century, German psychology had been pre-eminent, capitalizing on the rich legacies of Helmholtz and Wundt, and German Universities were training schools for leaders of US psychology such as James McKean Cattell, Titchener, and Edwin Boring. These remarkable scientists returned to set up departments in the great American universities to which brilliant young German scholars were, in their turn, glad to emigrate. The flow of talent from Germany to the USA became a flood during the 1930s when a Nazi-driven academic Diaspora depleted German departments of psychology, leaving behind figures such as Jaensch who could combine an intelligent preoccupation with eidetic imagery with an expedient interest in cognitive and behavioural differences between north European and Mediterranean chickens. During the 1950s academic psychology in Germany was moribund and the post-war travail of the restructuring of the German economy and the rigidities of the German academic system delayed its gradual return to its current distinction. In France, psychology, like all academic disciplines, had been impoverished by the war and occupation. A strong tradition in clinical neuropsychology was maintained by individuals such as Hecaen, and consolidated by funding from the Centre National de la Recherche Scientifique (CRNS). Human experimental psychology was much less strong, although outstanding individuals such as Michotte and Fraisse earned international reputations. The number of distinguished younger scientists was increased with the establishment of a CRNS research centre in Marseilles. Although Piaget was Swiss, his massive influence may also be annexed to the French academic tradition. In Italy, human experimental psychology, and later cognitive psychology, were weakened by the war, and for much longer by the traditions of departments combining Psychology with Philosophy and also with Education. However, Italian neuropsychology was, and is, outstanding, and gifted practitioners such as Carlo Umilta and Cornoldi, and their many students, have developed links between cognitive psychology and neuropsychology.

The comparatively sluggish development of human experimental psychology and, later, of cognitive psychology in Germany, Italy, and France contrasts with a much more vigorous growth in Britain and North America, the (then) USSR, Holland, and Belgium. At first sight the strength of the Russian tradition seems anomalous as the USSR had suffered an academic depletion, through war and political purges, cumulatively even greater than in Germany. The harsh post-war economic and social climate of the then USSR is also notorious. But there were also robust foundations on which to build. The most widely recognized is the work of I. P. Pavlov, which had the advantages of scientific rigour and wide recognition by behaviourists abroad and also domestic acceptability by a political establishment committed to the dogma that all behaviour, and most especially human behaviour, can be controlled by appropriate techniques—and so perfected in terms of the Marxist–Leninist ideal—also to the bias of an academic establishment that valued both physiology and education. The Western recognition of Pavlovian conceptualizations was advanced in the West by Jeffrey Gray's translations and exegeses of his and that of his successors (e.g. Gray and Eysenck 1964). In contrast, while another brilliantly creative Russian intellect, Vygotsky, became a strong influence on Western developmental and educational psychologists, he was much less appealing to his political masters. Russian neuropsychology was widely read and became influential in the West, largely because of the scientific and literary talents of Luria who, with his colleagues, published widely in Western journals (e.g. Luria and Tsvetkova 1964; Luria and Vinogradova 1959; Luria et al. 1966) and with Western collaborators (e.g. Luria et al. 1964). Besides the originality of Luria's translated academic books (e.g. Luria 1961), he also wrote more accessible works for a Western readership (e.g. Luria and Yudovitch 1971) and his *The Mind of a Mnemonist* (Luria 1968) almost anticipated the current popular acclaim of Oliver Sach's 'The man who mistook his wife for a hat'. The recognition of Russian psychology in the West was promoted by the work of distinguished enthusiasts who also happened to be Russian linguists: Neil O'Connor, who commissioned reviews of the Soviet literature' (e.g. O'Connor 1961) and Jeffrey Gray who, besides his own reviews and commentaries on Russian work, and his incorporation of this literature in his personal research output, for many years edited a journal of translations of selected papers from Russian journals 'Soviet Psychology' published by Pergamon Press. These papers, largely reproduced from 'Voprosi Psikhologii' ('Problems of Psychology') offered a strange and cautionary insight for Western academics into the realities of state control of scientific discourse— and how these could be circumvented. Each article began with a dense and ingeniously argued preamble, illustrated by lengthy, and usually embarrassingly irrelevant quotations, purporting to show how the issues that the authors were about to raise were not only completely consistent with, but were actually inspired by, the principles of Marxist Leninism. This ritual obeisance was abruptly followed by descriptions of work of striking cleverness and originality, often developing the new cybernetic models much further than was then usual in Western journals.

Reviews and translations brought to Western notice the work of figures such as A. N. Leontiev, who was a frequent attendant at meetings in Western Europe and contributed to O'Connor's (1961) compilation of reviews, *Recent Soviet Psychology*. A translation of selected papers by N. I. Bernstein on applications of cybernetic control theory to motor skills, published by Pergamon Press, also became widely influential.

Once translated, the work of these Russian scientists was immediately understood by psychologists in Britain and the USA because they shared the experience of applying their science to military problems during World War II—an activity then loosely classified as 'ergonomics' and later as 'human factors research'. For example, N. I. Bernstein had spent the war advising on the design of footbridges and prosthetic limbs. Unfortunately, the administrations of Kruschev and Breznev intensified the Cold War and curtailed contacts with these and other talented colleagues.

I believe that the ways in which applications of psychology during World War II altered and enriched our subject, both intellectually and financially, have not been stressed sufficiently. Involvement in the war effort benefited psychologists, and thereby psychology, in three different ways. First, we were obliged to find something useful to say about how people actually cope with very complex scenarios and systems, about how to improve selection and training of personnel, and about how to optimize the design of systems and equipment so that they could be used to the best advantage. These new demands stretched imaginations beyond the small scope of the experimental paradigms invented to illustrate and test impoverished models of human performance. A corollary was that research had to be empirical (see Donald Broadbent's 1973 *In Defence of Empirical Psychology*). Success was defined as discovering how to make practical improvements that others, besides the experimenters, could recognize. This resulted in new ways of interpreting the bases of performance, notably visual perception, as evidenced by James Gibson's conceptual use of the devices he tested to improve landing on awkward airstrips (Gibson 1966) and Adelbert Ames' arguments for perception as a process of 'transactions' between the observer and the environment (Ames 1949; Cantril *et al.* 1949). An even more important benefit was that applied research forced collaborations with engineers, physicists, mathematicians, and physiologists. One consequence of this was that the psychologists were obliged to assimilate the theories and applications of cybernetic and information processing that guided their post-war thinking about their own subject. A second was that, during these forced collaborations, psychologists gained respect from engineers and workers in more established sciences and countered the widespread prejudice that psychology is a 'pseudo-science', by achieving conspicuously useful practical results. From increasing recognition grew tolerance and the crucial benefit of access to decision-making bodies and so to funding.

This wartime involvement in applied science and in the wider scientific community provided common ground for psychologists in America, Canada, Britain, and Australia. In Australia, the work of applied psychologists such as Ron Cumming on aircraft landing gained more than local reputation. American involvement in military applied psychology launched the distinguished careers of 'Tex' Garner, Howard Egan, John Webster, Chas Baker, Pierce, Karling and, perhaps pre-eminently, Paul Fitts. In Britain, Sir Frederick Bartlett's success in directing applied work during both World Wars I and II allowed him to assemble and deploy extraordinarily talented people, notably Derek Russell Davis, G. C. Grindley, William Hick, Norman Mackworth (who came from, and eventually returned to, Canada), and, most famously, Kenneth Craik, whose monograph *The Nature of Explanation* both captured and anticipated the development of 'black box' engineering, cybernetic and information-processing models. The quality of the work of these individuals encouraged considerable public investments. In Britain, this included the financing of Sir Frederick Bartlett's Applied Psychology Research Unit (APRU), through the Medical Research Council (MRC), initially under the directorship of Kenneth Craik and, after his premature death, by Norman Mackworth and then Donald Broadbent, as well as the inclusion of active groups of psychologists attached to aviation medicine at Farnborough and the National Physical Laboratory. In America, there was government investment in large research groups with a predominantly applied agenda, perhaps most strikingly in Paul Fitt's group in Ann Arbor, Michigan. In the USA, in contrast to the UK, business investment also became important. The distinguished history of relatively unfettered 'blue sky' research in Bell Laboratories in auditory and vision sciences (for instance the career of Bela Julesz) and in perception and immediate memory (George Sperling, Averbach, and, in the late 1960s, Saul Sternberg) is a central theme in histories of this period. The emergence of large, independent, private, applied research consultancies, such as Bolt Beranek and Newman (Dick Pew, Ray Nickerson), which were partly supported by public funding agencies for which they successfully wrote proposals, is also a phenomenon of the time. Generous and prolonged funding for work that sometimes stretched putative 'applications' to the borders of fantasy from the US Defense Advanced Research Projects Agency (DARPA), and from the US Office of Naval Research, supported both private and academic research not only in the USA but also in the UK and Canada, as did, from the 1960s through the 1970s, funding fallout from NASA's first panicky dash in the 'space race'. In Canada, the Defence Research Agency, based in Toronto, played a similar role to the MRC's Applied Psychology Unit (APU) in Britain, juggling the demands for applied solutions from the military and for theoretical advances from academic colleagues.

Younger colleagues who have frisked throughout their working lives in the lush pastures of public funding and in large and prosperous departments cannot easily comprehend the micro-economics of psychology before the 1950s. For example, in Cambridge and in the University of Western Australia, the departmental accounts still displayed in cabinets of memorabilia show annual totals of less than £200. In other departments budgets were even more meagre. The Cambridge Department bought its first electrically driven adding machine in 1958 and its first 'Dekatron' centi-second timer in 1959 (although the traditional 'Hipp Chronoscope' had tarnished for years in a display cupboard). Competition for both machines was fierce. In the UK, from the 1950s through the 1970s, university departments housed talented and influential individuals, but were tiny by US standards, with between six and eight tenured staff. These individuals were, by necessity of undergraduate teaching, experts in quite different parts of the syllabus, so that collegiate respect usually failed to spark into research synergy. A footnote on that time is the surprising rarity of active collaboration between members of different departments, even those that might be less than a hundred miles apart. The change in the current ethos is certainly due to the much greater size of departments but also, we may speculate, a direct benefit of otherwise accursed e-mail.

Dearth of funding also meant that the age distribution in departments was positively skewed because, except in the largest departments, there were seldom more than one or two postdoctoral researchers and research students enrolled in any given year. In many years, many departments enrolled none.

This shaped the social environment in uncomfortable ways. In all but a few prestigious departments visitors from abroad were also rare. Career opportunities were proportionately limited and most university lecturers could not expect geographical or professional mobility, and expected to retire in the departments in which they had begun their careers. Promotions to senior lectureships and readerships were slow and infrequent and, until the 1970s, nearly all departments had only a single professor. Election to a chair meant a perpetual stint as department head. The numbing weight of this administrative burden is revealed by chronology of individuals' research output against their trajectories of academic advancement.

Compared with the USA, Britain had few 'stand alone' research centres. In the University of London Institute of Psychiatry, the Department of Psychology, a distinguished graduate school, mounted a vigorous challenge to psychotherapy and began the first attempt to relate individual differences in introversion and extraversion and neuroticism to differences in physiology and to human performance. However, these forays stemmed from the genius, energy and scary self-confidence of a single individual, Hans Eysenck, whose interests turned to ingenious polemics against assumptions of risk from smoking and proposals that reaction times might be the 'biological basis of intelligence'. As his age and public visibility increased, his mainstream academic influence waned. Public funding was linked to assumptions of useful applications, and channelled mainly through the MRC. Peter Warr's occupational psychology unit in Sheffield prospered, but age research units in Liverpool and Bristol did not. The MRC developmental psychology unit in London, first directed by Neil O'Connor and then by John Morton, exercised an influence disproportionate to its size. From the 1950s through the 1990s, the MRC APU in Cambridge was certainly the most influential single institution in British psychology. This was due partly to the personal distinction of the first four directors: very briefly Kenneth Craik, followed by Norman Mackworth, Donald Broadbent, and Alan Baddeley. From 1958 through 1996, the latter two were uniquely influential through their personal research, but also as advisers on appointments to many, if not most, of the chairs that became available in Britain as national prosperity and government support for academia grew through the 1960s and 1970s. Baddeley's vision expanded not only the APU but also, by example, the horizons of ambition of some university departments by using the marked increases in funding available from 1972 through 1996 gradually to liberate the APU from its total commitment to military applications, post office research, road traffic research, and research on human factors in IT to basic research in memory and attention, on language, neuropsychology and Alzheimer's disease, and clinical psychology. Another, less top-driven, influence of the APU on British psychology was a result of the economics of a large research unit that dictate that, although only the most talented young staff available should be recruited, necessary restrictions to growth mean that even these must expect to leave on expiry of brief contracts. This made the APRU/APU a national launching pad for distinguished careers in research and in the leadership of departments such as those of Alan Baddeley himself, who went first to Sussex and then to Stirling before returning as director; Vicky Bruce, professor and vice-chancellor at Stirling and now at Edinburgh; Martin Conway at Bristol and now Leeds; Derek Corcoran to chairs in Halifax Nova Scotia and then Glasgow; Bob Hockey to Hull and then Leeds; Phil Johnson-Laird to Princeton; Tony Sanford at Glasgow; and Andy Smith to Cardiff. The APU also enriched British psychology through the fleeting but vivid passage of very many distinguished visitors from the USA, who could there find both sabbatical sanctuary and stimulation during which their visits also enlivened most university departments in the UK. These are too many to begin to record but, to the generous acknowledgements of the influence of the APU on their personal careers made by Andries Sanders and Paul Bertelson, it should be added that the benefits were, to say the very least, bilateral. Sanders' career, in particular, illustrates the strong link between applied research and the general health of the subject in a Dutch context. The long successes of the Institute for Perception in Soesterburg and also of its sister Institute in Eindhoven, producing both useful solutions to real-life problems and important theoretical advances, exemplify this. Among Sanders' many contributions was the initiation in 1966 of the very long series of 'Attention and Performance' conferences, and their published proceedings, which have tracked the progress of human experimental psychology, cognitive psychology, and, more recently, cognitive neuropsychology in Europe and North America throughout our working lifetimes.

The mutual dependencies between psychology and neuroscience during this period are too extensive and obvious to cover here, but our contributors allow an interestingly oblique perspective on them through the unexpected influence of philosophy (a respectable discipline that I may seem to have slighted by emphasis on applied rather than theoretical research and by stress on the negative influence of Russian Marxist Leninism). Max Coltheart recalls his enjoyment of, and debt to, John Anderson, David Armstrong, John Mackie, and Alan Stout in Sydney. Richard Gregory regrets arriving too late at Cambridge to encounter Wittgenstein and records his debts to C. D. Broad, R. Braithwaite, and John Wisdom. Alan Allport also recalls the pleasure of Cambridge lectures by John Wisdom, the looming presence of Gilbert Ryle at Psychology Society seminars, and of Karl Popper's and Stephen Toulmin's commentaries on the nature of scientific endeavour—as do many of his colleagues, including myself. Whether these were only optional, extracurricular entertainments or shaped our approach to psychology is an interesting question that I cannot decide. Decades of editorials to the journal *Perception* leave no doubt of Richard Gregory's answer. The traditional common ground between philosophy and psychology has been perception, particularly visual perception, but, as Mary Warnock's monograph illustrates, increasingly also memory and, as shelves of books by Pinker and others demonstrate, language. During our lifetimes the territory shared with philosophy has been expanded in to the area of consciousness by explorations of the effects of lesions in human patients leading to discoveries such as Larry Weiskrantz's demonstration of discrimination without conscious awareness ('blindsight') and by Mike Gazzaniga's long exploration of the shared and separate consciousnesses of the two hemispheres. With accelerating development of non-invasive real-time brain imagery it is, almost weekly, becoming more clear that the relatively early completion of the decisions that we make, and the tardiness of our subsequent awareness of what we have decided to do, now offers a rich return of fruitful questions to philosophers in exchange for the inspiration and entertainment that they have afforded so many of us.

References

Ames, A. (1949). Psychology and scientific research. I. The nature of scientific enquiry. *Science* Nov: 461–4.

Attneave, F. (1954). Some informational aspects of visual perception. *Psychological Review* 61: 183–93.

Attneave, F. (1955). Symmetry, information and memory for patterns. *American Journal of Psychology* 68: 209–22.

Attneave, F. (1959). *Applications of information theory to psychology: a summary of basic concepts, methods and results*. New York: Holt.

Broadbent, D. E. (1973). *In defence of empirical psychology*. London: Methuen.

Cantril, H., Ames A., and Hastorf, A. H. (1949). Psychology and scientific research. The transactional view in psychology. *Science* Nov: 517–22.

Gibson, J. J. (1966). *The senses considered as perceptual systems*. New York: Houghton Mifflin.

Goldstein, K. (1939). *The organism: a holistic approach to biology derived from pathological data in man*. New York: American Books.

Gray, J. A. and Eysenck, H. J. (1964). *Pavlov's typology: recent theoretical and experimental developments from the laboratory of B. M. Teplov*. New York: Franklin Books.

Hake, H. W. and Garner, W. A. (1951). The amount of information in absolute judgements. *Psychological Review* 58(6): 446–459.

Hake, H. W. and Hyman, R. (1953). Perception of the statistical structure of a random series of binary symbols. *Journal of Experimental Psychology* 45: 64–74.

Hebb, D. (1949). *The organisation of behaviour: a neuropsychological theory*. New York: John Wiley.

Hick, W. E. and Bates, J. A. V. (1949). *The human operator of control mechanisms*. Inter-departmental Technical Committee on Servo-Mechanisms, Great Britain, Shell Mex House.

Hick, W. E. (1952). On the rate of gain of information. *Quarterly Journal of Experimental Psychology* 4: 11–26.

Hubel, D. H. and Wiesel, T. N. (1959). Receptive fields of single neurones in the cat's striate cortex. *Journal of Physiology* 148: 574–91.

Hubel, D. H. & Wiesel, T. N. (1962). Receptive fields, binocular interaction and functional architecture in the cat's visual cortex. *Journal of Physiology* 160: 106–54.

Hyman, R. (1953). Stimulus information as a determinant of reaction time. *Journal of Experimental Psychology* 45: 188–96.

Jeffress, L. A. (ed.) (1951). *Cerebral mechanisms in behavior: The Hixon Symposium*. New York: Wiley.

Luria, A. R. (1961).The role of speech in the regulation of normal and abnormal behaviour. Oxford: Pergamon Press.

Luria, A. R. (1968). *The mind of a mnemonist* (trans. L. Solotaroff). Cambridge, MA: Harvard University Press.

Luria, A. R. and Tsvetkova, L. S. (1964). The programming of constructive activity in local brain injuries. *Neuropsychologia* 2: 95–108.

Luria, A. R. and Vinogradova, O. S. (1959). An objective investigation of the dynamics of semantic systems. *British Journal of Psychology* 50: 89–105.

Luria, A. R. and Yudovitch, F. (1971). *Speech and the development of mental processes in the child*. Harmondsworth: Penguin.

Luria, A. R., Pribram, K. H., and Homskaya, E. D. (1964). An experimental analysis of the behavioural disturbance produced by a left-frontal arachnoid endothelioma (meningioma) *Neuropsychologia* 2: 257–80.

Luria, A. R., Karpov, B. A., and Yarbuss, A. L. (1966). Disturbances of active visual perception with lesions of the frontal lobes. *Cortex* 2: 202–12.

McCulloch, W. S. and Pitts, W. (1943). A logical calculus of the ideas immanent in nervous activity. *Mathematical Biophysics* 5: 115–33.

Miller, G. A. (1958). Free-recall of redundant strings of letters. *Journal of Experimental Psychology* 56: 485–91.

O'Connor, N. (1961). *Recent soviet psychology*. Oxford: Pergamon Press.

Shannon, C. E. (1948). A mathematical theory of communication. *Bell System Technical Journal* 27, 379–423, 623–656.

Shannon, C. E. and Weaver, W. (1949). *The mathematical theory of communication*. Urbana, IL: University of Illinois Press.

1

The ups and downs of cognitive psychology: attention and other 'executive functions'

Alan Allport

A few books I read as a student shaped my youthful idea of what a new experimental science of mind might—or ought—to be like. Arthur Koestler's *The Sleepwalkers*, about Tycho Brahe and Keppler, offered a delightful image of obsessive amateurs, groping their way into inventing a science of the solar system. Could psychology ever be like that? A new Copernican revolution, sweeping away not the old Ptolomeic epicycles, but the old folk-psychology conceptions such as perception, memory, will, consciousness, self—and transforming them into radically new ways of understanding mind? The thought was dizzying! In 1959 even to have a second-row seat in the gallery while such a conceptual revolution was going on seemed an exciting prospect. Was it possible? Ross Ashby's *Cybernetics* (1956), and that extraordinary symposium published in cardboard covers, *Mechanisation of Thought Processes* (National Physical Laboratory 1959), suggested that it was. In contrast, the experimental psychology that I was mostly supposed to study as an undergraduate (Woodworth and Schlosberg 1954) seemed a bizarre, atheoretical, and almost totally shapeless subject, an arbitrary collection of behavioural phenomena tagged to experimental paradigms: serial position curves and rate-of-decay of spiral after-effects. It was a big disappointment. I almost gave up and went back to South America.

I'll explain. Before going to university (in 1958) I had done my two years of National Service, ending up in Guyana ('*British* Guiana', in those days). My conscript sentence over, I stayed on for a six-month walkabout through northern Amazonia (Venezuela, Brazil, finally Peru), travelling with Akawaio Indians, hunting, fishing, living with them in the bush. I climbed Mount Roraima, contracted malaria, got comprehensively lost in the Pakaraima highlands. Eventually I re-emerged, got to hospital, recovered, and found myself with a life-long passion for biodiversity. I wanted to be a biologist. But arriving at Oxford with a scholarship to read modern languages did not make it easy. My profoundly traditional school had encouraged me to drop science at the age of 13. A transfer to biology without chemistry or mathematics? No chance! Philosophy and Psychology ('PPP'), on the other hand, had no apparent academic prerequisites whatever. So I slipped in. (Jeffrey Gray had found his way into psychology by the identical route, a couple of years earlier.)

Regretfully, after graduation, I still couldn't figure out how to finance a life as a nineteenth century-style naturalist in Amazonia. Instead, not knowing what else to do, I took a job as a 'probationer' clinical psychologist, at £512 per annum. I was given singularly little to do aside from administering occasional IQ tests, so I started doing experiments. It was fun. *Surprising* fun! Perhaps experimental psychology was what I should do, after all, rather than studying orchids or orthoptera.

I embarked on a PhD at Cambridge, with Richard Gregory as my supervisor, which in practice meant a free rein to do whatever I liked. I spent a few weeks wandering around the science area wearing a crash helmet with a steel rod bolted across the top, and a set of sliding mirrors that could give me an effective 2-, 4-, or 6-foot spacing between the eyes. (That felt the sort of thing to be doing in a lab run by Richard. The idea was to study Ivo Kohler-style visuomotor adaptations.) But after trying out my apparatus on a bike, with seriously injurious results, I decided a shift of research track might lead to a longer-lived career.

I had just discovered Karl Popper's *Logic of Scientific Discovery* (1959). It was a revelation. I decided that, for me, the primary goal of research should be to do my damnedest to *falsify* theories (other people's theories, mostly, but my own too, just as enthusiastically—if I ever had any). For this purpose, the broader the scope of the theory the better. The *ideal*, if it could be achieved, would be to group possible theories of a given domain into two (or more) broad categories, and then to find a way to falsify—experimentally to rule out—one whole category. Donald Broadbent wrote a paper to this effect. I was impressed. At this ideal, or idealized, level, the falsificationist strategy becomes a kind of experimental *conceptual surgery* ('natural philosophy' in its truest form), which I continue to find hugely attractive.

Obviously, there are at least two major difficulties before the conceptual surgeon can bring her scalpel effectively to bear. First of all, the question (or theoretical dichotomy) has to be well posed. Supposing it is *not* (as in questions like: 'Is attentional selection early or late?' aka 'Where is the attentional bottleneck?'),[1] then the attempts to falsify one or other alternative are

---

[1] Just for the record, there are several reasons why the 'early/late selection' question was ill posed: (As posed by Donald Broadbent, for whom 'early selection' *meant*, i.e., logically

doomed to go round and round without ever reaching closure (see Allport 1993). Usually the problem lies in the *underlying* assumptions—the sort that may not even be recognized as such, hence seldom, if ever, seriously questioned. A typical example, related to the above, is the idea that 'attention' is (must be?) the name of an identifiable subset of causal, neurocognitive control operations ('shift', 'select', 'disengage', etc.) If so, it could make sense to try to localize these control functions in the brain (as in so many recent publications in *Nature: Neuroscience*). But what if 'attention' is properly an outcome state—a resultant—rather than a causal process, as first mooted by William James (1890), and by Johnston and Dark (1986) a century later? What if, for example, the reaction-time costs attributed to these supposed control operations ('disengage', etc., etc.) are simply indicators of conflict anywhere in the system? In that case, what one is localizing (e.g. on the basis of increased parietal or frontal activations following an 'invalid' spatial pre-cue, etc.) might be simply the sites of maximum (here, spatial) conflict. Nothing more. It is clearly these 'bedrock' assumptions that the conceptual surgeon needs to examine first of all.

The second major difficulty for the would-be falsificationist is one that is common to experimentalists in practically every field, at least in the non-standard or exploratory phases of research. It is how to invent or design an experimental procedure that can do the job. All too often, alas, experimental invention is just not up to it. In other cases, however, it is because the theory is so ambiguously specified as to be genuinely unfalsifiable. An example, in my opinion, is Alan Baddeley's 'central executive', aka Norman and Shallice's 'supervisory attentional system', aka 'the Will', which is supposedly called in, like some obliging Auntie, whenever the children (i.e. the lower-level systems) are engaged in 'non-routine' (or 'dangerous') activities. Given that we are told essentially nothing about what Auntie actually does, still less how she does it,

---

entailed, 'no semantic processing of 'unattended' stimuli') the 'early/late' dichotomy rested on the underlying assumption that so-called 'physical' stimulus attributes—including location—were necessarily analysed *prior to* any 'semantic' attributes. On the contrary, if, for example, there are parallel streams of 'what' and 'where' processing (or anything like it), that assumption falls, and the dichotomy with it. More fundamentally, the dichotomy rested on the assumption that there is some discrete operation, *'selection'*, that occurs once only at a specific stage or level of processing. This assumption, in turn, rests on the idea that 'selection' occurs (obligatorily) because of the need to avoid, or protect, a postulated 'processing bottleneck', the 'limited-capacity central channel'. On the contrary, if all we are talking about (re 'selection') is *any* sort of selective modulation or biasing (enhancement, attenuation, etc.) it seems obvious that such modulation can (and *does*) operate at every possible processing level. Indeed, isn't that what 'processing' *is*?

nor any other of her properties besides 'limited capacity', I am led to infer that claims to her existence, like that of fairies, do not belong at the present time within the domain of science.

But I digress. (Glimpse a passing hobby-horse and hitch a ride. As Ogden Nash said, '*Shake and shake the ketchup bottle: first none will come and then a lot'll.*')

I did my PhD work on John Stroud's (1955) theory of the discrete 'psychological moment', essentially the hypothesis that psychological time is discontinuous. And I was lucky. Besides a series of largely descriptive experiments, I stumbled on a method that provided essentially a disproof of the hypothesis (Allport 1968). Since then, so far as I know, the theory has not mounted a come-back.

I thought I had a post-doc job in Edinburgh from September 1965, to work on schizophrenia, but at the last minute the funding fell through. I had just got married to my beautiful Virginia, and suddenly had no job and no prospects. I hurriedly scanned the job adverts in the Edinburgh municipal library, and spotted one for an assistant lecturer in psychology, in Aberdeen. Again, I was lucky. Aberdeen is a wonderful place to live if you enjoy the grey North Sea and the wild, sea-bird-haunted cliffs, crocuses in May, and skiing on wet porridge in the Cairngorms. I was assigned to lecture on developmental psychology, which surprised me as I knew nothing about the subject. But I was happy to learn—I did so mostly a day or so ahead of my students.

By some quirk of economics the University had one or two 'professorial' houses to rent at that time, but no professorial takers for them; so we became the occupants of a draughty eighteenth century mansion, Tillydrone House, right opposite St Machar's Cathedral, complete with a moat and four-acre garden. The rent was £4 a month.

The Aberdeen department (then) was not particularly encouraging of research, but I managed to acquire a three-field tachistoscope and started a series of experiments, inspired by George Sperling's (1963) masking paradigm. There was not the slightest pressure to publish, so I didn't, aside from a couple of short reports. (Several of those experiments, I confess, remain unpublished to this day.) Mowing the grass on our four-acre estate, watching the sea-birds, playing with our first child, and skiing the Devil's Elbow took up too much of my time. We had four extraordinarily happy (and unstressed) years there. But by then it seemed time to move, and I found a job at Reading University with some stimulating company: Leslie Henderson, Max Coltheart, Lizanne Bainbridge, and over the years a series of marvellous students, who quickly became colleagues, such as Derek Besner, Ruth Campbell, and Elaine Funnell. Under their stimulus, and some years past my thirtieth birthday, I began to be almost hopeful about psychology.

I had ten pleasant years in Reading, before moving to Oxford in 1979—a rash move in several respects. Pat Rabbitt left more or less the moment I got there, and Jerry Bruner had departed in clouds of smoke just before: there was still smoke everywhere. I found myself the sole lecturer in the department teaching the experimental psychology of cognition—language, memory, skill, attention, word recognition, AI, etc.—constituting four full undergraduate courses. It was hard going, and remained so for several years. On the other hand, of all the cities I know well, Oxford is for me the most liveable, the quirkiest, the richest in strange and unexpected talents. I have spent more than thirty years of my life there and would not now wish to live anywhere else.[2] As well as many, rewardingly challenging, Oxford undergraduates (Felix Wichmann, now a Professor in Berlin, perhaps the cleverest of the lot), I had some wonderful graduate students from whom I learnt immeasurably, many of them much abler and more professional than me: people like Liz Styles, Shulan Hsieh, Ian Dennis, Jon Driver, Steve Tipper, Geoff Ward, Renata Meuter, and Glenn Wylie. I am grateful to them all.

But back to Reading, 1970. Pursuing my Popperian agenda I recruited a couple of bright undergraduates, Barbara Antonis and Pat Reynolds, to run the experiments we subsequently published together as a 'disproof of the single channel hypothesis' (Allport *et al.* 1972). What (if anything) did it '*disprove*'? (There's a lesson here, somewhere.) The core idea of Broadbent's famous (1958, 1971) model was that, in the sensory control of action, and as regards *all* access to long-term memory, the brain constituted a unitary processing channel, *defined by* its limited informational capacity, i.e. in terms of 'bits per second'. The postulated capacity limit was, explicitly, independent of the type, modality, or 'content' of the information involved—visual, auditory, linguistic, spatial … what you will. In other words, the single (or 'central') channel was a 'general purpose' processor, with unmistakeable resemblance to the Von Neumann architecture of the general-purpose digital computer. (Why anyone might suppose such a thing perplexed me even then, given what classical neurology had long since discovered about the degree of specialization for different high-level cognitive processes in different cerebral areas.)

---

[2] I even have a ten-acre jungle—the 'Trap Grounds'—on my North Oxford doorstep, complete with dragonfly pool, glow-worms, and reed-warblers, over which we fought a four-year legal battle all the way to the House of Lords to save it from the 'developers'. I can now half-assuage my distant longings for Amazonia by stalking the mini-beasts there with a macro lens.

The canonical evidence put forward in support of Broadbent's hypothesis was the (apparent) inability of subjects to follow (to remember or respond to) more than one verbal message at a time, as first reported by Cherry (1953). Because the information rate of speech is so high, the argument went, letting in more than one speech stream would seriously overload the informational capacity of the central channel; hence all but one input stream must be 'filtered out' at an earlier stage. But (I wondered) what if, while 'shadowing' one speech stream, you tried to follow a second high-bit input in a *different* processing domain—pictorial, musical, etc.? The answer we reported was simple: even after minimal practice people could carry out both tasks concurrently with almost no loss of information transmission in either task. Broadbent's response to this was completely disarming. Rather than fully loading the 'central channel', as previously supposed, he now suggested that speech shadowing actually bypassed it altogether, via its own domain-specific pathway. Experimental falsification is clearly not a one-stop shop. One 'non-central' pathway down, how many more to go?

Meanwhile, the explanation for Cherry's 'dichotic listening' limitation presumably had to be sought somewhere *other than* the supposed capacity limit of a 'single channel', such as in the eminently special-purpose constraints of sentence processing? (There *is* a lesson here.)

In that case (you may well ask) why is attention—or awareness—so narrowly focused, so *selective*? (What *is* 'selective attention', anyway, and what purpose does it serve?) It's all very well rejecting one type of model: give us a better one!

Fair enough. Here are a few ideas that I and others have explored. I like to think of them as preliminary steps toward a 'theory of consciousness'. (But they can be sketched here only briefly; for more argument and experimental evidence—still very incomplete—see Allport 1987, 1989.)

 (i) Consciousness is inseparable from 'very short-term memory', that is, from cognitive states that *persist* (at least for some hundreds of milliseconds), which in turn is a precondition for longer-lasting memory encoding.

 (ii) Only *coherent* cognitive states can persist. Non-coherent (e.g. mutually incompatible or conflicting) states are intrinsically unstable and are swiftly modified or suppressed. (This is a basic property of brain function; see 'parallel distributed processing', below.)

(iii) Which cognitive states dominate at any moment—hence can persist, hence enter awareness—is of course the central *explanandum* of psychology as the 'science of mental life'. Innumerable different factors can contribute to this cognitive 'control'. (More on this, below, as well.)

However, in most behavioural experiments, for example where a speeded sensory–motor response is required, the physical constraints of *action* itself are a major controlling factor. It works like this. At any one moment I can speak only one word, grasp one object, foveate one point in space, etc. Thus, if *one* set of stimulus parameters (among other competing ones) has to guide or specify that unique action—as in selective naming, grasping, eye movement, yes/no monitoring tasks, etc.—then the neural coding of *those* stimulus parameters must be enhanced, relative to any others potentially competing for control of the *same* class of action. (I call this '*selection-for-action*', Allport 1987; for a particularly elegant illustration, see Deubel and Schneider 1996.) In all such cases, the need for selection (selective prioritization) among sensory inputs is a direct consequence of the demands of *action*—nothing to do with limited processing capacity. On the other hand, where different effectors (e.g. eyes, hands, voice, locomotion) can be guided by *different*, appropriately compatible, sense inputs (hence without significant cross-talk between them), 'dividing attention' between ongoing tasks shows no such limitation. Similar constraints, I believe, apply to 'selection-for-memory', but I have not done nearly enough work on this.

Thinking about contemporary cognitive science, it is interesting to reflect on where it has come from over the past forty-plus years. The 1970s (give or take a few years) were the hey-day of 'information processing' psychology. Dozens of new behavioural phenomena were reported and canonized, each one linked to its particular experimental paradigm. RT (reaction time) methods predominated, many of elegant ingenuity. (Sternberg's high-speed memory scanning, from the 1960s, is perhaps the prototype; Shepard and Metzler's linear rate of 'mental image rotation' is another, as is Anne Treisman's 'conjunction search'.) And research became increasingly phenomenon driven. Uncomfortably, however, as time went by and countless (small or large) variations on the experimental paradigms were explored, the underlying phenomena came to look less and less robust, their original interpretations less and less convincing. Very few of these micro-worlds, if any, seemed genuinely to consolidate, still less to link up convincingly with other research lines, based on other 'phenomena'. The topic of 'attention' was certainly no exception.

Around that time two new developments rescued me from a gathering disillusion. The first was the emergence of cognitive neuropsychology, combining the traditions of classical neurology with these newer information-processing concepts and methods. Marshall and Newcombe, and Warrington and Shallice, were already busily inventing the approach in the 1960s. For me, the conviction that I wanted to join in dates from a paper in 1975 by Marin,

Saffran and Schwartz. And by 1980, with '*Deep Dyslexia*', cognitive neuropsychology seemed to me clearly the way to go. Hot on its heels, however, came the connectionist revolution, with a swirl of publications from 1981 onwards, emerging from San Diego and elsewhere. Earlier AI approaches—particularly Production Systems—had seemed to offer a promising language for cognitive theory but remained brittle, rule based, incapable of spontaneous generalization, generally failing to match behavioural data at any real level of detail. Suddenly the prospect looked different: it was the most optimistic moment of my career. Was this—at last—the beginning of a conceptual revolution for psychology, the one of which I had dreamed when I first embarked on the subject? Well, in part, yes, I still believe, but with narrower scope than I had hoped—still hope. For another twenty years, at least, the emergence of connectionism had surprisingly little impact on how cognitive psychologists—for the most part—continued to think about (or not think about) the 'central' problems of psychology: attention, consciousness, voluntary decision, 'executive control'; nor on the traditional boundaries between specialisms (e.g. 'attention' *vs* 'memory'; 'cognition' *vs* 'motivation').

Parallel distributed processing (PDP) brought three conceptual leaps forward, all closely interlinked: 'memory' and 'processing' were no longer separate—or separable—components; memory itself was no longer a filing system, a passive store-place of declarative data, to be 'searched or 'scanned' by the processor, but a (purely dispositional) 'processing landscape' embodied in a network of local connection-weights or biases; and 'processing' was radically distributed throughout these memory structures, as a process of integrated 'constraint satisfaction'. This last property also had important implications for thinking about 'control'. According to the traditional information-processing approach, some kind of *additional*, supervisory control was necessary to ensure that all ongoing processing and decision-making remained mutually consistent and coherent. From the PDP perspective, however, mutual consistency was the essence of what was computed, and 'integration' was a byproduct.

Perhaps understandably, PDP modellers tended to concentrate on particular micro-domains, chosen to be broadly consistent with the kind of functional modularity postulated by cognitive neuropsychology (visual word recognition, face recognition, past-tense morphology…). Ironically, the results of experimentally 'lesioning' these models frequently challenged the ultra-modularity inferred (hitherto) from neuropsychological deficits (in the caricature, a new 'box' to be added to a box-and-arrow schema, for each new deficit reported). A lot of 'boxes' had to go. But the conceptual challenge from PDP ran a lot deeper than that.

A dominant concept (perhaps *the* dominant concept) in the neuropsychology of language at that time was that of a 'mental lexicon' (*logogen* system, in John Morton's theoretical coinage). However, in the new PDP models the idea of explicit word-form representations ('dictionary units') disappeared entirely, leaving only systems of connection-weights linking *supralexical* 'semantic features' with *sublexical* phonological and/or orthographic features. The 'word forms' themselves had become attractor states, purely *emergent* properties of the action of the network as a whole. An essay by Stephen Monsell (1987) on 'lexical input and output pathways' is one of the monuments of the period: an iconic Laokoon struggle with the entangling serpents of connectionism and the neuropsychologists' concept of *lexicon*. (Stephen protested that his essay provoked more words of commentary from me, as its editor, and the other referees than were contained in the final chapter. Well, Stephen, they were—and are—cunning serpents. And the wrestling still goes on: see Max Coltheart's chapter here.)

And what about 'executive control'? The way any field of enquiry starts out, early in its history, inevitably has profound effects on how that field subsequently develops. The 'information processing' approach, rooted in the concept world of sequential computational operations and routines, with separate 'processor' and 'memory', imposed a distinctive and instantly recognizable mind-set on the whole of cognitive psychology, the legacy of which has persisted for more than half a century. Three of the key elements of this mind-set were the following:

(a) The basic units of analysis for cognitive psychology were specifiable, discrete '*cognitive operations*', whose duration (and perhaps other properties) were to be inferred through appropriately cunning RT methodology.

(b) These cognitive operations were assumed to run sequentially, and generally unidirectionally, from 'stimulus' to 'response'.

(c) 'Control' was something intrinsically *centralized* (as in the 'central executive'), and imposed on the basic cognitive operations from outside—from 'above'. (What exactly was meant by 'central' has never been clear to me; the fundamental idea, in any case, was that such 'control' emanated from a control *system* (or systems?) *separate* from the lower-level ('slave') processing systems; control was thus mysterious, and came from outside—from 'elsewhere'.)

Why elsewhere?

From the earliest days, the heartland topics of information-processing psychology were speeded performance, attention, working memory, 'executive control'.

By contrast, learning and memory ('*long-term* memory') was a separate specialism. Researchers who studied attention and speeded performance seldom also worked on learning or long-term memory, and *vice versa*. (There were of course honourable exceptions: students of priming and 'automaticity', for example, have formed something of a bridge between these otherwise surprisingly divergent fields.) This separation was evident half a century ago, back in the 1950s and 1960s, and remains enshrined to this day in separate scientific journals, separate research groups and symposia, separate textbooks, separate undergraduate courses. Even the connectionist revolution has failed to overturn it altogether. And over the same half century, until very recently, an even deeper gulf divided the 'information processing' field from the field of emotion and motivation. (Indeed, the very idea of 'cognitive' psychology was *defined by* this latter separation.)

Suppose, as I do, that 'control' (like attention, like consciousness) is an emergent property, a resultant rather than a cause. Suppose that what is causal are the multitudinous constraints (biases) *within* the system, constraints arising, that is, from anywhere and *everywhere*: from the sensory environment; from ongoing and intended action; from the entire processing history of the organism encoded in memory; from current and long-term goals in so-called 'working' memory (*long-term* working memory, for sure); and from all the rest of the immensely powerful, inbuilt emotional/motivational biases woven throughout the system. It is curious to reflect that, from the perspective of (early) information-processing psychology, *all* of these sources of control were conceptually *outside* of what was originally thought of as *basic* information processing—that is, memory-less, motive-less, and certainly emotion-less 'cognitive operations'! No wonder, then, that 'control' had to come from *outside*—from 'elsewhere'!

You may say that this is a caricature. It is. All a caricature does is to exaggerate (slightly) the true features of the object.

It is undeniable that, for over fifty years, the search has been on to identify (and measure the time-course of) discrete 'control operations' (spatial attention shifts, shifts of set, etc.), imposed from above upon the stupid and ignorant (inevitably, because memory-less) 'basic processing systems'. And as cognitive psychology morphed into cognitive neuroscience, the search has continued, to try to localize the source of the postulated control operations—the 'attentional control systems'—in parietal or prefrontal cortex, the anterior cingulate, or wherever.

Just consider the research effort expended over the past three decades in measuring the supposed duration (the 'time cost') of a shift of spatial attention; or the, by now, almost comparable research effort expended on attempts to measure the duration of a *shift of 'set'*, using the various task-switching paradigms. Belief in the reality of discrete 'control operations', whose endogenous time-course can be measured, seems as deep-rooted as the corresponding belief in the reality of 'basic' cognitive operations. As one small but revealing symptom of this belief bias: in the task-switching literature, the difference between RTs on 'task-switch' and 'task-repetition' trials is almost invariably described as a task-switch cost, rather than a task-repetition benefit, although the two are logically equivalent.

So can experimental falsification work, in this sort of case?

One thing we discovered about these RT 'switch costs' is their dependence on learned associations between individual stimuli and 'tasks'. For example, even one previous experience of a given stimulus—in the context of the *other* RT task (the task to be switched *from*)—can be enough to double the so-called switch cost in some cases, even after hundreds of intervening RT trials (Allport and Wylie 2000; Waszak *et al.* 2003)—a good example of 'bottom-up' rather than 'top-down' control, and of the inseparability of processing and implicit memory.

Another thing we discovered about task-switching, using an 'RSVP' (rapid serial visual presentation) method for visual search, is that the control operation supposedly needed to shift 'set' (e.g. from one type of search target to another) does not actually have an intrinsic time-course of its own, but is simply paced by the presentation rate of the RSVP stimuli (Allport and Hsieh 2001). Many other observations about *RT* switch costs, likewise, run strongly counter to the popular intuition that they reflect the time taken—by a *central executive*: the ego, the self, the will?—to reconfigure the subordinate-level processing pathways from one task 'set' to another. Here's just one. When naming 'Stroop' stimuli (e.g. the word 'RED' written in green ink), you can name either the word (an easy task) or the colour (a much harder task; see MacLeod 1991). Intriguingly, switching to the easy task turns out here to have a very big time-cost (or is it a big repetition-benefit?), whereas switching to the harder task has a small (sometimes even zero) 'switch cost' (Allport and Wylie 1999, 2000; Allport *et al.* 1994). Does all this amount to a Popperian falsification of the executive control model, as regards RT 'switch costs'? It is hard to see why not. But I suspect the folk intuitions about the nature of volition are too deeply entrenched. Even if their time-course can't be measured by RT switch-costs (and they certainly can't), executive control operations must surely exist, mustn't they?

Well—I wonder.

References

Allport, D. A. (1968). Phenomenal simultaneity and the perceptual moment hypothesis. *British Journal of Psychology* 59: 395–406.

Allport, A. (1987). Selection-for-action: some behavioural and physiological considerations of attention and action. In: H. Heuer and A. F. Sanders (ed.) *Perspectives on perception and action*, pp. 395–419. Hillsdale, NJ: Erlbaum.

Allport, A. (1989). Visual attention. In: M. I. Posner (ed.) *Foundations of cognitive science*, pp. 631–82. Cambridge, MA: MIT Press.

Allport, A. (1993). Attention and control: Have we been asking the wrong questions? A critical review of twenty-five years. In: D. E. Meyer and S. Kornblum (ed.) *Attention and performance XIV*, pp. 183–218. Cambridge, MA: MIT Press.

Allport, A. and Hsieh, S. (2001). Task-switching: using RSVP methods to study an experimenter-cued shift of set. In: K. Shapiro (ed.) *The limits of attention: temporal constraints on human information processing*, pp. 36–64. Oxford: Oxford University Press.

Allport, A. and Wylie, G. (1999). Task-switching: positive and negative priming of task-set. In: G. W. Humphreys, J. Duncan, and A. Treisman (ed.) *Attention, space and action: studies in cognitive neuroscience*, pp. 273–96. Oxford: Oxford University Press.

Allport. A. and Wylie, G. (2000). Task switching, stimulus-response bindings and negative priming. In: S. Monsell and J. Driver (ed.) *Control of cognitive processes: attention and performance XVIII*, pp. 35–70. Cambridge, MA: MIT Press.

Allport, A., Styles, E. A., and Hsieh, S. (1994). Shifting intentional set: exploring the dynamic control of tasks. In: C. Umiltà and M. Moscovitch (ed.) *Attention and performance XV*, pp. 421–52. Cambridge, MA: MIT Press.

Allport, D. A., Antonis, B., and Reynolds, P. (1972). On the division of attention: a disproof of the single channel hypothesis. *Quarterly Journal of Experimental Psychology* 24: 225–35.

Ashby, W. R. (1956). *An introduction to cybernetics*. London: Chapman and Hall.

Broadbent, D. E. (1958). *Perception and communication*. London: Pergamon Press.

Broadbent, D. E. (1971). *Decision and stress*. London: Academic Press.

Cherry, E. C. (1953). Some experiments on the recognition of speech, with one and with two ears. *Journal of the Acoustical Society of America* 25: 975–9.

Deubel, H. and Schneider, W. X. (1996). Saccade target selection and object recognition—evidence for a common attentional mechanism. *Vision Research* 36: 1827–37.

James, W. (1890). *Principles of psychology*. 2 vols. Reprinted 1950. New York: Dover.

Johnston, W. A. and Dark, V. J. (1986). Selective attention. *Annual Review of Psychology* 37: 43–75.

MacLeod, C. M. (1991). Half a century of research on the Stroop effect: an integrative review. *Psychological Bulletin* 109: 163–203.

Marin, O. S. M., Saffran, E. M., and Schwartz, M. F. (1975). Dissociations of language in aphasia: implications for normal function. *Annals of the New York Academy of Sciences* 280: 868–84.

Monsell, S. (1987). On the relation between lexical input and output pathways for speech. In: A. Allport, D. G. Mackay, W. Prinz, and E. Scheerer (ed.) *Language perception and production: relationships between listening, speaking, reading and writing*, pp. 273–311. London: Academic Press.

National Physical Laboratory (1959). *Mechanisation of thought processes*. Proceedings of a Symposium in the National Physical Laboratory. London: HMSO.

Popper, K. R. (1959). *The logic of scientific discovery.* London: Hutchinson.

Sperling, G. (1963). A model for visual memory tasks. *Human Factors* 5: 19–31.

Stroud, J. M. (1955). The fine structure of psychological time. In: H. Quastler (ed.) *Information theory in psychology*, pp. 174–205. Glencoe, IL: Free Press.

Waszak, F., Hommel, B., and Allport, A. (2003). Task-switching and long-term priming: role of episodic stimulus-task bindings in task-shift costs. *Cognitive Psychology* 46: 361–413.

Woodworth, R. S. and Schlosberg, H. (1954). *Experimental psychology* (2nd edn). New York: Holt, Rinehart and Winston.

2

Psychology in the 1950s: a personal view

Alan Baddeley

I was initially asked to write about the development of the concept of working memory. However, having just completed such an article (Baddeley and Hitch, 2007) for a symposium marking the 30th anniversary of our 1974 paper, I opted for a different task, that of trying to give an overview of psychology in the 1950s, in hope that this might provide a useful background to the rest of the book. It is a personal view, but reasonably widely based, on time spent during the 1950s in five different research centres: University College London (UCL), Princeton, the University of Southern California, the Burden Neurological Institute in Bristol, and the Medical Research Council (MRC) Applied Psychology Unit (APU) in Cambridge. In each case I was a student or graduate student, and try to give a flavour of that experience.

I began my study of psychology as a first year student at UCL in 1953. It was an exciting time, in which 'schools of psychology' were being overtaken by new developments, both empirical and theoretical. In my first year, our basic text was Woodworth's *Experimental Psychology*, published in 1938 and comprising 889 flimsy pages (paper was scarce) that covered an enormous range of experimental work, much of it using methodology that was no longer regarded as acceptable. Things changed with the publication of Osgood's (1953) *Method and Theory in Experimental Psychology*, an exciting but even-handed blend of the old and the new.

So, what had happened in the years intervening between Woodworth and Osgood? First came the demise of Gestalt psychology, a distinctive approach to experimental psychology, strongly influenced by the Gestalt principles of perception, such as continuity and proximity, and their extensions to cover animal behaviour (Köhler 1925), reasoning (Wertheimer 1945), social psychology (Lewin 1951), and memory (Katona 1940). Theoretically, Gestalt psychology was strongly influenced by developments in physics, adopting a 'field' theory within which stimuli had a tendency to form structured wholes, the Gestalt principle. However, with the rise of the Nazis, most of the influential German psychologists, many of whom were Jewish, were forced to flee the country, principally to North America. Although the USA provided a welcome haven, Gestalt psychology became fragmented and did not flourish in the neo-behaviourist atmosphere that characterized the USA at that time.

Gestalt psychology did, however, form an important, although not large, part of the syllabus at UCL, principally reflected through translations of books by the major Gestalt psychologists such as Koffka (1935), Köhler (1925, 1940), and Wertheimer (1945). I myself found it an attractive approach to psychology, although I was less convinced by the proposed physiological basis in terms of electrical fields on the surface of the cortex. This was tested by Lashley, Chow, and Semmes (1951), who placed strips of highly conductive gold foil over the visual cortex of a monkey and found no evidence of disturbed perception, a result that had few implications for the basic psychological principles, which remain valid, but which cast doubt on the whole Gestalt enterprise. In my own case it has made me cautious about tying psychological concepts too firmly to physiological speculation.

By far the most active region in experimental psychology at this time was the USA, where the influence of behaviourism was still very strong. A major focus of our course at UCL was theories of learning, of which there were a number of prominent contenders, summarized in Hilgard's (1948) classic text, and virtually all based on experiments performed on rats. The most influential was that of Clark L. Hull, whose theory involved the establishment of stimulus–response associations based on reward, and was expressed in terms of postulates and equations explicitly aimed to imitate Newton's Principia. Hull's principal opponent was Edward C. Tolman, who argued that rats learned mazes, not by establishing stimulus–response associations, but by developing mental maps. By the early 1950s, the controversy had moved on to the next generation, with Hull's position being defended by Spence (1956), and challenged among others by Bitterman (1957). As an undergraduate, this controversy was a godsend, given that the broad outline of Hull's model was easy to learn, and the critical experiments could readily be generated by imagining oneself in the position of the rat and selecting experimental paradigms for which one's own response would be inconsistent with Hull's principles.

My first published experiment, carried out during a year at Princeton, was generated on this basis, and used hooded rats borrowed from Bitterman. Tolmanians tended to use hooded rats that were considerably more visually oriented, and perhaps less intellectually challenged, than the albino rats favoured by Hullians. My rats had to learn to choose one of two doors for a food reward. In the crucial condition, whenever they made an error they could see food being delivered to the correct side but could not, of course, reach it.

Would the sight of food act as a secondary reinforcer for the response, as Hull's theory would predict, and simply make the rats even more likely to make the wrong response in future? Or would they behave like sensible Tolmanians? True to form, my rats proved cleverer than they ought to be, and I published a paper to this effect anticipating that the Hullians would come down on me from a great height. In fact, absolutely nothing happened, and this is, I believe, my paper's third citation (Baddeley 1960). By this time the whole controversy appeared to have been abandoned as a nil–nil draw. The Tolmanian maps implied some form of unseen internal representation, whereas Spence's alternative also involved invisible internalised stimuli and responses. Neither kind of internal representation was regarded as respectable within the neo-behaviourist canon, so, instead of agreeing to investigate the nature of such representations, theorists abandoned the field.[1]

The theoretical approaches discussed so far were already highly active in the 1930s. There were, however, some very exciting new ideas that had developed during the war years when psychologists had been required to move away from their ivory towers and tackle practical problems such as how to train a pilot, why radar operators showed a decline over time in detection rate, and how physiological stressors influenced human performance. One effect was to focus attention on the richness of the real world environment and the importance of taking this into account, a view strongly advocated by the German psychologist Egon Brunswik (1947), who argued vigorously, though in somewhat turgid prose, for ecological validity based on 'representative design', a method that required the investigator to go out into the field and measure the environment in considerable detail before designing experiments that reflected this complexity. Sadly Brunswik died before taking his views further, although they have continued to have an influence in the area of decision-making (Hammond 2007). Considerably more broadly influential was the work of J. J. Gibson (1950), who also emphasized the need to measure and specify the stimulus, taking as one of his inspirations the task of a pilot attempting to land a plane, utilizing the expanding flow of information in his visual field as the plane approached the ground, an approach that continues to be highly influential through his enthusiastic disciples (Turvey *et al.* 1981).

One of the most influential new developments came through the information-processing approach to the study of human cognition. This reflected a number of separate but related sources. One of these was through communication theory and the attempt by Claude Shannon (Shannon and Weaver 1949) to

---

[1] A much more detailed and informed account of this period of learning theory and beyond is given by Bob Boakes in Chapter 3.

measure the flow of information through an electronic communication channel in terms of the capacity of a message to reduce uncertainty, which was in
turn measured in terms of binary choices or bits. This led to the concept of the
human as a limited-capacity information-processing device, an approach that
led to Hick's (1952) classic multi-choice reaction time experiment, in which
he showed that the time to respond was a logarithmic function of the number
of response alternatives. This finding, tagged as 'Hick's Law', suggested that
perception involved the flow of information through a channel of limited
capacity, while Paul Fitts (1954) showed a comparable function for motor
behaviour, 'Fitt's Law'. The attempt to measure channel capacity was also
applied to a wide range of other topics, such as perceptual judgements (Miller
1956) and immediate memory (Davis *et al.* 1961; Miller 1956).[2]

A related source of excitement during the early 1950s was the development
of cybernetics, stimulated by attempts to optimize the automatic control of
weapons. In North America its most influential advocate was Norbert Wiener
(1950), whose book *The Human Use of Human Beings* speculated on the possible social implication of such developments. In Britain, the most influential
cyberneticist was probably W. Grey Walter, a very creative and persuasive
physiologist, whose inventions ranged from developing methods of using elec-
toencephalography (EEG) to locate epileptic foci by triangulation, to inventing a machine called 'the tortoise' that was capable of searching a room in
order to find a source of electricity to recharge its batteries (Walter 1953). One
advantage of this ingenious toy was that it allowed one to refute the objection
to the concept of purpose, made by many philosophers at the time. If a simple
machine could show purposeful behaviour, why not people and animals?
In my own case, however, the strongest influence ultimately was one that I did
not encounter until I had left UCL and gone to Cambridge, where I encountered the ideas of Kenneth Craik (1943) on the development of models of
human behaviour based on computing and the information-processing
metaphor. I will return to this later.

When I arrived at UCL, it was in process of transition, from a department
chaired by Sir Cyril Burt, emphasizing the psychometric study of intelligence,
to one chaired by Roger Russell, an American experimental psychologist
who had worked in London during the war. He had appointed a bright and
enthusiastic group of young lecturers, most of them pre-PhD, who managed
to convey a sense of the excitement in the field.

---

[2] Andries Sanders gives a more detailed account of this approach and its subsequent development in Chapter 19.

We learned about Barlett's concept of schema, which was respectfully but sadly dismissed as probably untestable, although Carolus Oldfield in Oxford subsequently suggested that computers might be programmed to simulate schemata, a view also proposed by George Miller, and of course subsequently developed by Schank and Abelson (1977).

The question of the testability of theories loomed large at the time. A. J. Ayer's (1936) *Language, Truth and Logic* presented a readily accessible version of the approach to philosophy taken by the Vienna Circle of logical positivists, presenting the view that a theory that was not verifiable was not meaningful. Gilbert Ryle's (1949) book *The Concept of Mind* was also influential in applying the approach to philosophy based on a careful analysis of everyday language that was dominant in Oxford at the time and for many years afterwards. Although this was not, I think, a very constructive approach to psychology in the long term, it did at that time provide a very useful training in the need to avoid conceptual traps set by the unthinking use of language.

There was also a great deal of interest in the philosophy of science at the time and how it related to psychology. We were presented with two contrasting approaches, one by Braithwaite (1953), who took Newton's Principia as a model, and appeared to evaluate a science by the extent to which it fitted this mathematico-deductive pattern. The other, rather more modest, approach was presented by Stephen Toulmin (1953), who argued that theories were essentially like maps—useful as ways of capturing what we know, steering us through the world, and helping us develop better maps. I myself was, and have remained, a Toulmin cartographer.

I was therefore fortunate to arrive at UCL at an exciting time, into a rejuvenated department that combined a range of British approaches to psychology with that from teachers who were refugees from Europe, such as Hans Eysenck, who was developing his psychometrically based approach to personality at the time, and Karl Flugel, a charming psychoanalyst who taught us about pre-war European psychology. Among other things, he wrote a book on the psychology of clothes, proposing that in future people would wear rather fewer of them. On his death, he was commemorated on the front page of one of the tabloid newspapers as 'Author of the brave nude world dies'. Because of Roger Russell's influence, we also got a good grounding in a range of North American approaches to psychology, which I subsequently found invaluable, particularly when I later became involved in the controversy over trace-decay versus a stimulus–response interference interpretation of short-term forgetting.

After graduating from UCL, I spent a year at Princeton, where I learned more about the history of psychology from Carrol Pratt, a psychophysicist who had been trained as an introspectionist by Titchener. Dr Pratt was responsible for ensuring that all graduate students could translate psychological papers from both French and German. The latter involved retranslating a page from a translation into German of one of Titchener's introspectionist tomes, which taught us such useful vocabulary as *eindringlichkeit*—'thingness'. I also learned to run rats in Skinner boxes and on jumping stands, failed psychometrics, but passed psychoanalysis, and got by on my UCL training, being duly awarded an MA. I spent the summer in Los Angeles, paid by the US Office of Naval Research, to do a literature search for research on human–computer interaction (there wasn't any), before returning to England, where I hoped to do a PhD on partial reinforcement in rats. Instead, after a summer on a grant from Guinness concerned with finding some positive effects of alcohol, I found myself in 1958 with a job investigating postal codes at the MRC APU in Cambridge, experiencing at first hand what has subsequently been called the cognitive revolution.

Although the term 'cognitive revolution' is widely used, opinions differ as to where and when it started. My impression is that, in North America, the seminal events are seen as Chomsky's (1959) review of Skinner's (1957) book *Verbal Behavior* and Neisser's (1967) book *Cognitive Psychology*. In the UK, my impression is that Skinner's views on language were never taken very seriously, and I see Chomsky's work as an unfortunate but temporary distraction from the scientific study of language.[3] Neisser's book was certainly very important. It unified a wide range of exciting new developments under the term 'cognitive psychology', brilliantly conveying the excitement of the new field. However, as Neisser himself makes clear, he was able to do so because such developments were already taking place. They had their roots in the 1940s and 1950s, and one place where such roots developed was in Cambridge at the MRC APU.[4]

A seminal figure was the first director of the APU, Kenneth Craik, tragically killed in a cycling accident in 1944. Craik was a remarkable scientist whose book *The Nature of Explanation* (Craik 1943) introduced the concept of the model as an approach to theory development, and who saw the potential of the computer as a way of developing such models. Digital computers were just being developed, but analogue computers were available, and were used by Craik to model empirical data from gun-aiming in what was probably the earliest computational model in experimental psychology, published after his death (Craik and Vince 1963).

---

[3] The chapter by Bob Boakes gives a somewhat different view of these events from Harvard, where Skinner, George Miller, Chomsky, and their students made Cambridge Mass a very exciting place to be at that time.

[4] Chapter 19 provides a view of the APU at this time as seen from the Netherlands.

When I joined the APU in 1958, it was clear that Craik's and related ideas permeated the unit. They were reflected most coherently in Donald Broadbent's (1958) book *Perception and Communication*, which was published just before I arrived. Donald had just become director, and must have found rather tedious my constant attempts to buttonhole him to discuss this view or that claim from this exciting new book; 'friends' told me he regarded me as rather immature. I still am. My badgering was concerned largely with theories of vigilance, though in retrospect I have been influenced much more by Donald's model of short-term memory.

I recently decided to re-read the relevant section of *Perception and Communication*, and found it surprisingly hard going. It reflects detailed arguments that attempt to make sense of a complex range of data on attention and memory, using a conceptual framework that was still developing. His model includes two components, the *p* system and the *s* system. Somewhat confusingly, the *p* system involves *serial* and the *s* system *parallel* processing. I suspect the confusing labels reflect the fact that the terms serial and parallel processing were not common at the time, and that *p* probably refers to perception and *s* to storage. A further complication came from the fact that the initial diagram in the 1958 book was printed upside down, turning the *p* system into a *d* system. It is only in the final chapter summary that all becomes clear.

> Information is held in a short-term store with a very limited time span. From this store it may be passed selectively by filter, through some mechanism of limited capacity from which it is returned to the store ... Only information that passes the filter can be stored for long periods

> Broadbent 1958, p. 242

Neisser (1967) explains Broadbent's model, by then further developed, much more clearly—a model that continues to influence the field, as elaborated by Atkinson and Shiffrin (1968), and in my own work (Baddeley 2007; Baddeley and Hitch 1974).

Although the work of Broadbent and the APU was influential, as Neisser (1967) illustrates, similar ideas were developing elsewhere, typically in laboratories with an applied link, notably Bell Labs, with the work of Sperling (1960) and Sternberg (1966) being highly influential. Within Europe, the link between information-processing theory and its practical application was very well represented by the TNO Laboratory at Soesterberg in the Netherlands, as described by Andries Sanders in Chapter 19.

Within the US university sector, the closest in spirit to the APU was the group led by Paul Fitts at Ohio State. Sadly, Fitts died at an early age, but fortunately the tradition was carried on by his young colleague Michael Posner, who was, of course, instrumental, not only because of his role in promulgating the information-processing approach within mainstream experimental psychology, but also for his crucial role in developing the next major revolution in the field, cognitive neuroscience. But that is another story. Happily, a story that is told by Mike Posner himself in Chapter 15.

References

Atkinson, R. C. and Shiffrin, R. M. (1968). Human memory: a proposed system and its control processes. In: K. W. Spence and J. T. Spence (ed.) *The psychology of learning and motivation: advances in research and theory*, vol. 2, pp. 89–195. New York: Academic Press.

Ayer, A. J. (1936). *Language, truth and logic*. London: Gollacz.

Baddeley, A. D. (1960). Enhanced learning of a position habit with secondary reinforcement for the wrong response. *American Journal of Psychology* 73: 454–7.

Baddeley, A. D. (2007). *Working memory: thought and action*. Oxford: Oxford University Press.

Baddeley, A. D. and Hitch, G. J. (1974). Working memory. In: G. A. Bower (ed.) *Recent advances in learning and motivation*, vol. 8, pp. 47–89. New York: Academic Press.

Baddeley, A. D. and Hitch, G. J. (2007). Working memory: past, present … and future? In: N. Osaka, R. Logie & M. D'Esposito (ed.) *Working memory – behavioural & neural correlates (the cognitive neuroscience of working memory)* pp. 1–20. Oxford: Oxford University Press.

Bitterman, M. E. (1957). Review of K. W. Spence's behavior theory and conditioning. *American Journal of Psychology* 70: 141–5.

Braithwaite, R. B. (1953). *Scientific explanation*. Cambridge: Cambridge University Press.

Broadbent, D. E. (1958). *Perception and communication*. London: Pergamon Press.

Brunswik, E. (1947). *Perception and the representative design of psychological experiments*. Berkeley: University of California Press.

Chomsky, N. (1959). Review of B F Skinner's 'Verbal Behavior'. *Language* 35: 26–58.

Craik, K. J. W. (1943). *The nature of explanation*. Cambridge: Cambridge University Press.

Craik, K. J. W. and Vince, M. A. (1963). Psychological and physiological aspects of control mechanisms. *Ergonomics* 6: 419–40.

Davis, R., Sutherland, N. S., and Judd, B. R. (1961). Information content in recognition and recall. *Journal of Experimental Psychology* 61: 422–9.

Fitts, P. M. (1954). The information capacity of the human motor system in controlling the amplitude of movement. *Journal of Experimental Psychology* 47: 381–91.

Gibson, J. J. (1950). *The perception of the visual world*. Boston, MA: Houghton Mifflin.

Hammond, K. R. (2007). *Beyond rationality*. Oxford: Oxford University Press.

Hick, W. E. (1952). On the rate of gain of information. *Quarterly Journal of Experimental Psychology* 4: 11–26.

Hilgard, E. R. (1948). *Theories of learning*. New York: Appleton-Century-Crofts.

Hull, C. L. (1943). *The principles of behaviour*. New York: Appleton-Century.

Katona, G. (1940). *Organizing and memorizing: studies in the psychology of learning and teaching*. New York: Hafner.

Koffka, K. (1935). *Principles of Gestalt psychology*. New York: Harcourt, Brace & World.

Köhler, W. (1925). *Mentality of apes* (trans. E. Winter). London: Routledge & Kegan Paul.

Köhler, W. (1940). *Dynamics in psychology*. New York: Liveright.

Lashley, K. S., Chow, K. L., and Semmes, J. (1951). An examination of the electrical field theory of cerebral integration. *Psychological Review* 58: 123–36.

Lewin, K. (1951). *Field theory in social science*. New York: Harper.

Miller, G. A. (1956). The magical number seven, plus or minus two: some limits on our capacity for processing information. *Psychological Review* 63: 81–97.

Neisser, U. (1967). *Cognitive psychology*. New York: Appleton-Century Crofts.

Osgood, C. E. (1953). *Method and theory in experimental psychology*. New York: Oxford University Press.

Ryle, G. (1959). *The concept of mind*. London: Hutchison.

Schank, R. C. and Abelson, R. (1977). *Scripts, plans, goals and understanding*. Hillsdale, NJ: Lawrence Erlbaum Associates.

Shannon, C. E. and Weaver, W. (1949). *The mathematical theory of communication*. Urbana, IL: University of Illinois Press.

Skinner, B. F. (1957). *Verbal behavior*. New York: Appleton-Century-Crofts.

Spence, K. W. (1956). *Behavior theory and conditioning*. New Haven: Yale University Press.

Sperling, G. (1960). The information available in brief visual presentations. *Psychological Monographs: General and Applied* 74: 1–29.

Sternberg, S. (1966). High-speed scanning in human memory. *Science* 153: 652–4.

Tolman, E. C. (1932). *Purposive behavior in animals and men*. New York: Century.

Toulmin, S. (1953). *An introduction to the philosophy of science*. London: Longmans, Green.

Turvey, M. T., Shaw, R. E., Reed, E. S., and Mace, W. M. (1981). Ecological laws of perceiving and acting: in reply to Fodor and Pylyshyn. *Cognition* 9: 237–304.

Walter, W. G. (1953). *The living brain*. London: Norton.

Weiner, N. (1950). *The human use of human beings*. Boston: Houghton Mifflin.

Wertheimer, M. (1945). *Productive thinking*. London: Tavistock.

3

Learning theory and the cognitive revolution, 1961–1971: a personal perspective

Robert A. Boakes

This chapter is about the ten years after I first started to study psychology, a period of unusually rapid change in the fields in which I became involved. When the 1960s began, behaviourism dominated American psychology. This entailed accepting that the study of learning is central to psychology because every important aspect of human psychology is overwhelmingly determined by environmental events during an individual's life. Furthermore, it was very widely believed—and not just by researchers working in rat laboratories—that fundamental principles of learning could be discovered only by carrying out conditioning experiments with animals.

Such views were not widely held in the UK. In particular, in Cambridge, where I first studied psychology, the 1960s continued with excitement over information theory (see Chapters 2 and 19). This was one of several developments that led to a cognitive revolution that rejected behaviourism and marginalized the study of learning. Nevertheless, during this period research in animal learning produced important discoveries and theories that have had a tremendous influence ever since.

As a PhD student at Harvard, I was exposed both to radical behaviourism and to the new US-based cognitive science. The first 'Cognitive Center' was founded by Bruner and Miller at Harvard in 1960, and at the other end of town a number of linguists, philosophers, and psychologists at the Massachusetts Institute of Technology (MIT) were exploring the implications of Chomsky's theories of grammar (Boden 2006).

Cambridge

As a teenager I once mentioned to a friend the passing idea of becoming a psychologist. She found this hilarious. Neither of us really had much idea of what psychology was about or what psychologists did—perhaps only hazy ideas of listening carefully to what mentally ill people had to say and then 'analysing them'. (It was probably the thought of me as an attentive listener that was unconvincing.) Until the late 1960s few people in the UK knew much about psychology, and there were few universities where one could obtain a degree in the subject. I was lucky that, after choosing to become an engineer, I went to Cambridge, because—unlike most British universities—it allowed unusual flexibility in the choice of subjects. Discovery that engineering was not for me was followed by an exciting year of philosophy and then a year of psychology.

This last change followed lectures by Alan Watson on experimental psychology given especially for philosophy students. I found the content fresh and exciting, especially his summary of current debates over Hullian learning theory. His lectures inspired me both to transfer to psychology and to obtain a copy of Broadbent's (1961) book, *Behaviour*. After switching to studying psychology full time I discovered Broadbent's more widely known and extremely influential book, *Perception and Communication* (Broadbent 1958). He and colleagues from the Applied Psychology Unit gave lectures on short-term memory and selective attention that made the topics fascinating. In contrast, Alan Watson's extremely detailed treatment of learning theory was disappointingly dull—but at least his lectures were well organized.

Most lectures series were a shambles, partly reflecting the Cambridge belief that lectures were not important. What really mattered were the weekly 1-hour one-on-one meetings with a supervisor and the essays to be written for these intensive meetings. Good supervisors would set their students essays on potential exam topics that no lecturer may have even touched on. As a result, I read, for example, Tinbergen's (1951) *A Study of Instinct*, together with later books on the relationship between learning and instinct (e.g. Thorpe and Zangwill 1961). The nature of imprinting and of birdsong learning were of particular interest at that time, and in Cambridge interaction between psychologists and ethologists meant that questions, for example as to whether Hullian learning theory could account for various types of early learning, were likely to appear in the psychology exam.

During my final year at Cambridge Skinner came into my life. Throughout the 1940s and 1950s the neo-behaviourism of Hull and Spence had maintained a strong intellectual and political grip on American psychology. By 1960, there were growing doubts about both the core theoretical assumptions S–R–reinforcement theory made about rat behaviour and its relevance to many important aspects of human psychology (Leahey 2004). In its place Skinner's radical behaviourism had become increasingly attractive, especially following publication of *Science and Human Behavior* (Skinner 1953), with its analysis of everyday behaviour in terms of operant conditioning principles and its promise of solutions to a wide range of individual and social problems. At Cambridge the general attitude, as reflected, for example, by Watson's lectures and Broadbent's (1961) book, was that Hull–Spence theory was an intellectually exciting, but ultimately inadequate, account of learned behaviour in non-human animals, one that had some, albeit limited, relevance to aspects of human behaviour. Skinner's ideas were less well regarded. I do not believe that his analysis of language and communication in *Verbal Behavior* (Skinner 1957)—an area where few behaviourists had previously dared venture—was even noted. Instead, I became interested in Skinner's applications of reinforcement principles, particularly in relation to education and his invention of the 'teaching machine'.

Skinner came to Cambridge to give a lecture. At the end there was an opportunity for a mere undergraduate like myself to ask a question. 'How do you explain latent learning?', I asked. It was clearly not a topic of much interest to Skinner and he brushed my question aside. On the other hand, he was attentive after the lecture when I told him about my interest in teaching machines. He described a new research centre on 'programmed instruction' and encouraged me to apply to Harvard.

Harvard

Graduate students entering Harvard's Department of Experimental Psychology in September 1963 were made well aware of a tradition stretching back to Wundt. Having studied in Leipzig with Wundt, Titchener set up an early American department of psychology at Cornell University. His student, Boring, a historian of psychology (e.g. Boring 1950), moved to Harvard, where his student, Stevens, known for his analysis of measurement in psychology (Stevens 1939) and for his psychophysical Power Law (Stevens 1961), was very much in control when I arrived. One aspect of this tradition was the 'pro-seminar', a weekly meeting that all first-year graduate students had to attend and that was dominated by the tenured faculty, notably Stevens and Herrnstein. Their highly atheoretical approach contrasted with presentations by Bruner and discussions, led by Norman, of the entirely new idea that computers might be used to model psychological processes.

Another requirement was that all graduate students complete a 'practicum', an experiment in some area other than that of their intended PhD topic. The admirable intention was that our research focus did not become too narrow too soon. It also had the benefit of providing the faculty with unpaid labour to run their experiments. Stevens was particularly keen on this system, and a large number of students ended up—as I did—completing some kind of psychophysical experiment. Stevens was an enthusiastic skier, obsessed by the virtues of short skis. As a result, learning to ski on short skis—a very sensible way to begin—combined with learning to run and report psychophysical experiments formed part of many a graduate student's first-year experience.

A further tradition was to require that students be able to read articles in either German or French. One of my few early contacts with Skinner was when he conducted my oral exam in French. Skinner had a research fellowship that allowed him to spend most of his time at home where he had a recorder attached to his typewriter in order to measure his output rate. He was rarely seen in the department and had no contact that I ever detected with the Center of Programmed Instruction. I worked there as a part-time research assistant until decreasing faith in the future of teaching machines helped to turn me from experiments on learning by undergraduates to learning by pigeons.

Only a few students continued with psychophysics after their practicum. Most returned to the subjects that had attracted them to Harvard in the first place. Many were there because of George Miller. Like Broadbent, Miller had been an early enthusiast for the application of information theory (e.g. Miller 1956). He had written a book on *Language and Communication* (Miller 1951) that promoted these ideas, and also endorsed the operant analysis of language acquisition and performance developed in Skinner's (1957) *Verbal Behavior.* Following Chomsky's (1959) devastating review of Skinner's book and caustic dismissal of behaviourist psychology in general, Miller had undergone a St Paul-like conversion, his road to Damascus being in California (Miller *et al.* 1960). On his return to Harvard—now bearded, leading Herrnstein to comment that Miller had left Occam's Razor behind—Miller almost single-handedly brought back to life the Lazarus of psycholinguistics, an area of research that had remained effectively unvisited by a generation of American psychologists.

By 1963 this enterprise was in full swing. Miller's students tested whether Chomsky's syntactic analysis could be applied to understanding and remembering sentences. For example, I helped with an experiment to test whether the difference in deep structure between sentences like 'John is eager to please' and 'Jack is easy to please' would affect how well they were remembered. (We found that logical subjects, e.g. John, were more effective prompts than logical objects, e.g. Jack; Blumenthal and Boakes 1967.) Meanwhile I attended courses given by Brown, whose studies of the development of syntactic knowledge—for example at what stage did children acquire the rule for generating plurals? (Brown and Bellugi 1964)—stimulated an enormous growth of such research. Another converted Chomskian gave equally challenging lectures on the neuropsychology of language (Lenneberg 1967).

There was ongoing debate between the psycholinguistics students and those who had come to Harvard because of Skinner. By the 1960s, several American psychology departments, most notably that at Columbia University, had become strongly influenced by Skinner's behaviourism and in turn imbued many of their undergraduates with an almost religious-like dedication to these ideas. Some entered Harvard and were disappointed to find that Skinner was almost inaccessible. Instead they came under the powerful influence of Herrnstein.

With hindsight I can see that I arrived at a turning point in the history of operant conditioning. The research programme that Skinner had initiated in the 1930s (Skinner 1938), one that explored the properties of operant conditioning in an atheoretical way, had run its course. It had been very fruitful in the 1950s, but arguably the last important studies of this kind were those on discrimination learning undertaken at Harvard before I arrived (Honig 1966). For example, Terrace (1966) had just left after completing for his PhD an influential set of experiments on errorless learning in pigeons. After Skinner, Herrnstein was the only researcher in operant conditioning who remained at Harvard and eventually obtained a tenured position. During my time there he ran the operant laboratory and was adviser to the large group of graduate students working with rats and pigeons. The mid 1960s happened to be a particular creative period for Herrnstein; his research from that period has had an enormous influence on subsequent generations of Skinnerian researchers (Boakes 2002). Most notably, he and his students ran experiments that gave pigeons two response keys to peck at and measured their choice between different reinforcement schedules. This research gave rise to the 'Matching Law' which, in its original simple form, claimed that the relative rates with which animals made different responses matched the relative rates of reinforcement obtained by those responses (Herrnstein 1970).

Herrnstein maintained Skinner's dismissal of all attempts to infer any underlying processes, but in other respects his approach was quite different. Unusually for a behaviourist, he advocated strong hereditarian views on human differences. In addition, unlike Skinner, he displayed little interest in applications of operant conditioning and believed that science was about establishing quantitative relationships between observable events. In this last respect he resembled Stevens, who had been at least as important a mentor to Herrnstein as had Skinner. In the 1960s the term 'Law of Science' already appeared old fashioned. The Matching Law seemed to me an attempt at a behavioural equivalent to Stevens' Power Law and, probably because I had been immunized against the appeal of purely quantitative descriptions by my Cambridge training, I was never convinced that either provided much further understanding of either behaviour or perception.

Two visitors stand out from my final year at Harvard. One was a student from the University of Pennsylvania named Rescorla, who gave a brilliant talk about his research on Pavlovian conditioning. His whole approach was so alien to that of the prevailing intellectual climate at Harvard that it was no surprise that he ended up at Yale instead. The other was an Englishman, Sutherland, who had recently left Oxford to establish experimental psychology at the new University of Sussex, but was currently on sabbatical at MIT. We spent an afternoon discussing my research and then he invited me to a party that evening. Unusually powerful Manhattans were served and I spent most of the evening vomiting in a toilet. Later I learned that this day had served as an interview process and that I was appointed as an assistant lecturer at Sussex, despite my display of low tolerance to alcohol.

Sussex

Psychology departments began to proliferate in the UK during the 1960s. Appointment of academic staff was generally made in a similar manner to the choice of animals for a small seaside zoo, namely, picking representative animals from widely disparate species (P. Rabbitt, open letter to Jerry Bruner). In contrast, Sutherland's policy for experimental psychology at Sussex was to concentrate on the few areas of psychology he considered to have intellectual merit. These included his core interest, developed at Oxford, in animal discrimination learning, together with mechanisms of selective attention ranging from the level of behaviour to physiological processes in perception; recent discoveries on cortical organization (e.g. Hubel and Wiesel 1962) were particularly exciting in this respect. Sutherland's visit to MIT added psycholinguistics and artificial intelligence to his set of enthusiasms. As a result, I arrived at Sussex in October 1966 to find a very active animal laboratory in which all three of my new colleagues were carrying out research and, as the Laboratory of Experimental Psychology expanded over the next few years, we were joined by other biologically minded researchers and an increasing number of cognitive scientists.

Discrimination learning was the major topic for our rat and pigeon experiments. Research assistants trained rats in a jumping stand to test the attentional theory of learning that Sutherland was developing in long range collaboration with his former student, Mackintosh (Sutherland and Mackintosh 1971). Others of us used Skinner boxes to analyse effects such as behavioural contrast—an increase in responding to a reinforced stimulus produced by introducing a second, non-reinforced stimulus—that had been uncovered by Terrace and other Harvard students just before my time there.

The latter research was transformed by the discovery of autoshaping in Jenkins' laboratory at McMaster University. After decades of experiments in which the delivery of grain had been made contingent on pigeons pecking at an illuminated plastic response key, it was found that such pecking could be maintained even when it had no effect on the delivery of grain. All that was needed was a classical conditioning contingency whereby a light appearing for ten seconds or so served as a reliable signal for the delivery of grain (Brown and Jenkins 1968). A dramatic demonstration that autoshaped pecking was a classically conditioned response equivalent to salivation by Pavlov's dogs was that, under an 'omission' contingency, pigeons would persist in pecking even when such responses prevented the arrival of grain (Williams and Williams 1969). These results opened up the possibility that a large range of puzzling phenomena could be explained in terms of interactions between instrumental and classical conditioning. Halliday and I began to test the idea that behavioural contrast could be explained in this way (e.g. Halliday and Boakes 1972).

Autoshaping challenged Pavlov's principle of 'equipotentiality'; put simply, it does not matter what kind of stimulus, response, reinforcer, or species a researcher uses in an experiment, the same basic principles of learning will apply. This assumption was implicit in the agreement between Hull and Tolman—who differed in most other respects—that understanding the behaviour of a rat at the choice point in a maze would illuminate most of the interesting problems in psychology. It was behind Skinner's simple generalizations, for example from the behaviour of pigeons to that of children in a classroom. Equipotentiality was increasingly attacked in the 1960s by ethologically influenced critics, who cited findings such as autoshaping as examples of 'constraints on learning'.

The most substantial body of research of this kind, and the one that had most lasting impact, began in the 1950s at a US Navy research station in Hawaii (e.g. Garcia et al. 1955). Garcia's experiments examined the ways in which exposure to gamma radiation led rats to avoid their food or flavoured solutions. As such, they were quite different from the standard maze or Skinner box experiments of that era. Moreover, Garcia's conclusions and data were treated with great scepticism by journal editors, so that his early articles did not appear in mainstream journals (Garcia 1981; Revusky 1977). Consequently this research was ignored for a decade or more. Despite my relatively intensive exposure to learning theory at Cambridge, Harvard, and Sussex, I did not come across taste-aversion learning until the late 1960s. By then the data clearly indicated that such learning had very different properties from standard conditioning. Most notably, nausea-based learning displays a high degree of stimulus selectivity so that a rat can learn in a single trial to associate a taste with sickness, but not to associate a sound or visual signal with sickness, whereas this last kind of stimulus can be easily associated with a shock, while tastes are associated with shocks only with great difficulty (Garcia & Koelling 1966).

Equipotentiality could be taken to imply that, given appropriate training, an ape might acquire some kind of language. A few early attempts to provide such training had been unsuccessful. This provided support for the Chomskian claim that language acquisition is a uniquely human trait and no amount of research on learning in non-human animals can help towards understanding this ability. In this context, the visit to Sussex of a husband and wife team, the Gardners, who had trained a chimpanzee, Washoe, to produce and respond appropriately to a hundred signs or more, was particularly exciting. This success was sensational and, even more so, was their claim that Washoe had started to string signs together in a meaningful way and so display the 'creativity' that Chomsky had emphasized as a hallmark of human language (Gardner and Gardner 1969). Washoe inspired other projects of this kind over the next few years, but later the enterprise suffered a major blow from Terrace's (1979) discovery that his team's chimpanzee, Nim Chimpsky, produced interesting strings of signs only when unintentionally cued by a trainer.

Terrace was on sabbatical at Sussex, along with Jenkins and Neisser, who had recently published the first book called *Cognitive Psychology* (Neisser 1967), at a time when Sutherland organized a weekly seminar to discuss a preprint he had just received, the first paper by Rescorla and Wagner (1972) to describe their theory. All of the now six academic staff attended, along with the visitors and the particularly talented group of postgraduate students; it was clear to everyone that the Rescorla–Wagner theory was of major importance. It provided a model that made sense of data indicating that, in classical conditioning, cues compete for 'strength' of association with some outcome, and how well a cue competes depends on its relative validity as a signal of the outcome. Impressively, the model made some interesting new predictions that Rescorla and Wagner had started to confirm. We had already heard about Kamin's (1968) blocking effect and his conclusion that conditioning took place to the extent that an outcome was surprising. (The use of terms such as 'surprise' and 'expectancy' in an article on conditioning was still a little shocking; they would never have been allowed by the behaviourists who so very recently had dominated learning theory.) What Rescorla and Wagner did was to turn these loose ideas into a precise model that also captured various results from their own separate laboratories, including data providing the first real insights into conditioned inhibition since Pavlov's time (e.g. Rescorla and LoLordo 1965).

This seminar and a conference on inhibition and learning that Halliday and I organized later in 1971 (Boakes and Halliday 1972) were followed by nine years of exciting learning research at Sussex. It was a period when cognitive research also flourished there. Things were different elsewhere, as I began to learn. Research within the Skinnerian tradition, mainly following Herrnstein's lead, became even more isolated from the rest of psychology. Skinner had never replied to Chomsky's attack. The latter was widely perceived as having demolished the intellectual foundations of radical behaviourism, and the several practical achievements of behaviourist psychology were modest compared with the early ambitious claims. As belief in the importance of animal research declined, so did the number of psychology departments that included increasingly expensive animal laboratories. How learning theory later revived is another story (Boakes, in preparation).

Acknowledgements

I am very grateful to Margaret Kirkwood, Ben Colagiuri, Emyo Wang, and Justin Harris for their comments on earlier drafts of this chapter.

References

Blumenthal, A. L. and Boakes, R. A. (1967). Prompted recall of sentences. *Journal of Verbal Learning and Verbal Behavior* 6: 674–6.

Boakes, R. A. (In preparation). *Pavlov's legacy*.

Boakes, R. A. (2002). From programmed instruction to pigeons. *Journal of the Experimental Analysis of Behavior* 77: 374–6.

Boakes, R. A. and Halliday, M. S. (1972). *Inhibition and learning*. London: Academic Press.

Boden, M. A. (2006). *Mind as machine: a history of cognitive science*, vol. 1. Oxford: Oxford University Press.

Boring, E. G. (1950). *A history of experimental psychology* (2nd edn). New York: Appleton-Century-Crofts.

Breland, K. and Breland, M. (1961). The misbehavior of organisms. *American Psychologist* 16: 681–4.

Broadbent, D. E. (1958). *Perception and communication*. Elmsford, NY: Pergamon.

Broadbent, D. E. (1961). *Behaviour*. London: Eyre and Spottiswoode.

Brown, R. and Bellugi, U. (1964). Three processes in the child's acquisition of syntax. *Harvard Educational Review* 34: 133–151.

Brown, P. L. and Jenkins, H. M. (1968). Auto-shaping of the pigeon's key-peck. *Journal of the Experimental Analysis of Behavior* 11: 1–8.

Chomsky, N. (1959). Review of B. F. Skinner's *Verbal Behavior*. *Language* 35: 26–58.

Garcia, J., Kimmeldorf, D. J., and Koelling, R. A. (1955). A conditioned aversion towards saccharin resulting from exposure to gamma radiation. *Science* 122: 157–8.

Garcia, J. and Koelling, R. A. (1966). Relation of cue to consequences in avoidance learning. *Psychonomic Science* 20: 123–4.

Gardner, R. A. and Gardner, B. T. (1969). Teaching sign language to a chimpanzee. *Science* 165: 664–72.

Halliday, M. S. and Boakes, R. A. (1972). Discrimination involving response-independent reinforcement: implications for behavioural contrast. In: R. A. Boakes and M. S. Halliday (ed.) *Inhibition and learning*, pp. 73–97. London: Academic Press.

Herrnstein, R. J. (1970). On the law of effect. *Journal of the Experimental Analysis of Behavior* 13: 243–66.

Honig, W. K. (1966). *Operant behavior: areas of research and application.* New York: Appleton-Century-Crofts.

Hubel, D. H. and Wiesel, T. N. (1962). Receptive fields, binocular interaction and functional architecture in the cat's visual cortex. *Journal of Physiology (London)* 160: 106–54.

Kamin, L. (1968). Attention-like processes in classical conditioning. In: M. R. Jones (ed.) *Miami symposium on the prediction of behavior: aversive stimulation*, pp. 9–33. Miami: University of Miami Press.

Leahey, T. H. (2004). *A history of psychology* (6th edn). Upper Saddle River, NJ: Pearson.

Lenneberg, E. H. (1967). *Biological foundations of language.* Cambridge, MA: MIT Press.

Mackintosh, N. J. (1974). *The psychology of animal learning.* London: Academic Press.

Miller, G. A. (1951). *Language and communication.* New York: McGraw-Hill.

Miller, G. A. (1956). The magic number seven, plus or minus two: some limits on our capacity for processing information. *Psychological Review* 63: 81–97.

Miller, G. A., Galanter, E., and Pribram, K. (1960). *Plans and the structure of behavior.* New York: Holt.

Neisser, U. (1967). *Cognitive psychology.* New York: Appleton.

Rescorla, R. A. and LoLordo, V. M. (1965). Inhibition of avoidance behavior. *Journal of Comparative and Physiological Psychology* 59: 406–12.

Rescorla, R. A. and Wagner, A. R. (1972). A theory of Pavlovian conditioning: variations in the effectiveness of reinforcement and nonreinforcement. In: A. H. Black and W. F. Prokasy (ed.) *Classical conditioning II: Current research and theory*, pp. 64–99. New York: Appleton-Century-Crofts.

Skinner, B. F. (1938). *The behavior of organisms.* New York: Appleton-Century-Crofts.

Skinner, B. F. (1953). *Science and human behavior.* New York: Macmillan.

Skinner, B. F. (1957). *Verbal behavior.* New York: Appleton-Century-Crofts.

Stevens, S. S. (1939). On the problem of scales for the measurement of psychological magnitudes. *Journal of Unified Science* 9: 94–9.

Stevens, S. S. (1961). To honor Fechner and repeal his law. *Science* 133: 80–6.

Sutherland, N. S. and Mackintosh, N. J. (1971). *Mechanisms of animal discrimination learning.* New York: Academic Press.

Terrace, H. S. (1966). Stimulus control. In: W. K. Honig (ed.) *Operant behavior: areas of research and application*, pp. 271–344. New York: Apppleton-Century-Crofts.

Terrace, H. S. (1979). *Nim*. New York: Knopf.

Thorpe, W. H. and Zangwill, O. L. (1961). *Current problems in animal behaviour*. Cambridge: Cambridge University Press.

Tinbergen, N. (1951). *A study of instinct*. Oxford: Oxford University Press.

Tolman, E. C. (1932). *Purposive behavior in animals*. New York: Century.

Williams, D. R. and Williams, H. (1969). Automaintenance in the pigeon: sustained pecking despite contingent non-reinforcement. *Journal of the Experimental Analysis of Behavior* 12: 511–20.

4

Face recognition in our time

Vicki Bruce

This chapter is dedicated to the memory of Hadyn
Ellis, father of this field.

When I was an undergraduate student in the early 1970s there was much talk
and some surprise expressed at the apparently great capacity and accuracy of
picture memory, recently rediscovered after years of neglect (e.g. Shepard
1967). Pictures of faces seemed particularly well remembered compared
with other categories of similar objects such as houses (Yin 1969). At about
the same time, many cases of wrongful conviction in courts—often from
mistaken eye-witness identification—were attracting public attention. This
seeming paradox—of good memory for pictures of faces and poor memory
for faces in everyday life—set the scene for much subsequent work on memory for faces.

When visual memory was rediscovered, it seemed difficult to do good
experiments using pictures in contrast to words, where for decades research
had established the importance of dimensions such as imageability, frequency,
and so forth. The important dimensions of variation in appearance and
significance for picture memory were not known, and before the development
of image processing tools it was extremely difficult to vary systematically
the composition of pictures of natural scenes and real objects. So pictures in
general, and faces in particular, seemed challenging from the perspective of
cognitive psychologists such as Hadyn Ellis seeking theoretical insight into the
processes of remembering such items. For psychophysicists, too, the face
seemed a strange distraction. Soon after I started working with Alan Baddeley
on my PhD, Fergus Campbell, FRS, a brilliant Scots physiologist who was in
Cambridge at that time, looked at me curiously and said, 'Well Vicki, the face
is very interesting, but you can't do a whole PhD on it …'. Fergus, and most
other visual scientists, studied how the mammalian visual system responded
to grating patterns. More complex natural images such as faces were difficult
to control.

Fergus was wrong. Although a search in Web of Science reveals only 12 articles with titles mentioning 'face recognition' or 'face perception' during the period of my PhD research between 1974 and 1977 (one of these was Hadyn Ellis's seminal review of the topic in 1975), this had risen more than 80-fold to over 850 in the years from 2003 to 2006. In my research lifetime, the study of human faces and how we perceive and recognize them has become an extremely hot topic. In this chapter I try to describe why this happened, and a little about what we have learned and what remains to be discovered.

Why did faces become a hot topic?

In 1976, Lord Devlin reported on a number of cases of mistaken identity in which the wrong person had been convicted of a crime. It became clear that eye-witnesses, who might be very sincere and credible people, were quite often wrong when they selected suspects from line-ups or sets of photographs. The case of Laszlo Virag was striking. Apprehended as the man responsible for armed robberies in Liverpool and Bristol, several independent witnesses picked him from photo-spreads or live line-ups. A police witness testifying in court said, 'His face is imprinted on my brain'. But later, another man, George Payen, who bore some resemblance to Virag, confessed to these along with other crimes. So one impetus for research into face recognition was the need to find ways to ensure that eye-witness testimony could help more reliably with the apprehension of criminals. I will return to this later. In the years since the Devlin report many other application areas have influenced the kind of scientific questions people pose about faces.

The issue of mistaken identity is part of a broader theme to do with 'security'. Computer scientists competed to develop programs that can recognize faces as well as (or preferably better than) humans can. In theory such programs could allow automatic screening for identity at work, at cash machines, at airports. In the late 1990s an international competition—the FERET evaluation (Face Recognition Technology)—was held to compare different systems developed at that time, For example, Phillips and co-workers (1998) examined how well an automatic or semi-automatic face recognition algorithm could find matches in a large gallery of 1196 images of faces when probed with variant images of the same people. When the variants were photographs taken on the same day and with the same camera (but some difference in expression), matching was only 80% accurate with the *best* of the systems. When probes were of the same people taken under different lighting conditions or at different times, performance of all systems was extremely poor. Whatever the popular press would have us believe, we are still far from having camera systems at airports that can scan for known terrorists, but the challenge of doing so remains a strong driver behind some of the research.

Another growth area over the 30 years or so since I finished my PhD has been in the area I will loosely term 'cosmetics'. Facial appearance is big business and the effects on appearance of a change in hairstyle, lipstick, or even shape of nose can now be modelled in computer graphics and shown to clients before they submit to superficial or more radical treatments. Some of the most interesting and challenging work I was involved with was in the 1980s when my own group in Nottingham worked in collaboration with Alf Linney's group at University College London. Alf is a medical physicist who had developed a laser scanning device to measure the three-dimensional (3D) shape of the face surface, so that such shapes could be pulled over 3D models of the skull to predict the effects on facial appearance of surgical operation. Alf's 3D scanning and visualization software—quite novel at that time—allowed us to try to investigate faces as 3D surfaces rather than as 'flat' patterns, and we made some modest progress in understanding aspects of face perception in this way (Bruce et al. 1993a,b; Bruce and Langton 1994; Burton et al 1993; Hill et al. 1995).

The development of good ways to display 3D surfaces of faces was also relevant to the hugely important *entertainments* and *communications* industries. It is now possible to generate reasonably convincing human-like moving heads (avatars) which are used in video games or even automated customer service applications. There is still room for considerable improvement in the realism of such images, and it is particularly challenging to create detailed realistic speech-related movements (for a review, see Bailly et al. 2003). In terms of theory, the widespread uptake in recent years of mobile telephony, video, and even virtual conferencing leads us to ask new questions about non-verbal communication. In what ways is face-to-face communication different from telephone communication? Is a video-phone a good or a poor substitute for 'real' face-to-face communication?

Face recognition research did not develop just because of applications interest; it was theoretically timely too. In the early 1970s vision scientists had been investigating how human and animal brains perceived simple grating patterns, so developing our understanding of early cortical processing in vision. But discoveries by a number of scientists in the USA and UK of cells in monkey cortex apparently tuned to natural images such as monkey paws (Gross et al. 1972) and human and monkey faces (Gross et al. 1972; Perrett et al. 1982, 1984) were intriguing.

Rare but fascinating neuropsychological impairments in brain-injured humans were also important. 'Prosopagnosic' patients (Bodamer 1947) apparently lost their capacity to recognize individual faces, while still recognizing person identities by different routes such as voice or name recognition. Such patients could fail to recognize their friends or family—even their own faces in the mirror may appear unfamiliar (De Renzi 1986; Young 1998). Although prosopagnosic patients usually have other problems too, the apparent specificity of face processing problems, coupled with the observation of selective responses to faces in monkey cortex, led to the idea that face processing relies on dedicated neural machinery.

Prosopagnosia is just one of a number of deficits that affect face processing and interpersonal perception, and that have helped theorists explore the logic of the neural systems that decipher facial messages. For example, recognition of the identity of a face and recognition of facial expressions often dissociate, suggesting logical and/or physical independence of the systems used for person recognition and emotion interpretation (Young *et al*. 1993). Campbell and colleagues (1986) described a fascinating example of a double dissociation between expression recognition and lip-reading that led to further theoretical differentiation. Using the 'box and arrow' kind of model imported to cognitive psychology from computer science in the 1960s and 1970s, fairly elaborate models of face perception and recognition were first developed on paper in the 1980s (e.g. Bruce and Young 1986) and then further refined and implemented with connectionist modelling techniques in the 1990s (e.g. Burton *et al*. 1990, 1999). But computer power influenced the field in other ways too, as we shall see.

New methodologies for investigating face perception

Just as the area of face recognition was getting increasingly interesting theoretically, so new methodologies allowed us systematically to vary facial appearance.

When I was working on my PhD, doing experiments with faces was rather tedious. I was investigating the process of visual search for specific target faces. In one set of studies I asked the photographer to copy lots of faces from books into inch-square prints. I mounted these into arrays five faces deep by three wide, had these results rephotographed on to cards, covered these with transparent film, and presented them manually in a tachistoscope, one at a time (Bruce 1979). To manipulate the appearance of an individual face in any way generally involved taking scissors to it. I'm sure that's what Peter Thompson was doing when he accidentally discovered the Thatcher illusion (Thompson 1980), though quite why an academic should be taking scissors to a picture of Margaret Thatcher's face in the late 1970s of course remains mysterious.

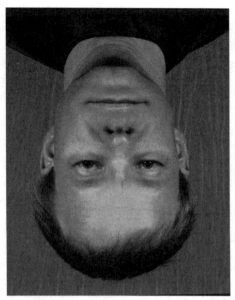

Figure 4.1 This face looks normal until you turn the page upside down. Image created by Peter Hancock, University of Stirling, of himself.

The Thatcher illusion is an extremely neat way of demonstrating our inability to see the configuration of a face when it is turned upside down. It doesn't have to be Thatcher's face, of course. Figure 4.1 illustrates using the face of my colleague, Peter Hancock. Printed as it is, upside down, his face looks quite normal. Turn the book around and you'll see what he's allowed the program Adobe Photoshop to do to him. When the face is upside down, individual features such as eyes or mouth are processed rather independently, so the mismatch in their orientation does not become apparent. This kind of manipulation can be done more easily in Photoshop, but Thompson's work with scissors made the same point.

For my visual search experiments I wanted also to be able to merge different facial identities. Some kinds of merging were easy—using scissors again. That is how Andy Young and colleagues discovered the face composite effect. Young, Hellawell, and Hay (1987) found that if the top half of one celebrity's face was paired up with the bottom half of another, as in Figure 4.2, it was extremely difficult to identify to whom each half-face belonged, unless the two halves were misaligned, when the individual identities became more readily identifiable. This, like the Thatcher illusion, again shows the critical importance of the relationship between individual features in an upright

Figure 4.2 It is difficult to identify the top or bottom half of this face. Cover up one half and you'll find the other easier to recognize. Image created by Peter Hancock, University of Stirling.

face—Tony Blair's eyes just don't look like Tony Blair when paired with George (W) Bush's chin.

Other things were less easy to do without computer graphics and had to wait till the 1980s. Careful manipulations of the effects of displacing different face features on facial appearance could be done properly only with photographs of faces using computers (Haig 1984, 1986; Hosie *et al.* 1988). But other kinds of novel manipulations involving merging faces became possible with computer graphics. About 20 years ago, Dave Perrett and his colleagues at the University of St Andrews first developed means of producing photographic quality caricatures of faces. This involved developing some of the first software for 'morphing' faces (e.g. Benson and Perrett 1991). Such techniques allow different images of faces to be blended without blurring. A set of control points are marked on each face image (such as the corners of the mouth, the tip of the nose, etc.) and the spatial locations of these points can be averaged. Points are joined in triangles and the colour/texture in each triangle can be averaged (see http://perception.st-and.ac.uk/Software/research.htm).

It is possible to average together many different male faces and many different female faces to create the average male and average female. Caricaturing techniques then make it possible for an individual face to be made more feminine or masculine in appearance. Similar techniques can be used to age faces—to predict what an individual might look like 10 or 20 years later (Burt and Perrett 1995). Although some of these applications are frivolous, such techniques also have practical application, for example to manipulate an image of a person missing for several years as they might appear today.

The capacity to blend different faces has also been used theoretically to investigate whether expressions and identities are seen 'categorically'. It is possible to produce an ordered series of images that vary in terms of how much of each face is present in the blend. For example, we can create faces with a 50% 'happy' expression and a 50% 'sad' expression, or a face that is 80% Paul Newman and 20% Robert Redford. Morphed continua of variations can be produced in this way, for example stepping in 10% increments from a face that is 100% happy to one that is 100% sad. By examining how detectable differences between images on such series are, and how readily variants can be categorized, evidence has been found that emotional expressions (Young *et al.* 1997) and familiar identities (Beale and Keil 1995) are seen categorically. That is, it is easier to categorize images at the extremes than nearer the centre of the continua, and harder to discriminate between small variants at the extremes than near the middle of these continua.

A practical application of morphing in the context of eye-witness testimony was published by my own group quite recently (Bruce *et al.* 2002). We have been working on ways to help witnesses to produce better face 'composites'— remembered images of faces seen at crimes. Even with today's very realistic electronic composite systems such as E-Fit and Pro-fit, it is extremely rare that a recognizable composite can be produced from memory (Frowd *et al.* 2005a,b).

We reasoned that, although witnesses produce composites that are error prone, there is no reason to suppose that the errors produced by different witnesses working independently would be correlated. Thus, combining such memories should reinforce the correct aspects of the face and minimize the influence of the errors. So we hypothesized that where two or more witnesses had seen the same crime, and could each produce a composite image working independently, morphing their composites together should produce a better likeness and be more likely to trigger recognition. Laboratory experiments confirmed this prediction (Bruce *et al.* 2002) and this has led to a modification in the acceptable ways in which composites can be used by police investigators in the UK.

The experience of translating a laboratory experimental result to real-world practice was also very instructive. It is easy to forget within the synthetic and somewhat sterile laboratory context the complexity of the situation within which a real eyewitness may encounter a criminal. For example, when my colleagues and I first urged those drafting the guidelines for police to allow more than one witness composite to be collected and combined, the question was asked, 'How do you know each witness is describing the same face?'. In the laboratory, of course, you know—there is only a single target the 'mock' witness could be describing, so the issue had not occurred to us as a problem. The resulting guidelines are clear in allowing composite combination only where there is good reason to suppose that the witnesses are describing the same person.

Perhaps even more significant than the developments in computer graphics have been those enabled more recently by human brain imaging. In addition to the earlier neuropsychological and neurophysiological findings, there is now considerable evidence that there is an area in the human temporal cortex that responds particularly vigorously and selectively to faces. The properties and significance of the 'fusiform face area' (Kanwisher *et al.* 1997) currently remain hotly debated. Some suggest that the area is also involved in making fine ('expert') discriminations within other categories whose members share overall similar appearance, such as bird shapes or dog shapes when discriminated by ornithologists or dog judges (Gauthier et al. 1999, 2000; McKone *et al.* 2007). Others emphasize that many other areas of the brain are involved in face processing too, and so the fusiform face area can be only a component in a much more extended system for deriving meaning from faces (e.g. Gobbini and Haxby 2007; Haxby et al. 2000).

The complexity of the neurological underpinnings of face recognition and perception should not be surprising. More than 20 years ago, Andy Young and I (Bruce and Young 1986) described how any adequate theory of face processing would have to articulate properly what is meant by 'face recognition' (the face, or the picture?) and the relationships between the derivation of the many different kinds of meaning from faces. If we want to ask about whether face processing involves 'special' neural underpinnings we need to ask what we mean by 'special' (Young 1998), and also to be clear about what aspects of face processing we are trying to describe. In this respect, the work of Jim Haxby and his collaborators stands out as exemplary.

What have we learned?

Thirty years after the Devlin report, I think we understand more about the reasons why witnesses find it hard to recall and recognize faces, and we have found some ways to help them do it a little (though not much) better. We also have cameras in almost all our streets and other public places recording the actions and appearances of passers-by. These camera images also provide new opportunities for mistaken identification, however. Bruce and co-workers (1999) showed that participants were surprisingly bad at deciding whether a high-quality video image matched one of the people shown in an array of photographs below it. Different images of the same person can look very different, and images of different people can look very similar. Apparent resemblance between a camera image and a suspect should not be used to prove identity, just as the memorial resemblance between Laszlo Virag and George Payen should not have been used to signal identity either.

So recent work on the matching of CCTV images really confirms the paradox that stimulated my entry to the field some 30 years ago: remembering or matching individual *pictures* is very good, but recognizing 'real' faces in the world can be very difficult. Recent theoretical and cognitive neuroscientific work suggests that robust representations of familiar faces must be built over time from flimsy image-specific descriptions of initially glimpsed items. Computer modellers are showing how this can be done (Burton *et al.* 2005). Because our initial internal representations of faces are so tied to specific image properties, we are bad at matching across different images, even if there is no memory load.

The past 30 years have seen us make some progress at understanding some of the reasons why we can be both good at familiar face recognition but poor at dealing with unfamiliar ones. We have also made considerable progress at understanding how meaningful interpretations of personal identities are derived (e.g. Bruce and Young 1986; Burton *et al.* 1999a).

The next decade will, I think, see us spreading out from the simple interpretation of static face images. I would expect to see much more theoretical work in three areas: *dynamic* image processing (e.g. Lander and Bruce 2000, 2003; Pilz *et al.* 2006); the *integration* of information from faces, bodies, and voices into full 'person' recognition; and the *interaction* between different kinds of emotional, social, and cognitive systems involved in person perception and recognition. On these last two, interrelated, themes there has already been some excellent work in the new field of 'cognitive neuropsychiatry'. This owes much to Hadyn Ellis's research on conditions such as Capgras syndrome (e.g. Ellis and Lewis 2001; Ellis and Young 1990). Capgras patients think their friends and relations have been replaced with imposters or cunningly disguised aliens or robots. They recognize the people correctly, but claim they are not really who they seem to be. Explaining such conditions requires an understanding of the interaction between perceptual–cognitive and affective–autonomic systems in the normally functioning brain, an understanding that may also illuminate the much older questions arising from eye-witness testimony. There's still plenty to occupy another generation or two of PhD students.

References

Bailly, G., Berar, M., Elisei, F., and Odisio, M. (2003). Audiovisual speech synthesis. *International Journal of Speech Technology* 6: 331–46.

Beale, J. M. and Keil, F. C. (1995). Categorical effects in the perception of faces. *Cognition* 57: 217–39.

Benson, P. J. and Perrett, D. I. (1991). Perception and recognition of photographic level caricatures: implications for the recognition of natural images. *European Journal of Cognitive Psychology* 3: 105–35.

Bodamer, J. (1947). Die Prosopagnosie. *Archiv fur Psychiatrie und Nervenkrankheiten* 179: 6–53.

Bruce, V. (1979). Searching for politicians. An information-processing approach to face recognition. *Quarterly Journal of Experimental Psychology* 31: 373–95.

Bruce, V. and Langton, S. (1994). The use of pigmentation and shading information in recognising the sex and identities of faces. *Perception* 23: 803–22.

Bruce, V. and Young, A. W. (1986) Understanding face recognition. *British Journal of Psychology* 77: 305–28.

Bruce, V., Burton, A. M., Hanna, E., *et al.* (1993a). Sex discrimination: How do we tell the difference between male and female faces? *Perception* 22: 131–52.

Bruce, V., Coombes, A., and Richards, R. (1993b). Describing the shapes of faces using surface primitives. *Image and Vision Computing* 11: 353–63.

Bruce, V., Henderson, Z., Greenwood, K., Hancock, P. J. B., Burton, A. M. and Miller, P. (1999). Verification of face identities from images captured on video. *Journal of Experimental Psychology: Applied* 5: 339–60.

Bruce, V., Ness, H., Hancock, P. J. B., Newman, C., and Rarity, J. (2002). Four heads are better than one: combining face composites yields improvements in face likeness. *Journal of Applied Psychology* 87: 894–902.

Burt, D. M. and Perrett, D. I. (1995). Perception of age in adult Caucasian male faces: computer graphic manipulations of shape and colour information. *Proceedings of the Royal Society of London* B259: 137–43.

Burton, A. M., Bruce, V., and Johnston, R. A. (1990). Understanding face recognition with an interactive activation model. *British Journal of Psychology* 81: 361–80.

Burton, A. M., Bruce, V., and Dench, N. (1993). What's the difference between men and women? Evidence from facial measurement. *Perception* 22: 153–76.

Burton, A. M., Bruce, V., and Hancock, P. J. B. (1999). From pixels to people: a model of familiar face recognition. *Cognitive Science* 23: 1–31.

Burton, A. M., Jenkins, R., Hancock, P. J. B., and White, D. (2005). Robust representations for face recognition: the power of averages. *Cognitive Psychology* 51: 256–84.

Campbell, R., Landis, T., and Regard, M. (1986). Face recognition and lip reading—a neurological dissociation. *Brain* 109: 509–21.

De Renzi, E. (1986). Current issues on prosopagnosia. In: H. D. Ellis, M. A. Jeeves, F. Newcombe, and A. Young (ed.) *Aspects of face processing*, pp. 243–52. Dordrecht: Martinus Nijhoff.

Ellis, H. D. (1975). Recognizing faces. *British Journal of Psychology* 66: 409–26.

Ellis, H. D. and Lewis, M. B. (2001). Capgras delusion: a window on face recognition. *Trends in Cognitive Sciences* 5: 149–56.

Ellis, H. D. and Young, A. W. (1990). Accounting for delusional misidentifications. *British Journal of Psychiatry* 157: 239–48.

Frowd, C. D., Carson, D., Ness, H., et al. (2005a). A forensically valid comparison of facial composite systems. *Psychology, Crime and Law* 11: 33–52.

Frowd, C. D., Carson, D., Ness, H., *et al.* (2005b). Contemporary composite techniques: the impact of a forensically-relevant target delay. *Legal and Criminological Psychology* 10: 63–81.

Gauthier, I., Behrmann, M., and Tarr, M. J. (1999). Can face recognition really be dissociated from object recognition? *Journal of Cognitive Neuroscience* 11: 349–70.

Gauthier, I., Skudlarski, P., Gore, J. C., and Anderson, A. W. (2000). Expertise for cars and birds recruits brain areas involved in face recognition. *Nature Neuroscience* 3(2): 191–7.

Gobbini, M. I. and Haxby, J. V. (2007). Neural systems for recognition of familiar faces. *Neuropsychologia* 45: 32–41.

Gross, C. G., Rocha-Miranda, C. E., and Bender, D. B. (1972). Visual properties of neurons in inferotemporal cortex of the macaque. *Journal of Neurophysiology* 35: 96–111.

Haig, N. D. (1984). The effect of feature displacement on face recognition. *Perception* 13: 505–12.

Haig, N. D. (1986). Exploring recognition with interchanged facial features. *Perception* 15: 235–47.

Haxby, J. V., Hoffman, E. A., and Gobbini, M. I. (2000). The distributed human neural system for face perception. *Trends in Cognitive Sciences* 4: 223–33.

Hill, H., Bruce, V., and Akamatsu, S. (1995). Perceiving the sex and race of faces: the role of shape and colour. *Proceedings of the Royal Society of London* B261: 367–73.

Hosie, J. A., Ellis, H. D., and Haig, N. D. (1988). The effect of feature displacement on the perception of well known faces. *Perception* 17: 461–74.

Kanwisher, N., McDermott, J., and Chun, M. M. (1997). The fusiform face area: a module in human extrastriate cortex specialised for face perception. *Journal of Neuroscience* 17: 4302–11.

Lander, K. and Bruce, V. (2000). Recognising famous faces: exploring the benefits of facial motion. *Ecological Psychology* 12: 259–72.

Lander, K. and Bruce, V. (2003). The role of motion in learning new faces. *Visual Cognition* 10: 897–912.

Lord Devlin (1976). *Report to the Secretary of State for the Home Department of the Departmental Committee on Evidence of Identification in Criminal Cases.* London: HMSO.

McKone, E., Kanwisher, N., and Duchaine, B. C. (2007). Can generic expertise explain special processing for faces? *Trends in Cognitive Sciences* 11: 8–15.

Perrett, D. I., Rolls, E. T., and Caan, W. (1982). Visual neurons responsive to faces in the monkey temporal cortex. *Experimental Brain Research* 47: 329–42.

Perrett, D. I., Smith, P. A., Potter, D. D., *et al.* (1984). Neurones responsive to faces in the temporal cortex: studies of functional organisation, sensitivity to identity and relation to perception, *Human Neurobiology* 3: 197–208.

Phillips, P. J., Moon, H., Rizvi, S., and Rauss, P (1998). The FERET evaluation. In: H. Wechslerm, P. J. Phillips, V. Bruce, F. F. Soulie, and T. S. Huang (ed.) *Face recognition: from theory to applications*, pp. 244–61. NATO ASI Series F. Berlin: Springer.

Pilz, K. S., Thornton, I. M., and Bulthoff, H. H. (2006). A search advantage for faces learned in motion. *Experimental Brain Research* 171: 436–47.

Shepard, R. N. (1967). Recognition memory for words, sentences and pictures. *Journal of Verbal Learning and Verbal Behaviour* 6: 156–63.

Thompson, P. (1980). Margaret Thatcher: a new illusion. *Perception* 9: 483–4.

Yin, R. K. (1969). Looking at upside-down faces. *Journal of Experimental Psychology* 81: 141–5.

Young, A. W. (1998). *Face and mind*. Oxford: Oxford University Press.

Young, A. W., Hellawell, D. J., and Hay, D. C. (1987). Configural information in face perception. *Perception* 16: 747–59.

Young, A. W., Newcombe, F., De Haan, E. H. F., Small, M., and Hay, D. C. (1993). Face perception after brain injury—selective impairments affecting identity and expression. *Brain* 116: 941–59.

Young, A. W., Rowland, D., Calder, A. J., *et al.* (1997). Facial expression megamix: tests of dimensional and category accounts of emotion recognition. *Cognition* 63: 217–313.

5

Cognitive science now and then

Max Coltheart

A science that is no better now then it was fifty years ago—that offers no greater illumination of its subject matter now than it did then—hardly excites. But that does not mean that we would like currently exciting science to have been worthless half a century ago. On the contrary: if some of the ideas favoured currently are ideas that were also favoured then, these have stood the test of time—which must testify to their worth, surely?

Are there any such ideas in cognitive science?

I was a feckless youth. Memory tells me that the reason I went to university from the small country town (population 4999) where I attended high school was because I had been offered a government scholarship that would pay me a living allowance sufficient to keep me alive for the three or four years in which my University studies were to be pursued. Which meant that I didn't need to think about having to get a job straight after I'd finished school.

As my best school subject was English, I chose without further consideration to study English at university; I thought also that studying English would have the advantage that it would allow me to become a novelist and to live the kind of life that my then favourite novelists lived, in the South of France, Paris, London, or Capri.

University regulations prescribed that I would have to choose two other subjects for first-year study. I chose philosophy (because to be studying philosophy seemed an impressive thing for a boy from the bush to be doing) and psychology (because that seemed something that a novelist ought be able to make use of).

English I at the University of Sydney in 1957 was a shock. The subject was taught in a desiccated and disdainful way. Never expressed was the idea that books were there to be read for enjoyment; books were for criticizing, not for enjoying. I found this dull and distasteful, and limped through to a Pass in the subject.

Psychology I and Philosophy I, on the other hand, were glorious. The Professor of Philosophy at that time, John Anderson,[1] was in his last year

---

[1] http://en.wikipedia.org/wiki/John_Anderson_%28philosopher%29

before retirement. He did all the wrong things as a lecturer: his Glaswegian accent was near to impenetrable, and he read his lectures straight from his lecture notes, looking up only occasionally. Yet his lecture course on the pre-Socratic philosophers was enthralling, and his last lecture received a lengthy round of applause from the students. I was astonished to learn that there were people thinking about thought two and a half millennia ago—and that we could today still know something about the views they had. No less astonishing was that it was possible to do scientific experiments on thought, as I learned in the practical classes in Psychology I. The study of English, and all ideas of being a novelist, were discarded, and the rest of my undergraduate career was devoted to a double major in psychology and philosophy.

Though there was a slight interruption: three months of National Service before returning to university. I don't need to describe what that was like, because Clive James has done so, unforgettably, in Chapters 14 and 15 of *Unreliable Memoirs* (James 1980). He and I shared that experience, as well as sharing Psychology I (which he thoroughly disliked) and English I (which was more to his taste than to mine).

John Anderson was not the only exciting philosophy teacher in the University of Sydney at that time. I learned a great deal from David Armstrong,[2] John Mackie[3] (themselves both much influenced by Anderson), and Alan Stout, son of G. F. Stout[4] (Monro 1983). But the one person whose intellectual influence on me was enormous was a temporary lecturer and PhD student in the Department of Psychology, a man called Peter Kenny, whom I met in my second year at University.

Kenny was a little older than most PhD students, having previously spent some time training for the priesthood, although by the time I met him he had become an ex-Catholic (as had I, Anderson having done an effective job of corrupting this particular youth[5]). His speciality was psychometrics, and he and I published a paper on factor analysis while I was an undergraduate (Kenny and Coltheart 1960). As part of this work, I even did a little programming on

---

[2] http://en.wikipedia.org/wiki/David_Malet_Armstrong

[3] http://en.wikipedia.org/wiki/J._L._Mackie

[4] Alan Stout's father was Wilde Reader in Mental Philosophy at Oxford when Stout was born in 1900; this post, now become Wilde Professor in Mental Philosophy, has had a long association with psychology and for some time now has been held in the Department of Experimental Psychology at Oxford. I have published with the current incumbent of this post while having been taught by the son of a previous incumbent.

[5] With some assistance from others; see http://en.wikipedia.org/wiki/Sydney_Push

the first digital computer in an Australian University, SILLIAC.[6] It was gigantic (2.5 m high, 3 m wide, and 0.6 m deep), primitive (paper tape was the input and output medium), and slow; but it was an electronic computer, and I was being allowed to program it. Eighteen months before I had been shooting rabbits in the bush and skinning them for dinner.

Kenny's interests turned out to be much wider than just psychometrics; crucially, he was particularly interested in what today would be called cognitive science.

Cognition was not part of the undergraduate curriculum at Sydney in those days, of course, since the Cognitive Revolution was only just beginning then; Broadbent's *Perception and Communication* appeared in the same year I met Kenny. But Kenny knew of and told me about much significant work in cognitive science that had already been published. He was studiedly insolent to his academic seniors, and a notorious libertine, and so (to my regret) soon vanished from the academic scene; but I read all of the material he recommended, and it fixed permanently the kind of work I subsequently did and still do.

I will mention here some of this work that I still particularly remember being deeply attracted to. The earliest was the paper by McCulloch and Pitts (1943) with the gorgeous title 'A logical calculus of the ideas immanent in nervous activity'. Pitts was a philosopher of logic and McCulloch a neuroscientist. This was probably the first paper on artificial neural nets (and hence on computational modelling, which is something I am still doing). The possibility set out in that paper of abstracting computational procedures from the physical systems that implement them, and the implication that the same procedure can be run on many different kinds of physical system and so is independent of particular physical realizations, seems to me still to be one of the most important ideas in cognitive science—and I was exposed to this idea fifty years ago.

Then there was the Hixon Symposium (Jeffress 1951), which was held at Caltech in September 1948; the symposiasts came from psychology, philosophy, psychiatry, neurology, mathematics, biology, and zoology. Every paper in this volume is a classic, but one might single out Lashley's 'The problem of serial order in behaviour', McCulloch's 'Why the mind is in the head', and von Neumann's 'The general and logical theory of automata' (it is believed that the first occurrence of the term 'black box' was in von Neumann's paper: '*I shall, therefore, view a neuron as a "black box" with a certain number of inputs that receive stimuli and an output that emits stimuli*' (von Neumann 1951, p. 22).

----

[6] http://en.wikipedia.org/wiki/SILLIAC

Across the Atlantic ten years later, at Teddington on the Thames near London, a symposium on 'Mechanisation of Thought Processes' was held (National Physical Laboratory 1959). This book, which I read as avidly as I had the Hixon Symposium volume, also contains some classics in cognitive science, including Selfridge's paper on Pandemonium, Minsky's 'Some methods of artificial intelligence and heuristic programming', McCarthy's 'Programs with common sense' and Rosenblatt's paper on Perceptrons. Well over 200 people attended this meeting, including Sir Frederick Bartlett, John Morton, Stuart Sutherland, Horace Barlow, Richard Gregory, Fergus Campbell, Donald MacKay, Peter Ladefoged, and J. Z. Young.

And then there was *Perception and Communication* (Broadbent 1958). Not only did it use flowcharts to express models of cognition (see pp. 216 and 219 of the book), but it made a clear and explicit statement of cognitive science as abstracting computational procedures from the physical systems that implement them:

> *The proper relation between the physiologist and the psychologist may be regarded as analogous to that between the automobile mechanic and the test driver. Each of these men has his own domain of knowledge … for many purposes a knowledge of the mechanism is not essential to the driver; no more so than a knowledge of the problems of driving is essential to the mechanic. (In the scientific field, one may note, the psychologist usually knows much more of physiology than the physiologist does about behaviour.)*

Broadbent 1958, p. 306

Broadbent could have pursued his example further by pointing out that the driver does not care, nor need to know, what metal carburettors are made from, or even whether they are made from metal at all, whereas these are matters of intense interest to the mechanic—which illustrates the implication that the same processing procedure (in this case, aerating the petrol) can be run on many different kinds of physical system and so is independent of any particular physical realization.

I was as an undergraduate spared ultra-behaviourism. Learning was taught in the third year of the psychology course at the University of Sydney by a person who had obtained his MA from the University of Iowa under the supervision of Kenneth Spence, and could be described as an ultra-Hullian. But he was away that year on sabbatical leave, and the psychology of learning was taught instead by a visitor from the American University of Beirut, J. D. 'Peter' Keehn, a man of wide interests who introduced me to some thoroughly cognitive theorizing about animal behaviour—the work of Tolman, whose research interests would today be referred to as 'Animal Cognition', and whose paper 'Cognitive maps in rats and men' (Tolman 1948) counts as another early classic in cognitive science.

Having pursued my undergraduate studies with mixed success (finishing top in the Psychology class in each of my first three years, but collapsing into Second Class honours in my fourth), I went on from being an undergraduate to being a PhD student. Why? Because I had been offered a postgraduate scholarship that paid me a living allowance sufficient to keep me alive for the three years in which my PhD studies were to be pursued. Which meant that I didn't need to think about having to get a job straight after finishing my first degree.

In the years when I was a PhD student (1962–1964) my thesis topic was the Perceptual Moment Hypothesis—the idea that psychological time is quantized, the quantum often argued to be something like 100 milliseconds. My interest in this came from reading John M. Stroud's 1956 chapter 'The fine structure of psychological time' (Stroud 1956).[7] There must have been some serious morphic resonance going on here, because at this time both Alan Allport and Tim Shallice were working on exactly this topic for their PhDs.

Both Tim and Alan went on to publish their work on this (Allport 1968; Shallice 1964). I didn't. My three years as a full-time PhD student on a scholarship were spent mostly playing tournament and rubber bridge in clubs in downtown Sydney. I did find time to read a lot of cognitive science, and to do a desultory experiment or two, but I never saw my PhD supervisor and wrote nothing of my PhD thesis. In the last few weeks before my scholarship was due to expire—at the end of 1964—I therefore had nothing to show for it and no plans for employment. One day during those last few weeks, though, the head of my department, as he was passing me in the corridor, remembered that one of his staff members was about to go on sabbatical leave for the whole of the next year, and that he had forgotten to arrange a replacement. I was therefore asked on the spot whether I would like a temporary lectureship in the department for the year 1965. It was easy to accept, and that meant that I didn't need to think about having to get a job straight after finishing my PhD scholarship.

This lectureship was renewed for 1966. My main responsibility in those two years was lecturing to Psychology 1, and I seem to recall being required to deliver to these first-year students 63 hours of lectures covering every aspect of psychology. During this period I must have decided that I did need to have a PhD, because I embarked on a new PhD topic—the interaction of size and distance information in visual space perception—and during the two years I was a temporary lecturer I completed enough experiments (mainly at night)

---

[7] Interestingly, Stroud had been an Additional Participant at the 1948 Hixon Symposium 'as a kind of renegade physicist' (his words), and was even publicly quizzed by McCulloch about the perceptual moment hypothesis (Jeffress 1951, pp. 97–99).

to be able to write up later a (short) PhD thesis. This work was stimulated by Ross Day, then a Reader in the Sydney Psychology Department. He had taught me perception during my second undergraduate year, with a valuable historical perspective (it was from him that I learned about the Hemholtzian concept of unconscious inference in perception, an idea still important in current cognitive science). He was remarkably tolerant of youthful intellectual overenthusiasm (my lab report after our practical class on Wohlgemuth and reversible perspective was 103 pages long, rather than the requested 10. It was returned to me imperturbably, with comments on most pages, but no comment on its length).

Although the work for my real PhD was on perception, in retrospect I can see that its flavour was highly cognitive—even in some ways computational. My subjects viewed a disc of light, monocularly, through a pinhole, in a completely dark room, without any visual cues as to how far away it was, and were asked to judge its distance from them. To ensure that the subjects could not even use knowledge of the size of the room to establish a maximum possible distance for the stimulus, I made certain that they did not know what room they were in by meeting them elsewhere, blindfolding them, leading them around the building until they were completely disoriented, and then into the room where the experiment was conducted. Hence the only information the subject had that was relevant to judging the distance of the disc was the size of its retinal image. That information is completely ambiguous: a big far object and a small near object would produce retinal images of the same size, despite being at different distances.

So I provided disambiguating information that was non-visual—it was either verbal size information ('That disc you are seeing is three inches across') or haptic size information ('Here's a cardboard disc to feel: it is the same size as the disc you are looking at'). Combining information about the size of the retinal image with the second source of information about disc size allows distance to be unambiguously determined—in principle. But can people perform such computations? At that time, it was argued by many that people are not sensitive to the absolute size of the retinal image of an object and hence that absolute size can play no role in visual perception. If that were so, then varying the size of the retinal image while holding constant the nonvisual size information would have no effect on the subject's judgement of distance: if the subject was told that the disc was six inches across, a 3-inch disc 10 feet away would be judged to be at the same distance as a 12-inch disc 10 feet away (as the only difference between these two conditions is the absolute size of the retinal image). If, on the other hand, subjects *can* use the absolute size of the retinal image to perform such computations, they will judge the smaller disc to be more distant (it must be more distant since its retinal size is small relative to its objective size as specified in the non-visual size information). I did find such effects. This yielded a paper in *Nature* (Coltheart 1969).

In 1965, Ross Day was offered the Foundation Chair of Psychology at Monash University in Melbourne, and I accepted an offer of a lectureship in that department in 1967. Upon arrival I found the atmosphere electric. People were there at all hours of the day and night. Everybody was doing research. Everybody was publishing. Everybody was enthusiastic about their subject. I met Ken Forster. I wrote up and submitted my PhD thesis, the degree being awarded in June 1969.

Two months after that date I had left Monash. The siren songs from the South of France, Paris, London, and Capri had eventually proven too seductive. I didn't manage to move to Europe, but at least Waterloo, Ontario, was a lot closer to those places than Melbourne, Australia. I arrived at the Waterloo Psychology Department as a cognitive scientist of theoretical persuasion with a background in visual perception, and this generated a paper in *Psychological Review*, written while I was there (Coltheart 1971); but what I mostly did at Waterloo was work on a tachistoscopic report of unpronounceable random letter strings. I worked on that simply because there was an enthusiastic group already there working on it: Phil Merikle, Phil Bryden, and their graduate students. What they were doing looked like fun, and so I joined in. It was this experience that led to my later research interest in letter strings that are words, and letter strings that are not words but which are nevertheless pronounceable.

The next year, at last, I got to Europe: an extended European summer holiday trip including some time in (still slightly) swinging London. Europe was all I had hoped for and more, but it took me another two years to find a job there, a Readership at the University of Reading. John Morton and John Marshall had been at Reading but were gone by then; however, I found Alan Allport in post. Over the next three years I spent many absorbing hours in conversation with him about the foundations of cognitive science, his characteristically slightly jaundiced attitude helping to curb my characteristic over-enthusiasm. One product of our extensive interactions was one of the most embarrassing footnotes imaginable. This was to do with experimental work I did with my PhD students at Reading (notable amongst whom was Derek Besner) and published as Coltheart, Davelaar, Jonasson, and Besner (1977). This paper has had a large number of citations—about 585 at present—largely because of the experiment in it which investigated the effects of orthographic neighbourhood size on lexical decision. This variable is now often called 'Coltheart's N'. The footnote says: '*We thank Alan Allport for suggesting this experiment and Nick Davison for running the subjects'*. No one seems to have noticed this footnote. At least, no one has ever said to me, 'Tell me, Max, if the experiment was Alan's idea, and the subjects were run by Nick, then your own contribution was …?'.

An offer of a Chair in the Psychology Department of Birkbeck College at the University of London meant that, at last, I would actually be able to *live* in London. A house was therefore bought in Tufnell Park, one street away from where Clive James had inhabited a squalid bedsit fifteen years before—he got to London long before I did—and I took up my new post in 1975. By then I had become immersed in work on the psychology of reading and in developing a dual-route model of reading based on ideas first put forward by Forster and Chambers (1973) and Marshall and Newcombe (1973).

As well as proposing some dual-route ideas, the Marshall and Newcombe paper made a claim that was completely new to me. It was that one might be able to learn something about how reading is normally accomplished by studying people in whom the processes of reading had been perturbed by brain damage. Their demonstrations seemed to me completely persuasive. So I wanted to start doing research immediately with people with acquired dyslexia. Or, as I soon appreciated, research with people with any acquired disorder of cognition. I realized this when, as I was interviewing Jane Riddoch for entry to the undergraduate programme at Birkbeck, she told me about dressing apraxia (she was a physiotherapist at the time).

I had no idea how to go about finding patients to work with, but when I mentioned this to Maria Wyke, a neuropsychologist at the Institute of Psychiatry whom I happened to know, she invited me to do some work with her and a patient of hers, KC. He was a charming elderly man of letters who had been at Oriel College in his youth, whose language was cultured and fluent, but who had an almost complete inability to repeat single words: a severe conduction aphasia. I thought it would be interesting to investigate the role of working memory in sentence comprehension with this man, and we did. Having completed an extensive set of experiments with him, I went to read the aphasiological literature on this topic, to find that everything I had done with him had already been done before, and thoroughly. I wasn't too downhearted: at least this showed that I knew how to do cognitive neuropsychology, a field of work to which I was by then deeply committed.

I was also fortunate at Birkbeck to encounter Morag Stuart. She had been a schoolteacher for many years, and eventually found that she needed a degree in psychology to advance further in her profession, so she enrolled at Birkbeck for that purpose. However, she never returned to teaching, having acquired a taste for research from her undergraduate studies at Birkbeck, and gone on to do a PhD there. She is now a Professor in the University of London. Through being her supervisor I acquired some understanding of learning to read and developmental disorders of reading, and so extended my research interests in reading into these new areas.

I had left Sydney in 1967. Twenty years later it had become a different place—in 1987 it had become as glittering a destination as London had seemed to me in 1967. So I returned, to a Chair in the Psychology Department at Macquarie University, a position from which I retired last month. In fact, I had been on leave from that position since January 1 2000, when I became Director of the Macquarie Centre for Cognitive Science, a position in which I am continuing.

My work on reading continued apace at Macquarie, particularly in collaboration with my PhD students, Kathy Rastle (with whom I worked on computational modelling of reading; she is now a Professor at the University of London) and Anne Castles (with whom I worked on learning to read and developmental dyslexia; she is now a Professor at Macquarie University). But I also acquired a completely new research interest, the study of delusional belief, which was the subject of my recent Bartlett Lecture to the Experimental Psychology Society (Coltheart, 2007).

This happened because a student in the department who was working on schizophrenia, Robyn Langdon, lost her supervisor to another university, and asked me to take on this role. I demurred, explaining to her that I knew nothing about schizophrenia,[8] but she said that she would teach me about that, which she has done, and continues to do. Shortly afterwards, the same thing happened again: a clinical neuropsychologist of my acquaintance, Nora Breen, told me about two remarkable men she had come across in her clinic who each had the fixed belief that the person he saw when he looked into the mirror was not him but some complete stranger who looked like him. She wanted to do a PhD on delusional belief including these men as part of her project, and wanted me to supervise her, assuring me that she would take responsibility for filling in all the gaps in my flimsy knowledge of neuropsychiatry and clinical neuropsychology. This she did with great success. This work resulted in the formulation of a two-factor theory of delusional belief (see e.g. Coltheart 2007; Coltheart Langdon and McKay, 2007), according to which delusional beliefs arise when two cognitive abnormalities are present simultaneously. The first of these is what causes the delusional thought to occur to the

---

[8] Although, as it happened, I had given a lecture on this topic once, in Bilbao in 1975 (Coltheart 1977).

person in the first place, and the second is an impairment to the normal processes of belief evaluation which, if intact, would have allowed the person to reject the thought that had occurred to them rather than accepting it as a belief. Each of these two impairments is, of course, associated with some particular form of brain damage, but the theory has been described, and tested, at a level that abstracts away from such facts about the neural implementation of the relevant cognitive systems.

Cognitive science then and now

I'm happy to see that certain ideas about cognitive science that I liked so much almost fifty years ago are still popular The idea that computational procedures can be abstracted from the physical systems that implement them, the implication that the same procedures can be run on many different kinds of physical system and so are independent of particular physical realizations, and the consequence that the operation of any such procedure can be described at (at least) two different levels, are still very strong in cognitive science.

That is not to say that there are not barbarians at the gate; there are, and they belong to several different tribes.

There are the *eliminative materialists* (e.g. Churchland 1981), whose view is that there is no such thing as cognitive science; there is only cognitive neuroscience. They identify cognitive psychology with folk psychology, and argue that the more we learn about the brain the less we will need folk psychology to discuss cognition, until eventually folk psychology will have withered away and the folk will use only brainspeak to discuss cognition.

Then there are the *connectionists*, currently too numerous to mention. They reject the idea that computational procedures should be studied by abstracting them away from the physical systems that implement them. The models of cognition they offer are described as 'brain-like' or 'neurally plausible', and elements of their models are often described as 'neurone-like'. So their models are not attempts at describing cognition in a way that abstracts away from the physical system upon which cognition depends.

And then there are contemporary neo-behaviourists of a Wittgensteinian persuasion such as Bennett and Hacker (2006), who repudiate the very concept of mental representation; these authors indeed assert that any attempt at describing mental activities in the form of flowcharts or box-and-arrow diagrams is 'misleading', 'confused', 'a mythological redescription', 'incoherent', 'a mythical tale', and 'risible' (this is just a selection from the numerous derogatory epithets sprinkled throughout their paper). And this paper doesn't hesitate to name names: amongst those whom the paper accuses of risible myth-making are Willem Levelt, John Morton, and Anne Treisman.

But these gates, I am delighted to see, are still being defended fervently by such luminaries of cognitive science as Ned Block, Saul Sternberg, and Jerry Fodor.

Cognitive scientists often say that the mind is the software of the brain

Block 1995, p. 21

During the second half of the century there was a change in the kinds of questions that psychologists asked and in the acceptable answers. This change was influenced by the growth of computer science, which persuaded psychologists that programming concepts might be acceptable as precise descriptions of information processing by people as well as by machines. Also the software–hardware distinction supported the legitimacy of theories couched in terms of abstract information processing operations in the mind rather than only neurophysiological processes in the brain. In the "human information processing" approach, complex activities of perception, decision, and thought, whether conscious or unconscious, came to be conceptualized in terms of functionally distinct and relatively independent ("modular") sub-processes responsible for separate operations such as input, transformation, storage, retrieval, and comparison applied to internal representations— modules whose arrangement was expressed in systematic flow charts.

Sternberg (submitted)

It isn't, after all, seriously in doubt that talking (or riding a bicycle, or building a bridge) depends on things that go on in the brain somewhere or other. If the mind happens in space at all, it happens somewhere north of the neck. What exactly turns on knowing how far north? It belongs to understanding how the engine in your auto works that the functioning of its carburetor is to aerate the petrol; that's part of the story about how the engine's parts contribute to its running right. But why (unless you're thinking of having it taken out) does it matter where in the engine the carburettor is? What part of how your engine works have you failed to understand if you don't know that?

Fodor 1999, p. 69

It would have been interesting to have been present when the engineer Broadbent and the philosopher Fodor opened the bonnet of Fodor's car and began a discussion of carburettors, carburetion, and cognitive science.

References

Allport, D. A. (1968). Phenomenal simultaneity and the perceptual moment hypothesis. *British Journal of Psychology* 59: 395–406.

Bennet, M. R. and Hacker, P. M. S. (2006). Language and cortical function: conceptual developments. *Progress in Neurobiology* 80: 20–52.

Block, N. (1995). The mind as the software of the brain. In: D. Osherson, L. Gleitman, S. Kosslyn, E. Smith, and S. Sternberg (ed.) *An invitation to cognitive science*, pp. 21–83. Cambridge, MA: MIT Press.

Broadbent, D. E. (1958). *Perception and communication*. London: Pergamon Press.

Churchland, P. M. (1981). Eliminative materialism and the propositional attitudes. *Journal of Philosophy* 78: 67–90.

Coltheart, M. (1969). The effects of two kinds of distance information upon visual judgments of absolute size. *Nature 221*: 383.

Coltheart, M. (1977). Attention and schizophrenia. *Gaceta Medica de Bilbao* 74: 577–582.

Coltheart, M. (2007). The 33rd Bartlett Lecture: Cognitive neuropsychiatry and delusional belief. *Quarterly Journal of Experimental Psychology* 60: 1041–1062.

Coltheart, M., Davelaar, E., Jonasson, J.T., and Besner, D. (1977). Access to the internal lexicon. In: S. Dornic (ed.) *Attention and performance VI*, pp. 535–556. Hillsdale, NJ: Lawrence Erlbaum Associates.

Coltheart, M., Langdon, R. and McKay, R. (2007). Schizophrenia and monothematic delusions. *Schizophrenia Bulletin* 33: 642–647.

Fodor, J. A. (1999). Diary. *The London Review of Books* 21(10): 68–69.

Forster, K. I., and Chambers, S. M. (1973). Lexical access and naming time. *Journal of Verbal Learning and Verbal Behavior* 12: 627–635.

James, C. (1980). *Unreliable memoirs*. London: Picador.

Jeffress, L. A. (ed.) (1951). *Cerebral mechanisms in behavior: The Hixon Symposium*. New York: Wiley.

Kenny, P. B. and Coltheart, F. M. M. (1960). The effect of sampling restriction on factor patterns. *Australian Journal of Psychology* 12: 58–69.

Marshall, J. C. and Newcombe, F. (1973). Patterns of paralexia: A psycholinguistic approach. *Journal of Psycholinguistic Research* 2: 175–199.

McCulloch, W. S. and Pitts, W. (1943). A logical calculus of the ideas immanent in nervous activity. *Mathematical Biophysics* 5: 115–33.

Monro, D. H. (1983). Obituary: Alan Ker Stout, 1900–1983. *Australasian Journal of Philosophy* 61: 337–9.

National Physical Laboratory (1959). *Mechanisation of thought processes*. Proceedings of a Symposium in the National Physical Laboratory. London: HMSO.

Patterson, K. E., Seidenberg, M. S., and McClelland, J. L. (1989). Connections and disconnections: dyslexia in a computational model of reading. In: P. Morris (ed.) *Parallel distributed processing: implications for psychology and neuroscience*, pp. 131–181. Oxford: Oxford University Press.

Shallice, T. (1964). The detection of change and the perceptual moment hypotheses. *British Journal of Statistical Psychology* 17: 113–35.

Sternberg, S. (submitted). Modular processes in mind and brian. Ms submitted for publication.

Stroud, J. M. (1956). The fine structure of psychological time. In: H. Quastler (ed.) *Information theory in psychology: problems and methods*, pp. 174–207. New York: Free Press.

Tolman, E. C. (1948). Cognitive maps in rats and men. *Psychological Review* 55: 189–208.

von Neumann, J. (1951). The general and logical theory of automata. In L. A. Jeffress (ed) *Cerebral mechanisms in behavior: The Hixon Symposium*, pp. 1–41. New York: John Wiley.

6

Ageing memory: ageing memories

Fergus I. M. Craik

In 2008, fifty years will have passed since the publication of two books that had a major impact on the field of cognitive ageing: Broadbent's *Perception and Communication* (1958) and Welford's *Ageing and Human Skill* (1958). Broadbent's classic book was a main source of the shift from S-R behaviourism to information-processing approaches. This paradigm shift had a strong influence on studies of age-related changes in human performance, as the early work in this area was carried out by mainstream experimental psychologists who simply added individual differences in ageing to their studies. Welford's book is a classic in the narrower field of ageing research, reporting a systematic programme of laboratory and field studies carried out in Cambridge between 1946 and 1956. The many findings are grouped under such headings as skill, speed and accuracy, translation processes, perception, memory, and problem-solving; the findings are also linked by reference to underlying theoretical concepts and how these concepts change in the course of ageing. Welford's book is quite theoretical in fact, and in that sense stands in contrast to the mostly descriptive studies of age-related differences in memory and cognition of the time. I will survey that empirical scene after saying some words about my own entry to the field.

A personal perspective

To my mild embarrassment, the year 2008 also marks the 50-year anniversary of my own involvement in experimental psychology. I completed my undergraduate degree at the University of Edinburgh in 1960, having taken courses in memory from Ian Hunter and in perception from James Drever. My first experiment (looked back on as fondly as a first love!) was on time perception. I was very impressed by George Miller's 'Magical number 7' paper (Miller 1956), and so measured information-processing rates in bits per second while subjects made absolute perceptual judgements involving various degrees of complexity for about 12 minutes, and were then unexpectedly asked to estimate how long the task had taken. I obtained a nice function relating rate of processing to subjective time estimates, although I never got around to publishing the data. But I did keep remembering the result, to the point that Janine Hay and I conducted and published a more sophisticated version of it with younger and older adults many years later (Craik and Hay 1999).

After Edinburgh I joined the Medical Research Council (MRC) Unit on Occupational Aspects of Ageing, attached to the Psychology Department at the University of Liverpool, established to carry on Welford's useful work on ageing, but in a more applied industrial setting. The Director, Alastair Heron, asked me to explore the idea that older adults' performance may be limited by lack of confidence and feelings of inadequacy. It's an interesting but complex problem, undoubtedly involving personality, developmental, social, and contextual factors. The last aspect was made obvious to me while testing a very anxious and timid older woman who, when tea was served during a break, immediately took command of the situation and ordered everyone else about, only to revert to her previous 'personality' when testing resumed! After inconclusive experiments using Rotter's 'level of aspiration' framework, I discovered signal detection theory (Swets *et al.* 1961) and investigated age-related differences in caution-riskiness by examining criterion placement (β) in a tone-detection paradigm. The results suggested that older adults require stronger evidence of a signal before committing themselves to a response, a result that was in line with an influential study by Botwinick and colleagues (1958). These authors had subjects judge which of two simultaneously exposed lines was the shorter; as the difference in length between the lines was reduced, decision latencies increased—substantially more so for older than for younger adults. This result was obtained when the lines were exposed for 2 seconds, but when exposure time was shortened to 0.15 seconds the age difference in latencies greatly diminished. It thus seemed that older adults *preferred* to take more time before committing themselves to a decision, but that this extra time was not necessary.

Being a member of an MRC unit enabled me to make contact with the MRC Applied Psychology Unit (APU) in Cambridge, directed by Donald Broadbent. I visited the Cambridge unit on several occasions, making the acquaintance of such youthful researchers as Alan Baddeley, John Morton, and Patrick Rabbitt, as well as the demi-gods Broadbent and Conrad! In their dichotic listening studies, Broadbent and Gregory (1963) had shown that diversion of attention away from a stimulus reflects a decrease in d′—a reduction in effective signal strength. Inglis and Caird (1963) had carried out dichotic listening experiments on younger and older adults, with the main finding that older adults showed a substantial age-related loss in recall of items from the second ear reported, but with no loss in first ear recall, concluding that ageing increases memory loss from simultaneous interference, in this case recall of the first half-set. This was in line with Welford's (1958) earlier suggestion that an age-related decrement in short-term memory, attributable to simultaneous interference, is a major cause of age-related declines in learning, memory, and problem-solving. Broadbent and Gregory's result made me wonder whether the reduction in d' associated with divided attention might not be greater in older adults; in other words, whether the Inglis and Caird result might reflect an attentional as opposed to a memory problem.

This thought led me to design a dual-task study in which one task was auditory signal detection and the other was short-term recognition memory. Both tasks were presented auditorily, but from different loudspeakers. The memory task consisted of seven successive digit pairs followed immediately by a probe pair; the subject had to decide whether the probe was one of the preceding pairs. The signal detection task consisted of 10 seconds of white noise overlapping the digit-pair presentation; the signal was a 1000-Hz tone lasting for 1 second and occurring at an unpredictable time during the noise. The signal strength was adjusted for each subject to yield 75% detectability, and the signal was present on 50% of the trials, independently of the presence or absence of the memory probe. Thus, on each trial the subject decided yes or no with regard to both tasks, yielding a d' value for each task. The tasks were performed both separately (full attention) and together (divided attention), and we compared groups of young, middle-aged, and older subjects.

One reason for running the study was to see whether divided attention (DA) was particularly detrimental to performance in older adults, but there was a further interest in examining the hypothesis with signal detection measures. Taylor and colleagues (1967) suggested that d'^2 may be considered a measure of processing capacity, and that when two or more discrimination tasks are performed simultaneously the sum of individual values of d'^2 should add to a constant total. More accurately, for tasks T_1 and T_2, performed either alone or together, Taylor et al. suggested that

$$\frac{d'^2(T_1 \text{ together})}{d'^2(T_1 \text{ alone})} + \frac{d'^2(T_2 \text{ together})}{d'^2(T_2 \text{ alone})} = 1.0$$

If subjects can perform each task as well in the shared condition as they can perform it alone, each component ratio would be 1.0 and the sum will be 2.0; but if there is a constant processing capacity that must be shared among simultaneous tasks then the sum of the ratios ($\Sigma d'^2$) should approximate 1.0. In fact, Taylor and colleagues found the sum to be 0.85 and suggested that 15% of capacity must be devoted to managing the division of attention. It seemed possible that if older adults are especially penalized by DA situations they would require more of their capacity to 'programme' the division of attention, and that 'DA costs' would be larger than 15% for them.

The results of the signal detection/memory study are shown in Table 6.1A. Neither the memory task nor the detection task showed age differences when carried out alone, but the $\Sigma d'^2$ values showed a systematic drop with age. The fact that $\Sigma d'^2$ values are greater than 1.0 suggested that these particular tasks did not require extensive cognitive analysis—this would be particularly true of the tone detection task which (following Treisman 1964, 1969) could presumably be carried out by relatively peripheral analysing mechanisms. Accordingly, I carried out a more 'cognitive' version of the experiment in which one task was

Table 6.1 Values of d' and $\Sigma d'^2$ for young, middle-aged, and older adults in two dual-task experiments (Craik 1973)

Experiment 1	Detection	Memory	$\Sigma d'^2$
Young			
Together	1.35	1.08	1.58
Alone	1.39	1.35	
Middle-aged			
Together	1.02	1.28	1.39
Alone	1.82	1.23	
Older			
Together	1.22	0.94	1.05
Alone	1.59	1.38	
Experiment 2	**Letters**	**Digits**	**$\Sigma d'^2$**
Young			
Together	0.62	1.14	0.42
Alone	2.38	1.93	
Middle-aged			
Together	0.76	1.00	0.31
Alone	2.21	2.29	
Old			
Together	0.28	0.56	0.11
Alone	1.70	1.91	

Detection = detection of tone in noise; memory = short-term recognition memory for digit pairs; letters = short-term recognition memory for visual letters; digits = detection of three successive odd digits, presented auditorily visual recognition memory (seven letters presented serially at a 1-second rate, followed immediately by a recognition probe letter) and the other was auditory monitoring (a string of 14 digits presented at 2 digits/second, which subjects monitored for the presence or absence of three successive odd digits (e.g. 935 or 173). Table 6.1B shows the values of d' and d'^2. There are no marked age differences in performance of the digit task by itself, but in this case performance on the recognition memory task does decline with age, possibly owing to the less salient visual presentation. But now all tasks show marked losses when they are performed simultaneously, with the older subjects being especially penalized. Values of $\Sigma d'^2$ are now much less than 1.0, interpreted as reflecting the greater depth of cognitive processing necessary to carry out the tasks. The situation is therefore more complex than envisaged by Taylor *et al.* (1967) with 'processing capacity' apparently depending *inter alia* on tasks, age of subjects, task combinations, and age by task interactions. These conclusions will not surprise readers in 2008, but they do perhaps illustrate how our conceptions of attention and processing capacity have changed in the past 40 years.

I have described this study at some length as it gives a sense of the British interest in attention and short-term memory in the 1960s and early 1970s. I presented the two experiments shown in Table 6.1 at an American Psychological Association meeting in 1973, in a session devoted to the application of signal detection theory to ageing. The person doing the commentary was a psychophysical fundamentalist unfortunately, and he heavily criticized other speakers for using stimuli that were not pure sinusoids. Turning with some distaste to my paper, he commented, 'And then there was the person who used *verbal* stimuli …'—further words failed him! I found this such a traumatic experience that I never followed up on the ideas, although Martin Taylor later comforted me by saying that d' is just a statistical measure, like *t* or *F*.

My own interests in cognitive ageing shifted gradually from studies of attention and dichotic listening to experiments on age differences in primary and secondary memory. The general finding (e.g. Craik 1968) was that the amount recalled from primary memory is not sensitive to ageing, and indeed the same insensitivity is found in amnesia (Baddeley and Warrington 1970). These results make sense from the perspective that primary memory largely reflects recall of items that have been held in mind by means of subvocal rehearsal; they are held in the articulatory loop in terms of the Baddeley and Hitch (1974) working memory model. Recall from secondary memory (or 'long-term memory') *is* sensitive to ageing, however, presumably owing to age-related inefficiencies in both encoding and retrieval. One early observation, following from Murdock's (1960) classic work on factors influencing free recall, was that recall (R) is a linear function of list length (L); that is,

$$R = m + kL$$

where m is a constant reflecting primary memory and k is a further constant reflecting encoding and retrieval factors in secondary memory. Craik (1968) reported that m is unaffected by ageing, by word length, and list length, but that k *is* affected by age and by the size of the set from which the words are drawn—k is larger for younger adults and for smaller sets.

I left the Liverpool Unit in 1965 to take a job as lecturer at Birkbeck College, London, where I remained until 1971 when I moved to Toronto. During the late 1960s and early 1970s I focused largely on mainstream studies of memory and attention, as I was no longer required to study ageing. However, in 1973 I was invited by Jim Birren and Warner Schaie to contribute a chapter on age-related differences in memory to the first edition of their *Handbook of the Psychology of Aging* (1977), and this rekindled my interest in the area. I received some helpful comments on the first draft from the English–Canadian psychologist David Schonfield who, among other points, noted the difficulty that older adults have in 'remembering to remember'—a notion that grew into the current research topic of prospective memory. It is interesting to reflect that Schonfield was thinking about such issues in the 1970s. I had also asked Alan Welford whether he had some new memory data to include in the review. He replied that he did not, but that he was surprised to see that my address was now Toronto and regretted that I was now apparently 'lost to Britain'. The guilt that this mild admonishment might have induced was mitigated, however, by the fact that Welford's letter came from Adelaide, South Australia!

Attention, memory, and ageing, 1960–1980

Studies of ageing memory in the 1960s tended to describe some difference in performance between younger and older adults without much consideration of *mechanism*. Many experiments were carried out in the verbal learning tradition, although mercifully few involved nonsense syllables—perhaps older learners had too much robust good sense to tolerate such pointless exercises! This early work thus dealt more with *learning* than with *memory*, in keeping with the dominant paradigm of the times. Many results were interesting and informative. Wimer and Wigdor (1958) found that age differences occurred mainly at acquisition, and that if initial learning was equated retention and rates of forgetting did not differ. There was much interest in the

conditions of learning. Rate of presentation in the recall phase of paired-associate learning is age sensitive, for example, with older learners especially penalized by fast testing rates (Taub 1967). Hulicka and Grossman (1967) discovered
that, whereas older learners could profit from the use of imagery, they did not
generate image mediators spontaneously. This echoes similar findings in
young children, studied under the label of production deficiency. Experiments
from this era are well described in Donald Kausler's comprehensive
Experimental Psychology and Human Aging (1982).

The new information-processing approach radically changed topics and
paradigms, with a new focus on age differences in the ability to process and
retain information. Experiments showed that older adults processed information less rapidly (Welford 1958), were less able to ignore irrelevant information (Rabbitt 1965), and were more likely to concentrate on one channel
rather than share processing resources between two channels in a dual-task
situation (Broadbent and Heron 1962). Memory comparisons now focused on
possible differences in the capacity, coding characteristics, and forgetting
functions associated with various memory stores—sensory, short-term and
long-term. The answers in brief, and with the benefit of hindsight, are that age
differences are slight in both sensory and short-term memory—with the
exception of an age-related decrement in dichotic listening, as mentioned previously. The idea of limited capacity did not seem relevant to long-term memory, so researchers shifted focus gradually to the processes of encoding and
retrieval. Organizational processes were in vogue at the time, following the
pioneering work of George Mandler, Endel Tulving, and others; in this con-
nection Hultsch (1974) showed that older adults were less effective organizers,
and that this processing inefficiency was one factor contributing to their
poorer long-term memory performance. Other evidence pointed to age-
related retrieval deficits, however. Laurence (1967) found that older adults
showed a disproportionate benefit from receiving cues at retrieval, and
Schonfield and Robertson (1966) reported that, whereas *recall* of verbal material fell off progressively with increasing age, *recognition* memory did not—
implying that the information is still available in the older memory system,
but is not accessible, except with the help of powerful cues. A strong case for
an age-related retrieval deficit being the root cause of memory loss in older
adulthood was made by Burke and Light (1981).

The 1960s and 1970s were thus characterized by a move away from 'verbal
learning' paradigms and from its roots in learning theories. Compared with
America, British psychology was much less under the thrall of learning theory,
so information theory approaches made an earlier start there. Once cognitive
theories became established in the 1960s there was a great liberalization of

ideas and methods, and these gradually trickled down to studies of cognitive ageing. A particularly fresh and insightful programme of studies was carried out by Harry Bahrick and his collaborators (e.g. Bahrick 1979; Bahrick *et al.* 1975). He assessed *very* long-term memory for real-life information, such as names and faces of high-school colleagues (recognition holds up well for at least 25 years but recall falls off earlier—c.f. Schonfield and Robertson, 1966), and for knowledge of places and languages learned many years before. There was also a move towards *models* of memory (e.g. Atkinson and Shiffrin 1968; Baddeley and Hitch 1974; Craik and Lockhart 1972; Crowder and Morton 1969; Waugh and Norman 1965), with the models acting, not so much as representations of 'the truth' (although perhaps they were considered to be so at the time!), but more as points of view that suggested particular lines of experimentation. Two other shifts in the general area were first an attempt to specify *mechanisms* of memory, and second a gradual awakening of interest in the brain and a realization that our behavioural and cognitive notions must ultimately be compatible with brain processes and mechanisms. Two examples of this latter trend are, first, Marcel Kinsbourne's (1980) speculation that interference effects increase with age owing to a reduction in funct-ional distance between cortical representations because of age-related cellular and synaptic loss; competing representations are less easily held apart in the ageing brain. Second, Albert and Kaplan (1980) drew attention to the fact that frontal lobe efficiency declined with age and that this in turn was likely to reduce the efficiency of cognitive control—a very current idea at the present time!

Slowing, inhibition, and resources: cognitive ageing in the 1980s and 1990s

The area of cognitive ageing really took off in the 1980s. New theoretical ideas were proposed and a multitude of experiments conducted to test them. Age-related declines were variously attributed to slowing of cognitive opera-tions (Salthouse 1982, 1996), to a decline in inhibitory processes (Hasher and Zacks 1979, 1988), and to a reduction in available processing resources (Craik and Byrd 1982). Although proponents of these different perspectives argued in favour of their point of view and against alternative positions, the strong likelihood is that *all* of these theoretical ideas have some merit. We are still awaiting an adequate 'unified theory' of cognitive ageing in 2008, however.

My lab in the 1980s was located at Erindale College in the University of Toronto; we worked both on general problems of memory, stemming from the levels of processing ideas suggested by Craik and Lockhart (1972), and on problems of memory and ageing, exploring the hypothesis that ageing is associated with a reduction in available processing resources. The concept of 'processing resources' was left a little vague (to say the least!), but has a lot in common with both general arousal and with the information-processing notions of selective attention and channel capacity. One line we pursued is that, if reduced attentional resources is a major problem of ageing, the effects of ageing might be mimicked by reducing resources in young adults—by placing them in a dual-task situation, for example (Craik 1982). After a number of successful studies on this theme Moshe Naveh-Benjamin has persuaded me that older adults also have an additional memory problem over and above resource attenuation, namely a deficit in establishing and utilizing associative information (Naveh-Benjamin 2000, 2002). Further, the notion that resources must be *allocated* efficiently between tasks is obviously similar to the concept of cognitive control, and my friend Larry Jacoby has patiently told me over the years that 'control' is really the relevant variable. Perhaps, but back in the 1980s we believed firmly in resources, suggested how the idea applied to ageing and memory (e.g. Rabinowitz *et al.* 1982) and to older adults working in dual-task situations (e.g. McDowd and Craik 1988).

If one consequence of ageing is reduced ability to process information rapidly and powerfully, how might that affect memory? It seems plausible that difficult, complex operations requiring a great deal of supervision and control will suffer badly while easy automated operations will be relatively unaffected. This was the message of an important paper by Hasher and Zacks (1979), who presented persuasive evidence that ageing spares automatic mental processes but severely impairs controlled processes. Procedural learning and priming are two types of retention that can apparently be executed in the relative absence of cognitive control, and it was shown by Light and Singh (1987) that priming declined little with age. Two other notions that fit this general analysis are, first, the proposal by Jacoby and colleagues (e.g. Dywan and Jacoby 1990; Jacoby 1991; Jennings and Jacoby 1993) that memory processes can be dissociated into the components of recollection and familiarity. Recollection requires conscious control whereas familiarity does not, and Jacoby has demonstrated that recollection is age sensitive whereas familiarity is not (Jennings and Jacoby 1993). Second, I have suggested that, when remembering is not well supported by either the external or internal environments, a person can nevertheless run off appropriate and effective retrieval operations by mustering 'self-initiated' mental activities (Craik 1983, 1986). Such self-initiated activities are effortful, however; they probably involve frontal lobe processes and apparently decline in the course of ageing (Craik 2002). I am therefore suggesting that ageing is associated with a reduction in either (or both) processing resources or cognitive control, that this simple notion fits well with observed differential age-related losses, and also fits the basic ideas of a number of theorists (Craik 1983, 1986; Hasher and Zacks 1979, 1988; Jacoby 1991; Jennings and Jacoby 1993). There may be more latent agreement in the area than we have all acknowledged!

The current scene

I will end this nostalgic exercise in retrospective memory by pointing to a few topics of current interest in the area of age-related changes in memory, again focusing on topics that have been of greatest interest to me and my collaborators. Undoubtedly the main shift in research activity from previous decades is the current interest in brain mechanisms and their relations to behavioural and experiential variables. One aspect of this approach is neuropsychology— studying the effects of neural pathology on cognitive measures—and one focus here is to find parallels with the normal ageing process. Theories and findings in the area are well described in review chapters by Moscovitch and Winocur (1992) and Prull *et al.* (2000). Current conjectures include the notion that many age-related problems in working memory and cognitive control can be related to inefficiencies of frontal lobe functioning (West 1996), although this remains controversial (Phillips and Henry 2005). Rubin (1999) has suggested that Parkinson's disease and subcortical damage might provide a better model for cognitive ageing; this suggestion may be quite compatible with the frontal hypothesis, however, given the strong links provided by frontal–striatal circuits.

The area of cognitive neuroscience has been revolutionized by the development of various neuroimaging technologies, and this type of evidence is now an obligatory component of any current description of memory functioning. It still makes perfect sense to develop models based entirely on behavioural data, but it will be progressively more necessary for such models to be compatible with the rapidly accruing evidence from functional magnetic resonance imaging (fMRI) and other brain-scanning techniques. Evidence and theoretical notions relating to the cognitive neuroscience of memory and ageing are still in the early stages of development, although interesting work is being reported by Cheryl Grady, Roberto Cabeza, Denise Park, and other colleagues. Useful reviews of the current scene are provided by Grady and Craik (2000) and in a book edited by Cabeza, Nyberg, and Park (2005).

But many interesting things are happening in purely behavioural studies. One topic that has generated lively debate is 'prospective memory'—remembering to carry out some planned action at a future time—'remembering to remember' in Schonfield's (1982) phrase. I had suggested in 1983 that prospective memory necessarily involved self-initiated activities and should therefore be one type of memory that falls off steeply with age (actually, John Harris made this point to me after hearing the talk on which the paper was based). However, Einstein and McDaniel (1990) reported a study finding *no* age-related decrement in prospective memory, which clearly went against Schonfield's and Craik's (and Harris's!) intuitions. Later work by Einstein and McDaniel's group *did* find an age difference in time-based tasks (remembering to carry out an action at some nominated time), which the investigators characterized as being high in self-initiated retrieval, but no age differences in event-based tasks (remembering to carry out a planned action when a nominated cue is encountered later) (Einstein *et al*. 1995). Studies from my own lab *have* found age-related differences in event-based prospective memory, however (Rendell and Craik 2000), so the issue is still unresolved.

Context is an important concept in memory studies, and my own work has related it to ageing in two rather different ways. First, encoding context may be regarded as the source of some piece of acquired information—you know the facts, but were they learned from a friend, read in a newspaper, or seen on TV? Following work by Dan Schacter, a study by McIntyre and Craik (1987) showed that older adults are less able to recollect where and when they learned some information; that is, older adults show a mild form of 'source amnesia'. Further, the degree of source amnesia is related to their performance on tests of frontal lobe functioning (Craik *et al*. 1990). This latter study thus ties in difficulties of recollection to frontal lobe efficiency, and possibly again to age-related problems with self-initiated activities. Given this evidence of age-related problems in recollecting context, it is apparently paradoxical to claim that older adults' memory is *more* dependent on reinstatement of the encoding context than is the case for younger adults. Yet the evidence also shows that older people benefit *more* than do their younger counterparts from 'environmental support' at the time of retrieval (Craik 1983, 1986; Luo *et al*. 2007). This is not a paradox in my opinion, however; both cases reflect an age-related difficulty in initiating appropriate encoding and retrieval operations in the absence of external cues and guidance.

Age-related inefficiencies of cognitive control are still regarded as the root cause of cognitive decline at the present time, even though the precipitating factors remain a matter of fierce debate. Candidates include general slowing (Salthouse, 1996), less effective inhibitory or control powers (Hasher *et al*. 1999; Hay and Jacoby 1999), and a decline in working memory operations (Park *et al*. 2002). Even the vaguely defined notion of attentional resources is beginning to receive support from some neuroscientists (e.g. Sarter *et al*. 2006),

so this too remains a viable candidate. The next phase in theoretical development will be to show how these various constructs map on to one another; my
own bet is that many will be shown to be aspects of the same basic neurobiological mechanism. One last puzzle is the role of consolidation in age-related
memory problems. I have taken the view that, if processing is sufficiently
rich and meaningful during encoding, good memory follows automatically,
but this position was *not* supported in some studies of divided attention
(Craik and Kester 2000). So it seems possible that, as with amnesic patients,
older adults may process information deeply and elaborately, yet still
show later memory decrements. Alan Baddeley has suggested this to me on
several occasions.

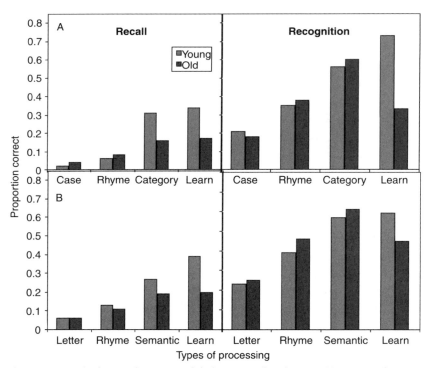

Figure 6.1 Levels then and now. Part (A) shows recall and recognition scores for
younger and older adults after encoding in terms of case, rhyme, and semantic incidental orienting tasks or intentional learning (Craik 1977). Part (B) shows recall and
recognition performance after generation of the first letter, a rhyming word or a
semantic association to presented names, or intentional learning of such names
(Troyer *et al.* 2006).

Conclusion

So what has changed in 50 years? My retrospective scan through the area suggests that terminology and methods have changed a great deal, but that fundamental ideas have changed much less. Welford's (1958) point that many problems of ageing are attributable to an increased vulnerability to interference in short-term memory can be readily translated into age-related problems with working memory and executive functions. In my 1977 review paper, I reported a levels-of-processing experiment with younger and older adults. The main result of interest was that older adults performed as well as younger adults when a semantic orienting task at encoding was combined with a well supported (recognition) task at retrieval (Figure 6.1A). In recent work with Angela Troyer and others, we again used levels of processing in an attempt to bolster name learning in older adults, and again contrasted later recall with later recognition. The similarities with the earlier study are striking (Figure 6.1B), and I leave it to the reader to decide whether this represents brilliant foresight in 1977 or total stagnation in 2007!

Acknowledgements

Preparation of this chapter was facilitated by a grant from the Natural Sciences and Engineering Research Council of Canada.

References

Albert, M. S. and Kaplan, E. (1980). Organic implications of neuropsychological deficits in the elderly. In: L. W. Poon, J. L. Fozard, L. S., Cermak, D. Arenberg, and L. W. Thompson (ed.) *New directions in memory and aging*, pp. 403–32. Hillsdale, NJ: L. Erlbaum Associates.

Atkinson, R. C. and Shiffrin, R. M. (1968). Human memory: a proposed system and its control processes. In: K. W. Spence and J. T. Spence (ed.) *The psychology of learning and motivation: advances in research and theory*, vol. 2, pp. 89–195. New York: Academic Press.

Baddeley, A. D. and Hitch, G. (1974). Working memory. In: G. H. Bower (ed.) *The psychology of learning and motivation: advances in research and theory*, vol. 8, pp. 47–89. New York: Academic Press.

Baddeley, A. D. and Warrington, E. K. (1970). Amnesia and the distinction between long- and short-term memory. *Journal of Verbal Learning and Verbal Behavior* 14: 575–89.

Bahrick, H. P. (1979). Maintenance of knowledge: questions about memory we forgot to ask. *Journal of Experimental Psychology: General* 108(3): 296–308.

Bahrick, H. P., Bahrick, P. O., and Wittlinger, R. P. (1975). Fifty years of memory for names and faces: a cross-sectional approach. *Journal of Experimental Psychology: General* 104(1): 54–75.

Birren, J. and Schaie W. (1977). *Handbook of the psychology of aging*. New York: Van Nostrand Reinhold.

Botwinick, J., Brinley, J. F., and Robbin, J. S. (1958). The interaction effects of perceptual difficulty and stimulus exposure time on age differences in speed and accuracy of response. *Gerontologia* 2: 1–10.

Broadbent, D. E. (1958). *Perception and communication*. London: Pergamon Press.

Broadbent, D. E. and Gregory, M. (1963). Division of attention and the decision theory of signal detection. *Proceedings of the Royal Society of London, Series B* 158: 222.

Broadbent, D. E. and Heron, A. (1962). Effects of a subsidiary task on performance involving immediate memory by younger and older men. *British Journal of Psychology* 53(2): 189–98.

Burke, D. M. and Light, L. L. (1981). Memory and aging: the role of retrieval processes. *Psychological Bulletin* 90(3): 513–46.

Cabeza, R., Nyberg, L., and Park, D. (ed.) (2005). *Cognitive neuroscience of aging: linking cognitive and cerebral aging*. New York: Oxford University Press.

Craik, F. I. M. (1968). Two components in free recall. *Journal of Verbal Learning and Verbal Behavior* 7(6): 996–1004.

Craik, F. I. M. (1973). Signal detection analysis of age differences in divided attention. Paper presented to a meeting of the American Psychological Association, Montreal, 1973.

Craik, F. I. M. (1977). Age differences in human memory. In: J. E. Birren and K. W. Schaie (ed.) *Handbook of the psychology of aging*, pp. 384–420. New York: Van Nostrand Reinhold.

Craik, F. I. M. (1982). Selective changes in encoding as a function of reduced processing capacity. In: F. Klix, J. Hoffmann, and E. van der Meer (ed.) *Cognitive research in psychology*, pp. 152–61. Amsterdam: North Holland.

Craik, F. I. M. (1983). On the transfer of information from temporary to permanent memory. *Philosophical Transactions of the Royal Society of London, Series B* 302: 341–59.

Craik, F. I. M. (1986). A functional account of age differences in memory. In: F. Klix and H. Hagendorf (ed.) *Human memory and cognitive capabilities, mechanisms, and performance*, Part A, pp. 409–22. Amsterdam: Elsevier Science.

Craik, F. I. M. (2002). Human memory and aging. In: L. Bäckman and C. von Hofsten (ed.) *Psychology at the turn of the millennium*, pp. 261–80. Hove: Psychology Press.

Craik, F. I. M. and Byrd, M. (1982). Aging and cognitive deficits: the role of attentional resources. In: Craik, F. I. M. and S. E. Trehub (ed.) *Aging and cognitive processes*, pp. 191–211. New York: Plenum Press.

Craik, F. I. M. and Hay, J. F. (1999). Aging and judgments of duration: effects of task complexity and method of estimation. *Perception and Psychophysics* 61(3): 549–60.

Craik, F. I. M. and Kester, J. D. (2000). Divided attention and memory: impairment of processing or consolidation? In: E. Tulving (ed.) *Memory, consciousness, and brain: the Tallinn Conference*, pp. 38–51. New York: Psychology Press.

Craik, F. I. M. and Lockhart, R. S. (1972). Levels of processing: a framework for memory research. *Journal of Verbal Learning and Verbal Behavior* 11(6): 671–84.

Craik, F. I. M., Morris, L. W., Morris, R. G., and Loewen, E. R. (1990). Relations between source amnesia and frontal lobe functioning in older adults. *Psychology and Aging* 5(1): 148–51.

Crowder, R. G. and Morton, J. (1969). Precategorical acoustic storage (PAS). *Perception and Psychophysics* 5(6): 365–73.

Dywan, J. and Jacoby, L. (1990). Effects of aging on source monitoring: differences in susceptibility to false fame. *Psychology and Aging* 5(3): 379–87.

Einstein, G. O. and McDaniel, M. A. (1990). Normal aging and prospective memory. *Journal of Experimental Psychology: Learning, Memory, and Cognition* 16(4): 717–26.

Einstein, G. O., McDaniel, M. A., Richardson, S. L., Guynn, M. J., and Cunfer, A. R. (1995). Aging and prospective memory: examining the influences of self-initiated retrieval processes. *Journal of Experimental Psychology: Learning, Memory, and Cognition* 21(4): 996–1007.

Grady, C. L. and Craik, F. I. M. (2000). Changes in memory processing with age. *Current Opinion in Neurobiology* 10(2): 224–31.

Hasher, L. and Zacks, R. T. (1979). Automatic and effortful processes in memory. *Journal of Experimental Psychology: General* 108(3): 356–88.

Hasher, L. and Zacks, R. T. (1988). Working memory, comprehension, and aging: a review and a new view. In: G. H. Bower (ed.) *The psychology of learning and motivation: advances in research and theory*, vol. 22, pp. 193–225. San Diego, CA: Academic Press.

Hasher, L., Zacks, R. T., and May, C. P. (1999). Inhibitory control, circadian arousal, and age. In: D. Gopher and A. Koriat (ed.) *Attention and performance XVII: Cognitive regulation of performance: interaction of theory and application*, pp. 653–75. Cambridge, MA: MIT Press.

Hay, J. F. and Jacoby, L. L. (1999). Separating habit and recollection in young and older adults: effects of elaborative processing and distinctiveness. *Psychology and Aging* 14(1): 122–34.

Hulicka, I. M. and Grossman, J. L. (1967). Age-group comparisons for the use of mediators in paired-associate learning. *Journal of Gerontology* 22: 46–51.

Hultsch, D. F. (1974). Learning to learn in adulthood. *Journal of Gerontology* 29(3): 302–8.

Inglis, J. and Caird, W. K. (1963). Age differences in successive responses to simultaneous stimulation. *Canadian Journal of Psychology* 17(1): 98–105.

Jacoby, L. L. (1991). A process dissociation framework: separating automatic from intentional uses of memory. *Journal of Memory and Language* 30(5): 513–41.

Jennings, J. M. and Jacoby, L. L. (1993). Automatic versus intentional uses of memory: aging, attention, and control. *Psychology and aging* 8(2): 283–93.

Kausler, D. H. (1982). *Experimental psychology and human aging*. New York: Wiley.

Kinsbourne, M. (1980). Attentional dysfunction and the elderly: theoretical models and research perspectives. In: L. W. Poon, J. L. Fozard, L. S. Cermak, D. Arenberg, and L. W. Thompson (ed.) *New directions in memory and aging*, pp. 113–29. Hillsdale, NJ: Erlbaum.

Laurence, M. W. (1967). Memory loss with age: a test of two strategies for its retardation. *Psychonomic Science* 9(4): 209–10.

Light, L. L. and Singh, A. (1987). Implicit and explicit memory in young and older adults. *Journal of Experimental Psychology: Learning, Memory, and Cognition* 13(4): 531–41.

Luo, L., Hendriks, T., and Craik, F. I. M. (2007). Age differences in recollection: three patterns of enhanced encoding. *Psychology and Aging* 22(2): 269–80.

McDowd, J. M. and Craik, F. I. M. (1988). Effects of aging and task difficulty on divided attention performance. *Journal of Experimental Psychology: Human Perception and Performance* 14(2): 267–80.

McIntyre, J. S. and Craik, F. I. M. (1987). Age differences in memory for item and source information. *Canadian Journal of Psychology* 41(2): 175–92.

Miller, G. A. (1956). The magical number seven, plus or minus two: some limits on our capacity for processing information. *Psychological Review* 63(2): 81–97.

Moscovitch, M. and Winocur, G. (1992). The neuropsychology of memory and aging. In: F. I. M. Craik and T. A. Salthouse (ed.) *The handbook of aging and cognition*, pp. 315–72. Hillsdale, NJ: Lawrence Erlbaum Associates.

Murdock, B. B. J. (1960). The immediate retention of unrelated words. *Journal of Experimental Psychology* 60(4): 222–34.

Naveh-Benjamin, M. (2000). Adult age differences in memory performance: tests of an associative deficit hypothesis. *Journal of Experimental Psychology: Learning, Memory, and Cognition* 26(5): 1170–87.

Naveh-Benjamin, M. (2002). The effects of divided attention on encoding processes: underlying mechanisms. In: M. Naveh-Benjamin, M. Moscovitch, and H. L. Roediger III (ed.) *Perspectives on human memory and cognitive aging: essays in honour of Fergus Craik*, pp. 193–207. Philadelphia: Psychology Press.

Park, D. C., Lautenschlager, G., Hedden, T., Davidson, N S., Smith, A D., and Smith, P. K. (2002). Models of visuospatial and verbal memory across the adult life span. *Psychology and Aging* 17: 299–320.

Phillips, L. H. and Henry, J. D. (2005). An evaluation of the frontal lobe theory of aging. In: J. Duncan, L. Phillips, and P. McLeod (ed.) *Measuring the mind: speed, control, aging*, pp. 191–216. Oxford: Oxford University Press.

Prull, M. W., Gabrieli, J. D. E., and Bunge, S. A. (2000). Age-related changes in memory: a cognitive neuroscience perspective. In: F.I.M. Craik and T.A Salthouse (ed.) *The handbook of aging and cognition* (2nd edn), pp. 91–153. Mahwah, NJ: Lawrence Erlbaum Associates.

Rabbitt, P. M. A. (1965). An age decrement in the ability to ignore irrelevant information. *Journal of Gerontology* 20: 233–7.

Rabinowitz, J. C., Craik, F. I. M., and Ackerman, B. P. (1982). A processing resource account of age differences in recall. *Canadian Journal of Psychology* 36(2): 325–44.

Rendell, P. G. and Craik, F. I. M. (2000). Virtual week and actual week: age-related differences in prospective memory. *Applied Cognitive Psychology* 14: 43–62.

Rubin, D. C. (1999). Frontal–striatal circuits in cognitive aging: evidence for caudate involvement. *Aging, Neuropsychology, and Cognition* 6(4): 241–59.

Salthouse, T. A. (1982). Adult cognition: an experimental psychology of human aging. New York: Springer.

Salthouse, T. A. (1996). The processing-speed theory of adult age differences in cognition. *Psychological Review* 103(3): 403–28.

Sarter, M., Gehring, W. J., and Kozak, R. (2006). More attention must be paid: the neurobiology of attentional effort. *Brain Research Reviews* 51(2): 145–60.

Schonfield, D. (1982). Attention switching in higher mental process. In: F. I. M Craik and S. E. Trehub (ed.) *Aging and cognitive processes*, pp. 309–16. New York: Plenum Press.

Schonfield, D. and Robertson, B. A. (1966). Memory storage and aging. *Canadian Journal of Psychology* 20(2): 228–36.

Swets, J. A., Tanner, W. P. J., and Birdsall, T. G. (1961). Decision processes in perception. *Psychological Review* 68(5): 301–40.

Taub, H. A. (1967). Paired associates learning as a function of age, rate, and instructions. *Journal of Genetic Psychology* 111(1): 41–6.

Taylor, M. M., Lindsay, P. H., and Forbes, S. M. (1967). Quantification of shared capacity processing in auditory and visual discrimination. In: A. F. Sanders (ed.) *Attention and performance*, pp. 223–9. Amsterdam: North Holland.

Treisman, A. M. (1964). Selective attention in man. *British Medical Bulletin* 20(1): 12–16.

Treisman, A. M. (1969). Strategies and models of selective attention. *Psychological Review* 76(3): 282–99.

Troyer, A. K., Häfliger, A., Cadieux, M. J., and Craik, F. I. M. (2006). Name and face learning in older adults: effects of level of processing, self-generation, and intention to learn. *Journals of Gerontology: Series B: Psychological Sciences and Social Sciences* 61(2): 67–74.

Waugh, N. C. and Norman, D. A. (1965). Primary memory. *Psychological Review* 72(2): 89–104.

Welford, A. T. (1958). *Ageing and human skill*. Oxford: Oxford University Press.

West, R. L. (1996). An application of prefrontal cortex function theory to cognitive aging. *Psychological Bulletin* 120(2): 272–92.

Wimer, R. E. and Wigdor, B. T. (1958). Age differences in retention of learning. *Journal of Gerontology* 13: 291–5.

7

Psycholinguistics in our time

Anne Cutler

A nostalgic vignette

It's hard to deny that some of the most radical changes in our scientific lives over the past decades have been in the mundane trappings of our daily work. The last words on the last page of my—beautifully formatted—PhD thesis (Cutler 1975) are: 'This dissertation was typed by Arlene Walker'. That is how we prepared documents in 1975—remember? We had someone else do it. Now, I venture to suppose that all chapters in the present book were typed straight into a computer by the authors.

Like other branches of science, the practice of psychology thus no longer offers employment to substantial numbers of secretaries. Careers like that of Arlene Walker don't happen any more (having put herself through college with part-time secretarial work, she did a PhD at Cornell with Eleanor J. Gibson, and is now full professor of psychology and associate provost at the University of Montana: http://psychweb.psy.umt.edu/www/faculty).

Of course, psychologists are not alone in having had their daily existence transformed by technological advance. Perhaps more than many others, though, we endure change in the very content of our work as a result of what technology offers; the computer as a model information processor is one obvious case. Psycholinguistics, my niche in contemporary psychology and in this book, has certainly been immensely technology-driven. See the section 'Technology in the driving seat' below for more on this. But first, some background on psycholinguistics and why it is a little different from many other areas of psychology in our time, and an account of how, somewhat against the odds, I found my perfect niche there.

A brief history of psycholinguistics

The biggest change involving psycholinguistics is that it exists now, and 50 years ago it didn't. As I write this in 2007, it is 50 years since the publication of Chomsky's *Syntactic Structures* (Chomsky 1957). By launching the notion of a grammar as a device for generating the sentences of a language,

Chomsky made linguistics suddenly exciting in a way it had never been before, and this new excitement in linguistics was one of the reasons for the growth of psycholinguistics as a recognizable field of study in its own right. Each of the parent disciplines, psychology and linguistics, boasts an independent research tradition going back centuries, but psycholinguistics itself was born only in the second half of the twentieth century.

Psycholinguists want to know how language structure relates to language use. A psycholinguist like me is primarily a psychologist, seeking to understand the mental structures and processes involved in the use of language. Other psycholinguists who are primarily linguists are more concerned with the patterning of language itself. The common factor that makes us psycholinguists, though, is the cross-disciplinary contact. Thus, I need to wonder about why language has certain universal characteristics, how it can vary in language-specific ways, and how these aspects of structure impinge upon the way language is processed; my linguistic colleagues must be interested in explaining patterns of language performance, and must also be open to evidence from laboratory studies with highly controlled processing tasks. We all need to be interdisciplinary if psycholinguistics is to succeed in solving its core problems.

The relation between psycholinguistics' two parent traditions has changed several times over the years, and has differed across different areas of the field. Language acquisition had a long and strong tradition, for observational techniques predate experimental labs. This early research tradition, from the nineteenth and early twentieth centuries (think of Stern and Stern, think of Piaget), viewed language acquisition as part of the general cognitive and social development of the child. Many hold this view today. But a separate parallel line of research (also still going strong) arose from Chomsky's proposal of an innate and universal 'language acquisition device', and this, in principle, made acquisition a central topic in the study of the human language faculty. It also provided basic assumptions that strongly influenced all the rest of psycholinguistics at the time.

Indeed, owing to the Chomskyan revolution, linguistics was able to set the tone as adult-language psycholinguistics got started in the 1960s. Much empirical research was aimed at deriving processing predictions from linguistic models, in particular from grammar models. The Derivational Theory of Complexity is the best known of these. It proposed that the complexity of grammatical derivations of sentences in transformational grammar could directly predict the processing complexity of the same sentences. Experimental support for this proposal was found (e.g. Miller and McKean 1964), and psycholinguists of the time also did their best to test rival grammatical theories against one another (e.g. Clifton and Odom 1966).

This period ended when the linguistic theories changed—solely in response to linguistic argumentation and not at all in response to the growing body of processing evidence. This was, understandably, not a little frustrating to psycholinguists, who had spent years gathering the relevant evidence. The result was a period when psychological studies of language processing tried to maintain independence from linguistic theory, with the tone set by psychological issues alone. Linguistics returned to psycholinguistics only in the 1980s, with a new growth of research in sentence processing, including processing models that were intended as linguistic proposals (e.g. Frazier and Fodor 1978). Current psycholinguistic research is more integrated still.

Two formative influences

In most universities the parent disciplines I referred to are located in separate faculties, so that psycholinguists generally come to the field via courses taken in a psychology department or a linguistics (or language) department. But the establishment of such courses began in America only in the 1960s, and elsewhere even later. When I started my university course, psycholinguistics was unheard of in Australia.

Recent neurophysiological discoveries suggest that an ability to discriminate foreign speech sounds depends in good part on white matter endowment in the auditory cortex (Chee *et al.* 2004; Golestani *et al.* 2006). Armed with this new knowledge, I now view my grandfather's enthusiastic involvement in the early days of radio in Australia and my own secondary-school foreign-language results as offshoots of the same genetic heritage. But at university all that was on offer for the bearer of such a heritage was preparation for a school teaching career. The associated school teaching scholarship further constrained my choice of courses. Psychology was not so much a choice (my choice would have been biology, but the timetable made it impossible) as a necessary evil to fulfil the 'science subject requirement' in a general arts degree.

The introductory psychology lectures at the University of Melbourne in 1962 were chiefly aimed at convincing the suffering recipients that psychology really was a 'science subject'. Rats (not known for communicating in language, of course) figured largely. The main message to me was clear: psychology was not for me.

Enter, quite by accident, formative influence number 1. I was swotting for the final exam in the library but couldn't take one word more of what I was reading—my memory tells me it was Cohen and Nagel (1934) on scientific method, which is unfair to an excellent treatise, but revealing about the sort of department that expects first-year students to read it. Wandering around the library I came across the new acquisitions shelf, where I picked up a big blue–green book. It proved to contain: an article about an American Indian tribe who expressed concepts like 'house' and 'water' as verbs; an account of how to produce intelligible speech from patterns painted on glass; proof that children could invent the correct plural forms of new words that they had never heard before, such as *wug* or *wuck*; a grammar machine that could generate an infinite number of sentences, with the further proposal that speakers could be thought of as embodiments of such a machine. And much more. So—all this was psychology too? Was it perhaps worth going on with this subject after all?

It was years later that I worked out that the book must have been Saporta's collection of readings called *Psycholinguistics* (a title that would have said nothing to me at the time). Blessings upon the University of Melbourne library for having a book published in 1961 as a new acquisition in November 1962, and for putting the new acquisitions on a shelf where the first-years could freely read them.

Saporta thus ensured that I stuck with psychology (and the many more rats) right through to my degree. My ignorance of psycholinguistics, though, was still not disturbed by any of the courses I took. In America, by now, a few forward-thinking universities had started cross-faculty PhD programmes sponsored jointly by linguistics and psychology departments (not easy then, just as it is not easy today). One such programme was at the University of Illinois, and one of its early graduates was Australian, Ken Forster. He returned to Melbourne as a postdoc and taught a series of lunchtime seminars on psycholinguistics in my final year, and he needed a research assistant who could speak German, exactly at the moment that I needed some short-term employment to bridge a gap between my exams and my departure on a scholarship to Europe. That RA time was formative influence number 2—see Forster and Clyne (1968) for evidence that it wasn't time wasted. Those who know Ken—among them a substantial population of Australian psycholinguists he has launched in the field—will know his gift of talking to everyone at the same level. I cultivated the habit of greeting him each day with coffee, to receive in return remarks like: 'What do you think of this idea I had this morning…'. There was no chance that he ever got a useful comment back, but golly, did I learn a lot about how to formulate and test scientific ideas.

The Forster experience sent me, after some necessary detours (for school teaching scholarships have to be paid off in teaching time), to America to do a PhD in psycholinguistics. It was a good time to be a psycholinguist interested in spoken language, and with a polyglot background, because there were few like me. It was a good time to be in this new field, because it had attracted the attention of the Max Planck Society, whose institute for psycholinguistic research was set up roughly coincident with my emergence from graduate school. That institute (where eighteen years later I became a director) was and still is dedicated to bringing psychological and linguistic expertise together, and without it, advances in psycholinguistics would have been much harder to achieve.

Technology in the driving seat

Technological advance prompted many of the changes in the field. Procedures for chronometric analysis in experimental psychology had first prompted research interest in language processing anyway. The tape recorder made possible controlled and replicable research on spoken language, and from the 1970s onwards digital signal processing techniques made computer-based analysis, storage, and presentation of speech possible. While visual word recognition, based mainly on evidence from lexical decision and word naming, started first, and continues to be a minor industry in itself, word recognition is now almost as well studied in the auditory as in the visual modality.

Besides the early visual/auditory imbalance, there was another. So dominant was language comprehension over language production as a research topic in early psycholinguistics that it was possible for another of this volume's contributors to maintain in the *Annual Review of Psychology*: '*The fundamental problem in psycholinguistics is simple to formulate: what happens when we understand sentences?*' (Johnson-Laird 1974). The reasons for the dominance of comprehension studies were obvious: control over the conditions in which an experiment is conducted is paramount, and control over stimuli presented for comprehension is trivially easy to achieve whereas control over spontaneous language production seems at first glance nigh on impossible. But some concentrated efforts, especially by MPI founder Levelt and colleagues (Bock 1995; Bock and Levelt 1994; Levelt 1992), produced new techniques for studying the production of words, phrases, and sentences. Research on production is now competitive with research on comprehension.

Back with technology, another revolution was brought about by computer-readable vocabularies and large language corpora. They provided a reality test for models of spoken-word recognition and sentence processing. Models of word recognition that were modality independent (e.g. Morton 1969) had been joined, in the late 1970s, by models that attempted to capture the temporal nature of spoken-word processing in particular (Cole and Jakimik 1978; Marslen-Wilson and Welsh 1978). These models saw speech understanding as a sequence of word recognition acts; as soon as one word was identified, it would allow the beginning of the next word to be located for its processing to begin. However, the availability of the electronic dictionaries, from the mid-1980s, pulled the rug out completely from under this view (Cutler and Carter 1987; Luce 1986; Pisoni *et al.* 1985). Vocabulary analyses showed that words in speech were hardly ever unique objects. Thus *recognition* begins with *wreck* followed by *a*; how would a simple sequential processor know *not* to recognize *wreck*?

Technology provided the way out of this problem too. The programming techniques developed in engineering and mathematics—in particular, connectionist modelling—altered the type of modelling undertaken in all cognitive psychology, psycholinguistics included. The growing knowledge of vocabulary statistics called for new models that could simultaneously entertain the multiple possibilities that speech turned out to consist of, and—right on cue—connectionism provided them (e.g. McClelland and Elman 1986). For the past 20 years, all models of spoken-word recognition have allowed for concurrent activation of multiple word candidates, with some form of competition resolving the eventual selection (Gaskell and Marslen-Wilson 1997; McClelland and Elman 1986; Norris 1994). In such models, *recognition*, *wreck*, *a*, and many more fully and partially supported candidates (*rest*, *wrecker*, etc.) could all be evaluated simultaneously, and support for any one of them could automatically modulate the support received by the others without the need for intervention by a separate decision process. The past two decades in spoken-word recognition research have been unusually harmonious as a result of the agreement on this fundamental architecture (though not on the flow of information within it; see Norris *et al.* 2000, and its 31 largely dissenting companion commentaries).

This harmony may disappear as new types of model challenge the currently accepted structure (e.g. Norris and McQueen, submitted). In addition, today's main technological driving force, in psycholinguistics as in all areas of cognitive psychology, is supplied by the techniques of neuroscience. Cognitive neuroscience methods are currently being embraced by psycholinguists, as by researchers in all other branches of cognitive psychology, and imaging evidence is almost as desirable in linguistics as in psychology (though the first linguistic model based on such evidence is yet to be seen). As yet, neuroscience has had no effect on the structure of psycholinguistic models. Alas, the reverse is also true; I am probably not the only contributor to this book to hope that the structure of psychological models will come to have greater influence on cognitive neuroscience research in the future.

The universal substrate

The biggest change *within* psycholinguistics concerns the interpretation of the shared basic assumption—we saw it already in the section on history—that the language-processing system is universal. The most significant fact about language acquisition is that the language a child acquires is the language the environment makes available. The child's specific genetic endowment brings no leanings towards one language rather than another. This suggests that the processing involved in language acquisition—to whatever extent it involves innate specialization for linguistic structure, or exploits general cognitive abilities—is much the same in all humans: universal rather than language specific. By extension, the basic architecture of adult language processing (for instance, the multiple activation and competition of spoken-word recognition described above) should be common to all.

As translated into the experimental practice of the 1970s, this seemed to imply that the characteristics of the language-processing system could be studied in any language to equal effect. Although the acquisition of language-specific structure was obviously an important topic for investigation (e.g. see Slobin 1985), the basic goal was an account of the universal system that dealt with the variable inputs. In consequence, early studies of adult processing were conceived as, in principle, independent of the language in which they happened to be carried out. It was entirely possible for an experiment carried out in one language to be followed up, supported, or countered by an experiment in another language, without any reference being made to whether the difference in language might play a role in the processing being examined. Example 1: the lexical ambiguity effect in phoneme monitoring, established in English (Cairns and Kamerman 1975; Foss 1970; Foss and Jenkins 1973; Swinney and Hakes 1976), but attacked via experiments in French (Mehler *et al.* 1978). Example 2: the debate on 'units of perception', in which experiments were variously carried in English (e.g. Foss and Swinney 1973; Healy and Cutting 1976; Savin and Bever 1970), French (e.g. Segui *et al.* 1981), and Portuguese (e.g. Morais *et al.* 1979). The language in which the experiment was done was never referred to as an important factor in any of the cited papers.

Things have changed now, and I was there as it happened. When I graduated there were few people working on spoken language, and not many of the ones working in America had a polyglot background, as I have already described. My PhD topic was the processing of stress, and it doesn't take a very wide acquaintance with other languages to realize that English-like stress is absolutely not a universal phonological feature. So I came to wonder about how to fit my stress findings into a universal framework. While I was wondering, Jacques Mehler and his colleagues put forward a claim (Mehler *et al.* 1981) that speech is segmented for lexical access in terms of syllabic units. My own findings convinced me, however, that segmentation of speech was based on stress. Moreover, my first reaction on hearing about Mehler's experiment was that it would not work in English. The short version of the story is that indeed it didn't; English listeners not only didn't produce the same results with materials in their native language, they didn't even produce the same results with the original French materials from Mehler's study. Extraordinarily (to us, then), however, French listeners did produce the same syllabically motivated pattern when presented with the English materials.

This suggested that listeners from different language backgrounds command different routines for processing speech, and against the background of psycholinguistic universalism the finding was startling enough to appear in *Nature* (Cutler *et al.* 1983). Clearly it was no longer possible to assume that every part of adult processing should be shared by all language users; French listeners segmented in syllabic units, but English listeners used stress. Presumably, some parts of every listener's processing system might be language specific. But the argument for a universal basis retains its force—all children begin from the same point, so in some sense the system must be universal. The next challenge, therefore, was to seek the underlying universal commonality that is susceptible to language-specific implementation. For stress in English and syllables in French, the common factor is language rhythm. For instance, French and English poetic forms are, respectively, based on syllable patterning and on stress beats.

This universal substrate of language specificity is what I've spent the last quarter of a century working on, one way and another. I am far from the only one, because just as there were others in the 1980s who were looking at the psycholinguistic implications of cross-linguistic variation (e.g. Byrne and Davidson 1985; Werker and Logan 1985), so there have been many since, across a wide spectrum of psycholinguistic approaches, who have wrestled with the reconciliation of the universal and language-specific (Bowerman 1994; Emmorey 2002; Grimshaw 1997; Imai and Gentner 1997; Newmeyer 1998; Thornton *et al.* 1998). The difference with the point where I started is that it would be unthinkable now to counter an experiment in Language A with an experiment in Language B without any mention of the language switch; even more satisfyingly, cross-language comparisons are found in all the psycholinguistic journals. The general 1970s' acceptance of a universal common processor has been replaced in psycholinguistics by widespread recognition that cross-linguistic differences might be the key to understanding the possible variation in, and thus the true universal nature of, the system.

References

Bock, J. K. (1995). Sentence production: from mind to mouth. In: J. L. Miller and P. Eimas (ed.) *Handbook of perception and cognition: speech, language, and communication*, vol. 11, pp. 181–216. Orlando, FL: Academic Press.

Bock, K. and Levelt, W. J. M. (1994). Language production: grammatical encoding. In: M. A. Gernsbacher (ed.) *Handbook of psycholinguistics*, pp. 945–84. New York: Academic Press.

Bowerman, M. (1994). From universal to language-specific in early grammatical development. *Philosophical Transactions of the Royal Society of London, Series B* 346: 37–45.

Byrne, B. and Davidson, E. (1985). On putting the horse before the cart: exploring conceptual bases of word order via acquisition of a miniature artificial language. *Journal of Memory and Language* 24: 377–89.

Cairns, H. S. and Kamerman, J. (1975). Lexical information processing during sentence comprehension. *Journal of Verbal Learning and Verbal Behavior* 14: 170–9.

Chee, M. W., Soon, C. S., Lee, H. L., and Pallier, C. (2004). Left insula activation: a marker for language attainment in bilinguals. *Proceedings of National Academy of Sciences of the USA* 101: 15265–70.

Chomsky, N. (1957). *Syntactic structures*. Den Haag: Mouton.

Cohen, M. R. and Nagel, E. (1934). *An introduction to logic and scientific method*. New York: Harcourt Brace.

Cole, R. A. and Jakimik, J. (1978). Understanding speech: how words are heard. In: G. Underwood (ed.) *Strategies of information processing*, pp. 67–116). London: Academic Press.

Clifton, C. J. and Odom, P. (1966). Similarity relations among certain English sentence constructions. *Psychological Monographs: General and Applied* 80: 1–35.

Cutler, A. (1975). *Sentence stress and sentence comprehension*. PhD dissertation, University of Texas.

Cutler, A. (ed.) (2005). *Twenty-first century psycholinguistics: four cornerstones*. Hillsdale, NJ: Erlbaum.

Cutler, A. and Carter, D. M. (1987). The predominance of strong initial syllables in the English vocabulary. *Computer Speech and Language* 2: 133–42.

Cutler, A., Mehler, J., Norris, D., and Segui, J. (1983). A language-specific comprehension strategy. *Nature* 304: 159–60.

Emmorey, K. D. (2002). *Language, cognition and the brain: insights from sign language research*. Mahwah, NJ: Erlbaum.

Forster, K. and Clyne, M. (1968). Sentence construction in German–English bilinguals. *Language and Speech* 11: 113–19.

Foss, D. J. (1970). Some effects of ambiguity upon sentence comprehension. *Journal of Verbal Learning and Verbal Behavior* 9: 699–706.

Foss, D. J. and Jenkins, C. M. (1973). Some effects of context on the comprehension of ambiguous sentences. *Journal of Verbal Learning and Verbal Behavior* 12: 577–89.

Foss, D. J. and Swinney, D. A. (1973). On the psychological reality of the phoneme: perception, identification, and consciousness. *Journal of Verbal Learning and Verbal Behavior* 12: 246–57.

Frazier, L. and Fodor, J. D. (1978). The sausage machine: a new two-stage parsing model. *Cognition* 6: 291–325.

Gaskell, M. and Marslen-Wilson, W. D. (1997). Integrating form and meaning: a distributed model of speech perception. *Language and Cognitive Processes* 12: 613–56.

Golestani, N., Molko, N., Dehaene, S., Le Bihan, D., and Pallier, C. (2006). Brain structure predicts the learning of foreign speech sounds. *Cerebral Cortex* 17: 575–82.

Healy, A. F. and Cutting, J. E. (1976). Units of speech perception: phoneme and syllable. *Journal of Verbal Learning and Verbal Behavior* 15: 73–83.

Imai, M. and Gentner, D. (1997). A crosslinguistic study of early word meaning: universal ontology and linguistic influence. *Cognition* 62: 169–200.

Johnson-Laird, P. N. (1974). Experimental psycholinguistics. *Annual Review of Psychology* 25: 135–60.

Levelt, W. J. M. (1992). Accessing words in speech production: stages, processes and representations. *Cognition* 42: 1–22.

Luce, P. A. (1986). A computational analysis of uniqueness points in auditory word recognition. *Perception and Psychophysics* 39: 155–8.

Marslen-Wilson, W. D. and Welsh, A. (1978). Processing interactions and lexical access during word recognition in continuous speech. *Cognitive Psychology* 10: 29–63.

McClelland, J. L. and Elman, J. L. (1986). The TRACE model of speech perception. *Cognitive Psychology* 18: 1–86.

Mehler, J., Segui, J., and Carey, P. (1978). Tails of words: Monitoring ambiguity. *Journal of Verbal Learning and Verbal Behavior* 17: 29–35.

Mehler, J., Dommergues, J. Y., Frauenfelder, U., and Segui, J. (1981). The syllable's role in speech segmentation. *Journal of Verbal Learning and Verbal Behavior* 20: 298–305.

Miller, G. A. and McKean, K. O. (1964). A chronometric study of some relations between sentences. *Quarterly Journal of Experimental Psychology* 16: 267–308.

Morais, J., Cary, L., Algeria, J., and Bertelson, P. (1979). Does awareness of speech as a sequence of phones arise spontaneously? *Cognition* 7: 323–31.

Morton, J. (1969). Interaction of information in word recognition. *Psychological Review* 76: 165–78.

Newmeyer, F. J. (1998). *Language form and language function*. Cambridge, MA: MIT Press.

Norris, D. (1994). Shortlist: a connectionist model of continuous speech recognition. *Cognition* 52: 189–234.

Norris, D. and McQueen, J. M. (2008). Shortlist B: a Bayesian model of continuous speech recognition. *Psychological Review* 115: 357–395.

Norris, D., McQueen, J. M., and Cutler, A. (2000). Merging information in speech recognition: feedback is never necessary. *Behavioral and Brain Sciences* 23: 299–370.

Pisoni, D. B., Nusbaum, H. C., Luce, P. A., and Slowiaczek, L. M. (1985). Speech perception, word recognition and the structure of the lexicon. *Speech Communication* 4: 75–95.

Saporta, S. (1961). *Psycholinguistics: a book of readings*. New York: Holt, Rinehart & Winston.

Savin, H. B. and Bever, T. G. (1970). The nonperceptual reality of the phoneme. *Journal of Verbal Learning and Verbal Behavior* 9: 295–302.

Segui, J., Frauenfelder, U., and Mehler, J. (1981). Phoneme monitoring, syllable monitoring and lexical access. *British Journal of Psychology* 72: 471–7.

Slobin, D. I. (1985). *The crosslinguistic study of language acquisition*, vol. 1: *The data*. Vol. 2: *Theoretical issues*. Hillsdale, NJ: Erlbaum.

Swinney, D. A. and Hakes, D. T. (1976). Effects of prior context upon lexical access during sentence comprehension. *Journal of Verbal Learning and Verbal Behavior* 15: 681–9.

Tesar, B., Grimshaw, J., and Prince, A. (1999). Linguistic and cognitive explanation in optimality theory. In: E. Lepore and Z. Pylyshyn (ed.) *What is cognitive science?*, pp. 295–326. Malden, MA: Blackwell.

Thornton, R., Gil, M., and MacDonald, M. C. (1998). Accounting for crosslinguistic variation: a constraint-based perspective. In: D. Hillert (ed.) *Syntax and semantics*, vol. 31: *Sentence processing: a crosslinguistic perspective*, pp. 211–25. San Diego: Academic Press.

Werker, J. F. and Logan, J. S. (1985). Cross-language evidence for three factors in speech perception. *Perception and Psychophysics* 37: 35–44.

8

Two brains—my life in science

Michael S. Gazzaniga

Understanding anything large comes from understanding one aspect of that thing in the greatest possible detail and with the greatest possible clarity. In my case, my study of cognitive neuroscience has been enabled by a life's work on a particular topic—studying subjects whose brains have been split into two parts. During almost a half century of working with such patients, I have come to realize that scientific stories are never as they first appear. New combinations of scientific personalities, experimental opportunities, and empirical data cause both questions and answers to be revised and expanded, seemingly in perpetuity. And that, of course, is as it should be; scientists are paid to doubt, to challenge, and to reassess. I suppose good lawyers are paid to do the same, but the difference is that they must be partisan, whereas science is concerned with what is true for everyone, not what is beneficial for just one person. That is what makes a life in science so fulfilling.

Forty-six years ago, I examined a robust and charming man, WJ, who was about to undergo cerebral commissurotomy, the so-called split-brain surgery, to control his otherwise capricious epilepsy. He was the sort of level-headed person to instil respect in a young, green, graduate student like myself. I had just started graduate school at Caltech under the direction of Professor Roger W. Sperry. Dr Joseph Bogen, a resident at the time, had critically reviewed the medical literature and was convinced that split-brain surgery would have beneficial effects. Dr P. J. Vogel, a professor of neurosurgery at the Los Angeles-based Loma Linda Medical School, performed the surgery, and my chore was to quantify the psychological and neurological changes, if any, in the way WJ behaved once the connections between his hemispheres had been sectioned. The conventional wisdom suggested that nothing would happen. Several studies by a gifted young neurologist at the University of Rochester, A. J. Akelaitis, twenty years earlier had found that callosal section in human subjects produced no behavioural or cognitive shifts. Karl Lashley had seized on this finding to push his idea of mass action and 'equipotentiality' of the cerebral cortex; discrete circuits of the brain were not important, he claimed—only cortical mass.

After all, he concluded, cutting the massive nerve bundle that connected together the two halves of the brain appeared to have no effect on interhemispheric transfer of information.

I learned about the split-brain world as a young undergraduate summer fellow at Caltech the summer between my junior and senior year. Inspired by the excitement of the ongoing animal research on split-brain cats and monkeys, I returned to Dartmouth College determined to go to graduate school at Caltech. Although my summer project was focused on trying to anaesthetize a half-brain of a rabbit I couldn't help but become captivated by the question of what would happen to humans with callosal sections. During my senior year at Dartmouth I had the idea to try to retest those Aklaitis' patients in nearby Rochester, New York, during my spring break. I designed many experiments and exchanged letters with Sperry about the ideas and the plan. I applied to the Mary Hitchcock Foundation at Dartmouth Medical School and received a small grant to rent a car and to pay for my stay in Rochester.

In the end I didn't see the Rochester patients, even though my car was loaded with borrowed taschistoscopes from the Dartmouth psychology department. The effort to reveal the effects of callosal disconnection in humans would come later. As soon as I arrived at Caltech, for my first day of graduate work, the assignment was given to me by Sperry. The split-brain experiments I had designed during my senior year at Dartmouth would finally be implemented, but on Caltech patients rather than Rochester patients. Nothing can possibly replace a singular memory of mine: the moment when I discovered that WJ could no longer verbally describe, using his left hemisphere, stimuli presented to his freshly disconnected right hemisphere. An experiment I had designed, executed, and carried out as a mere graduate student at Caltech had worked. With it the modern human split-brain story began and I spent the next five years in a sort of sublime state, working every day at the finest scientific institution in the world with one of the greatest biologists of all time, Roger Sperry.

These electrifying beginnings of the human work might have been predicted by dozens of experiments on animals. Study after study had shown that corpus callosum section profoundly altered brain function in cats, monkeys, and chimpanzees. Specifically, information presented to one brain hemisphere remained isolated in that hemisphere. It was as if dividing the great cerebral commissure produced an animal with two minds, neither of which was aware of the workings of the other. Ronald E. Myers and Sperry had already coined the term 'split brain' to describe such animals. Yet, the idea that callosal section would produce a similar condition in humans seemed bizarre.

Preoperatively, WJ could name stimuli presented to either visual field or placed in either hand. With his eyes closed, he could understand any command and carry it out with either hand—in short, he was entirely normal. The stage was ideally set to investigate what would happen following the disconnection of his cerebral hemispheres. The scientific context and the time were right for us to ask the right questions: Could it be that a disconnected right hemisphere was as conscious as a disconnected left hemisphere? Could it be that a state of co-consciousness could be produced in a human being? Where would positive answers to either or both of those enquiries lead us?

When WJ returned for testing after surgery, I experienced, as I said, one of those pivotal moments in life. First, and to no one's surprise, the subject normally named and described stimuli that were presented to his left hemisphere. Then came the critical test: what would happen when information was flashed to his verbally silent and physically isolated right hemisphere? Akelaitis' work predicted that the subject would describe the stimulus normally, as his studies suggested that the corpus callosum played no essential role in the interhemispheric integration of cerebral information. On the other hand, the animal work suggested that something interesting might emerge. As it happened, something interesting did emerge: the idea that splitting the human brain produced two separate conscious systems. It was a revolutionary idea, and over forty years later it is one that still needs study and clarification.

It is curious that, despite centuries of study and speculation about consciousness, there is no general agreement even about what the term means. If you asked twenty students of the problem to finish the sentence, 'Consciousness is…', twenty different definitions would result. Still, most of us would agree that the term refers to that subjective state we all possess when awake and to our feelings about our mental capacities and functions. As is typical with vast and ill-defined concepts, it is easy to offer simple examples of what it means to be conscious, but, at the same time, lifetimes of inquiry will not divulge the entirety of its nature.

When the first split-brain patients were studied we avoided confronting the essential definitional question in favour of measuring the separate capacities of each half-brain. Following my initial encounter with WJ, I have spent the last forty-six years trying to characterize the nature of conscious mechanisms in these patients. I have attempted here to track the major findings in split-brain research that relate to the problem of consciousness. Clearly our understanding of the problem is constantly evolving and new dimensions continually present themselves. I should say from the start that the gift of launching these studies with Roger Sperry at Caltech and the continuing capacity to study other patients like WJ with dozens of other students and colleagues has been a joy.

The first decade: basic principles

True to our expectations, and like all right-handed split-brain cases that followed, WJ normally named and described information presented to his left speaking hemisphere. What was surprising was his seeming lack of response to stimuli presented to his surgically isolated right hemisphere—it initially seemed as though he was blind to stimuli presented to the left visual field. To investigate this idiosyncrasy further, I devised a series of tests that allowed WJ to respond to visual stimuli using a reaction-time Morse code key with his left hand (controlled by his right hemisphere) rather than verbally (using his speaking left hemisphere). I flashed a light, and WJ said he didn't see anything, even though his left hand responded to the stimulus by pressing on the key!

An early conclusion from these results was that, following callosal section, each brain hemisphere behaved entirely independently of the other. Information experienced by one side seemed unavailable to the other and, moreover, each half-brain seemed specialized for particular kinds of mental activity. The left was superior in terms of language ability, whereas the right seemed more able to carry out visuospatial tasks. Hemispherical separation had isolated two structures with distinct and complex functions. The capacities demonstrated by the left hemisphere came as no surprise. However, when the first experiments showed that split-brain patients were able to read using the right hemisphere and to use the information thus gained as the basis for decisions, the case for a double conscious system seemed strong indeed. We could even elicit emotional responses from the right hemisphere. Dozens of studies that I carried out on split-brain patients during the following five years confirmed this dramatic state of affairs. After separating the human cerebral hemispheres each half-brain seemed to work and function outside the conscious realm of the other. Each could independently learn, remember, emote, and carry out planned activities.

Although these findings were dramatic, they posed even more questions than they answered about the essential nature of dual consciousness. Splitting the brain into two consciousnesses presented us with two systems that we didn't understand, instead of the single cryptic system we had started with. At this point, the field was too new to have developed depth by pushing the upper limits of right-hemisphere mental capacities, nor had it developed sufficient breadth, by examining a large enough pool of patients, to reveal the rich variation in right hemisphere capacities that has since been discovered.

Most importantly, however, the challenge to define consciousness itself lingered in the backs of all our minds, as yet we hadn't addressed it.

The second decade: origins of modular concepts and the interpreter

By the 1970s, the passage of time had provided more studies and more patients, and the original nature of split-brain studies had been modified substantially. The field had drifted into thinking about different kinds of consciousness, and the notion that mind left dealt with the world differently than mind right was the major conclusion of studies during this era. Though interesting in its own right, this characterization of how each hemisphere processes information still begged the question of what consciousness actually was and how the brain enabled it to be experienced.

In many ways, the work in the early 1970s was misleading. Reports with chimaeric stimuli found that split-brain patients favour the right hemisphere for 'gestalt' stimuli and the left hemisphere for 'analytical tasks', and our hypotheses briefly took on a new direction. We began to argue that it wasn't so much that there were separate conscious systems following commissure section but simply that each hemisphere possessed a different cognitive style. This characterization was short lived in the scientific community, but has been annoyingly persistent in the popular press. The paper that triggered this trend in left brain/right brain thinking used stimuli that were already well known to elicit preferred hemisphere functioning. Demonstrating through another stimulus preparation medium that the left hemisphere preferred language-based stimuli and the right hemisphere preferred faces merely replicated existing results and was a distraction from new research.

During the mid-1970s, a number of reports emphasized an additional feature of right hemisphere specialization. Milner and Taylor reported superior performance in the right hemisphere on non-verbal tactile stimuli. Joseph LeDoux and I found the manipulations of a stimulus to be critical in bringing out right hemispheric superiorities. For example right hemispheric superiority was only revealed in a block design test in which the patient manipulated the blocks to make the patterns required; in an equivalent, "match to sample" test in which patterns were only visually inspected right superiority disappeared. While these new observations were challenging enough to the simple view of hemispheric functioning and to ideas about dual consciousness, the new conceptual framework was even more antithetical to existing concepts about the unity of conscious experience. In brief, the new view suggested that the brain was organized in a modular fashion with multiple subsystems active at all levels of the nervous system, and that each subsystem could process data outside the realm of conscious awareness. These modular systems were fully capable of producing behaviours, mood changes, and cognitive activity. Such activities were in turn monitored and collated by a special system in the left hemisphere that Ledoux and I called the 'interpreter'.

We first revealed the interpreter using a simultaneous concept test. In this type of test, the subject is shown two pictures—one exclusively to the left hemisphere and one exclusively to the right. The subject is then asked to choose pictures that are associated with those lateralized images from an array of pictures placed in full view in front of them. For example, a picture of a chicken claw is flashed to the right visual field, and a picture of a snow scene to the left visual field. Of the pictures placed in front of the subject, the obviously correct association is a chicken for the chicken claw and a snow shovel for the snow scene.

Accordingly, subject PS responded by choosing the chicken picture with his right hand and the snow-shovel picture with his left. The left brain hemisphere, however, was aware only of the chicken-claw image, while the right hemisphere was aware only of the snow-scene image. When asked why he chose these items, his speaking left hemisphere replied, 'Oh, that's simple. The chicken claw goes with the chicken, and you need a shovel to clean out the chicken shed.' The left brain, observing the left hand's response, interpreted that response only in the context of its own sphere of knowledge—a sphere that did not include information about the left visual field snow scene.

In a related experiment, we lateralized written commands by presenting them tachistoscopically to the subject's left visual field. In an example where the command was 'laugh', the patient laughed and, when asked why, replied, 'You guys come up and test us every month. What a way to make a living!'. If the command 'walk' was flashed to the right hemisphere, the patient would stand up from their chair and start to leave the testing van. When asked where they were going, the left brain might say, 'I'm going into the house to get a cola.' Again, the left hemisphere observes and interprets the actions of the isolated right hemisphere in order to create a verbal response.

Over the past several years my search for corroborative evidence has taken me to the neurosurgical wards of New York Hospital, where a procedure called angiography is carried out routinely on patients about to undergo brain surgery. A long catheter is fed up one of the main arteries that supply the brain from an entry point on the leg, and a radio-opaque dye is injected that flows through either the left or right half-brain. X-ray pictures are taken at that precise moment, and abnormalities in the arterial system are thereby revealed to

the surgeon. It turns out that while the catheter is in position for this procedure it is frequently advisable to determine whether or not the hemisphere
about to undergo surgery is dominant for language and speech. The Wada
test, as the procedure is known, is performed by injecting anaesthetic through
the catheter, and for approximately two minutes, one side of the brain falls
asleep while the other remains alert. Most frequently it is the left, language-
dominant, hemisphere that must be tested.

My idea was to give the right hemisphere something to remember while the
left hemisphere was asleep. Then, after the left brain woke up, I would ask it
whether or not it knew about the information I had given to the right. What
we discovered was that if we allowed a non-verbal response of which the non-
verbal right hemisphere is capable, such as pointing to make a choice between
stimuli, the correct decision was always made. If we required a verbal response,
the patient was incapable of supplying it. Therefore, even in normal patients,
it is possible for right-hemisphere information to be encoded in such a way
that it cannot be accessed by the left hemisphere's language system.

At this point, our research had shown that there are many ways to influence
the left brain interpreter, and we were still interested in determining whether
emotional states present in one brain hemisphere would have an effect on the
affective tone of the other hemisphere. It was at this point that we met VP,
a dazzling 28-year-old woman with a keen sense of life who was a patient of
Dr Mark Rayport of the Medical College of Ohio. She is introspective about
her medical history and articulate in expressing her feelings. When we first
met her, her right hemisphere skills were limited to simple writing of answers
and the capacity to carry out verbal commands. Flash the command 'smile' to
her right hemisphere and VP could do it. Ask her why she was smiling and her
left hemisphere would concoct an answer.

But two years later, VP's right hemisphere could directly tell us why, because
by then it had developed the capacity to talk. During the time when only her
left brain could speak, however, we were able to set up mood states in her non-
talking hemisphere and study whether or not the talking hemisphere was
aware of the mood, and, if so, how it dealt with the induced mood. From all of
the other studies, of course, it was clear that the left brain was not directly
knowledgeable about the actual pictures or movies that had been shown to the
right brain. But could it detect the mood?

Using a very elaborate optical computer system that detects the slightest
movement of the eyes, we were able to project a movie exclusively to the left
visual field. If the patient tried to cheat and move her right eye toward the
movie image, the projector was automatically shut off. The movie her right
hemisphere saw was about a vicious man pushing another man off a balcony

and then throwing a fire bomb on top of him. It then showed other men trying to put out the fire. When VP was first tested on this problem, she could not access speech from her right hemisphere. When asked about what she had seen, she said, 'I don't really know what I saw. I think just a white flash.' I asked, 'Were there people in it?' VP replied, 'I don't think so. Maybe just some trees, red trees like in the fall.' I asked, 'Did it make you feel any emotion?' VP: 'I don't really know why, but I'm kind of scared. I feel jumpy. I think maybe I don't like this room, or maybe it's you, you're getting me nervous.' Then VP turned to one of the research assistants and said, 'I know I like Dr Gazzaniga, but right now I'm scared of him for some reason.'

This experimental evidence merely illustrates a rather extreme case of a phenomenon that commonly occurs to all of us. Our mental systems set up a mood that alters the general physiology of the brain. In response, the verbal system notes the mood and attributes cause to the feeling based on available evidence. Once this powerful mechanism is clearly demonstrated, given the complexity of real-life emotional stimuli, one cannot help but wonder how often we are victims of spurious emotional/cognitive correlations.

Although our split-brain subjects always possess at least some understanding of their surgery, they never say things like, 'Well, I chose this because I have a split brain and the information went to the right, non-verbal hemisphere.' Even patients who have exceptional IQs tend to view their responses as behaviours emanating from their own volitional selves. As a result, they incorporate those behaviours into theories to explain why they behave as they do. One can imagine that, at some point, a patient might be studied who might choose not to interpret such behaviours because of an overlying psychological structure that prevented the response. Or one can imagine a patient learning by rote what a 'split brain' is all about and why, therefore, a certain behaviour most likely occurred. Such a circumstance would certainly complicate the role of the researcher, and such subjects might well not be able to offer explanations for their behaviours.

There are occasions when a patient who is having trouble controlling his or her left arm due to a transient state of dyspraxia will tend to dismiss anything that he or she does under the direction of the right brain. This makes the simultaneous concept test inappropriate. In such situations, a single set of pictures is presented and only one hand is allowed to make the response. For example, the word 'pink' is flashed to the right hemisphere and the word 'bottle' to the left. Placed in front of the subject are pictures of at least ten bottles of different colours and shapes, and the subject is required to respond using the right hand.

When this test was run on split-brain subject JW, on a particular day when he said that he could not control his left hand, he immediately pointed to the pink bottle with the right hand. When asked why he had done this, JW said, 'Pink is a nice colour.' In this case, JW responded to a stimulus that had been presented to his right hemisphere using his right hand, in defiance of our expectation that he would be unable to do so. When he was pressed to explain how he had done it, his left-hemisphere speech apparatus was unable to provide an explanation, and so the interpreter responded as best it could, claiming that the subject had made a simple aesthetic choice.

It has been well established that the human brain follows a modular organization, and that those 'modules' do manifest themselves through function-specific physical regions of the brain. The precise nature of the neural networks that carry out those functions is less clear, however. What is apparent is that they operate largely outside the realm of awareness, and that they announce their computational products to various executive systems that result in behaviour or cognitive states. Managing and interpreting all of this constant and parallel activity is the role of the left hemisphere's interpreter module.

The interpreter is of primary importance to our identity as human beings; it is what allows for the formation of beliefs, which in turn yield mental constructs that allow us to do more than simply respond to stimuli. It does not appear, however, to be the system that articulates the content of consciousness—it does not generate *feelings* about our thoughts. I have much more to say about this property of the left hemisphere below.

The third decade: variations in patterns

In the 1980s, reports of more split-brain cases made it possible to begin to study the degrees and types of variation among subjects, particularly with regard to hemisphere specialization patterns. What was striking in these new studies was that the patients all reported that they felt mentally unchanged from their preoperative state. In other words, although their surgery had caused brain function to be redistributed in various ways, they all held in common the notion that their consciousnesses had not changed significantly.

There was also increasing interest during the 1980s in the possible role of subcortical processes in unconscious brain activity. Some studies tried to demonstrate that the split-brain human was not, in fact, so very 'split' at all—that common subcortical mechanisms integrate high-level information between the hemispheres, independent of the corpus callosum.

The effort to integrate all of these strands of research helps to define a set of issues that must be resolved as part of the attempt to reach a functional definition of consciousness *per se*. It is necessary to determine whether or not there are actual structural differences in how each individual brain processes information. Equally important is to examine more closely how variations in cortical organization may impact on demonstrable aspects of personal consciousness. Finally, the possible role of subcortical systems in unconscious mechanisms must be examined.

It has always been difficult to quantify the costs to cognitive ability incurred by callosal section. Early studies showed no changes in reaction time, ability to perform simple discriminations, verbal IQ, or capacity to form hypotheses. There have since been some reports that negative effects can be registered on memory function, although other studies have disputed this. Some studies have shown that hemispheric disconnection actually provides for supernormal capacity to apprehend perceptual information by allowing each half-brain to function without perceptual interference from the other. In short, various modes of research are challenging the original view that each half-brain is a functioning, independent system, the functioning of which is relatively unaffected by callosal section. The old view was based on the behavioural profiles of split-brain subjects who possessed language in each hemisphere. In that small group of subjects, each hemisphere seemed capable of responding in its own way to a wide variety of stimuli.

Cases where post-callosotomy right-hemisphere verbal performance is poor to non-existent raise the question of whether right-hemisphere verbal skills are entirely absent, or whether they are merely unable to manifest themselves after disconnection from the dominant left hemisphere. That possibility has led to the hypothesis that such patients possess the perceptual capacity and engrams necessary to generate speech, but lack the capacity to operate on them. Prior to split-brain surgery, EB performed a number of tests, including the nonsense wire figure test of Milner and Taylor. She was able to perform this task, which is designed to tap into right-hemisphere specialized systems, with either hand when the objects were presented out of view. Her intact callosum, it would appear, assisted in distributing information from her left brain over to the specialized system in the right hemisphere. At least, that is how we have come to think about these kinds of results.

After the posterior half of the corpus callosum had been cut EB was unable to name objects placed in her left hand in typical split-brain fashion. The fibres crucial for the interhemispheric transfer of tactile information had been severed, and, as a result, what the right hemisphere knew the left knew not. EB also proved to lack right-hemisphere language capability. Although she was able to find points of stimulation on her left hand by touching them with her left thumb, thereby demonstrating good right-hemisphere cortical somatosensory function, she was unable to retrieve an object named by the examiner with her left hand. Such a task would be easily managed by a patient with right-hemisphere language capability. Most importantly, however, EB could no longer perform the wire figure task with either hand.

As EB could perform the task before but not after surgery, it is clear that her right hemisphere possessed a specific capacity when it was connected to the left that it lacked once it had been disconnected. As we have noted, findings of this nature suggest that the left brain may normally contribute certain executive functions to specialized systems in the right brain. The capacity to carry out such non-verbal tasks, which was thought to be the product of one integrated system, is actually dependent upon the interaction of at least two systems, each of which is located in a different brain area.

The evidence to date suggests that there are separable factors active in what at first appear to be unified mental activities. One must envision that something on the order of executive controllers are active in manipulating the data of specialized processing systems. These controllers normally tend to be lateralized in the left brain, and when the right brain becomes isolated from their influence the specific functions of the right brain become hard to detect by testing the right hemisphere alone. Yet the impact of all of the newly discovered variation in left-hemisphere organization on the patient's own sense of consciousness following split-brain surgery is virtually nil. If consciousness reflects the felt state about specialized capacities, a neural system can be aware of only those capacities it possesses—it cannot sense the absence of a cognitive feature that it lacks. Observations such as these have led me to the conclusion that consciousness is not learned, and is best thought of as an intrinsic property of a neural network.

The fourth decade: establishing the evolutionary context

It was not until late in the 1980s that I became convinced that our understanding of consciousness is best enabled by placing the phenomenon in an evolutionary perspective. That context causes certain truths to emerge for me that give rise to the idea that, at its core, human consciousness is a *feeling* about specialized capacities. Throughout the development of split-brain research, one salient fact has remained: disconnecting the two cerebral hemispheres, while eliminating direct interaction between the halves of the cortex, does not typically disrupt cognitive and verbal intelligence.

The left hemisphere remains the dominant cognitive entity following such surgery, and this dominance seems to be sustained not by the entire cortex, but by specialized circuits within the left hemisphere. In short, the unique properties of the inordinately large human brain are engendered by its circuitry, not simply by its inordinate size. It is the accumulation of specialized brain circuits, then, that accounts for the human conscious experience. Furthermore, our sense of being conscious never changes during the normal ageing process. Taken together, these two views lead to the conclusion that what we refer to as 'consciousness' is nothing more or less than a collection of feelings that we have about our specialized capacities. We have feelings about people and objects we interact with, and about our capacities to think, to believe, and to use language.

In other words, consciousness is not a distinct system—it reflects the affective component of specialized systems that have evolved to enable human cognitive processes. Combined with the human inferential system, which seems to be limited to the left hemisphere, it empowers all sorts of mental activity. Our consciousness of those mental activities depends on our capacity to assign feelings to them, and that is what distinguishes human consciousness from everything else, including the electronic artefacts with which we surround ourselves.

Naturally, viewing consciousness as a myriad of feelings about specialized abilities predicts that the consciousness emanating from one hemisphere would differ radically from that emanating from the other. Whereas left-hemisphere consciousness would reflect what we refer to as normal conscious experience, right-hemisphere consciousness would vary as a function of the specialized circuitry that half-brain possesses. Mind left, with its complex cognitive machinery, can distinguish between the states of sorrow and pity, for instance, and it appreciates the feelings associated with each state. The right hemisphere does not possess the cognitive apparatus to create such distinctions and, as a consequence, its state of self-awareness is relatively low. Specific types of reduced right-hemisphere capacity, therefore, have specific implications for the states of consciousness of the subjects in which they are found.

Patients with a split brain without right-hemisphere language capability exhibit a limited capacity to respond to patterned stimuli that ranges from no capacity at all to the ability to make simple matching judgements at above-chance levels of performance. Patients who possess the capacity to make perceptual judgements that do not involve language do not exhibit the ability to make a simple same/different judgement within the right brain when both stimuli are lateralized simultaneously. In other words, when two simultaneously presented figures required the judgement 'same', the right hemisphere failed. This profile is commonly seen in all kinds of patient with a silent right hemisphere, and it seems to be independent of overall subject intelligence.

This minimal-capacity profile stands in marked contrast to that of patients who possess right-hemisphere language. The right brain of these patients is responsive, and their overall capacity to respond to both language and non-language stimuli has been well catalogued and reported. In the East Coast series of patients we study, this observation includes the case of JW, whose right hemisphere has understood language and has had a rich lexicon throughout our association with him, as assessed by the Peabody Picture Vocabulary Test and other specialized tests. Until recently, however, JW could not generate speech from his right hemisphere. Studies with VP and PS revealed that these patients were able to understand language and to speak from either half-brain. It would be reasonable to suppose that this extra skill would add to their right-brain capacities to think, which is to say to interpret the events of the world.

It turns out, however, that the right hemispheres of both patient groups are poor at making simple inferences. The subjects were tested by being asked semantically to combine the content of two pictures that were presented one after the other to their left visual fields. Presented with a picture of a match and then a picture of a woodpile, for example, neither group was successful in deducing that a burning woodpile was the correct result. In another test, simple words were presented one after another to the subject's left visual field, and the subject was instructed to choose the word that reflected the causal relationship between them from a list of six possible answers. The subjects also failed these trials, a typical one of which might consist of the words 'pin' and 'finger' being flashed to the right brain, the correct answer being 'bleed'. Although the right hemisphere could always find a close lexical associate of a word that was given by itself, it could not perform the interpretive function necessary to recognize relationships between two words.

In this light, it is hard to imagine that the left and right hemispheres have similar conscious experiences. The right cannot make inferences and, as a consequence, is extremely limited in what it can have feelings about. The left hemisphere, on the other hand, constantly and almost reflexively labels stimuli, making causal inferences and carrying out a host of other cognitive activities. Recent studies have shown that the left brain carries out visual search tasks in a methodical manner, whereas the right hemisphere tends to perform haphazardly. The evidence surrounds us that the left hemisphere is predisposed to analyse and differentiate the workings of the world, whereas the right hemisphere simply monitors its surroundings.

The fifth decade: it never ends

I was recently asked by a *Time Magazine* reporter: 'If we could build a robot or an android that duplicated the processes behind human consciousness, would it actually be conscious?'. It is a provocative question and it is one that persists, especially as one tries to capture the differences between the spheres of consciousness that exist between separated left and right brains. Much of what I have written here has appeared before in other forums and, for students of split-brain research, is not all that new. Yet, I find the way we all nuance our understanding of complex topics to be ever changing, as none of us holds the true answers in our hip pocket. I found myself answering the reporter with what I feel is a new twist.

Underlying this question is the assumption that consciousness reflects some kind of process that brings all of our zillions of thoughts into a special energy and reality called personal or phenomenal consciousness. That is not how it works. Consciousness is an emergent property and not a process in and of itself. It is the taste of salt that is the emergent and unpredictable product of sodium and chloride coming together. Our cognitive capacities, memories, dreams, etc. reflect distributed processes throughout the brain and each of those entities produces its own emergent state of consciousness. Consider one fact. A human split-brain patient who has had the two halves of her brain disconnected from one another does not find that one side of the brain misses the other. Her left brain has lost all consciousness about the mental processes managed by her right brain, and vice versa. This is just as with ageing or with focal neurological disease. We don't miss what we no longer have access to. The emergent conscious state arises out of each capacity. If they are disconnected or damaged, there is no underlying circuitry from which the emergent property arises.

The thousands, if not millions, of conscious moments that we experience each reflect one of our networks being 'up for duty'. When it finishes, the next one pops up and the pipe organ-like device plays its tune all day long. What makes emergent human consciousness so vibrant is that our pipe organs have lots of tunes to play, whereas rats, in contrast, have few. And the more we know, the richer the concert becomes. That's my story and for now I am sticking to it.

Bibliography

Baynes, K. B., Eliassen, J. C., Lutsep, H., and Gazzaniga, M. S. (1998). Modular organization of cognitive systems masked by interhemispheric integration. *Science* 280: 902–5.

Bogen, J. E. and Gazzaniga, M. S. (1965). Cerebral commissurotomy in man: minor hemisphere dominance for certain visuospatial functions. *Journal of Neurosurgery* 23: 394–9.

Corballis, P. M., Funnell, M. G., and Gazzaniga, M. S. (2000). An evolutionary perspective on hemispheric asymmetries. *Brain and Cognition* 41: 222–7.

Corballis, P. M., Funnell, M. G., and Gazzaniga, M. S. (2002). Hemispheric asymmetries for simple visual judgments in the split brain. *Neuropsychologia* 40: 401–10.

Funnell, M. G., Corballis, P. M., and Gazzaniga, M. S. (2000). Cortical and subcortical interhemispheric interactions following partial and complete callosotomy. *Archives of Neurology* 57: 185–9.

Gazzaniga, M. S. (1971). Right hemisphere's language. *Neuropsychologia* 9: 479–88.

Gazzaniga, M. S. (1989). Organization of the human brain. *Science* 245: 947–52.

Gazzaniga M. S. (1995). The emergence of the capacity to name left visual field stimuli: implications for functional plasticity. *Neuropsychologia* 33: 1225–42.

Gazzaniga, M. S. and Freedman, H. (1973). Observations on visual processes after posterior callosal section. *Neurology* 23: 1126–30.

Gazzaniga, M. S. and Hillyard, S. A. (1971). Language and speech capacity of the right hemisphere. *Neuropsychologia* 9: 273–80.

Gazzaniga, M. S. and Smylie, C. S. (1983). Facial recognition and brain asymmetries: clues to underlying mechanisms. *Annals of Neurology* 13: 536–40.

Gazzaniga, M. S. and Smylie, C. S. (1984). Dissociation of language and cognition: a psychological profile of two disconnected right hemispheres. *Brain* 107: 145–53.

Gazzaniga, M. S. and Sperry, R. W. (1967). Language after section of the cerebral commissures. *Brain* 90: 131–48.

Gazzaniga, M. S., Bogen, J. E., and Sperry, R. W. (1962). Some functional effects of sectioning the cerebral commissures in man. *Proceedings of the National Academy of Sciences* 48: 1765–9.

Gazzaniga, M. S., Bogen, J. E., and Sperry, R. W. (1963). Laterality effects in somesthesis following cerebral commissurotomy in man. *Neuropsychologia* 1: 209–15.

Gazzaniga, M. S., Bogen, J. E., and Sperry, R. W. (1965). Observations on visual perception after disconnection of the cerebral hemispheres in man. *Brain* 88: 221–36.

Gazzaniga, M. S., Bogen, J. E., and Sperry, R. W. (1967). Dyspraxia following division of the cerebral commissures. *Archives of Neurology* 16: 606–12.

Gazzaniga, M. S., Risse, G. L., Springer, S. P., Clark, E., and Wilson, D. H. (1975). Psychologic and neurologic consequences of partial and complete cerebral commissurotomy. *Neurology* 25: 10–15.

Gazzaniga, M. S., LeDoux, J. E., and Wilson, D. H. (1977). Language, praxis, and the right hemisphere: clues to some mechanisms of consciousness. *Neurology* 27: 1144–7.

Gazzaniga, M. S., Sidtis, J. J., Volpe, B. T., Smylie, C., Holtzman, J., and Wilson, D. (1982). Evidence of para-callosal verbal transfer after callosal section: a possible consequence of bilateral language organization. *Brain* 105: 53–63.

Gazzaniga, M. S., Holtzman, J. D., and Smylie, C. S. (1987). Speech without conscious awareness. *Neurology* 37: 682–5.

Holtzman, J. D. and Gazzaniga, M. S. (1982). Dual task interactions due exclusively to limits in processing resources. *Science* 218: 1325–7.

Holtzman, J. D. and Gazzaniga, M. S. (1985). Enhanced dual task performance following callosal commissurotomy in humans. *Neuropsychologia* 23: 315–21.

Holtzman, J. D., Sidtis, J. J., Volpe, B. T., Wilson, D. H., and Gazzaniga, M. S. (1981). Dissociation of spatial information for stimulus localization and the control of attention. *Brain* 104: 861–72.

Kingstone, A., Enns, J. T., Mangun, G. R., and Gazzaniga, M. S. (1995). Guided visual search is lateralized in split-brain patients. *Psychological Science* 6: 118–21.

Kosslyn, S. M., Holtzman, J. D., Farah, M. J., and Gazzaniga, M. S. (1985). A computational analysis of mental image generation: evidence from functional dissociations in split-brain patients. *Journal of Experimental Psychology: General* 114: 311–41.

LeDoux, J. E., Wilson, D. H., and Gazzaniga, M. S. (1977). Manipulo-spatial aspects of cerebral lateralization: clues to the origin of lateralization. *Neuropsychologia* 15: 743–50.

LeDoux, J. E., Wilson, D. H., and Gazzaniga, M. S. (1977). A divided mind: observations on the conscious properties of the separated hemispheres. *Annals of Neurology* 2: 417–21.

Luck, S. J., Hillyard, S. A., Mangun, G. R., and Gazzaniga, M. S. (1989). Independent hemispheric attentional systems mediate visual search in split-brain patients. *Nature* 342: 543–5.

Luck, S. J., Hillyard, S. A., Mangun, G. R., and Gazzaniga, M. S. (1994). Independent hemispheric attentional systems mediate visual search in split-brain patients. *Journal of Cognitive Neuroscience* 6: 84–91.

Phelps, E. A. and Gazzaniga, M. S. (1992). Hemispheric differences in mnemonic processing: the effects of left hemisphere interpretation. *Neuropsychologia* 30: 293–7.

Putnam, M. C., Wig, G. S., Grafton, S. T., Kelley, W. M., and Gazzaniga, M. S. (2008). Structural organization of the corpus callosum predicts the extent and impact of cortical activity in the nondominant hemisphere. *Journal of Neuroscience* 28: 2912–18.

Roser, M. E., Fugelsang, J. A., Dunbar, K. N., Corballis, P. M., and Gazzaniga, M. S. (2005). Dissociating causal perception and causal inference in the brain. *Neuropsychology* 19: 591–602.

Sidtis, J. J., Volpe, B. T., Wilson, D. H., Rayport, M., and Gazzaniga, M. S. (1981). Variability in right hemisphere language function after callosal section: evidence for a continuum of generative capacity. *Journal of Neuroscience* 1: 323–31.

Sidtis, J. J., Volpe, B. T., Holtzman, J. D., Wilson, D. H., and Gazzaniga, M. S. (1981). Cognitive interaction after staged callosal section: evidence for a transfer of semantic activation. *Science* 212: 344–6.

Turk, D. J., Heatherton, T. F., Kelley, W. M., Funnell, M. G., Gazzaniga, M. S., and Macrae, C. N. (2002). Mike or me? Self-recognition in a split-brain patient. *Nature Neuroscience* 5(9): 841–2.

9

A perception of perception

Richard L. Gregory

It is hard to know which early experiences initiate lifelong interests. My father was an astronomer, who spent most of his life measuring distances of stars to scale the space of the universe.[1] I have tried to understand how visual space is scaled, for seeing sizes and distances of earthly objects. Perhaps it was looking through my father's telescopes that made me question what is really out there, beyond the flickering images of light captured by telescopes and eyes. And isn't the inside of our heads even more mysterious than the surrounding universe?

The science of psychology has its roots in philosophy and, like a tree, would die if it lost its roots. Yet present-day philosophers and psychologists are generally at odds. I read philosophy and psychology at Cambridge just after World War II, after nearly six years in the RAF (signals). This was 1947, when sadly, Wittgenstein left Cambridge terminally ill, so I just missed him. I did attend Bertrand Russell's seminars.[2] The lectures, of C. D. Broad, Richard Braithwaite, and John Wisdom were truly memorable in their distinctive ways, and I remain in debt to Dr A. C. Ewing for criticizing my puerile weekly essays. I have continued to write no doubt puerile essays ever since, any rare exceptions reflecting Alfred Ewing's patience of sixty years ago. There seems to be no substitute for the Oxford and Cambridge tradition of individual tuition,

---

[1] My father C. C. L. Gregory was the first director of the University of London observatory at Mill Hill. Heliocentric parallax uses the diameter of Earth's orbit (186 000 000 miles) as a base for parallax shifts, measured from photographs taken at 6-month intervals.

[2] Bertrand Russell spent each Thursday in Cambridge, at the age of 76, giving two lectures—on non-demonstrative inference (induction), and ethics. He had just finished *Human Knowledge*, his last philosophy book. (After a discussion with me, when I asked why Keynes assumed a prior probability of 0.5 when there was no evidence, he handed one from a pile by his chair and signed it. I still treasure it.) He had become rather bored with symbolic logic, and was more concerned with the politics of Europe, especially as Russia moved into Berlin. He was surprisingly anxious that we (the then young) would not relegate him to second place by accepting Wittgenstein as the major philosopher of the twentieth century.

with its rigour avoiding rigor mortis, though impossible with the student numbers of most universities. This challenge is being met with new technologies of communication, the remarkably successful Open University showing the way.

This post-war, post-Wittgenstein period of Cambridge philosophy is captured with its fascinating characters by David Edmonds and John Eidenow in *Wittgenstein's Poker* (2001). The title refers to a Moral Sciences Club meeting, when Karl Popper visited from London, speaking to this hallowed centre of Cambridge philosophy for the first and only time.[3]

Whether a poker was really raised against him is just one of many unanswered questions. Although as students we were concerned mainly with contemporary analytical philosophy, we did read some classics. The eighteenth century empiricists—John Locke, George Berkeley, David Hume—excited interest in epistemology and perception, although the accounts of perception by contemporary philosophers were not so inspiring. For example, explaining why a coin looks circular from one position and elliptical from another by sense data, neither matter nor mind, supposed to exist between objects and eyes. (These strange entities were a product of Oxford rather than Cambridge philosophy!) Seeing this as unsatisfactory initiated a lifelong interest in how perceptions are related to objects, and the significance of illusions. Wittgenstein did have very interesting ideas on perception, as on everything else. But I read him later, as his unpublished 'Brown' and 'Blue' books were closely guarded secrets, available only to John Wisdom's students. *Philosophical Investigations*, with its deep thoughts, including interesting discussion of vision and its ambiguities, was not published until five years later.

Reading experimental psychology in the third year, I was one of Sir Frederic Bartlett's last students, being greatly influenced by him then and revering his memory ever since. Sir Fred (as we called him) was a genuinely great man. It was through his influence that we escaped the Behaviourism of the time, by accepting that the mindful brain is knowledge driven and driving, within Bartlett's favourite phrase 'effort after meaning'. So we escaped the tyranny of reflexes, seeing stimuli as informing rather than commanding behaviour. American Behaviourism was however useful, as it stressed the importance of objective methods for experiments, and provided concepts such as operant conditioning, which remain significant. But rejecting consciousness (largely

---

[3] Psychology at that time was in the Moral Sciences tripos, although it was mainly experimental. Among the last acts of Bartlett (which pleased him greatly) was moving psychology into the Natural Sciences tripos. ('Tripos' originates from the three-legged milking stool provided for candidates of oral examinations in the Middle Ages.)

for tactical reasons to make psychology look more like physics and so scientifically respectable), was not only throwing out both the baby and the adult with the bath water, it was cheating. Behaviourists admitted to toothache, and for finding criticism painful and even enjoying art. Behaviourism rejected not only consciousness, but also meaning. Bartlett's comment on the use of nonsense syllables for learning experiments was that they provide nice graphs, and so look 'scientific', but tell us nothing about psychology.[4]

This was in the Cambridge Psychology Department in the Downing Street laboratory site, then as now sharing a building with Physiology. Physiology was presided over by Lord Adrian, discoverer of the neural all-or-none code, and filled by luminaries with higher perches in the scientific pecking order than us in Psychology. Their work in vision was outstanding though confined to the retina, as the brain was practically inaccessible to physiological techniques at that time. There were, however, some physiologically plausible theories, especially the insights of Donald Hebb in Canada (Hebb 1949), suggesting active mechanisms for learning, that gave at least potential substance to Bartlett's dynamic 'schema' concepts of memory (Bartlett 1932).

Lessons from the experiences of psychologists in applying their knowledge during the recent war focused experiments and theories on the 'human operator', in control tasks such as flying and gun aiming, so experiments on tracking and anticipation were seen as important, and linked to attention and vigilance, as well as the limited capacity of information channels. Many experiments were carried out in the associated Applied Psychology Unit of the Medical Research Council—the APU—which moved at that time from the Psychology Department to a large house in Chaucer Road just outside central Cambridge.

Remarkably, it was found that vigilance would fail after as little as twenty minutes in service conditions, even while under genuine threat. Fortunately for laboratory experiments they generally gave similar results to real-life conditions, when subjects (now 'participants') entered into the game in imagination. Indeed, game playing was a major interest of psychologists, as well as economists, and there were simulators of many kinds. From the simple but effective Link Trainer, flight simulators became ever more elaborate until they could cost more than the aircraft they simulated. As an example of applied projects, I was seconded to the Royal Navy at Portsmouth for a year to run

---

[4] A joke of the time: The department secretary, who could not spell, put up a large notice for a practical class on nonsense syllables. Displayed for all passers by to see in a ground floor window, it read: NONSENSE SYLLABUS.

experiments on improving escape procedures from stricken submarines, following the Affray disaster in which two crews were lost. The conditions were simulated in a large pressure chamber with controlled atmosphere, gradually decreasing oxygen and increasing carbon dioxide, to find how long the crew could wait to be found by surface ships, before attempting to escape one person at time from the gun-tower hatch. If the person passed out or died, the remaining crew would be trapped. I designed, and with my technician built, a printing time-event recorder we called Thoth (Egyptian god of wisdom and language), to record dummy escape performance over ten or so hours. The inspiration was avoiding the labour of reading off marks on miles of moving paper.

A key figure was Kenneth Craik (1914–1947), who tragically died in a cycle accident outside his Cambridge college on the last day of the war. His ideas lived on, and his presence was felt in the Psychology Department for many years afterwards. Craik undertook experiments of lasting value on visual performance, including dark adaptation. It was found that the eyes could be fully dark adapted in normal lighting by wearing red filters—especially useful for submariners. Very differently, he wrote an essentially philosophical book, *The Nature of Explanation* (Craik 1943), suggesting that perception works with physical 'internal models' in the brain, representing the world of objects. This simple idea had lasting impact, though we would see them more as symbolic software.

Wartime technology was important for experimental techniques (we used to build our own apparatus from aircraft components, such as electrical relays and uniselector switches), as well as suggesting theoretical concepts. The new ideas for transmitting and processing information had major effects on theories of brain function, first from analogue devices of cybernetics, considerably later from digital devices which transformed computing and much of technology. Being fast though with slow components, parallel-processing analogue systems look much more like the brain. Specialized analogue processors may not be dead, and certainly biological feedback controls of cybernetics are essential for life.

A recurring theme was *localization of function*. Oliver Zangwill was a founder of localizing brain functions in Neuropsychology, working originally with wartime head injuries. I thought about localization of function from wartime experience of electronics, suggesting that it is not logically possible to localize functions without knowing what they are, which means understanding how the machine or brain works. For example one can say, dangerously like the phrenologists, that memory is in the parietal and visual processing is in the occipital cortex; but it is functions producing memory storage and vision that matter, and when interactive the functions cannot be simply localized, for they result from activities of many components. Further, these functions are sure to be very different from what they produce, at least if electronic systems are any guide to the brain.

Famously, Karl Lashley claimed, from experimental failures of ablation experiments to find specialized regions, that the brain works by 'mass action'. This was like assuming from not seeing in a fog that there is nothing to be seen. I wrote several papers on these issues (Gregory 1958), sometimes taken as criticisms of colleagues' ablation experiments, but this was far from intended, as I simply tried to point out that conceptual models of how systems work are necessary for interpreting such experimental results. An analogy was from localizing functions in a radio from the effects of removing components. The radio might howl, when a resistor is removed—but it does not follow that this component was a 'howl inhibitor'. The rest of the circuit can acquire new properties when a part is removed, as it is now a different circuit. Negative feedback can easily become positive, changing an amplifier into a howling oscillator. Where the brain is modular, these problems are not so severe—but the frontal lobes?

The electronics concept of random noise, limiting the sensitivity of detectors, was central to communications and radar, and became a central idea for thinking about sensory discrimination. Horace Barlow developed elegant theories based on retinal noise (Barlow 1956). Violet Cane and I tried to develop a signal/noise account of sensory thresholds (Gregory and Cane 1955), with the raised thresholds and slowing of behaviour associated with ageing, seen as due to increased neural noise, which we tried to measure (Gregory 1958). This idea does not seem to be generally accepted now (though at the age of 80+ I do seem to be noise-masked!). Measuring the effects of neural noise led to a speech-processing hearing aid (Gregory and Drysdale 1976), and to later papers with Alan Drysdale and Tom Troscianko. Unfortunately, the hearing aid was not manufactured.[5] It was exceedingly difficult to get university laboratory work accepted by industry, but this has greatly changed.

Ideas of probability and statistics were seen as fundamentally important for understanding perception, as with Claude Shannon's (Bell Labs) mathematical

---

[5] This was based on J. C. R. Licklider's (1946) previous finding, that the information of speech is in the time intervals of the zero energy cross-overs; so peak amplitudes are not useful for speech, but, when amplified, overload the sensory neural impaired ear. The method was to limit speech amplitude without distortion (which had seemed impossible), by heterodyning to a carrier frequency outside the speech frequency band, then to limit the amplitude, filter out the inevitable harmonic distortion components, and finally heterodyne back to audiofrequency.

theory of communication (Shannon and Weaver 1949). A notable Cambridge contribution was W. E. (William) Hick's (1952) 'rate of gain of information' experiment, producing Hick's Law, that choice reaction time increases by $(\log_2 +1)$ of n, the number of available choices.[6] These were very exciting ideas, dramatically changing psychological thinking, although they tended to divide the subjects into many specialized 'disciplines' without shared aims or paradigms. This had the merit that as a 'psychologist' one could work on almost anything!

'Schools' of perception

Psychology at that time was riddled with violently opposed and hotly defended 'schools' of, one has to say, beliefs. Indeed, psychology was hardly secular as evidence was tenuous (and often ignored), so beliefs were held with the insular fervour of religions. This is not, indeed, unknown in science, especially when there are large uncertain questions with small chances of finding reliable answers. The history of cosmology is not so different. And the history of medicine? The many schools of psychotherapy cartoon the science of mind.

Perception has the benefit of striking phenomena, many readily measured. So, although perceptions are 'subjective', they attract objective experiments. Paradoxically illusions are among the most attractive phenomena—and have been ever since Aristotle, who discussed several and appreciated their significance. As dreams were the stuff of psychoanalysis, so illusions woke philosophy and science to realities of perception. The fact that perceptions can depart so clearly from physical reality challenged established ways of thinking, and showed that, though subjective, the mind can be the object of experiments. Although perception was not the major topic of research that it is today, we were introduced when students to wonderful phenomena of illusions, to stereoscopic pictures, to delights of colour and sound, and attempts to understand them.

Most broadly, there were 'passive' and 'active' accounts. 'Active' included Gestalt theory, from pre-war German psychology (moved to America by quite direct pressure from Hitler), and the 'passive' Direct Perception of the American psychologist, James J. Gibson, at Cornell. It is important to include the wonderful visual demonstrations of Adelbert Ames (Ittelson 1952). Neither Ames nor, as we shall see, Helmholtz were ashamed of introducing 'childish' illusions into serious

---

6 The testing was an hour a day for several months, The author was the only subject to complete the experiment, the other subject being Hick, but he did not quite finish it as the apparatus broke down. So Hick's law is based on my nervous system!

science for casting light, with a light touch, into studies of vision. For many psychologists and philosophers, phenomena of illusions showed how tenuous are relations between the physical world and perceptions. Gibson, however, tried to deny illusions (Gibson 1950), for they should not occur if perceptions are related directly to objects. When pushed, he would say they only occur in artificial laboratory conditions, and so can be ignored. Yet normal conditions are rich with illusions. (Compare the vertical mast of a boat to when it is lying horizontal on the ground: the vertical appears much longer.)

Gibson had a remarkable following, with, one has to say, religious fervour, although a vocal minority of experimental psychologists (including myself) saw his ideas as setting back understanding, not only to before Helmholtz but back to the ancient Greeks, who did not appreciate that eyes have optical images (read, though not seen, by the brain). Gibson abandoned Helmholtz's Unconscious Inference, from evidence of retinal images and even denied retinal images altogether. (He was quite upset when shown a photograph of a retinal image, though he did finally accept them, if not their importance.) Although I was opposed to his 'school' of psychology, I liked Gibson and his family immensely, and he did important work and wrote influential books, though I do think his philosophy was wrong. Science benefits from people who are *clearly* wrong!

The founding father of psychological–physiological experiments on vision and hearing is the German polymath (physiologist, psychologist, physicist, and philosopher), Hermann von Helmholtz (1821–1894). Helmholtz's immense contribution was less in evidence fifty years ago than now. With many others, I see Helmholtz as the Master.

Whereas Gibson thought of perceptions as related directly to objects, Helmholtz and his followers saw the retina and other physiological complexities as lying between objects and perception, making vision indirectly related to the world of objects. As physiological links of neural channels are present for all the senses, this indirectness applies to them all, including touch. The notion is that sense organs are (in the language of electronic instruments) transducers, providing coded messages to the brain via neural channels, which introduce considerable delay, as measured by Helmholtz in 1850. As sensory information comes from the recent past, perception cannot possibly be 'direct'; yet behaviour is in real time—making ping-pong possible. Perceptions are richer than sensory data, and are predictive—into the immediate future, and to many unsensed features of objects. One might say that the brain is a knowledgeable detective, working along the lines of Sherlock Holmes, using small clues to suggest and test working hypotheses, which are our reality, (Gregory 2007). I like to think of perceptions as *hypotheses*, essentially like hypotheses of the sciences (Gregory 1958, 1981). Both are greatly affected by probabilities; both are subject to fashion; both are tenuously related to 'truth'. Both, indeed, are bedevilled and enriched by illusions.

This is very different from J. J. Gibson's direct 'pick up of information', especially as his notion of information is different from that of Helmholtz and his followers, which at least implicitly follows Thomas Bayes' eighteenth-century formulation of statistical inference, for selecting and testing hypotheses. Only recently has Bayesian theory been seen as a useful model for thinking and for perception. All Helmholtzian perceptual theory is, at least implicitly, Bayesian. I came to think in this way from Bertrand Russell's lectures at Cambridge, and from his book *Human Knowledge: Its Scope and Limits* (Russell 1942), writing an essay along these lines initially when a student (Gregory 1952/1974).

In the Special Senses laboratory in Cambridge, we worked on a variety of topics, 'pure' and 'applied,' including perceptual problems anticipated for the moon landing of 1969, for the US Air Force, just before NASA took over. The American government was incredibly generous in funding European research, getting science and so much else going after the war. This allowed us to build a simple space simulator, an electrically driven carriage running along the darkened corridor of the laboratory, with electronically linked displays for measuring Size Constancy dynamically. There was also a large parallelogram swing introducing small acceleration forces. We measured Constancy by shrinking the display while approaching, vice versa for receding, so it appeared constant—the required change giving a measure of visual scaling. (No required change would indicate 100% scaling.) The principle of visual scaling, going back at least to Descartes, became a key concept for explaining many visual illusions, when inappropriate.

Illusions

Which phenomena are 'physiological' and which 'cognitive'? This seemed a fundamental issue for physiological-psychology (or at least for the hyphen between these words). It was generally thought that distortion illusions, such as the Muller–Lyer 'arrows', were due to peripheral physiological effects such as lateral inhibition's neural sharpening of borders. This was important for sensory physiology, but for various reasons I did not believe that these distortions were related so directly to peripheral physiology. It seemed to me that we should look at what the physiology is doing in order to achieve perception of size and shapes of objects, and then ask whether these procedures can work appropriately in situations of illusion. In particular, how can procedures for three-dimensional objects work correctly for flat representations in pictures?

There are dangers, in any science, of seeing with some sort of tunnel vision. The tunnels change over time and also place, as they are set by what is prestigious at a given time and place. For neuroscience there is the temptation to see what is overtly visible as most 'real' and most reliable, such as nerves one can see with a microscope, and now brain regions shown as active by coloured regions of (functional magnetic resonance imaging—fMRI) pictures. Of course, these are very important, but so too are less tangible, more abstract, features and phenomena, such as reflex arcs, servo loops, inhibitors, and activators. Indeed, brain regions seen as active by fMRI may be either inhibiting or activating, so they are ambiguous, to be interpreted by conceptual models of what may be going on.

An interesting example of tunnel vision in the recent history of perception is illusory or 'subjective' contours. These were described and illustrated in the first years of the twentieth century by Schumann, but ignored almost entirely for half a century, until Geatano Kanizsa's beautiful examples in *Scientific American* (1976) attracted worldwide attention to these wonderful visual phenomena. Schumann's original example appeared in the most read text—R. S. Woodworth's *Experimental Psychology* (1938)—as Figure 191 on page 637, yet was ignored. It showed a ghostly rectangle with clear contours, though without brightness differences. The physicist Ernst Mach had appreciated in 1865 that contours are not simply changes of brightness or colour. Yet, for a long time, physiology and psychology viewed them through a tunnel of peripheral neural interactions, these being a popular research topic. People now see them as striking examples of Bayesian inference. I was not alone in thinking along these lines, following Kanizsa's striking examples (Gregory 1972). It is unlikely that the missing slices of the 'cakes' would line up exactly— more likely there is some nearer, triangle-shaped, occluding surface, which is conjured up by Bayesian inference and seen, though there is nothing there. It is visible fiction. Of course there will be an underlying physiology, but this account of what the physiology is *doing* is a useful explanation, although not complete.

I spent a lot of time thinking of distortion illusions as due to constancy scaling, when set inappropriately, by perspective or other clues signalling depth. This was different from physiological accounts or errors of neural signalling, as in lateral inhibition, for it concerned what perceptual processes are *doing*, for seeing objects in external space, rather than how the physiology works, or how it malfunctions. Although, of course, knowledge of physiology is essential, the action for explaining many phenomena is in what it is *doing*. Thus strategies can win or lose wars. Of course there must be weapons, but where they are directed is as important as what they can do. So, there are many kinds of illusory phenomena, which I tried to classify with a 'Peeriodic Table' (Gregory 2005). The major division is between 'bottom-up' signals from the senses and 'top-down' knowledge, for reading neural signals as evidence for what might be out there. Rules for reading objects from signals may be called 'sideways'.[7]

This approach to considering perception and illusions started with the fortunate experience of studying a rare case of adult recovery from blindness at birth—SB—with my research assistant Jean Wallace (Gregory and Wallace 1962). Following a corneal graft operation, SB had surprisingly good vision, with surprising lack of the usual distortion illusions. After fifty-two years of blindness, SB could immediately see a great deal not only from his new eye, but also from his years of touch experience. Still in the hospital he could tell the time visually, and read upper-case letters, from previous touch experience of feeling the hands of a watch and letters engraved on blocks of wood, taught in the blind school. All of this suggested that perception is largely cognitive, knowledge based.

SB disliked his wife's face, and his own in a mirror! Mirrors did, however, fascinate him, as the opposite of blindness, touch without sight. As described in the book *Mirrors in Mind* (Gregory 1991) I came to see mirrors through SB's eyes, to realize how amazing they are, as indeed is vision itself. Our finding that immediately after receiving sight, and later, SB had only small or no distortion illusions suggested that these are cognitive phenomena. Inspecting the various well known distortion–illusion figures showed that though they appeared flat they were perspective drawings of objects or scenes in depth. Whenever *distance* was represented, illusory *expansion* occurred.[8] The notion that distortions in pictures might be related to depth was not obvious at that time.

---

[7] The spelling of 'peeriodic' is a joke, from peering at things to see them clearly. Unfortunately a reviewer of the second edition of my *Oxford Companion to the Mind* (Gregory 2004) pointed it out as a reprehensible mistake! No doubt there were several, but doesn't this show that humour is dangerous, as unexpected in a science book. Yet, as lectures often have jokes—why not reference and text books?

[8] Being familiar with several illusion figures, from showing them to students, one day I looked at the ceiling of my office and noticed that the lines of the corner formed a Muller–Lyer figure, although it was clearly three-dimensional while the figures were and appeared to be flat. It was then obvious that other illusion figures—Ponzo (the most obvious), Zolner, Hering, Poggendorff—were all perspective drawings of familiar simple objects or scenes. I concentrated on the Muller–Lyer as it was easy to draw with various angles. My favourite experiment was with my colleague John Harris (Gregory and Harris 1975), showing that the distortion disappears when the figure is presented as a three-dimensional anaglyph. The interpretation for the 'inappropriate scaling' theory is that,

It is still sometimes resisted, perhaps because it implies and requires a particular way of thinking about perception. (It fits a Helmholtzian, but not a Gibsonian, approach.) A surprise was that size scaling could be set by clues to distance, even when distance was not seen, as when countermanded by the surface texture of the figure. This suggested that scaling can be set rather directly by depth clues, and also that there is more to perception than the conscious experience, so experiments are required to 'see' what is going on.

To identify bottom-up and top-down scaling experimentally, depth-ambiguous figures and objects (such as a wire cube) are useful, as they flip in seen depth without any change of bottom-up clues. These issues occupied my attention for several years, and still do. They do not seem trivial, if only because they are a magnifying glass to what the physiology is *doing*, as well as how it *works*. This can now be investigated with techniques of brain imaging. But MRI pictures of brain activity need related observations and experiments, with theoretical concepts to interpret them. Phenomena cannot speak for themselves!

The conclusion was that some phenomena of illusions are due to malfunctions of physiology, others, very differently, to misleading knowledge. These are very different kinds of cause, with different 'cures', although not all are easy to classify. I attempted to classify illusions in terms of Kinds and Causes. Why trouble with illusions? Many are highly suggestive phenomena, revealing principles of normal perception free from the restraints of the physical world. We learn to see from handling objects, but perception is not limited to experienced objects, as we can see paradoxes and even impossible fiction in illusions. Although probabilities are very important, remarkably we can see the impossible. This is the wonder of creative perception, allowing discoveries and empowering art.

It was a great privilege to work with the art historian Sir Ernst Gombrich. We set up a major exhibition at the Institute of Contemporary Arts in London, *Illusion in Nature and Art*, with a book of the same name (Gregory and Gombrich 1973). This included the distinguished neuroscientist Colin Blakemore's first published paper, 'The baffled brain', which remains interesting to this day, describing 'physiological' illusions arising from the properties

when depth is seen as it is signalled, the scaling is appropriate, so no distortion. An anomalous case was pointed out by two bright students, Michael Morgan and Nicølas Humphrey (1965), now both distinguished scientists. They pointed out that the Ponzo (railway lines, or tunnel illusion) reverses when the distorted lines are rotated by 90° to lie along, rather than across, the converging railway lines or tunnel walls. Why size scaling (if indeed this is the way to describe it) is asymmetrical is not understood.

of visual channels. I wrote a companion chapter 'The confounded eye' (Gregory 1973). This introduced the Hollow Face—the concave back of a mask, which appears convex like a normal face. Page 84 says of a photograph of the Hollow Mask, (Figure 34):

> *The nose is not sticking out, as it appears to be: it is hollow, going inwards. This extremely powerful effect holds for any lighting, and against a great deal of countermanding sensory data – provided one hypothesis only is extremely likely. This is best demonstrated not with a photograph of, say, a hollow face; but with the hollow mould itself. It continues to appear as a normal face until closely approached, with both eyes and full stereo depth information. When the observer then withdraws a little, it will suddenly return to appearing as a normal face – though he knows it is hollow. So we discover that intellec-tual knowledge of such perceptual situations does not always correct perceptual errors. In other words, perceptual hypothesis making is not under intellectual control'. If the percep-tually depth-reversed face is rotated, or if the observer moves round it, the face apparently rotates in the wrong direction. Motion parallax is being interpreted according to the false hypothesis – to generate a powerful illusion, which is improbable. So both the texture depth data from the hollow face, and the resulting illusion of motion, are inadequate as data to correct the hypothesis – against the extreme improbability of a face being hollow.*

Gregory 1973, p. 84

Appreciating this playing with probabilities surely gives us significant insights far removed from early stimulus-driven accounts of perception.

The Hollow Face may have been the first demonstration of this power of top-down knowledge. Although so dramatic, it took a surprisingly long time to be taken seriously and absorbed into perceptual theory. It has turned out to be a useful phenomenon for several experiments, including providing further evidence for David Milner and Mel Goodale's (1995) important notion of two cortical streams for visual processing—the dorsal stream for rapid uncon-scious behaviour (here, flicking targets on the hollow mask) and the ventral stream (slow hand tracing of the illusorily seen convex face)—which separate, the first being stimulus driven and the second from conscious perception. We may say that, much as bizarre phenomena of physics are keys to unlock secrets of matter, so illusions can reveal hidden processes of brain and mind.

Artificial perception

I left Cambridge in 1967, with the distinguished theoretical chemist Christopher Longuet-Higgins FRS (we were both Fellows of Corpus Christi College), to join Donald Michie in Edinburgh to help to start a new subject: Artificial Intelligence.

The dream of intelligent robots roused the imagination over forty years ago, to become serious research projects in America and Britain. The first AI depart-ment in Europe, at the University of Edinburgh, was run by Donald Michie,

Christopher Longuet-Higgins and myself, the founding professors. A robot, called Freddie, was built by Steven Salter. It assembled parts from a television camera eye into a model boat or a model car. It had some learning with flexibility in its behaviour. This was only part of the work of the department, which included neural nets, game theory, linguistics, and machine-aided design, and it initiated the careers of a number of very talented people.

Perhaps naively and certainly optimistically, we thought that by making computers perceive and learn and think intelligently, we would discover the tricks of the brain. The computers of that time were not up to it and, with exceptions, neither were we. Programming was a difficult art, which I never mastered. The joke was that a PhD student at a distinguished American university was asked to spend a summer term programming a computer to recognize objects from signals provided by a television camera—his supervisor apologizing that this was too easy and would not take all summer. Teams of brilliant computer engineers have been struggling ever since! Effective AI still looks fifty years ahead. But what we and others at that time discovered from relative failure was surprising and important: that the mind–brain is far more complicated and hard to understand than anyone had appreciated. The emphasis of most AI research was on algorithms (rules) for thinking and seeing. The idea was to describe mind by operating rules that might be carried out by brains are computers. This strategy had the great merit of making theories of mind explicit. So early AI served psychology better than the psychological theories of the time served AI. To the rescue came Kenneth Craik's notion of Internal Models—physical representations of sensed and imagined realities.

Some of us wanted to augment AI algorithms by developing computer models of mind along these lines. Rather as a joke, from irritation with the clumsy computers of the time, Christopher Longuet-Higgins made a model car steered with a slowly rotating cardboard cutout of the path it was to follow, the cutout being its 'internal model'. This joke worked, as it annoyed the computer buffs who claimed too much, and demonstrated very simply that sensed inputs are far more powerful when used, not directly for behaviour, but via even simple predictive internal models. I came to this from a rather different direction, from disagreeing with J. J. Gibson's account of perception as 'direct pick-up of information'. For I saw perceptions as brain-created hypotheses, predictive into the immediate future, so that behaviour anticipates what is likely to happen, and work in real time in spite of physiological delays in sensory signals and commands. Also predictive to many non-sensed properties of objects, though not always correctly. A perhaps uncomfortable consequence for psychology is that, as perceptions are not at all closely linked to stimuli, they are not readily described or explained with psychophysics. Perception is creative history.

In 1970 I left Edinburgh for the University of Bristol, with a laboratory in the medical school—the Brain and Perception Laboratory, funded by the Medical Research Council. Here, we more or less continued the Cambridge philosophy, with an emphasis on perceptions as hypotheses of brain and mind. This had clinical implications, initially for Ken Flower's work on Parkinson's disease, using eye–hand tracking with a moving target and a joystick. The idea was to continue tracking while the target was made invisible. Although no one knew then, as the secret of *Enigma* was guarded for fifty years, his father Tom Flowers had invented the computer Colossus that broke the German Enigma codes in World War II.

Human visual phenomena we studied included the effects of isoluminance—neighbouring regions of different colour with the same luminance—which have implications for the evolution of vision, as colour came late in the evolution of the mammalian brain. It might be said that primates have 'colour by numbers' added to ancient monochromatic form perception. With only colour there are striking losses of motion and form perception, and stereo vision (especially for random dot stereograms) is much impaired. So is visual stability, because borders and edges become uncertain and labile, with loss of what printers call 'registration' at borders. This led us to suggest that normally colour regions are locked to common luminance borders; but they are missing at isoluminance, so 'border locking' fails. This seemed to relate to one of our favourite distortion illusions—the Café Wall—found in the tiles of a nineteenth century café near our laboratory in Bristol. From models with sliding parts we found Laws of the Café Wall, relating to characteristics of neural channels. The dramatic distortions disappeared at isoluminance, presumably because border locking is lost. This is not a 'cognitive', but rather a 'physiological', illusion; the various channels for position, motion, and stereo having different characteristics, which we could measure (Gregory and Heard 1983).

The future?

Aristotle moved seamlessly from physics, to natural history, to psychology. I like this. Much of engineering and even quantum physics is relevant to how the brain works. In a classical experiment, Hecht, Schlear and Pirenne (1942) measured the minimum number of quanta that could produce a conscious flash of light. It turned out that, apart from not being perfectly transparent, the eye is as sensitive as theoretically possible, responding to a single quantum. Current brain sciences hardly notice quantum physics, although electronic components such as transistors are quantum devices. This needs watching.

The human visual system is just one of many possible engineering solutions, and many have been tried through evolution. We had a lot of fun investigating the single-channel scanning eye (as it turned out) of a microscopic copepod, *Copilia quadrata*, at Naples (Gregory et al 1962). Other scanning eyes, with a few more channels, have been discovered and studied more fully by the biologist Michael Land (Land and Nilsson 2001).

Kenneth Craik's notion of brain models (Craik 1943) can be realized very usefully in engineering terms. This occurred to me in a darkroom at Cambridge, while thinking about the difference between the two eyes' images in stereoscopic vision. In the enlarger, I placed a photographic negative from one lens of a stereo camera, as a sandwich on a positive transparency from the other lens. The sandwich gave a difference picture, as the dark regions of the negative occluded the transparent parts of the positive where they matched, leaving transparent difference regions. It struck me that this could be used to improve images degenerated by atmospheric disturbance, for astronomical telescopes. For if the fluctuating image was projected, through a long-exposure photographic negative, to a photomultiplier opening the shutter of a second camera when the image matched its negative, the shutter would open when the disturbance was small. So the second camera should build up a better picture, each time its shutter opened, than the first unsampled photograph.

We tried this in the laboratory with simulated disturbance (Gregory 1964), then, with the engineer Steven Salter, on the smallest, 100-year-old refractor in the Cambridge Observatory, and a large telescope in New Mexico. This was before there were adequate computers, and there were annoying problems with tracking, but the method is now used very effectively first by amateur astronomers with CCV cameras and graphic computers.[9] As this system made its own decisions in the light of evidence, it was possibly an early example of AI. We see the power of internal models most dramatically in satellite navigation (GPS), the map being essential for making the received data effective.

Hints and analogies from engineering are very useful but stop short of consciousness, for so far artificial intelligences are zombies. For all the clever people thinking about consciousness, we do not have a handle on qualia of sensations. John Locke suggested that sensations are tokens of physical events—although the sky looks blue, it is no more blue than the word 'cat' is like a cat. We need more insights to unlock the outsight of vision—from this understanding

---

[9] This technique is far simpler than active optics with deforming mirrors, and may have some advantages. They might be combined. The field of view might be larger, which would certainly be a plus.

perhaps to make conscious robots. I hope we will recognize their artificial qualia, and be kind to sentient machines.

As the future rests with coming generations, education is all important. The evident importance of interactive experience for learning to see suggests that hands-on learning is important for schools. Accepting this, we started and ran the Exploratory hands-on science centre in Bristol. This was the first in Britain, following Frank Oppenheimer's very successful Exploratorium in San Francisco.[10] Two million children and adults visited our Exploratory during its final ten years, before it was taken over by other people, with a rather different philosophy and major funding. Whether a change is advance or retreat, can be hard to judge for historical events—impossible for the future. It is no more than a hope that science will become central to human culture and reason will prevail.

References

Bartlett, F. C. (Sir Frederick). (1932). *Remembering.* Cambridge: Cambridge University Press.

Barlow, H. B. (1956). Retinal noise and the absolute threshold. *Journal of the Optical Society of America* 46: 634.

Craik, K. J. W. (1943). *The nature of explanation.* Cambridge: Cambridge University Press.

Edmonds, D. and Eidenow, J. (2001). *Wittgenstein's poker.* London: Faber and Faber.

Gibson, J. J. (1950). *Perception of the visual world.* Boston: Houghton Mifflin.

Gregory, R. L. (1952). A speculative account of brain function in terms of probability & induction. MRC APU-memo. Cambridge. (First published in *Concepts & Mechanics of Perception.* London: Duckworth, pp. 521–536).

Gregory, R. L. (1958). Increase in neurological noise as a factor in ageing. 4th congress of the International Association of Gerontology. Fidenza pp. 314–324.

Gregory, R. L. (1958). Models and the localization of function in the central nervous system. In: National Physical Laboratory, Symposium No. 10, *Mechanization of thought processes,* vol. 2, H.M.S. pp. 566–583.

Gregory, R. L. (1964). A technique for minimizing the effects of atmospheric disturbance on photographic telescopes. *Nature* 203: 274–275.

Gregory, R. L. (1966). *Eye and brain.* Oxford: Oxford University Press.

Gregory, R. L. (1968a). On how so little information controls so much behaviour. In: C. H. Waddington (ed.) *Towards a theoretical biology,* vol. 2: *Sketches.* Edinburgh: Edinburgh University Press.

---

[10] My interest in the public understanding (or 'appreciation') of science started at the end of the war, when I was posted by the Air Ministry to an exhibition in Oxford Street for showing wartime technologies—radar, jet engines, and so on—to the public, in 1946. I helped Frank Oppenheimer just after he started the Exploratorium. Science Centres are now to be found around the world. Perhaps the science is thin on the ground, but a few seeds can make a mighty forest.

Gregory, R. L. (1968b). Perceptual illusions and brain models. *Proceedings of the Royal Society, Series B* 171: 179–296.

Gregory, R. L. (1972). Cognitive contours. *Nature* 238: 51–2.

Gregory, R. L. (1981). Mind in science: A history of explanations of psychology & physics. London: Weidenfeld and Nicholson.

Gregory, R. L. (1991). *Mirrors in mind.* Oxford: Oxford University Press.

Gregory, R. L. (2004). *Oxford companion to the mind* (2nd edn). Oxford: Oxford University Press.

Gregory, R. L. (2005). Royal soc. Medawar Prize Lecture 'Knowledge for vision: vision for Knowledge'.

Gregory, R. L. (2007). The great detective. *Nature* 445:152.

Gregory, R. L. and Cane. (1955). A statistical information theory of visual thresholds. *Nature* 176: 1272.

Gregory, R. L. and Drysdale, A. E. (1976). Squeezing speech into the deaf ear. *Nature* 264: 748–51.

Gregory, R. L. and Gombrich. (1973). Illusion in nature and art. London: Duckworth.

Gregory, R. L. and Harris. (1975). Illusion-destruction by appropriate scaling. *Perception* 4: 203-220.

Gregory, R. L. and Heard, P. (1983). Visual disassociation of movement, position and stereo depth: some phenomenal phenomena. Quarterly Journal of exp. Psychology 35A: 217–237.

Gregory, R. L., Ross, H. E., and Moray, N. (1964). The curious eye of copilia. *Nature* 201: 1166

Gregory, R. L. and Wallace, J. G. (1962). Recovery from early blindness: a case study. *Experimental Psychology Monograph 2.* Cambridge: Heffers.

Hebb, D. (1949). The organisation of behaviour. London: Chapman & Hall. New York: Wiley.

Hecht, S., Schlear, S., and Pirenne, M. H. (1942). Energy, quanta and vision. *Journal of General Physiology* 25: 819.

Hick, W. E. (1952). On the rate of gain of information. *Quarterly Journal of Experimental Psychology* 4: 11–26.

Ittelson, W. H. (1952). *The Ames demonstrations in perception.* Princeton, NJ: Princeton University Press.

Kanisza, G. (1976). Subjective contours. *Scientific American* 234 (4): 48–52.

Land, M. F. and Nilsson, D. E. (2001). *Animal eyes.* Oxford: Oxford University Press.

Licklider, J. C. R. (1946). Effects of amplitude distortion upon the intelligibility of speech. *J. Acoust. Soc. Amer.* 18: 429.

Milner, D. and Goodale, M. (1995). *The visual brain in action.* Oxford: Oxford University Press.

Morgan, M. J. and Humphrey, N. K. (1965). Constancy and the geometrical illusions. *Nature* 206: 744–745.

Russell, B. (1942). *Human knowledge: its scope and limits.* London: Allen & Unwin.

Shannon, C. E. and Weaver, W. (1949). *The mathematical theory of communication.* Urbana, IL: University of Illinois Press.

Woodworth, R. S. (1938). *Experimental Psychology.* New York: Holt.

10

Social psychology in our time: from 'fun and games' to grown-up science

Miles Hewstone and Wolfgang Stroebe

Introduction

Social psychology in our lifetimes has encompassed the period since the end of the 1960s in which the discipline blossomed, investigating basic processes and applying insights from fundamental social psychology to problems outside the laboratory. In the following sections we consider specifically five changes in our lifetimes: the rise of European social psychology, developments in theory, methods, and statistics, and the perceived relationship between basic and applied research. Finally, we draw some conclusions, looking forward as well as back.

The content of social psychology: continuity and change

Topics studied within social psychology range from construction of the social world (e.g. attitudes and attributions), through social interaction (e.g. attraction and relationships), to social groups (e.g. group dynamics and intergroup relations), and applied social psychology (e.g. health and organizational psychology). Three new perspectives emerged in our lifetimes: the appearance of *social cognition, evolutionary social psychology*, and *social neuroscience.*

Social cognition research is an application of principles of cognitive psychology to the area of social psychology (see Devine *et al.* 1994). Social psychology has always placed strong emphasis on how individuals internally represent their social environments. Many of our theories have been labelled 'cognitive' (e.g. cognitive dissonance), and central concepts of social psychology (e.g. attitudes, beliefs, intentions) are cognitive constructs; social psychologists have also borrowed methods from cognitive psychology to study how social information is encoded and how the information is stored and retrieved from memory. This perspective led to major changes in theory and research on, *inter alia*, causal attribution, attitudes, and stereotyping.

Evolutionary social psychology (e.g. Burnstein and Branigan 2001; Buss and Kenrick 1998) applies evolutionary theory to social psychology. Evolutionary theory explains human behaviours from their reproductive value, that is, in producing offspring during our evolutionary history. Evolutionary psychology makes the basic assumption that if a given behaviour is (a) at least partly genetically determined and (b) increases the probability that an individual will produce offspring, the genes that determine this behaviour will become more prevalent in the gene pool of future generations. Evolutionary social psychologists have made important contributions to the study of interpersonal attraction, helping and cooperation, and aggression.

Social neuroscience studies the neural correlates of social-psychological phenomena (e.g. Cacioppo and Berntson 2005; Ochsner and Lieberman 2001). Such research studies participants' brains with non-invasive techniques while they are processing social information. Experiments have used such techniques to further our understanding of prejudice, for example the use of functional magnetic resonance imaging (fMRI) while people are shown race-relevant stimuli under different conditions. Such research has shown that there is a link between social categorization and the amygdala, a structure in the limbic system that has a role in response to stimuli that signal danger or threat. It is important to stress that involvement of biological processes does not imply something fundamental and unchangeable. In fact, social neuroscience emphasizes that *social* variables can *influence* biological processes.

The coming of age of European social psychology

Until the beginning of our working lifetimes the dominant approach to social psychology had been the individualistic American approach. Yet, even if some writers have exaggerated the extent to which social psychology is predominantly a North American phenomenon (e.g. Jones 1985; Worchel *et al.* 1988), the development of social psychology in Europe has been a significant phenomenon. The European perspective is most evident in what Henri Tajfel (1981) called 'the social dimension', with a focus on the large-scale social processes and events that shape, and are shaped by, human psychological functioning.

During our careers, scientific development in social psychology has changed from being a one-sided enterprise, with American ideas being adopted in Europe, to a mutual exchange, in which European ideas have also been taken up enthusiastically in the USA. The two most salient examples of European ideas influencing social psychology in the USA are research on intergroup behaviour and on minority influence.

Henri Tajfel, at the University of Bristol, developed the 'minimal group paradigm' that turned intergroup behaviour into a major research area (see Brown and Brewer 1998; Tajfel *et al.* 1971). This paradigm offered an easy and economical procedure for the study of intergroup behaviour in the laboratory, and led to the development of the major theory of intergroup relations, social identity theory (Tajfel and Turner 1979).

The second theoretical innovation was research on minority influence. Social influence research in North America had focused exclusively on conformity, that is, on explaining how majorities influence minorities. Serge Moscovici, in Paris, conducted clever studies showing that numerical minorities could influence numerical majorities, and he developed theory to explain why (e.g. Moscovici 1976; Moscovici *et al.* 1969).

Other notable signs of the maturity of European social psychology included the appearance of the *European Journal of Social Psychology* in 1970, the *European Monographs* book series, the *European Review of Social Psychology*, and textbooks written by Europeans for a specifically European market (e.g. Hewstone *et al.* 2007).

Theoretical developments: continuity, innovation, and lacunae

Pettigrew (1986) contended that, to date, the field has provided only narrow- to middle-range theories that are almost impossible to falsify. These theories, he claimed, lack boldness and hold back the discipline from uncovering new and unexpected facts and problems. Notwithstanding the profusion of mini-theories (illustrated in the index of most textbooks), social psychology has successfully generated broad, substantive theories that have stood the test of time. These include social comparison theory (Festinger 1954), social exchange theory (Kelley and Thibaut 1978; Thibaut and Kelley 1959), and social identity theory (Tajfel and Turner 1979).

One area where work is still needed is the development of broad, integrative, theoretical approaches, as opposed to developing isolated theories each designed to account for a specific and limited topic (see Mackie and Smith 1998). For example, Mackie and Smith stressed that theories and empirical approaches from the domains of attitudes are relevant to the study of intergroup relations, and that theory and research on interpersonal relations can, and should, be integrated with work on intergroup relations.

Notwithstanding theoretical progress and an increasing openness to integration, some potential users of social psychology (e.g. policy-makers) may still be frustrated by our inability to predict exactly when something will happen.

For example, although theoretical understanding of the causes, correlates, and consequences of intergroup bias has grown impressively (for a review see Hewstone *et al.* 2002), when asked if we can predict *when* the next outbreak of, say, genocide or ethnic cleansing, or even inter-racial strife in our cities, will occur we are unable to provide answers. But is this really a cause for embarrassment? According to the philosophers Gorovitz and MacIntyre (1976), we may be asking science, in this case social psychology, to do more than it is capable of, when asking it to move beyond explaining 'how things generally behave' to predicting 'how exactly a particular thing will behave' (see Gawande 2003). Social psychology should no more be expected precisely to predict outbursts of collective violence than modern medicine should be to say exactly *when* an individual who is at risk of, say, breast cancer will develop the condition.

Research methods: crisis, what crisis?

According to its critics, social psychology in the 1960s and 1970s had stumbled into a 'crisis' about its goals, methods, and accomplishments. Two prominent papers were published in 1967 and 1973.

First, Ring (1967) contrasted the vision of Kurt Lewin (1951) of a social psychology that would contribute to the solution of important social problems with what he called the 'fun and games' attitude of the social psychology of his days. He lambasted the overemphasis on 'clever' experimentation, 'exotic' topics, and 'zany' manipulations (Ring 1967, pp. 116–17).

Second, Gergen (1973) questioned the very scientific value of social psychology. His two most important arguments were (1) that knowledge of social-psychological principles could change our behaviour in ways that would negate these principles and (2) that because the basic motives assumed by many of our theories are unlikely to be genetically determined they might be affected by cultural change. Gergen saw these problems as the main reason why, as he claimed, social-psychological research often failed to be replicable, and hence did not result in a body of cumulative knowledge.

How was the crisis overcome? We mention just two developments initiated within mainstream social psychology which, over the years, helped to alleviate some of the problems highlighted by these critics. First, social psychologists began to demonstrate their ability to contribute to the solution of real-life problems by developing several applied areas, which contributed to resolving important societal problems (e.g. social-psychological contributions to health psychology; see Stroebe 2001).

Second, meta-analytic procedures allowing statistical integration of the results of independent studies of the same phenomenon demonstrated the reliability of findings across many independent investigations (see Johnson and Eagly 2000). The increasing use of meta-analysis in social psychology has shown that many social-psychological claims have, in fact, been confirmed over multiple studies, often conducted in different countries over many decades. This accumulation of evidence contradicts Gergen's claim.

Although social psychology has done well to slough off the 'fun-and-games' tag, the demise of highly involving 'impact' experiments is a cause for some regret. Perhaps it is necessary to create high-impact situations to study some important phenomena (Goethals 2003). Generally, there has been a huge increase in the use of 'judgement experiments' (Aronson *et al.* 1985), in which the participant is typically asked to classify, remember, or evaluate stimulus materials of a putative social nature presented by an experimenter.

It is important to emphasize, too, that many of the classic studies that might *appear* to be 'fun and games' were designed specifically to test a theory, had a deeply serious message, stimulated significant theorizing and further research, and/or have yielded applications. Examples include studies of the impact of the mere presence of others on performance (Markus 1978), and of group size on individual performance (e.g. Latané *et al.* 1979).

Whether in the form of impact or judgement experiments, experimentation remains the dominant research method in social psychology because it is the method best suited to testing theory rather than merely describing the world as it is. It permits researchers a great degree of *control* over possible random variation and, even more advantageously, allows them to assign research participants *at random* to experimental conditions. To its proponents, laboratory experimentation, allied to probabilistic statistics, has led to the discovery of reliable, counterintuitive effects, often specified in the form of an interaction between manipulated variables.

This is not to argue, however, that the experiment is the sole method of social psychology. Far from it. In fact, one of the great benefits of social psychology is its rich array of methods, including field studies, natural experiments, field experiments, natural groups in the laboratory, artificial groups in the laboratory, diary studies, and surveys. A frequent criticism of a unique reliance on laboratory experimentation, with undergraduate students as participants (see Sears 1986), is, however, that such research is unlikely to yield generalizable results (see Taylor 1998).[1] As Aronson *et al.* (1985) argued, all experiments should be conducted in a variety of settings,

---

[1] We suspect, too, that this reliance on experiments using undergraduate students as participants is also, in part at least, responsible for the comparatively low impact of social psychology (compared with sociology) on policy-making and governments. Try the thought experiment of sitting before a select committee of politicians arguing for the relevance of your work (e.g. on helping behaviour, aggression, intergroup conflict), armed with a database consisting purely of studies using undergraduate samples.

and hypotheses should be tested in both the laboratory and the field. They refer to the interplay between laboratory and field experimentation as 'programmatic research', a research programme that capitalizes on the advantages of each approach.

This proposed solution is best understood in terms of the distinction between internal and external validity. Internal validity refers to the confidence with which one can draw cause-and-effect conclusions from research results; external validity refers to the extent to which a causal relationship, once identified in a particular setting with particular participants, can be generalized to other times, places, and people. Ideally, it is argued, we should use many different experimental and non-experimental procedures to explore the same conceptual relationship, thus replacing the profusion of single, isolated studies with systematic, conceptual replications.

Although this advice is sound, it is typically based on the assumption that if findings have been replicated with different types of people and different methodologies they can be generalized to all types of people and all types of situation (i.e. have external validity). This assumption is based on murky epistemological reasoning. Our theories usually state that a given causal relationship applies to all people at all times. Yet our experiments test it only under very specific conditions. The notion that external validity can ever be established is an inductivist fallacy (Gadenne 1976)—the fact that the only swans we have ever seen are white does not exclude the possible existence of black swans (Popper 1968). Intersecting evidence from multiple methods, and conducting conceptual replications under a wide variety of conditions, increases our trust in the validity of the general assumptions made by our theories, but we can never be sure. None the less, the pursuit of external validity is a goal to which we should aspire.

Statistical sophistication: distinguishing mediating from moderating variables

An analysis of publication trends in our leading journals some years after the so-called crisis reported that, since 1968, published articles in the flagship *Journal of Personality and Social Psychology* had, *inter alia*, become longer, reported research based on more studies, used more participants per study, and used more complex statistical methods (Reis and Stiller 1992; see Berscheid 1992).

There was a time when main effects and interactions were sufficient, perhaps supplemented by internal analysis of simple correlations. But a significant trend is for studies to move—and editors/reviewers insist that authors move—a step further and identify the underlying psychological variables that bring about an effect, that is, the mediating variables. Although analyses of mediating variables had also been conducted earlier (e.g. Insko *et al.* 1973), the practice had been rare and the publication of an important paper by Baron and Kenny (1986) certainly accelerated this trend.

Baron and Kenny (1986) explain that mediator variables address 'how' or 'why' questions. (For example, *how* or *why* does exposure to 'strong' versus 'weak' arguments produce greater attitude change? Answer: because it increases the number of *message-congruent thoughts*, which produces the attitude change; see Petty and Cacioppo 1986). With the fairly recent development of structural equation modelling techniques and widely available packages for analyses, the search for mediating variables has also been pursued in correlational-survey, as well as experimental, research.

Baron and Kenny (1986) distinguished between mediator and moderator variables, and demonstrated the importance of this distinction for the field of social psychology. Moderator variables address 'when' questions. (For example, *when* does contact between members of different groups lead to an improvement in outgroup attitudes? Answer: when members of the two groups remain aware of respective group memberships; see Brown and Hewstone 2005). Moderation implies that the *level* of a third variable can change the relationship between the other two variables—and the explication of moderators has become central to any conclusive meta-analysis; for example, see masterly meta-analyses of the literatures on minority influence and intergroup contact, respectively, by Wood *et al.* (1994) and Pettigrew and Tropp (2006). In contrast, mediation implies that a third variable (typically a process) can be identified which is responsible for the relationship between two variables. The distinction between mediation and moderation matters, as Baron and Kenny explain, because it has implications for our choice of experimental designs, research options, and planned statistical analyses. We note, too, that it has affected the theories we develop, and has led to far more sophisticated and conclusive tests of theoretical propositions (for more recent developments, see Muller *et al.* 2005; Wegener and Fabrigar 2000).

To some readers of the social-psychological literature we can imagine that such developments have become a source of frustration. The discovery of a new effect, with all its attendant excitement, has been, to some extent, replaced with the less exciting, but painstaking explication of limiting conditions, perhaps even conditions under which the opposite to the original effect is found, and the sometimes frustrating search for mediators. But we take this development from 'it is' to 'it depends' as an indicator of the increased methodological sophistication of our discipline.

Basic and applied research: from separation to symbiosis

The great mathematician Euclid apparently believed in the search for mathematical truth for its own sake, and did not look for applications in his work. One story tells of a student who questioned him about the use of the mathematics he was learning. Upon completing the lesson, Euclid turned to his slave and said, '*Give the boy a penny since he desires to profit from all that he learns*' (Singh 1997, p. 49). He then dismissed the student from the class.

We do not wish to argue for the sanctity of basic research, nor indeed that all research must have applications, but the relationship between basic and applied research is critical and our period of review has seen significant changes in it. Notably, reduced funding for basic research and increased funding for research applied to specific social problems (e.g. AIDS, terrorism) has helped to break down '*the wall between basic and applied research*' (Berscheid 1992, p. 532).

According to Jonas and Lebherz (2007), whereas basic research develops and tests theories that explain relationships between social constructs, applied social psychology centres around a social problem and searches for solutions to this problem, We need, however, sound theories in order to derive sound hypotheses about how to intervene in a real-world problem.

Jonas and Lebherz argue that tackling real-world problems profits from basic research, because it uses theories, paradigms, and concepts from basic research, as well as its results, to guide the search for solutions. They contend, however, that successful application can also improve basic research and theory. Empirical confirmation in a real-world setting increases our confidence in the predictive power of that theory, whereas disconfirmation often shows us ways to improve the theory and thus promotes theoretical advancement. Improved theories will, in turn, enable us to suggest better solutions for change, when faced with future practical problems. Thus, basic and applied social psychology should not be viewed and implemented separately, but in a way that promotes the advancement of both.

Conclusions

In this chapter we have tried to give a sense of the progress made and to show that social psychology today is an exciting and thriving enterprise, which has made a unique contribution to the social and behavioural sciences. There have been significant developments in both theory and research methodology, and social psychologists are applying the understanding they have gained from their study of fundamental cognitive, emotional, and motivational processes to the solution of real-life problems. We are proud of the progress social psychologists have made during our working lifetimes, replacing speculation with sophisticated theory-guided empirical research. Of course, there remains room for improvement. We end by mentioning, briefly, some limitations of the journal publication process, the apparent illegitimacy of social psychology in the eyes of some other psychologists, and the remaining room for improvement in social-psychological research.

As scholars with decades of experience as journal editors we are committed to the peer review process, and happily acknowledge the improvements many reviewers and editors have made to our work. However, even though the quality of published research has improved against objective criteria (Reis and Stiller 1992), there remains room for improvement. Our review process is too slow, too pedantic, and many of our editors rely on too many reviewers' opinions. We are particularly frustrated at the editorial practice of selecting, say, three reviewers for the first version of a paper (based on which the authors then make revisions), and then the addition of some new reviewers (with often quite different opinions) to read the revision. The graph of manuscript improvement against number of revisions is one of diminishing returns; the initial improvements, we submit, are often huge, but the subsequent improvements are often quite minor—if indeed they are improvements. We enjoin editors (ourselves included) to remember that the article before them is written by the author and not the editor, and that the correlation between different reviewers is usually rather small (Daniel 1993). Finally, they should value innovation, ideas, and heuristic value, as well as perfect methodology.

Of course, these multiple revisions also increase the publication lag.[2] If we work as we should, at least some of the time, on important social problems, then we should be doing all we can to speed publication. Would we allow papers on new cancer drugs to languish so long in the editorial doldrums? The development of e-first publishing has helped (adopted in our own journal, the *European Review of Social Psychology*), but we call upon publishers, professional organizations, and editors to work towards leaner, faster dissemination.

What is the contemporary status of social psychology within the discipline as a whole? Berscheid (1992) argued that there had been an increase in status over the past quarter of a century. We agree, but we are not quite so sanguine. There still seems to be the whiff of illegitimacy about social psychology,

---

[2] The information given by many journals about publication lag is, in our experience, misleading, because of the practice of giving 'revise and resubmit' as a first decision date. The date, which is then reported in the journal as the date when a manuscript has been received, is typically the date of receipt of revision.

and many of our colleagues in other areas seem to feel it is an area of which they can afford to remain ignorant.

This reaction from other fields of psychology seems all the more remarkable, given what we can contribute to the study of significant social issues and societal problems: aggression and media violence, health promotion and AIDS, defeating the problem of prejudice, and so on. But are we, to some extent, to blame for the way we continue to conduct much of the research in the area? The tendency of social psychologists slavishly to emulate natural science techniques has led to the charge of irrelevance. No less an authority than Gordon Allport concluded that '*many contemporary studies seem to shed light on nothing more than a narrow phenomenon studied under specific conditions ... some current investigations seem to end up in elegantly polished triviality – snippets of empiricism, but nothing more*' (Allport 1968, p. 68). Another sage observer of the field, Dorwin Cartwright, opined that: '*impressive gains in technical competence have been... something of a mixed blessing, for the fascination with technique seems all too often to have replaced a concern for substantive significance*' (Cartwright 1979, p. 87). These critiques are, sadly, still relevant today, and threaten the potential impact of our research findings.

So, social psychology is still some way from being August Compte's ultimate discipline, the 'true final science' beyond sociology (Goethals 2003). To get anywhere close to that goal, social psychology will have to develop even further. Far too much research is still conducted, in Henri Tajfel's (1981) phrase, 'in a social vacuum'. We need to follow Pettigrew's (1981) vision of a *contextual social psychology*, paying attention to individual factors in the context of macrostructural factors, using simultaneously individual and social variables in both theory and research.

References

Allport, G. W. (1968). The historical background of modern social psychology. In: G. Lindzey (ed.) *Handbook of social psychology*, vol. 1, pp. 3–56. Reading, MA: Addison-Wesley.

Aronson, E., Brewer, M. B., and Carlsmith, J. M. (1985). Experimentation in social psychology. In: G. Lindzey and E. Aronson (ed.) *Handbook of social psychology* (3rd edn), vol. 1, pp. 441–86. New York: Random House.

Baron, R. M. and Kenny, D. A. (1986). The moderator–mediator variable distinction in social psychological research: conceptual, strategic, and statistical considerations. *Journal of Personality and Social Psychology* 51: 1173–82.

Berscheid, E. (1992). A glance back at a quarter century of social psychology. *Journal of Personality and Social Psychology* 63: 525–33.

Brown, R. and Brewer, M. B. (1998). Intergroup relations. In: D. T. Gilbert, S. T. Fiske, and G. Lindzey (ed.) *The handbook of social psychology* (4th edn), vol. 2, pp. 554–94. New York: McGraw-Hill.

Brown, R. and Hewstone, M. (2005). An integrative theory of intergroup contact. In: M. Zanna (ed.) *Advances in experimental social psychology*, vol. 37, pp. 255–343. San Diego, CA: Academic Press.

Burnstein, E. and Branigan, C. (2001). Evolutionary analyses in social psychology. In: N. Tesser and N. Schwarz (ed.) *Blackwell handbook of social psychology: intraindividual processes*, pp. 3–21. Oxford: Blackwell.

Buss, D. M. and Kenrick, D. T. (1998). Evolutionary social psychology. In: D. T. Gilbert, S.T. Fiske, and G. Lindzey (ed.) *The handbook of social psychology* (4th edn), vol. 2, pp. 982–1026. New York: McGraw-Hill.

Cacioppo, J. T. and Berntson, G. G. (ed.) (2005). *Social neuroscience*. New York: Psychology Press.

Cartwright, D. (1979). Contemporary social psychology in social perspective. *Social Psychology Quarterly* 42: 82–93.

Daniel, H.-D. (1993). *Guardians of science: fairness and reliability of peer review*. Chichester: Wiley.

Devine, P. G., Hamilton, D. L., and Ostrom, T. M. (ed.) (1994). *Social cognition: impact on social psychology*. San Diego, CA: Academic Press.

Festinger, L. (1954). A theory of social comparison. *Human Relations* 7: 117–40.

Gadenne, V. (1976). *Die Gültigkeit psychologischer Untersuchungen*. Stuttgart: Kohlhammer.

Gawande, A. (2003). *Complications: a surgeon's notes on an imperfect science*. London: Profile Books.

Gergen, K. (1973). Social psychology as history. *Journal of Personality and Social Psychology* 26: 309–20.

Goethals, G. R. (2003). A century of social psychology: individuals, ideas, and investigations. In: M. Hogg and J. Cooper (ed.) *Sage handbook of social psychology*, pp. 3–23. London: Sage.

Gorovitz, S. and MacIntyre, A. (1976). Towards a theory of medical fallibility. *Journal of Medicine and Philosophy* 1: 51–71.

Hewstone, M., Rubin, M., and Willis, H. (2002). Intergroup bias. *Annual Review of Psychology* 53: 575–604.

Hewstone, M., Stroebe, W., and Jonas, K. (ed.) (2007). *Introduction to social psychology: a European perspective* (4th edn.). Oxford: Blackwell.

Insko, C. A., Thompson, V. D., Stroebe, W., Shaud, K. F., Pinner, B. E., and Layton, B. D. (1973). Implied evaluation and the similarity-attraction effect. *Journal of Personality and Social Psychology* 25: 297–308.

Johnson, B. T. and Eagly, A. H. (2000). Quantitative synthesis of social psychological research. In: H. T. Reis and C. M. Judd (ed.) *Handbook of research methods in social and personality psychology*, pp. 496–528. New York: Cambridge University Press.

Jonas, K. and Lebherz, C. (2007). Social psychology in action. In: M. Hewstone, W. Stroebe, and K. Jonas (ed.) *Introduction to social psychology: a European perspective* (4th edn), pp. 316–344. Oxford: Blackwell.

Jones, E. E. (1985). Major developments in social psychology during the past four decades. In: G. Lindzey and E. Aronson (ed.) *Handbook of social psychology* (3rd edn), vol. 1, pp. 47–108. New York: Random House.

Kelley, H. H. and Thibaut, J. W. (1978). *Interpersonal relations: a theory of interdependence.* New York: Wiley.

Latané, B., Williams, K., and Harkins, S. (1979). Many hands make light the work: the causes and consequences of social loafing. *Journal of Personality and Social Psychology* 37: 822–32.

Lewin, K. (1951). *Field theory in social science.* New York: Harper & Row.

Mackie, D. M. and Smith, E. R. (1998). Intergroup relations: insights from a theoretically integrative approach. *Psychological Review* 105: 499–529.

Markus, H. (1978). The effect of mere presence on social facilitation: an unobtrusive test. *Journal of Experimental Social Psychology* 14: 389–97.

Moscovici, S. (1976). *Social influence and social change.* London: Academic Press.

Moscovici, S., Lage, E., and Naffrechoux, M. (1969). Influence of a consistent minority on the responses of a majority in a color perception task. *Sociometry* 32: 365–80.

Muller, D., Judd, C. M., and Yzerbyt, V. T. (2005). When moderation is mediated and mediation is moderated. *Journal of Personality and Social Psychology* 89: 852–63.

Ochsner, K. N. and Lieberman, M. D. (2001). The emergence of social cognitive neuroscience. *American Psychologist* 56: 717–34.

Pettigrew, T. F. (1981). Extending the stereotype concept. In: D. L. Hamilton (ed.) *Cognitive processes in stereotyping and intergroup behavior*, pp. 303–31. Hillsdale, NJ: Erlbaum.

Pettigrew, T. F. (1986). The intergroup contact hypothesis reconsidered. In: M. Hewstone and R. Brown (ed.) *Contact and conflict in intergroup encounters*, pp. 167–95. Oxford: Basil Blackwell.

Pettigrew, T. F. and Tropp, L. R. (2006). A meta-analytic test of intergroup contact theory. *Journal of Personality and Social Psychology* 90: 751–83.

Petty, R. E. and Cacioppo, J. T. (1986). The elaboration likelihood model of persuasion. In: L. Berkowitz (ed.) *Advances in experimental social psychology*, vol. 19, pp. 123–206. Orlando, FL: Academic Press.

Popper, K. (1968). *The logic of scientific discovery.* London: Hutchinson.

Reis, H. T. and Stiller, J. (1992). Publication trends in *JPSP*: a three-decade review. *Personality and Social Psychology Bulletin* 18: 465–72.

Ring, K. (1967). Experimental social psychology: some sober questions about some frivolous values. *Journal of Experimental Social Psychology* 3: 113–23.

Ross, E. A. (1908). *Social psychology.* New York: Macmillan.

Sears, D. O. (1986). College sophomores in the laboratory: influences of a narrow data base on social psychology's view of human nature. *Journal of Personality and Social Psychology* 51: 515–30.

Singh, S. (1997). *Fermat's last theorem.* London: Fourth Estate.

Stroebe, W. (2001). *Social psychology and health.* Buckingham, UK: Open University Press.

Tajfel, H. (1981). Human groups and social categories: studies in social psychology. Cambridge: Cambridge University Press.

Tajfel, H. and Turner, J. (1979). The social identity theory of intergroup behavior. In: W. G. Austin and S. Worchel (ed.) *The social psychology of intergroup relations*, pp. 33–47. Monterey, CA: Brooks/Cole.

Tajfel, H., Billig, M. B., Bundy, R. P., and Flament, C. (1971). Social categorization and intergroup behaviour. *European Journal of Social Psychology* 1: 149–78.

Taylor, S. E. (1998). The social being in social psychology. In: D. T. Gilbert, S. T. Fiske, and G. Lindzey (ed.) *The handbook of social psychology* (4th edn), vol. 1, pp. 58–95. New York: McGraw-Hill.

Thibaut, J. W. and Kelley, H. H. (1959). *The social psychology of groups.* New York: Wiley.

Wegener, D. T. and Fabrigar, L. R. (2000). Analysis and design for nonexperimental data. Addressing causal and noncausal hypotheses. In: H. T. Reis and C. M. Judd (ed.) *Handbook of research methods in social and personality psychology*, pp. 412–50. Cambridge: Cambridge University Press.

Wood, W., Lundgren, S., Ouellette, J. A., Busceme, S., and Blackstone, T. (1994). Minority influence: a meta-analytic review of social influence processes. *Psychological Bulletin* 115: 323–45.

Worchel, S., Cooper, J., and Goethals, G. R. (1988). *Understanding social psychology* (4th edn). Homewood, IL: The Dorsey Press.

11

Thirty years of object recognition

Glyn W. Humphreys

My perception, in the 1970s

I completed my undergraduate degree in 1976. I had started university when student protest was still common, buildings would be taken over, flags bravely unfurled and then abandoned, flapping lifelessly from windows. By 1976 this had begun to seem faintly silly. Rather than pulling things down for some vague goal, one wanted to see how things could be made to work.

I suppose I studied psychology because I wanted to understand how humans worked. I was fortunate to sit in social psychology lectures given by Henri Tajfel on group dynamics, fuelled by his own experiences as a wartime exile. I spent hours learning about various reinforcement regimes, which at least seemed factual and enabled a sort of understanding of which type of learning might apply in which situation. I even undertook a rare gem of a course on mathematical psychology covering topics such as Luce's choice theorem and Bayesian analyses of decision-making. But, though of course I received the statutory courses, I just didn't 'get' Perception. Although the classes were filled with enough demonstrations to satisfy even a Royal Society Christmas Lecture audience, I couldn't figure out what it all amounted to, what the mechanisms were. Things began to click together only when I attended a lecture on cognitive psychology, where I remember the idea of using converging operations was discussed. Suddenly some larger picture began to fall into place. The lecture introduced the Atkinson–Shiffrin model of short-term memory—my first encounter with a theory formulated in a box-and-arrows framework, where the representations inside the boxes were specified along the connections between the boxes. Here was something that could direct experiments and was open to empirical evaluation. Most excitingly, this approach could be tested (indeed a converging operations advocate would argue that it *should* be tested) using different lines of evidence—not just from studies of free and serial recall by normal participants, but also, for example, from patients whose brain lesion might mean that one part of the model may not function properly. If correct, the model should predict the pattern of impairment found in neuropsychological populations. The idea of using converging evidence to test models was a revelation, suggesting that one should be able to link together work from different fields to construct an overarching account of human cognition. Moreover it encouraged the idea that different lines of converging evidence could then be designed to assess different component processes in the cognitive system. All this was somehow lacking in my understanding of perception. Our lectures explained that adaptation was the psychophysicist's microscope, but, as it were, all I could see were single cells. I really had no idea of what a perceptual system might comprise.

It would be unfair if these comments were read as a specific criticism of perception as I was taught it, because the fragmented picture reflected something of the state of affairs at that time. There were many clever experiments and interesting, non-intuitive ideas on aspects of perception (the notion that visual coding might operate through spatial frequency analysis had begun to infiltrate the undergraduate curriculum), but it was rare to find the different strands of work being linked together. Failing to see what could be done in perception, I went on to conduct a PhD in an area that would subsequently become known as visual cognition—inspired by Michael Turvey's (1973) (to this day beautiful) work on how different forms of masking could be used to probe sequential stages of visual processing. I hoped to advance our understanding of letter recognition by analysing the time course over which different types of information were made available. I had friends who were perception guys. They studied after-effects and visual gratings. I spent hours in dark labs listening to BBC Radio 4 and trying to detect low contrast patterns. But the world my friends inhabited was a different one to mine. Their vocabulary was foreign.

The Marrian revolution

Then, during my PhD, my psychophysicist friends started to talk about someone called David Marr, who was taking ideas from their field with the aim of translating them into working computer models. What was interesting was that, to do this, you had not only to specify how inputs were coded but also how different codes might be integrated, to think about the order of events, and to specify how the evolving representation could access stored knowledge that might allow the model to do something useful—like recognizing an object. In other words, to have a working computer model, you had to think of perception as a system. Suddenly I could see an analogy with models with which I had grown familiar, particularly accounts such as the dual-route model of word recognition being proposed by Max Coltheart and colleagues (e.g. Coltheart 1978). Marr's ideas offered a new kind of scaffolding to link different aspects of perception together using converging operations from computer science as well as from visual psychophysics. It gave scientists coming with very different approaches a common language.

The initial paper that kindled my interest was Marr and Nishihara (1978), built on Marr's earlier proposals (Marr 1976; Marr and Hildreth 1980). Note the incremental approach: Marr had earlier dealt with feature coding, and now Marr and Nishihara went on to consider higher-level representations where features were integrated and then associated with past knowledge. This in itself felt a novel way of thinking—a reflection of a computational approach in which a complex system could be built by linking together modules that each performed their own particular job. Moreover, the proposals put forward by Marr and Nishihara, for how you might go from feature representation to code a surface-based description of an object, and then from that to a modal three-dimensional (3D) representation, specified mechanisms for how object recognition might actually take place. These mechanisms could be tested.

As I came to read more, it became clear that Marr was not the first person to think of constructing explicit theories of pattern and object recognition using ideas from psychology and physiology—proposals such as the Pandemonium model of Selfridge (1959) long predated the work—but Marr's arguments still felt revolutionary. In part I think this was because they came with a well worked-through philosophy for how different approaches to perception could be linked. Marr argued for the utility of having different levels of description. He proposed a computational level of theory which set out the constraints that would impact on any system that used vision for object recognition—as relevant to computers as to humans. For example, his work on developing a model for stereopsis (Marr and Poggio 1976) used constraints such as: no point in the world should be represented at more than one point in an internal representation of depth, to limit possible mappings between points in the two eyes. Similar constraints still influence computational models today, for example the Heinke and Humphreys (2003) account of visual selection.[1] Beneath the computational level of theory, Marr suggested that one could have an algorithmic theory, based on abstracted processing mechanisms, which could be implemented in different kinds of hardware. Further, underneath this, he suggested that there could be a theory of the hardware, which dealt with how particular algorithms were realized in different physical systems. As Coltheart notes in Chapter 5, much of subsequent cognitive science has been built on

---

[1] In Heinke and Humphreys' (2003) model, selection is constrained based on parts of objects being allowed to occupy only one position in an object-centred spatial representation.

the idea that theories can be abstracted from the hardware on which processes operate. Marr's framework for different levels of theorizing makes this explicit, and has had a profound influence on the field—though, as I shall describe, the boundaries between, for example, the algorithmic and hardware levels have become increasingly blurred over time.[2]

After my PhD, I was lucky to gain a lectureship at Birkbeck College where Max Coltheart had recently taken up a chair in psychology, and the department was a hotbed of research into aspects of reading. This work had a particular flavour. It employed functional accounts of performance, such as the dual-route model, to guide experiments, and it used data from neuropsychological patients with disorders of reading alongside data from normal participants. The neuropsychological work seemed especially exciting. Here theorists went outside the laboratory and addressed real-life problems that people experienced after brain lesions. The models could also be used to guide therapy (e.g. Coltheart *et al.* 1992), and so could be useful practically. As a young lecturer it was impossible not to become infected.[3] The functional account of cognition offered by the dual-route model could be thought of as an algorithmic level theory, in much the same way as Marr and Nishihara's proposed mechanisms underlying visual object recognition. It was thus not difficult to think of testing the Marr and Nishihara account using similar procedures to those used to test dual-route theory—with cognitive neuropsychological studies providing an important part of the empirical armoury. This was how my own work in this area started. It was not a profoundly original approach, and Graeme Ratcliff and Freda Newcombe were already embarked on a similar analysis (Ratcliff and Newcombe 1982). However, up to that date I think it is true to say that neuropsychological data had had little impact on theories of normal object recognition, and indeed there were still controversies within the neurological literature over whether 'true' disorders of visual object recognition could occur without contamination from peripheral visual disturbances or more profound cognitive impairments (Bender and Feldman 1972).

My own work was helped enormously on two counts. One was meeting Jane Riddoch, who was beginning a PhD under Max Coltheart's supervision as I came Birkbeck and who wanted to carry out neuropsychological studies of cognition. It was Jane's insights into patient disorders that helped frame the

---

2 Though this is not to everybody's taste—see Coltheart (Chapter 5, this volume).

3 A few years later one of the first of my own PhD students, Cathy Price, wrote in her thesis about becoming infected by cognitive neuropsychologitis. An apt term for the illness!

questions posed in our joint work, and her access to patients made the research possible. The second was meeting HJA, a profoundly agnosic patient with a wonderfully persevering nature. HJA had many low-level visual processes as well as high-level cognitive capacities preserved, refuting the argument that frank disorders of 'intermediate' visual processes could not exist (contra Bender and Feldman 1972). HJA subsequently loyally helped our research for over 25 years (e.g. Riddoch and Humphreys 1987a; Riddoch *et al.* 1999). Patients such as HJA, with selective disturbances of particular aspects of cognition, have made great contributions to the field, and single-case studies should not be overlooked despite current-day emphases on group-based lesion analyses (see The Biological revolution, below).

The first neuropsychological papers on disorders of object recognition that I read were those of Warrington and Taylor (1973, 1978). These distinguished between groups of patients who had deficits either in matching objects depicted in different views or in matching between physically different exemplars of objects used to perform the same basic function (e.g. a wheelchair and a deckchair, both of which serve the function of being used to sit on). Such data provided early suggestions that aspects of object recognition could be fractionated; for example, the ability to achieve viewpoint-independent matching was distinct from access to semantic/functional knowledge about objects. Moreover, the data indicated that some of the processes proposed by Marr and Nishihara had psychological reality (e.g. that there might be some process that derived common object structures across viewpoints). The basic fractionation made by Warrington and Taylor has also continued to influence much of the work in the field; indeed the question of how objects can be recognized across different points of view has generated enormous heat and perhaps rather less light than one would hope (see Biederman and Gehardstein 1993; Tarr and Bülthoff 1998). Interestingly, findings that patients with problems in matching objects across different viewpoints can retain an ability to recognize objects in prototypical views (e.g. Davidoff and Warrington 1999) remain perhaps one of the strongest pieces of evidence suggesting that Marr and Nishihara's account was not correct in its details. For example, according to Marr and Nishihara, some form of view-independent object representation needs to be constructed to enable recognition to occur. If patients cannot construct a view-independent representation, then their recognition of objects in all views should be impaired. However, perhaps the more important point is that, through formulating their account of the perceptual system underlying object recognition, Marr and Nishihara paved the way for questions about view-independent representation to be addressed in a theoretically coherent way.

After the first revolution

Following from Marr's work, subsequent theories of object recognition have differed in many critical ways. One distinction concerns whether surface-based and 3D representations of objects need to be coded for recognition to take place. For example, Biederman's (1987) influential 'Recognition by Components' theory supposed that object representations could be assembled directly from the edges of visual objects, without the need to generate any intermediate surface-based representations. Other theorists have proposed a more direct image-based approach to recognition, where multiple, view-specific, memory representations may be held and used to match objects appearing in different viewpoints (Edelman and Bülthoff 1992). Hybrid accounts, in which view-independent and view-specific procedures operate in parallel, have also been proposed (Hummel and Stankiewicz 1998). These hybrid models hold that view-independent coding requires attentional processes that ensure that the parts of objects are coded in appropriate relative spatial locations, bringing into the play the issue of how attention may play a modulatory role in object recognition. Studies in which attention is manipulated in normal participants, or which use patients who are limited in attending across all the parts of objects, have provided some support for hybrid accounts (e.g. Stankiewicz *et al.* 1998; Vernier and Humphreys 2006).

A further question highlighted by post-Marrian theories concerns the role of colour and surface texture on object recognition, as edge-based approaches to object recognition maintain that colour and surface texture should play little causal role. Here there is again converging evidence from studies with normal participants and with patients pointing to there being an influence of colour and surface texture at least for some object classes and for objects for which surface information is a reliable cue (e.g. Humphrey *et al.* 1994; Price and Humphreys 1989; Riddoch and Humphreys 2004; Tanaka and Presnell 1999; Wurm *et al.* 1993).

We can think of this empirical work as refining our ideas about what we might term the intermediate representations involved in object recognition, such as the surface- and 3D-model representations suggested by Marr and Nishihara (1978). In addition to this, converging experimental work with normal participants and patients has helped to 'flesh out' our understanding of how the input into these intermediate representations is coded (how perceptual features are integrating and organized) and also what later processes are required for object recognition (the involvement of different forms of stored knowledge). For example, we have argued that work with patient HJA distinguishes between processes that group oriented elements into edges, and subsequent processes that code the relations between edges within and across objects (Humphreys 2001; Humphreys and Riddoch 2006). HJA can perform normally on tasks requiring that local oriented elements are grouped (Figure 11.1), but he is profoundly impaired at encoding the correct relations between edges within and across shapes—indeed his recognition errors often involve inappropriate segmentation of shapes based on misinterpreting an internal edge as a segmentation cue (Giersch *et al.* 2000; Riddoch and Humphreys 1987a). It is thus possible to elaborate on different stages of visual grouping and perceptual organization. Work by Mary Peterson and colleagues also provides evidence that perceptual organization operates in a top-down as well as a purely bottom-up manner, so that processes such as edge assignment (in figures with ambiguous figure–ground relations) are influenced by whether the edge forms part of a known object representation (see Peterson and Skow-Grant 2003). This notion—that earlier visual processes can be 'penetrated' by top-down knowledge—is a critical point that contrasts with the ideas put forward by Marr and colleagues. In keeping with the idea of stand-alone computational modules, Marr proposed a bottom-up approach to object recognition whereby early processes were not affected by feedback from processes at higher levels of representation. The questions of whether, when, and how top-down processes might influence earlier stages of object recognition are ones that will drive research in this field for some time to come.

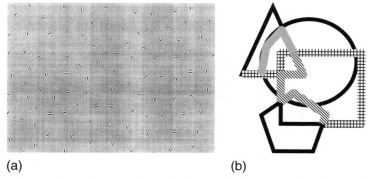

(a)   (b)

Figure 11.1 Example stimuli used by Giersch *et al.* (2000) to examine the grouping of oriented elements in the agnostic patient, HJA. HJA had a normal threshold for detecting a round group of elements aligned by collinearity, when shown against a 'noisy' background (see (a)). Nevertheless, HJA had major problems distinguishing between figures when they overlapped and had difficulty organizing lines within the context of complex shapes. Figure (b) illustrates how HJA assigned edges in shapes, when asked to colour different shapes in contrasting hues. Each shading pattern represents a different hue.

Distinctions between different forms of higher-level representations in object recognition have also been suggested. Evidence for structural representations of objects separate from semantic/functional representations in normal participants comes from reports by Schacter and Cooper (1993) that normal participants showed long-term priming for novel but plausible 3D shapes (with minimal semantic representations), but no priming for implausible shapes. They argue that plausible but not implausible 3D shapes must have persistent structural representations. In neuropsychological studies, several investigators (Fery and Morais 2003; Hillis and Caramazza 1995; Riddoch and Humphreys 1987b; Sheridan and Humphreys 1993; Stewart *et al.* 1992) have documented patients who can distinguish reliably between real objects and structurally similar non-objects, but who remain impaired at accessing semantic knowledge about the objects, for example in matching together semantically related objects. Such dissociations indicate a separation between stored structural representations of objects and stored semantic knowledge. The framework put forward by Marr and Nishihara (1978) needs to be expanded to take account of these additional distinctions.

One other major change in experimental and neuropsychological work on perception after the Marrian revolution has been to emphasize the importance of visual information for action. If you followed courses on Perception from the 1970s through to the mid-1990s you would have hardly thought that vision was used for anything other than describing the visual world and recognizing objects. Of course, in everyday life vision is used for much more than this—particularly for guiding our actions on the world. In the 1990s, David Milner, Mel Goodale, and colleagues (Milner and Goodale 1995; Milner *et al.* 1991) described the agnosic patient DF who showed an impairment apparently even earlier in the visual stream than that suffered by HJA, as she showed profound limitations when making perceptual judgements about groups of visual elements or the orientations of single lines. Strikingly, though, DF was able to reach and post a letter through a letterbox positioned at different orientations! Milner and Goodale argued that there is a distinction between the visual information that is used for conscious perceptual judgements and for object recognition (processes that are damaged in DF), and the visual information used for action (spared in DF). Subsequently, Goodale and associates have attempted to derive converging evidence from studies of visual illusions in normal participants. Here, it has been argued that our actions are much less susceptible to some illusions than our conscious perceptual judgements (e.g. Agolioti *et al.* 1995; Bridgeman 2002; Haffenden and Goodale 1998; for alternative views see Franz *et al.* 2000; Pavani *et al.* 1999). Other work has suggested that the actions we intend to make can modulate how we attend to objects, and, through this, alter how objects are coded (Linnell *et al.* 2005). The step towards thinking of what behavioural outcomes result from visual processing has to have been a healthy one in terms of thinking about real-world applications, and also one that now enables converging work to be developed between vision scientists and computer scientists and engineers working on robotic systems.

The biological revolution

There is one other change I believe worth highlighting, that has taken place after the Marrian revolution. This is that the neural basis of visual perception and object recognition (indeed, of all of cognition) is now taken much more seriously. One of the main drivers for this has been the development of functional brain imaging, which now allows us to assess which brain regions are active when we, for example, recognize particular types of object. My view is that brain imaging can contribute to our understanding of the functional basis of object recognition, not least because it brings another type of converging evidence to bear. The new evidence is concerned with *where* in the brain a given process operates. Now, because we have prior knowledge of what a given brain region is typically involved in, new information indicating that this area is recruited when a given stimulus is processed, can constrain our account of what kind of processing is involved. As a concrete example, Moore and Price (1999) contrasted the neural regions activated when participants named black and white line drawings relative to when they named colour images. They found differential activation in a number of posterior areas in the right hemisphere. One functional account of why coloured images can be easier to identify than black and white images of objects is that coloured images specifically facilitate name retrieval (Ostergaard and Davidoff 1985). A contrasting account is that colour images facilitate the object recognition process itself. Given that changes are observed in the right hemisphere, and that the right hemisphere is not usually thought to modulate name retrieval in normal right-handed participants, these imaging data suggest that the effects of colour are on object recognition itself. Arguments such as this, of course, start to blur Marr's distinction between the algorithmic level of description and descriptions of the hardware. Accounts of what particular regions of the 'hardware' are doing can be used to inform accounts of what algorithms might be involved. I find nothing ideologically objectionable in this. It seems simply to be a case of using extra (dare I say converging) evidence to help refine out arguments about complex processes such as object recognition.

This 'biological revolution' is still evolving, but some new emphases are apparent. Imaging data suggest that distinct brain regions may be recruited when different objects are recognized. This is perhaps most obvious when contrasting faces and other objects, given the highly reliable finding that small regions of the occipital cortex and fusiform gyrus show enhanced activity to faces compared with other stimuli (Grill-Spector *et al.* 2004; Kanwisher and Yovel 2006). However, neural specialization can be observed for other classes of object too. Haxby *et al.* (2001) raised the possibility that there are not generic 'object recognition procedures', but rather that contrasting processes may be called into play, depending on the object involved. This idea of recruitment may be important here. For example, there is evidence that there is activation of medial temporal cortex, left parietal and ventral frontal cortex when tools are recognized (Grabowski *et al.* 1998; Grafton *et al.* 1997). The interesting point that medial temporal cortex is associated with motion processing (Beauchamp *et al.* 2002), and parietal and ventral frontal regions are associated with tool use (Decety *et al.* 1994, 1997), suggests that associations with object motion and functional actions may come into play as we process tools, and these associations may even help us recognize the object involved. These suggestions from imaging sit alongside neuropsychological studies showing that patients can have selective deficits (or sparing) in processing faces versus other objects (Buxbaum *et al.* 1996; Riddoch *et al.* 2008; Rossion *et al.* 2003; Rumiati *et al.* 1994) or relatively impaired (or preserved) recognition of tools compared with living things (Riddoch and Humphreys 2004; Sirigu *et al.* 1991). Whereas the earlier emphasis from neuropsychological studies was primarily on the functional deficit involved, arguments about the lesion site now also become relevant. Of course, it can be difficult to argue about lesion site from single cases, given the (relative) idiosyncrasy of different brains, and so this also leads to a change in the way that research is done, moving work towards case series of patients rather than single cases (e.g. Humphreys and Riddoch 2003). Though, as I have argued, the continuing importance of single cases, and of functional dissociations, should not be lost when we add in further information about common lesion site over groups of patients.

One can caricature the box-and-arrow models that emerged during the Marrian revolution as being static, based on established representations in set boxes, and set connections between the boxes. However, an emergent emphasis from studying the biological basis of visual processing is that perceptual systems are not static but change dynamically over time. In studies of functional imaging, the importance of dynamic change has been highlighted by techniques such as adaptation (a return of the psychophysicist's electrode?), which have been developed to provide a finer-grained analysis of the neural substrates of processing (e.g. Kourtzi and Kanwisher 2001). Imaging studies show that neural areas responding to a stimulus have reduced activity if the same stimulus is adapted repeatedly. This would be consistent with the cells responding to that stimulus in that region entering a refractory state. The extent to which there is recovery of activity when the same stimulus is shown under different conditions (e.g. when the viewpoint changes) or when a new stimulus is presented, indicates both whether the same neurones in that region code the different stimuli, and whether the region contains different populations of neurones that can now be prized apart by the selective adaptation of the neurones to responding to one stimulus. Given the limited resolution of much of present-day functional imaging (e.g. using voxel sizes of 2×2×2 mm, say), adaptation has proved to be an important way of probing the selectivity of neural responding. But, perhaps even more than this, it indicates that dynamic changes operate continuously in perception, with both short- and longer-term changes being evident (see Kourtzi and DiCarlo 2006; Kourtzi and Kanwisher 2001). Understanding these dynamic changes is a critical issue for future research. The emphasis on dynamic change and learning also enables links to be formed with neural network models that incorporate dynamic fluctuations in activity as part of their normal operation, and with studies of how perceptual systems evolve as they develop. The importance of converging operations will not go away.

Acknowledgements

I thank Jane Riddoch for comments. The work was supported by the Medical Research Council and the Stroke Association (UK).

References

Aglioti, S., DeSouza, J. F. X., and Goodale, M. A. (1995). Size contrast illusions deceive the eye but not the hand. *Current Biology* 5: 679–85.

Beauchamp, M. S., Lee, K. E. Haxby, J. V., and Martin, A. (2002). Parallel visual motion processing streams for manipulable objects and human movements. *Neuron* 34: 149–59.

Bender & Feldman (1972).

Bender, M. B. and Feldman, M. (1972). The so-called visual agnosias. *Brain* 95(1): 173–186.

Biederman, I. (1987). Recognition-by-components: a theory of human image understanding. *Psychological Review* 94(2): 115–47.

Biederman, I. and Gehardstein, P. C. (1993). Recognizing depth-rotated objects: evidence and conditions for three-dimensional viewpoint invariance. *Journal of Experimental Psychology: Human Perception and Performance* 19: 1162–82.

Bridgeman, B. (2002). Attention and visually guided behaviour in distinct systems. In: W. Printz and B. Hommel (ed.) *Attention and performance XIX: Common mechanisms in perception and action*, pp. 120–135. Oxford: Oxford University Press.

Buxbaum, L. J., Gloser, G., and Coslett, H. B. (1996). Relative sparing of object recognition in alexia-prosopagnosia. *Brain and Cognition* 32: 202–5.

Coltheart, M. (1978). Lexical access in simple reading tasks. In: G. Underwood (ed.) *Strategies of information processing*. London: Academic Press.

Coltheart, M., Bates, A., and Castles, A. (1992). Cognitive neuropsychology and rehabilitation. In: G. W. Humphreys and M. J. Riddoch (ed.) *Cognitive neuropsychology and cognitive rehabilitation*, pp. 232–259. London: Psychology Press.

Davidoff, J. and Warrington, E. K. (1999). The bare bones of object recognition: implications from a case of object recognition impairment. *Neuropsychologia* 37: 279–92.

Decety, J., Perani, D., Jeannerod, M., *et al.* (1994). Mapping motor representations with PET. *Nature* 371: 600–2.

Decety, J., Grèzes, J., Costes, N., *et al.* (1997). Brain activity during observation of actions: influence of action content and subject's strategy. *Brain* 120: 1763–77.

Edelman, S. and Bülthoff, H. H. (1992). Orientation dependence in the recognition of familiar and novel views of three dimensional objects. *Vision Research* 32(12): 2385–400.

Fery, P. and Morais, J. (2003). A case study of visual agnosia without perceptual processing or structural description impairment. *Cognitive Neuropsychology* 20: 595–618.

Franz, V. H., Gegenfurtner, K. R., Bülthoff, H. H., and Fahle, M. (2000). Grasping visual illusions: no evidence for a dissociation between perception and action. *Psychological Science* 11: 20–5.

Giersch, A., Humphreys, G.W., Boucart, M., and Kovacs, I. (2000). The computation of occluded contours in visual agnosia: evidence for early computation prior to shape binding and figure-ground coding. *Cognitive Neuropsychology* 17: 731–59.

Grabowski, T. J., Damasio, H., and Damasio, A. R. (1998). Premotor and prefrontal correlates of category-related lexical retrieval. *Neuroimage* 7: 232–43.

Grafton, S. T., Fadiga, L., Arbib, M. A., and Rizzolatti, G. (1997). Premotor cortex activation during observation and naming of familiar tools. *Neuroimage* 6: 231–6.

Grill-Spector, K., Knouf, N., and Kanwisher, N. (2004). The fusiform face area subserves face perception, not generic within-category identification. *Nature Neuroscience* 7: 555–62.

Haffenden, A. M. and Goodale, M. A. (1998). The effect of pictorial illusion on prehension and perception. *Journal of Cognitive Neuroscience* 10: 122–36.

Haxby, J. V., Gobbini, M. I., Furey, M. L., Ishai, A., Schouten, J. L. and Pietrini, P. (2001). Distributed and overlapping representations of faces and objects in ventral temporal cortex. *Science* 293: 2425–30.

Heinke, D. and Humphreys, G. W. (2003). Attention, spatial representation and visual neglect: simulating emergent attentional processes in the Selective Attention for Identification Model (SAIM). *Psychological Review* 110: 29–87.

Hillis, A. E. and Caramazza, A. (1995). Cognitive and neural mechanisms underlying visual and semantic processing: implications from 'optic aphasia'. *Journal of Cognitive Neuroscience* 7: 457–78.

Hummel, J. E. and Stankiewicz, B. J. (1998). Two roles for attention in shape perception: a structural description model of visual scrutiny. *Visual Cognition* 5: 49–79.

Humphrey, G. K., Goodale, M. A., Jakobson, L. S., and Servos, P. (1994). The role of surface information in object recognition: studies in a visual form agnosia and normal subjects. *Perception* 23: 1457–81.

Humphreys, G. W. (2001). A multi-stage account of binding in vision: neuropsychological evidence. *Visual Cognition* 8: 381–410.

Humphreys, G. W. and Riddoch, M. J. (2003). A case series analysis of category-specific deficits of living things: the HIT account. *Cognitive Neuropsychology* 20: 263–306.

Humphreys, G. W. and Riddoch, M. J. (2006). Features, objects, action: the cognitive neuropsychology of vision from 1984–2004. *Cognitive Neuropsychology* 23: 156–83.

Kanwisher, N. and Yovel, G. (2006). The fusiform face area: a cortical region specialised for the perception of faces. *Philosophical Transactions of the Royal Society, Series B* 361: 2109–28.

Kourtzi, Z. and DiCarlo, J. J. (2006). Learning and neural plasticity in visual object recognition. *Current Opinion in Neurobiology* 16: 152–8.

Kourtzi, Z. and Kanwisher, N. (2001). The human lateral occipital complex represents perceived object shape. *Science* 24: 1506–9.

Linnell, K. J., Humphreys, G. W., McIntyre, D. B., Laitinen, S., and Wing, A. M. (2005). Action modulates object-based selection. *Vision Research* 45: 2268–86.

Marr, D. (1976). Early processing of visual information. *Philosophical Transactions of the Royal Society of London* B275: 483–524.

Marr, D. and Hildreth, E. (1980). Theory of edge detection. *Proceedings of the Royal Society of London* B200: 269–94.

Marr, D. and Nishihara, H. K. (1978). Representation and recognition of the spatial organization of three dimensional shapes. *Proceedings of the Royal Society of London* B200: 269–94.

Marr, D. and Poggio, T. (1976). Co-operative computation of stereo disparity. *Science* 194: 283–7.

Milner, A. D. and Goodale, M. A. (1995). *The visual brain in action.* New York: Academic Press.

Milner, A. D., Perrett, D. I., Johnston, R. S., *et al.* (1991) Perception and action in visual form agnosia. *Brain* 114: 405–28.

Moore, C. J. and Price, C. J. (1999). A functional neuroimaging study of the variables that generate category-specific object processing differences. *Brain* 122: 943–62.

Ostergaard, A. L. and Davidoff, J. B. (1985). Some effects of color on naming and recognition of objects. *Journal of Experimental Psychology: Learning, Memory and Cognition* 11: 579–87.

Pavani, F., Boscagli, I., Benvenuti, F., Ratbuffetti, M., and Farne, A. (1999). Are perception and action affected differently by the Titchener circle illusion? *Experimental Brain Research* 127: 95–101.

Peterson, M. A. and Skow-Grant, E. (2003). Memory and learning in figure-ground perception, In B. Ross. and D. Irvin (eds). *Cognitive Vinim: Psychology of Learning and Motivation* 42: 1–34.

Price, C. J. and Humphreys, G. W. (1989). The effects of surface detail on object categorisation and naming. *Quarterly Journal of Experimental Psychology* 41A: 797–828.

Ratcliff, G. and Newcombe, F. (1982). Object recognition: some deductions from the clinical evidence. In: A. W. Ellis (ed.) *Normality and pathology in cognitive functions.* London: Academic Press.

Riddoch, M. J. and Humphreys, G. W. (1987a). A case of integrative visual agnosia. *Brain* 110: 1431–62.

Riddoch, M. J. and Humphreys, G. W. (1987b). Visual object processing in optic aphasia: a case of semantic access agnosia. *Cognitive Neuropsychology* 4: 131–85.

Riddoch, M. J. and Humphreys, G. W. (2004). Object identification in simultanagnosia: when wholes are not the sum of their parts. *Cognitive Neuropsychology* 21: 423–42.

Riddoch, M. J., Humphreys, G. W., Gannon, T., Blott, W., and Jones, V. (1999). Memories are made of this: the effects of time on stored visual knowledge in a case of visual agnosia. *Brain* 122: 537–59.

Riddoch, M. J., Johnston, R. A., Bracewell, R. M., Boutsen, L., and Humphreys, G. W. (2008). Are faces special? A case of pure prosopagnosia. *Cognitive Neuropsychology* 25: 3–26.

Rossion, B., Caldara, R., Seghier, M., Schuller, A.-M., Lazeyras, F., and Mayer, E. (2003). A network of occipito-temporal face-sensitive areas besides the right middle fusiform gyrus is necessary for normal face processing. *Brain* 126: 2381–95.

Rumiati, R. I., Humphreys, G. W., Riddoch, M. J., and Bateman, A. (1994). Visual object agnosia without prosopagnosia or alexia: evidence for hierarchical theories of visual recognition. *Visual Cognition* 1: 181–225.

Schacter, D. and Cooper, L. (1993). Implicit and explicit memory for novel visual objects: structure and function. *Journal of Experimental Psychology: Learning, Memory and Cognition* 19: 988–1003.

Selfridge, O. G. (1959). Pandemonium: a paradigm for learning. In: *The mechanisms of thought processes.* London: Her Majesty's Stationary Office.

Sheridan, J. and Humphreys, G. W. (1993). A verbal-semantic category-specific recognition deficit. *Cognitive Neuropsychology* 10: 143–84.

Sirigu, A., Duhamel, J. R., and Poncet, M. (1991). The role of sensorimotor experience in object recognition. A case of multimodal agnosia. *Brain* 114: 2555–73.

Stankiewicz, B. J., Hummel, J. E., and Cooper, E. E. (1998). The role of attention in priming for left-right reflections of object images: evidence for a dual representation of object shape. *Journal of Experimental Psychology: Human, Perception, and Performance* 24(3): 732–44.

Stewart, F., Parkin, A. J., and Hunkin, N. M. (1992). Naming impairments following recovery from herpes simplex encephalitis. *Quarterly Journal of Experimental Psychology* 44A: 261–84.

Tanaka, J. W. and Presnell, L. M. (1999). Color diagnosticity in object recognition. *Perception & Psychophysics* 61: 1140–53.

Tarr, M. J. and Bülthoff, H. H. (1998). Image-based object recognition in man, monkey and machine. *Cognition* 67: 1–20.

Turvey, M. T. (1973). On peripheral and central processes in vision: inferences from an information processing analysis of masking with patterned stimuli. *Psychological Review* 80: 1–52.

Vernier, M.-P. and Humphreys, G. W. (2006). A deficit in contralesional object representation associated with attentional limitations after parietal damage. *Cognitive Neuropsychology* 23: 1104–29.

Warrington, E. K. and Taylor, A. M. (1973). The contribution of the right parietal lobe to object recognition. *Cortex* 9: 152–64.

Warrington, E. K. and Taylor, A. M. (1978). Two categorical stages of object recognition. *Perception* 7: 695–705.

Wurm, L. H., Legge, G. E., Isenberg, L. M., and Luebker, A. (1993). Color improves object recognition in normal and low vision. *Journal of Experimental Psychology: Human, Perception, and Performance* 19: 899–911.

12

Reasoning

Phil Johnson-Laird

Why do researchers become interested in one topic rather than another? The answer, at least for me, seems to have more to do with events in life than with personality or intellect. In 1961, I arrived at University College London (UCL) to study psychology. It came about in this way. One day when I was still at school, my father told me that he could no longer afford to go on paying the fees and that I would have to leave. With great disappointment, I left at the end of the term. I also left without being able to take the examinations necessary to enter university ('O-levels' and 'A-levels'). I worked for five years under contract as a quantity surveyor—a job whose tedium was alleviated only by my moonlighting as a pianist in a modern jazz quintet. (Our bass player, Ian Keen, is now a distinguished anthropologist.) When my contract expired, I quit surveying. My deferment from national service in the military expired, and I was immediately called up. One of my intellectual heroes, however, was Bertrand Russell, and his arguments had convinced me that Britain's possession of nuclear weapons was a moral and political mistake. So, I was a conscientious objector, and the tribunal that heard my case sent me to work for 'two years and sixty days in hospitals and other vital services'.

Towards the end of this period' when I was working in a bakery, I got married, and my wife and I realized that I needed a career. I wanted a job that would be interesting, and the way to get one, I thought, was to go to university. I should have liked to study science, but I needed O-levels and A-levels, and had to work for them by myself with no access to a laboratory. So, I had to study 'arts' subjects at A-level. But, an arts subject at university didn't seem likely to lead to an interesting job—a friend of mine had sat at the feet of Leavis in the Cambridge English Department, and now worked in a public library. The idea of a career within academia struck me as impossible—a realistic assessment, I think, for someone nearly 25 years old with no qualifications. I considered studying philosophy—the influence of Russell, again—but it too seemed unlikely to prepare me for a stimulating job. Then I discovered psychology. It led on to all sorts of interesting possibilities, from ergonomics to clinical practice. And so, as a result of these deliberations, I applied to UCL and, to my considerable amazement, was accepted.

For my subsidiary subject, I chose logic—in part, under the influence of Russell, and in part because I thought (wrongly) that it was easy—I had passed it at A-level after six weeks of study. The late Bernard Williams was the lecturer in introductory logic, and his wit and enthusiasm boosted my interest. But I discovered, as a subject in one of the late Peter Wason's experiments, that I was as susceptible as everyone else to logical error. Peter tested his own subjects, sitting in the corner of the room, smoking a pipe, and radiating more than a passing resemblance to Sherlock Holmes. Afterwards we chatted, and he explained where I had gone wrong. It was fascinating, and my interest in the psychology of thinking probably dates to that conversation.

The course at UCL had no lectures on reasoning, but textbooks had something to say on the topic: the 'atmosphere' of premises—the choice of words such as 'all' or 'none'—biased reasoners to draw certain conclusions rather than others. The texts, however, had nothing to say about the mental processes of reasoning. For that, one had to go to continental psychology and the works of Piaget. His theory was not easy to understand—an ominous sign was the existence of exegetical works purporting to explain it. But, in essence, he proposed that children's intellectual development culminated in a set of principles akin to those of formal logic (Inhelder and Piaget 1958).

I graduated well enough to be accepted for UCL's postgraduate programme, and Wason agreed to be my adviser. He had just returned from an exciting year at the Harvard Center for Cognitive Studies, co-directed by Jerome Bruner and George Miller, and he had carried out a pioneering study into the effects of negation in sentences, which helped to initiate the study of psycholinguistics. As an adviser, he had a miraculous way of getting his students to work on topics that interested him, without any overt direction on his part. And so I found myself working on the pragmatics of the passive voice. I didn't realize it at the time, but Wason was an extraordinary psychologist. He had a *genius*—no other word will do—for devising provocative experimental tasks. That was the one big purpose of his work, and so he had little interest in theories. His dictum was: psychologists should never quite know why they are carrying out an experiment. It took me a while to grasp that his way of doing psychology was unique.

The 1960s were a good time for budding academics, because there were more jobs than people to fill them. No sooner had I completed my doctorate than I was offered a lectureship at UCL. And, at last, I turned to reasoning as a research topic. I discovered a precursor to Piaget, the nineteenth century logician, George Boole, who had described what he took to be the 'laws of thought' in his algebra for the logic of *not, and,* and *or* (Boole 1854). The task for psychologists, it now seemed to me, was to carry out experiments to pinpoint the particular formal rules of inference in the mind. It would not be easy, because an indefinite number of different ways existed in which to formalize logic.

The idea of a tacit mental logic continues to have its adherents (e.g. Rips 1994), and it is implemented in many computer programs for proving logical theorems. But, Wason, though he did not realize it at first, had already made a major dent in this approach to reasoning. He had devised an ingenious task that required individuals to select evidence that could refute a hypothesis. Inhelder and Piaget (1958) had written that, given a hypothesis of the form:

If p then q

individuals should try to refute it by searching for a counter-example, namely the conjunction of p and not-q. Their view was that reasoning was '*nothing more than the propositional calculus*' (p. 305)—an interpretation of Boolean algebra in which variables such as p and q have values that are propositions. In Wason's (1966) experiment, the participants had to test the hypothesis:

If a card has a vowel on one side then it has an even number on the other side.

They had to select those cards that needed to be turned over to find out whether this hypothesis was true or false about four cards laid out on the table in front of them: A, B, 2, 3. They knew that each card had a letter on one side and an even number on the other. According to Piaget, they should select the A card (the p in *if p then q*), and the 3 card (not-q). They did indeed select A, but they almost all failed to select the not-q card.

Wason and I worked together for three years to try to find out what was going on. His most striking discovery was that when the task concerned a journey, and the hypothesis was 'If I travel to Manchester then I go by car', the participants were more likely to make the correct selections of p and not-q—the cards bearing 'Manchester' and 'train' (see Wason and Johnson-Laird 1972). Likewise, Paolo Legrenzi, Maria Sonino Legrenzi, and I observed a striking improvement when the hypothesis concerned potential violations to a postal regulation akin to one in force in the UK: 'If a letter is sealed then it has a 5 penny stamp on it.' We had unwittingly invented the so-called 'deontic' selection task. What struck us, however, was the utter failure of correct performance on this task to transfer to the standard selection task (Johnson-Laird *et al.* 1972).

The selection task has launched a thousand studies, but no consensus yet exists about what ability it taps. At the time, however, I had no doubt that the effect of content was an embarrassment to the view that the mind relies on a formal logic. Formal logic is blind to content, and so Wason's discovery marked a turning point in the study of reasoning. The question for psychologists now became: is there a theory that accounts for the effects of content? Such a theory now exists, but it emerged only over the course of some years. In pursuit of an answer, I spent a year working on the meanings of words with George Miller at the Institute for Advanced Studies in Princeton. Our paper on the topic turned over several years into a book (Miller and Johnson-Laird 1976)—a book so long that few individuals even claim to have read it.

With help from my work with Miller, I developed a theory of reasoning based on the idea that we understand the *meaning* of what we reason about. We use the meanings of words, the grammatical relations amongst the words, and general knowledge to compose the meanings of the premises. These meanings enable us to construct mental models of the possibilities compatible with the premises (Johnson-Laird 1983). Craik (1943) had argued that we construct mental models of the world in order to anticipate events, but he had taken for granted that reasoning depends on verbal rules. Several other theorists proposed that we represent discourse in models (e.g. van Dijk and Kintsch 1983), and the idea is no longer controversial (Garnham 2001). However, once we have constructed models to represent the situations that a discourse describes, we could use the same models as a basis for reasoning. A conclusion is valid if it holds in all the models of possibilities consistent with the premises. And the theory predicts that the more possibilities we have to represent, the harder reasoning should be. It therefore offers an explanation of errors in reasoning, and contrasts with the idea—revived in the 1990s—that naive individuals don't reason at all, but are either prey to 'atmosphere' effects or rely on probabilistic considerations. The current popularity of Sudoku puzzles seems to refute these accounts: the solution of the puzzles depends on pure deduction.

Consider this inference:

> *None of the artists is a beekeeper.*
>
> *All the beekeepers are chemists.*
>
> *What follows?*

Few of us draw the logically correct conclusion:

> *Some of the chemists are not artists.*

Why is the inference so difficult? The answer, according to the model theory, is as follows. We start by envisaging a possibility in which the first premise is true. We construct a model symbolized in the following diagram, where each line represents a separate individual, and the number of individuals is small but arbitrary:

artist

artist

beekeeper

beekeeper

Two of the individuals in the model are artists and two of them are beekeepers, but, of course, a real mental model represents individuals, not words, which I use here for simplicity. We use the second premise to update the model in as simple a way as possible:

artist

artist

beekeeper   *chemist*

beekeeper   *chemist*

This model suggests the conclusion that none of the artists is a chemist, or its converse, and many of us do draw these invalid conclusions. The 'atmosphere' of the premises supports these conclusions too, but according to the model theory they arise from the process of reasoning itself. In order to reach the correct conclusion, we need to realize that there can be chemists who are not beekeepers, and to envisage that these chemists could be artists:

artist   *chemist*

artist   *chemist*

beekeeper   *chemist*

beekeeper   *chemist*

This model refutes the conclusion that none of the artists is a chemist, and its converse. Yet, it does yield a conclusion also supported by the initial model: some of the chemists are not artists, namely, those who are beekeepers. In contrast, those problems that yield only a single model of the premises are easy for us, and even for children.

When I moved to the Medical Research Council's Psychological Research Unit in Cambridge, UK, Ruth Byrne came from Trinity College, Dublin, to work with me. We began with a study of simple spatial reasoning, which corroborated the model theory's main prediction. It was easier for the participants to reason from descriptions compatible with one layout than from descriptions compatible with multiple layouts (Byrne and Johnson-Laird 1989).

Subsequent studies showed the same effect for reasoning about temporal relations amongst events (e.g. Schaeken *et al.* 1996). But the main problem that Byrne and I confronted was to extend the model theory to the analogues of Boole's connectives in natural language: *if*, *or*, and *and*. It took three separate steps.

The first step was to postulate that individuals construct models of the possibilities compatible with assertions containing connectives. An 'exclusive' disjunction, such as:

> There is a king in the hand or else there is an ace, but not both.

is compatible with two possibilities. In one there is a king in the hand (and not an ace), and in the other there is an ace in the hand (and not a king). In contrast, an 'inclusive' disjunction, such as:

> There is a king in the hand or else there is an ace, or both.

is compatible with three possibilities: the two preceding ones, and the possibility in which both the king and the ace are in the hand. The model theory accordingly predicts that reasoning from an exclusive disjunction should be easier than reasoning from an inclusive disjunction. The prediction is crucial, because theories based on formal rules of inference make the opposite prediction. They treat an exclusive disjunction as a calling for an additional inference over and above an inclusive disjunction (e.g. Rips 1994). The results corroborated the model theory (Johnson-Laird and Byrne 1991; García-Madruga *et al.* 2001).

The second step depended on a major assumption: the principle of truth, which stipulates that mental models represent only what is true. Hence, the exclusive disjunction above has the mental models shown in this diagram, where each line denotes a separate possibility:

> *king*
>
> *ace*

Here, 'king' denotes that there is a king in the hand, and 'ace' denotes that there is an ace in the hand. Indeed, when individuals are asked to list the possibilities compatible with the assertion, they tend to list just these possibilities (Johnson-Laird and Savary 1999). However, the first model contains no information about the ace, and the second model contains no information about the king. 'Fully explicit' models of the two possibilities represent this information:

> *king*　　　　*not-ace*
>
> *not-king*　　*ace*

where 'not' is used to show that the corresponding affirmative propositions are false. In other words, the force of 'or else' is that one proposition in the disjunction is true and the other proposition is false. Only fully explicit models, however, represent the status of both propositions in both possibilities. The principle of truth eases the load on working memory, but it exacts an unexpected cost.

At each stage in its development, we implemented the model theory in computer programs, and just occasionally the output of these programs surprised us. The biggest surprise came from a program based on the principle of truth. Its output contained what seemed to be an egregious error. The premises were:

If there is a king then there is an ace, or else if there is not a king then there is an ace.

There is a king.

When the program followed the principle of truth, it represented the first premise in these mental models:

king   *ace*

not-king   *ace*

Given the second premise—the categorical assertion that there is a king—the program eliminated the second model and drew the conclusion: there is an ace. However, when the program used fully explicit models, representing both what is true and what is false, it drew the bizarre conclusion that there is *not* an ace.

Nearly everyone draws the conclusion that there is an ace (Johnson-Laird and Savary 1999). Yet, it is an illusion, and the program's conclusion from fully explicit models is correct: there is not an ace. To understand why, you need to recall two assumptions that I have already made. The first assumption is that one proposition in an exclusive disjunction is true and the other proposition is false—they can't both be true. The second assumption is that a conditional of the form, if p then q, is false in the possibility in which p and not-q occur. Granted that the first premise in the inference above is an exclusive disjunction, it can be abbreviated as:

If king then ace, or else if not-king then ace.

Suppose that the first conditional, if king then ace, is true. The second conditional is therefore false (i.e. not-king and not-ace both hold). This case is compatible with the truth of the first conditional, and so one possibility is:

not-king   *not-ace*

Now, suppose that the second conditional, if not-king then ace, is the one that is true. The first conditional is therefore false (i.e. king and not-ace both hold).

This case is compatible with the truth of the second conditional, and so another possibility is:

> king not-ace

The premises allow only these two possibilities, and so, even granted the presence of the king, it follows that there is not an ace.

You may think of an alternative rationale leading reasoners to infer to the contrary, that there is an ace. Perhaps they interpret the disjunction, not as exclusive but as inclusive. Perhaps they interpret the conditional as implying its converse. But, even granted either of these interpretations, or both of them, it still doesn't follow that there's an ace. Another possibility is that reasoners take the first premise to mean:

> *If there is a king or if there isn't a king then there is an ace.*

Yet, the fallacy occurs even when the two conditionals are stated separately and the participants are told, 'One of these assertions is true and one of them is false'. A more powerful result, however, is that illusions of many other sorts are predicted by the principle of truth, and reasoners are highly susceptible to them (Johnson-Laird 2006). A theory based on formal rules of inference might be able to explain the illusions. So far, no such theory has been forthcoming.

The third and most difficult step in formulating the model theory was to give a proper account of conditionals, that is, sentences of the form: if p then q, which have perplexed philosophers for millennia. Byrne and I, however, assumed that their complexities arise from interactions among a number of simple components (Byrne 2005; Johnson-Laird and Byrne 2002). We proposed that the core meaning of a conditional, such as 'If there is a king then there is an ace', is compatible with three possibilities:

> king   ace
>
> not-king   ace
>
> not-king   not-ace

In fact, children start by interpreting conditionals as compatible with just the first of these possibilities, later they add the third possibility, and by early adolescence they list all three possibilities (Barrouillet *et al.* 2000). But, the meanings of the clauses in conditionals, and general knowledge, can modulate the core interpretation. One effect of modulation is to prevent the construction of a possibility. For example, the conditional, 'If they played a game then it wasn't soccer', is compatible with only two possibilities: in one, they played a game that wasn't soccer, and in the other they didn't play a game.

Another effect of modulation is to establish various relations between the situations described in a conditional. For example, the conditional, 'If she put the ball onto table then it rolled off' is compatible with a temporal and spatial scenario in which she put the ball on the table and then it rolled off on to the surface below the table. The upshot is that the system for interpreting conditionals and other connectives, such as *and* and *or*, must take into account the meanings of the clauses that they interconnect, the entities that the clauses refer to, and general knowledge. The system cannot work in the way in which logic assigns interpretations to connectives, which concerns only whether propositions are true or false.

An alternative account of conditionals is that the if-clause invites us to make a supposition, and that we evaluate the then-clause in this hypothetical case (e.g. Evans and Over 2004). Some conditionals elicit suppositions, but not all do. As someone once said to me in Manhattan, 'If it's as hot as this now [in April] then it will be even hotter in the summer.' There was nothing hypothetical about the situation described in the if-clause. The model theory allows that individuals often make suppositions about clauses in conditionals and in other sorts of assertion (van der Henst *et al.* 2002). But suppositions cannot be the whole story. They fail to explain why individuals list three possibilities for simple conditionals, and why, as Ormerod and his colleagues have shown, they paraphrase a conditional of the form: if not p then q, as a disjunction, p or q, and vice versa (e.g. Ormerod and Richardson 2003).

Logic is built on Boolean connectives and on quantifiers such as 'all' and 'none', and so once the model theory had an account of reasoning based on these terms researchers began to investigate how it might be extended to other sorts of reasoning. It is impossible to describe all these developments, and so I mention only three diverse examples: reasoning about what is permissible (Bucciarelli and Johnson-Laird 2005); reasoning about relations, including those that appear to be transitive but are not, such as 'is a blood relative of' (Goodwin and Johnson-Laird 2005); and reasoning in psychological illnesses (Johnson-Laird *et al.* 2006).

Fifty years ago, cognitive psychology was in a nascent state. The story that I have told here is about a single strand in its subsequent development. I have focused on one approach to reasoning—the idea that it depends on constructing mental models of situations, from either perception or discourse. During the past decade, the theory has burgeoned, although it remains controversial. It began as a theory of deductive reasoning, but it now offers explanations of other sorts of reasoning—inductive reasoning, probabilistic reasoning, the detection and resolution of inconsistent beliefs, and the reasoning that underlies our ability to solve problems. The theory could be wrong. But, it has two strong empirical supports. The first is the ability of individuals to list what is possible given a description—this simple task lies beyond the scope of most alternative theories. The second is the consequences of the principle of truth: reasoning on the basis of mental models leads to systematic illusions. Finally, what makes the selection task difficult? It may be the lack of familiar counter-examples. The participants in the postal experiment were familiar with what violated the regulation. Those who don't know the regulation tend to err.

References

Barrouillet, P., Grosset, N., and Leças, J. F. (2000). Conditional reasoning by mental models: chronometric and developmental evidence. *Cognition* 75: 237–66.

Boole, G. (1854). *An investigation of the laws of thought: on which are founded the mathematical theories of logic and probabilities.* London: Walton and Maberley.

Bucciarelli, M. and Johnson-Laird, P. N. (2005). Naive deontics: a theory of meaning, representation, and reasoning. *Cognitive Psychology*, 50, 159–193.

Byrne, R. M. J. (2005). *The rational imagination: how people create alternatives to reality.* Cambridge, MA: MIT Press.

Byrne, R. M. J. and Johnson-Laird, P. N. (1989). Spatial reasoning. *Journal of Memory and Language* 28: 564–75.

Craik, K. (1943). *The nature of explanation.* Cambridge: Cambridge University Press.

Evans, J. St. B. T. and Over, D. E. (2004). *If.* Oxford: Oxford University Press.

García-Madruga, J. A., Moreno, S., Carriedo, N., Gutiérrez, F., and Johnson-Laird, P. N. (2001). Are conjunctive inferences easier than disjunctive inferences? A comparison of rules and models. *Quarterly Journal of Experimental Psychology* 54A: 613–32.

Garnham, A. (2001). *Mental models and the interpretation of anaphora.* Hove: Psychology Press.

Goodwin, G. and Johnson-Laird, P. N. (2005). Reasoning about relations. *Psychological Review* 112: 468–93.

Inhelder, B. and Piaget, J. (1958). *The growth of logical thinking from childhood to adolescence.* London: Routledge & Kegan Paul.

Johnson-Laird, P. N. (1983). *Mental models.* Cambridge, MA: Harvard University Press.

Johnson-Laird, P. N. (2006). *How we reason.* Oxford: Oxford University Press.

Johnson-Laird, P. N. and Byrne, R. M. J. (1991). *Deduction.* Hillsdale, NJ: Lawrence Erlbaum Associates.

Johnson-Laird, P. N. and Byrne, R. M. J. (2002). Conditionals: a theory of meaning, pragmatics, and inference. *Psychological Review* 109: 646–78.

Johnson-Laird, P. N. and Savary, F. (1999). Illusory inferences: a novel class of erroneous deductions. *Cognition* 71: 191–229.

Johnson-Laird, P. N., Legrenzi, P., and Legrenzi, M. S. (1972). Reasoning and a sense of reality. *British Journal of Psychology* 63: 395–400.

Johnson-Laird, P. N., Mancini, F., and Gangemi, A. (2006). A hyper emotion theory of psychological illnesses. *Psychological Review* 113: 822–41.

Miller, G. A. and Johnson-Laird, P. N. (1976). *Language and perception.* Cambridge, MA: Harvard University Press.

Ormerod, T. C. and Richardson, J. (2003). On the generation and evaluation of inferences from single premises. *Memory & Cognition* 31: 467–78.

Rips, L. J. (1994). *The psychology of proof.* Cambridge, MA: MIT Press.

Schaeken, W. S., Johnson-Laird, P. N., and d'Ydewalle, G. (1996). Mental models and temporal reasoning. *Cognition* 60: 205–34.

van der Henst, J.-B., Yang, Y., and Johnson-Laird, P. N. (2002). Strategies in sentential reasoning. *Cognitive Science* 26: 425–68.

Van Dijk, T. A. and Kintsch, W. (1983). *Strategies of discourse comprehension.* New York: Academic Press.

Wason, P. C. (1966). Reasoning. In: Foss, B. M. (ed.) *New horizons in psychology*, pp. 135–51. Harmondsworth: Penguin.

Wason, P. C. and Johnson-Laird, P. N. (1972). *The psychology of deduction: structure and content.* Cambridge, MA: Harvard University Press.

13

Weber's Law

Donald Laming

If X is a stimulus magnitude and $X + \Delta X$ is the next greater magnitude that can just be distinguished from X, then Weber's Law states that ΔX bears a constant proportion to X. As of 1958 (looking at my undergraduate notes), Weber's Law was attributed to a logarithmic transform somewhere in the brain. For, if ΔX bears a constant proportion to X, so also does $X + \Delta X$, and

$$\ln(X + \Delta X) - \ln X = \text{constant.} \tag{1}$$

This idea is due to Fechner (1860/1966), who envisaged a logarithmic transform as the interface between outer psychophysics (the domain of stimuli) and inner psychophysics (the domain of sensations). Fechner proposed that sensation should be measured in units of just noticeable differences, so that

$$S = \ln X + \text{constant,} \tag{2}$$

a relation known as Fechner's Law. This was the consensus in 1958. It led electrophysiologists to look for logarithmic relationships in sensory pathways and to place a quite disproportionate emphasis on a finding by Hartline and Graham (1932) recording from a single ommatidium in the king crab, *Limulus*. They found that the maximal frequency of discharge at onset increased as the logarithm of luminance over about three log units (though the sustained rate of discharge, measured after 3.5 s, followed a power law instead).

At about the same time Stevens (1957) asserted that on *prothetic* continua (continua for which stimulus magnitudes superpose) sensation was correctly reflected in magnitude estimates and was related to stimulus magnitude by a power law,

$$S = aX^{\beta}, \tag{3}$$

not a log law (eqn 2). And, of course, there was signal detection theory (Swets *et al.* 1961; Tanner and Swets 1954).

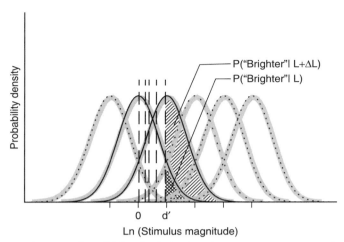

P("Brighter"| L+ΔL)
P("Brighter"| L)

Figure 13.1 The normal model for discriminations between two separate stimuli. The continuous density functions and the five criteria (dashed lines) model the 52-ms data in Figure 13.2(a). Additional density functions (dotted curves) can be added as required to generate a model for the entire continuum. The pale grey curves are density functions transposed from Figure 13.4. (Adapted from Laming, D. 'Fechner's Law: Where does the log transform come from?' © 2001, Pabst Science Publishers. Reproduced by permission.)

In combination with the logarithmic transform (eqn 1), the normal, equal variance, model of signal detection theory gives a superbly accurate account of the properties of discriminations between two separate stimulus magnitudes. The manner in which this is achieved is illustrated in Figure 13.1. The presentation of a stimulus of magnitude X is represented by a random sample from a normal distribution, mean $\ln X$, normal with respect to $\ln$(Stimulus magnitude). A discrimination between two magnitudes X and $X + \Delta X$ can then be modelled with two normal distributions, and the standard deviation, σ, is a free parameter at our disposal to adjust the discriminatory power of the model to the discriminability actually observed. The two continuous density functions in Figure 13.1 (means 0 and d') model the 52-ms data in Figure 13.2(a); d' has been set to 1.4 to generate the continuous operating characteristic in that figure, and the vertical broken lines in Figure 13.1 are the decision criteria that generate the data points. This model can be adapted to any stimulus difference ΔX:

$$d' = \ln(1 + \Delta X/X)/\sigma \qquad (4)$$

and the proportion of correct responses in a two-alternative forced-choice task increases as a normal integral with respect to d'. The stimulus difference

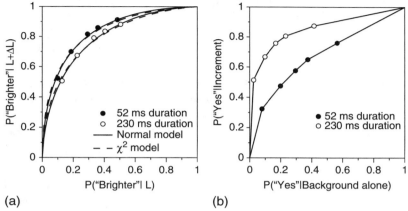

Figure 13.2 (a) Signal detection data for discrimination between two brief flashes of light differing in luminance by 26% (Nachmias and Steinman 1965, experiment III). The two sets of operating characteristics correspond to two different models: the normal (Figure 13.1) and χ^2 (Figure 13.4). (b) Corresponding data for detection of a bright line, 1.9-min arc in width and 18% greater than the background (Nachmias and Steinman 1965, experiment II). (Adapted from Laming, D. *Sensory analysis*, pp. 26 & 94. © 1986, Academic Press. Reproduced by permission.)

ΔX enters into the calculations only via the ratio $\Delta X/X$, so that Weber's Law obtains everywhere. The dotted density functions in Figure 13.1 represent other stimuli on the same continuum. This theory accounts for all the properties of discriminations between two separate stimulus magnitudes with a numerical precision rarely encountered in experimental psychology—but, I emphasize, only for discriminations between two *separate* stimulus magnitudes.

Two ideas have transformed our understanding of sensory discrimination and of sensation since 1958. The first says that sensory discrimination is differentially coupled to the physical world, so that only changes in sensory input are available as a basis for perception. The second idea says that there is no absolute judgement. Instead, judgements of stimuli presented one at a time depend on the preceding stimulus and the response assigned to it as a point of reference; in addition, comparison with that preceding stimulus is little better than ordinal.

Weber's Law

Signal detection theory prompted many authors in the 1960s to propose models for Weber's Law, usually with respect to some particular sensory modality.

For the most part, those models sought to explain the law without recourse to a logarithmic transform. An unpublished manuscript from 1975 reviews 27 such essays, of which one suggested the first of the ideas.

By the early 1960s, microelectrode technique enabled recording from primary fibres in the auditory nerve (Kiang 1965; Tasaki and Davis 1955). Such recordings revealed that primary discharges were synchronized with a specific phase of the stimulus tone, and comprised a Poisson-like stream of impulses. This suggested to McGill (1967) that auditory discrimination might be based on a counting of these impulses. After a deal of complicated mathematics, McGill derived Weber's Law for the discrimination of the intensity of Gaussian noise, but a square root law only for pure tones. Why the difference?

The difference results from the physical structure of the stimuli. A pure tone is a mathematical function of time, and discrimination between one amplitude of tone and another is limited only by the sensitivity of the discriminator. McGill's counting mechanism substituted a square root law for a constant ΔX. But Gaussian noise is a random function of time, each stimulus being randomly selected from a set of possible waveforms. A simple geometric argument shows that, to distinguish one level of noise from another, one must scale the set of waveforms by a constant multiplicative factor; that is, Weber's Law is a natural property of Gaussian noise.

Suppose, now, that the initial stages of transmission convert sensory input into a sample of Gaussian noise. Figure 13.3 shows how this is accomplished. Light is transmitted as a Poisson stream of energy. The topmost trace in Figure 13.3 is a sample from a Poisson process of density $1/2L$. Sensory neurones take both positive (excitatory) and negative (inhibitory) inputs, and this is the positive input. The negative input is represented by the second trace in panel A, another Poisson sample of density $1/2L$, but now inverted. Panel B shows the combination of these two inputs. The means, $\pm 1/2L$, cancel, and the sensory process is thereby differentially coupled to the physical process. But the quantal fluctuations do not cancel, because they are mutually independent. Instead, they combine in square measure to provide a combined input that is a close approximation to Gaussian noise of power L. Weber's Law results. McGill's (1967) study provided the source of the first idea, that sensory discrimination is differentially coupled to the physical world.

Sensory neurones, of course, emit action potentials of one polarity only, so a half-wave rectification follows. The positive-going excursions of the Gaussian noise are output as a maintained discharge. Half-wave rectification loses half the information in the original noise sample, but preserves the Weber Law property. So how does this explanation compare with the logarithmic transform (eqn 1)?

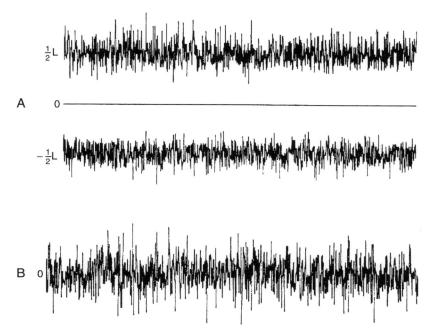

Figure 13.3 (A) Two Poisson traces of equal density and opposite polarity, representing the inputs respectively to the excitatory and inhibitory components of a receptive field. (B) Their sum, a Gaussian noise process centred on zero mean. (From Laming, D. *Sensory analysis*, p. 80. © 1986, Academic Press. Reproduced by permission.)

The answer is set out in Figure 13.4. The energy in a sample of Gaussian noise has a χ^2 distribution, and the χ^2 densities in Figure 13.4 parallel the normal densities in Figure 13.1. They each have 72 degrees of freedom, chosen, as before, to match the 52-ms data in Figure 13.2(a). The respective operating characteristics are so similar that no experiment will discriminate between them. This equivalence extends to all the properties of discriminations between two separate stimulus magnitudes. This is demonstrated in Figure 13.4 by reproducing the normal distributions from Figure 13.1, but now plotted as pale grey curves with respect to a linear (not the previous logarithmic) abscissa. They underlie the corresponding χ^2 densities. (Likewise the χ^2 distributions of Figure 13.4 are reproduced as the pale grey curves in Figure 13.1.) There are, therefore, two quite distinct theories that model the properties of discriminations between two separate stimulus magnitudes, each with superb numerical precision. How to choose between the two?

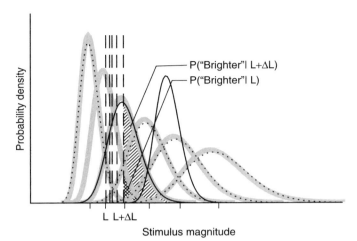

Figure 13.4 The χ^2 model for discrimination between two separate stimuli, analogous to the normal model of Figure 13.1. The continuous density functions and the five criteria (broken lines) again model the 52-ms data in Figure 13.2(a). The dotted curves indicate some of the additional density functions that can be added to model the entire continuum. The pale grey curves are the density functions transposed from Figure 13.1. (Adapted from Laming, S. 'Fechner's Law: Where does the log transform come from?'. © 2001, Pabst Science publishers. Reproduced by permission.)

The difference needed between two separate stimulus magnitudes, X and $X + \Delta X$, before they can be distinguished is typically 25% (see Laming 1986, Table 5.1, pp. 76–77). But if ΔX is added as an increment to a background magnitude X, a difference of 2% can be detected (Steinhardt 1936), and a sinusoidal grating can sometimes be detected with a contrast as small as 0.2% (van Nes 1968). Sensory systems are therefore peculiarly sensitive to boundaries and discontinuities in the stimulus field. Such sensitivity is achieved by differential coupling. Differential coupling is essential to the transition in Figure 13.3 from a Poisson input to Gaussian noise. It accommodates a wide range of phenomena for the detection of increments and sinusoidal gratings (Laming 1986, 1988) and generates an asymmetrical operating characteristic, skewed in the direction of the data in Figure 13.2(b).

The logarithmic theory in Figure 13.1 admits no such development, because it does not incorporate any differential relationship to the physical stimulus. So, although there are two theories that can each provide a superlative account of the properties of discriminations between separate stimulus magnitudes, only one of them can also accommodate the related properties of the detection of increments and sinusoidal gratings. The normal model with logarithmic transform happens to work because the logarithm of a χ^2 variable (with the number of degrees of freedom that are commonly needed to model sensory discriminations) happens to be approximated very closely by a normal variable (Johnson 1949). Fechner's Law derives solely from this mathematical relationship (Laming 2001).

The psychophysical law

A psychophysical law is a relation between physical stimulus magnitude and sensation. Equations (2) and (3) are psychophysical laws. Stevens (1957) argued that only direct methods (e.g. magnitude estimation) gave unbiased estimates of sensation. Subsequently Stevens (1966) showed that estimates of the exponent in (3) were approximately consistent as between magnitude estimation, magnitude production, and cross-modality matching. In view of the purely mathematical origin of Fechner's Law, this might appear to be correct. But that would be too simple.

Sometime in 1982 Christopher Poulton passed me a reprint (Baird *et al.* 1980) that contained Figure 13.5. This led to the second idea. After Stevens' death in 1972, magnitude estimation continued at Harvard University in the hands of

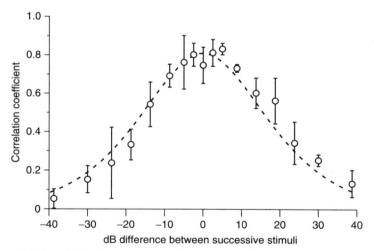

Figure 13.5 Correlations between successive log numerical estimates in the experiment by Baird *et al.* (1980). (Adapted with permission from Baird, J. C., Green, D. M., and Luce, R. D. Variability and sequential effects in cross-modality matching of area and loudness. *Journal of Experimental Psychology: Human Perception and Performance* 6: 286. © 1980, American Psychological Association, and reproduced with the permission of Oxford University Press from Laming, D. *The measurement of sensation*, p. 129. © 1997, Donald Laming.)

Duncan Luce, Dave Green, and their associates. Each participant now contributed many more trials than in Stevens' day, and autoregressive analysis revealed that successive log estimates were positively correlated. Figure 13.5 displays an example from the magnitude estimation of the loudness of 1-kHz tones.

When the stimulus value is repeated to within ±5 dB, the correlation is about +0.8; that is to say, the second log numerical assignment inherits about two-thirds of its variability from its predecessor. So the stimulus on the preceding trial and the number assigned to it must serve as a point of reference for the present judgement. That must still be so even when the difference between successive stimuli is large, because participants cannot know until they have judged the stimulus how it relates to its predecessor—large difference or small. The much smaller correlations when the difference between successive stimuli is large must therefore reflect a greatly increased variability of the comparison over large stimulus differences; such an increased variability would be observed if the exponent β in equation (3) or in

$$\log (N_n - N_{n-1}) = \beta \log (X_n - X_{n-1}) \tag{5}$$

were a random variable.

Let us throw Stevens' power law (eqn 3) away. Suppose, instead, that the comparisons between successive stimuli, $X_n - X_{n-1}$, are no better than ordinal. Equation (5) is then the mean resultant of a large number of ordinal comparisons and, with respect to individual comparisons, β takes on the properties of a random variable. The model curve in Figure 13.5 results. The data in Figure 13.5 suggest that (a) each stimulus is judged relative to its predecessor (a higher-level analogue to the differential coupling of sensory discrimination) and (b) those comparisons are little better than ordinal.

The ordinal character of sensory comparisons is confirmed by Braida and Durlach (1972, experiment 4). Participants were asked to identify stimuli from sets of ten 1-kHz tones, presented in different sessions at 0.25, 0.5, 1, 2, 3, 4, 5, and 6 dB spacing. Identification did not become more accurate as the spacing increased; instead, except for a purely sensory confusion at the closest spacings, errors of identification increased in proportion to the spacing of the stimuli (Laming 1997, pp. 150–3). This is what one would expect if the comparison of each stimulus with its predecessor were no better than < 'greater than', 'about the same as', 'less than' >. This idea supports quantitative models for a diversity of results from magnitude estimation and absolute identification experiments (Laming 1984, 1977).

It follows from these experiments that there is no empirical distinction between judging the stimulus and judging the sensation. Judgements are all relative to the preceding stimulus, and the comparisons are no better than ordinal. So judgements of stimuli and of sensations (assuming those judgements to be distinct) can always be mapped on to each other, and sensation does not admit measurement on a ratio or interval scale. In short, Stevens' power law (eqn 3) does not relate to internal sensation at all. How then does that relation arise?

Stevens' experiments nearly always used a geometric ladder of stimulus values—equally spaced on a logarithmic scale. His participants had received a Western scientific education and were well accustomed to ratios of numbers—approximately equally distributed on a logarithmic scale (see Baird *et al.* 1970). Purely ordinal comparisons between one stimulus and its predecessor lead to great variability in magnitude estimates, about 100 times the variability of threshold discriminations (Laming 1997, pp. 120–2). Figure 13.6 presents one set of data. The only meaningful relation between stimulus magnitude and numerical estimate is linear regression with respect to logarithmic scales, and this equates to a power law. Poulton (1967) and Teghtsoonian (1971) showed that Stevens' exponents bore an uncannily precise relationship to the log range of the stimulus variable—that is, Stevens' participants

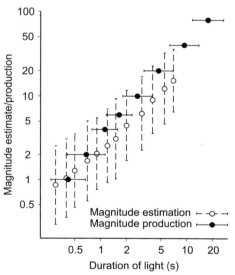

Figure 13.6 Matching of number to the duration of a red light. The open circles are geometric mean magnitude estimates and the filled circles magnitude productions. The vertical and horizontal lines through the data points extend to ±1 standard deviation of the distributions of log matches. (Data from Stevens and Greenbaum 1966, p. 444, Table 2.)

were fitting much the same range of numbers to whatever range of stimuli was presented for judgement.

Where are we now?

Present-day understanding of Weber's Law and of psychophysics is simpler now than it was 50 years ago.

Weber's Law

The key development has been the realization that the properties of a sensory discrimination—signal-detection operating characteristic, psychometric function, Weber fraction—depend on the configuration in which the two magnitudes to be distinguished are presented. Formerly it was argued (e.g. Holway and Pratt 1936) that Weber's Law represented no more than the minimum of a Weber fraction that increased at both low magnitudes and high. It is now clear that for discriminations between two separate magnitudes Weber's Law holds down to about absolute threshold, but that for the detection of an increment it tends to a square root relation at low magnitudes (e.g. Leshowitz *et al.* 1968).

The properties of sensory discriminations can now (Laming 1986, 1988) be related to a small number of basic principles—the differentiation of sensory input (see Figure 13.3), the background of Gaussian noise, half-wave rectification of cellular output, and a local smoothing/summation of the sensory process. These principles mean that discrimination is critically dependent on the spatial and temporal configuration in which two stimulus magnitudes are presented for comparison. The downside is that the mathematics needed to relate principles to predictions are more complicated than most experimental psychologists care to engage with. For example, many visual scientists (e.g. Klein 2001) use a Weibull function to approximate psychometric functions, notwithstanding that the basis ('probability summation') on which that function is derived has long been known to be contrary to experimental observation (Graham 1989, pp. 158–9). In view of the mathematical complexity, it is not surprising that the study of sensory discrimination is now out of fashion.

The psychophysical law

Fechner's (1860/1966) psychophysics was founded on an attempt to measure internal sensations. That can now be seen to have been misconceived. Fechner's Law can be identified with a purely mathematical relationship between the normal and $\log \chi^2$ density functions, but that is not the real point. What matters most is that human participants are unable to identify single stimuli absolutely, in isolation. Analysis of magnitude estimation and absolute identification data shows, first, that each stimulus is judged relative to its predecessor in the experiment and, second, that that comparison is little better than ordinal (Laming 1984, 1997). There is no empirical distinction between judging the stimulus and judging the sensation. It is true that magnitude estimates are still sometimes interpreted as measures of sensation (e.g. West *et al.* 2000), a practice that I have dubbed the '*sensation error*' (Laming 1997, p. 25), in reference to Boring (1921). But it is now clear that sensation cannot be measured in the sense that either Fechner or Stevens envisaged.

Two residual problems

Lest this survey should give the impression that in the matters of Weber's Law and the psychophysical law everything is now buttoned up, I finish with two fundamental problems that still require resolution.

Asymmetrical operating characteristics in signal detection

Figure 13.2 presents two sets of signal detection data from Nachmias and Steinman (1965). The left-hand diagram (a) shows the data from a discrimination between two 1° circular fields in Maxwellian view, differing in luminance by 26%. The right-hand diagram (b) relates to the detection of a fine vertical line, 1.9-min arc in width, and 18% greater in luminance, superimposed on the lesser background of diagram (a). All other details of the experimental procedure, including the observer, were the same. The operating characteristic for discrimination between two separate luminances (a) is symmetrical, whereas that for detection of the line (b) is asymmetrical. The superposition of the line is but a small perturbation of the input, yet it leads to an extreme asymmetry. Calculation based on existing theory says that, while the characteristic in (b) should, indeed, be asymmetrical, the degree of asymmetry should be so small as to be indistinguishable from symmetry (Laming 1986, pp. 256–62). So, where does the extreme asymmetry in detection of an increment come from?

The limit to absolute identification

Experiments on the absolute identification of single stimuli routinely give a limiting accuracy equivalent to the identification of five distinct magnitudes without error (2.3 bits of information, except for colour and orientation where there are, arguably, internal anchors; Garner 1962, Chapter 3). Pollack (1952) provides a particularly compelling example. Comparisons with the preceding stimulus are clearly not evaluated on an interval scale; indeed, if there is only that one point of reference, comparisons cannot be better than ordinal: <'greater than', 'about the same as', 'less than'> But the limit to accuracy is clearly five categories, not three. How are the two extra categories distinguished? Stewart and co-workers (2005, p. 892) propose that participants have an internal standard for scaling the logarithm of the ratio between successive stimulus magnitudes—an absolute judgement of log ratios, though not of magnitudes. But this proposal conflicts with the experiment by Braida and Durlach (1972), in which wider stimulus spacing produces a negligible increase in accuracy. The source of the limit to absolute identification is still to be resolved.

References

Baird, J. C., Lewis, C., and Romer, D. (1970). Relative frequencies of numerical responses in ratio estimation. *Perception & Psychophysics* 8: 358–62.

Baird, J. C., Green, D. M., and Luce, R. D. (1980). Variability and sequential effects in cross-modality matching of area and loudness. *Journal of Experimental Psychology: Human Perception and Performance* 6: 277–89.

Boring, E. G. (1921). The stimulus-error. *American Journal of Psychology* 32: 449–71.

Braida, L. D. and Durlach, N. I. (1972). Intensity perception. II. Resolution in one-interval paradigms. *Journal of the Acoustical Society of America* 51: 483–502.

Fechner, G. T. (1860/1966). *Elemente der Psychophysik*. Breitkopf and Härtel, Leipzig. *Elements of Psychophysics*, vol. 1 (trans. H. E. Adler). New York: Holt, Rinehart and Winston.

Garner, W. R. (1962). *Uncertainty and structure as psychological concepts*. New York: Wiley.

Graham, N. v. S. (1989). *Visual pattern analyzers*. New York: Oxford University Press.

Hartline, H. K. and Graham, C. H. (1932). Nerve impulses from single receptors in the eye. *Journal of Cellular and Comparative Physiology* 1: 277–95.

Holway, A. H. and Pratt, C. C. (1936). The Weber-ratio for intensive discrimination. *Psychological Review* 43: 322–40.

Johnson, N. L. (1949). Systems of frequency curves generated by methods of translation. *Biometrika* 36: 149–76.

Kiang, N. Y.-S. (1965). *Discharge patterns of single fibres in the cat's auditory nerve*. Cambridge, MA: MIT Press.

Klein, S. A. (2001). Measuring, estimating, and understanding the psychometric function: a commentary. *Perception & Psychophysics* 63: 1421–55.

Laming, D. (1984). The relativity of 'absolute' judgements. *British Journal of Mathematical and Statistical Psychology* 37: 152–83.

Laming, D. (1986). *Sensory analysis*. London: Academic Press.

Laming, D. (1988). Précis of *Sensory Analysis*. A reexamination of *Sensory Analysis*. *Behavioral and Brain Sciences* 11: 275–96, 316–39.

Laming, D. (1997). *The measurement of sensation*. Oxford: Oxford University Press.

Laming, D. (2001). Fechner's Law: Where does the log transform come from? In: E. Sommerfeld, R. Kompass, and T. Lachmann (eds.) *Fechner Day 2001*, pp. 36–41. Lengerich: Pabst.

Laming, D. (2004). *Human judgment: the eye of the beholder*. London: Thomson Learning.

Leshowitz, B., Taub, H. B., and Raab, D. H. (1968). Visual detection of signals in the presence of continuous and pulsed backgrounds. *Perception & Psychophysics* 4: 207–13.

McGill, W. J. (1967). Neural counting mechanisms and energy detection in audition. *Journal of Mathematical Psychology* 4: 351–76.

Nachmias, J. and Steinman, R. M. (1965). Brightness and discriminability of light flashes. *Vision Research* 5: 545–57.

Pollack, I. (1952). The information of elementary auditory displays. I. *Journal of the Acoustical Society of America* 24: 745–9.

Poulton, E. C. (1967). Population norms of top sensory magnitudes and S. S. Stevens' exponents. *Perception & Psychophysics* 2: 312–16.

Steinhardt, J. (1936). Intensity discrimination in the human eye. I. The relation of ΔI/I to intensity. *Journal of General Physiology* 20: 185–209.

Stevens, S. S. (1957). On the psychophysical law. *Psychological Review* 64: 153–81.

Stevens, S. S. (1966). Matching functions between loudness and ten other continua. *Perception & Psychophysics* 1: 5–8.

Stevens, S. S. and Greenbaum, H. B. (1966). Regression effect in psychophysical judgment. *Perception & Psychophysics* 1: 439–46.

Stewart, N., Brown, G. D. A., and Chater, N. (2005). Absolute identification by relative judgment. *Psychological Review* 112: 881–911.

Swets, J. A., Tanner, W. P. Jr., and Birdsall, T. G. (1961). Decision processes in perception. *Psychological Review* 68: 301–40.

Tanner, W. P. Jr. and Swets, J. A. (1954). A decision-making theory of visual detection. *Psychological Review* 61: 401–9.

Tasaki, I. and Davis, H. (1955). Electric responses of individual nerve elements in cochlear nucleus to sound stimulation (guinea pig). *Journal of Neurophysiology* 18: 151–8.

Teghtsoonian, R. (1971). On the exponents in Stevens' Law and the constant in Ekman's Law. *Psychological Review* 78: 71–80.

van Nes F. L. (1968). *Experimental studies in spatiotemporal contrast transfer by the human eye*. PhD thesis, University of Utrecht.

West, R. L., Ward, L. M., and Khosla, R. (2000). Constrained scaling: the effect of learned psychophysical scales on idiosyncratic response bias. *Perception & Psychophysics* 62: 137–51.

14

Fifty years of neuropsychological memory research. The score: methods 5–theory 2

Andrew Mayes

Compared with 50 years ago, how differently do we now think about the neural bases of human memory? Obviously, we know much about human memory today that was unknown in 1957 when Scoville and Milner first described HM, whose bilateral hippocampal damage permanently prevented him from acquiring new information, but has our basic theoretical thinking changed? There has certainly been one major change, but others have been more subtle. In the 1950s, researchers thought of memory as a unitary system, whereas today most researchers believe that there are different, hierarchically arranged, memory systems (e.g. conceptual priming < priming < non-declarative memory). Unfortunately, what is meant by 'memory system' is not as clear as it might be (see Foster and Jelicic 1999). To me, a memory system is an interconnected set of brain structures that work together to represent, store, and retrieve specific kinds of information. However, although there is little question that memory for different kinds of information is mediated by distinct (partially non-overlapping) parts of the brain, a more interesting, and far less fully resolved, issue is whether the distinct brain systems not only mediate memory for different information, but do so in *qualitatively* different ways.

Qualitative differences between two or more memory systems seem more likely if the cellular architecture (e.g. local circuitry) of the two systems is distinct and the synapse-altering intraneuronal processes that underlie consolidation and maintenance of long-term memory in distinct systems follow different learning rules. The involvement of different local circuitry and learning rules would suggest that the processes underlying information representation, storage, and retrieval are distinct. Since the early 1980s, parallel distributed processing (PDP)-style neural network modelling (see Rumelhart *et al.* 1986) has provided a potential means of using the constraints imposed by specific regional architectures and learning rules to check exactly how varieties of neural processing, specific to certain brain systems, mediate different kinds of memory. Such modelling also makes it possible to check how different memory systems excite, inhibit, or modulate one another. But, we are still at the early stages of these developments because the effectiveness of this approach depends on the degree to which anatomical, physiological, and other knowledge constrains the models we specify—and those constraints are still fairly minimal.

It is still not known how strong the constraints need to be before computational modelling becomes heuristically worthwhile. As knowledge of relevant constraints improves, model-based predictions will become more interesting. We already know enough about the psychological and brain processes that are necessary and sufficient for each memory system so that rather vague information processing and storage theories can be formulated. To progress to the further stage of building realistic computational models, we need to know still more about several issues. First, the precise functional role of each regional component of each memory system must be identified so that we know what role each region plays in the initial representation of incoming information (encoding), its consolidation and storage, and its retrieval. Second, how the individual regions of each memory system work together in a concerted fashion to allow memory also needs to be identified. Third, we need to know more about the firing patterns of each region's constituent neurones during memory tasks, as well as about their patterns of anatomical connectivity locally and with other regions, and how their synaptic connectivity changes are achieved (which will require isolating the intraneuronal biochemical processes that consolidate and maintain the synaptic alterations underlying long-term memory). Considerable advances towards all of these goals over the past 50 years have been enabled by powerful new techniques.

In my view, apart from the change to thinking explicitly about multiple hierarchically arranged memory systems, the major changes in the past half century have been methodological advances. For example, the idea that memory storage ultimately depends on changes in synaptic connectivity has been around since Hebb (1949). This framework has not changed greatly, but new techniques have filled in many of its details since World War II. So, while we are beginning to get a good preliminary understanding about how neuronal interactions trigger the complex and drawn-out biochemical cascades that lead to changes in neurones' synaptic structure and efficiency, we are still nowhere near formulating a theoretical account of precisely how these changes between neurones are related to the storage of information by different memory systems.

New techniques

When the modern era of research on memory neuropsychology began with Scoville and Milner's (1957) paper on the iconic amnesic patient, HM, knowledge of the medial temporal lobe (MTL) location of HM's lesion was based on Scoville's surgical notes. With non-surgical patients, precise lesion locations could be obtained for only the few patients whose brains underwent post-mortem analysis. For most research workers, including myself, this situation continued into the 1990s when structural magnetic resonance imaging (MRI) gradually improved to the point at which good volumetric measures of some key memory structures, such as the hippocampus, became feasible. As I was to discover in the late 1970s, although computed tomography (CT) had been invented earlier in 1972, CT images lacked the spatial resolution and contrast to identify the small diencephalic lesions that characterize patients with Korsakoff syndrome. When two patients with Korsakoff syndrome who had undergone CT earlier came to post-mortem analysis in the 1980s, there was little correspondence between what was found with the two methods (Mayes *et al.* 1988).

Today, research on amnesic patients depends on sophisticated structural MRI methods, which (like CT) have improved immensely since the mid-1980s. Although still not uncontroversial, automated procedures, such as voxel-based morphometry, make it possible to determine whether a patient's brain damage is relatively focal or more diffuse, spreading to several brain regions. Not only can the volumes of grey and white matter regions be measured, but tractography makes it possible to assess how intact fibre tracts are in patients (and how much they vary in intact brains). As human lesions are adventitious, it has proved helpful to explore cognition by using transcranial magnetic stimulation (TMS) to induce targeted transient disruptions or facilitations of relatively local neural activity. Unfortunately, this has not yet proved very helpful with memory research, because the regions involved often lie deep (as with the midline diencephalon, medial temporal lobes, and basal forebrain structures), and TMS or similar techniques have not yet proved able to affect deep structures selectively.

Despite these major methodological advances which have transformed research on human amnesic patients, research with animal models remains extremely important. This is because there are many manipulations, such as controlled lesions and single-unit recordings, that cannot be done in healthy humans but can be attempted in species with similar neuroanatomy, neurophysiology, and memory. There have also been major advances in methodology. For example, it is now possible to record from many neurones simultaneously while an animal is engaged in a memory task. Further, before the development of tractography in 2000, identification of fibre tracts was dependent largely on animal research with model species.

Although single-unit recordings are made only occasionally in human patients, cruder forms of human functional imaging are now possible. Initially, with positron emission tomography (PET) and then with functional MRI (fMRI), in the late 1980s and early 1990s respectively, it became possible to monitor indirect markers of brain activity in humans whilst performing memory tasks. In the 1990s, fMRI of memory, mainly in healthy humans, became more dominant than explorations of memory in amnesic patients. However, a convergent operations methodology is clearly essential because interpretations of each approach's findings are helped greatly by the findings of the other approach. For example, although fMRI may locate all regions comprising a memory system, it does not prove that each such region plays a key causal role in producing the relevant kind of memory. That depends on using lesion or TMS studies. Conversely, many believe that brain damage can lead to brain reorganization, so that memory functions are mediated in ways not seen in people with intact brains. This belief can be checked by fMRI studies of amnesic patients.

How has our knowledge about fact and episode memory's neural bases changed?

When I began research on amnesia in the 1970s, this was the main way of exploring the neural bases of memory, and my research history reflects that of the field. As amnesics have impairments of episodic and semantic memory, I will now focus on what has changed in our knowledge of these kinds of memory.

Although Korsakoff first described the amnesic syndrome in 1889, Scoville and Milner's (1957) description of HM rapidly established several ideas that had previously been only implicit. First, the central role of the MTLs in acquiring new and retrieving long-established episodic and semantic memory became a major concern. Second, continued testing of HM, and later of other amnesics, strongly suggested that the critical damage did not noticeably disrupt other cognitive processes, tapped by tests of intelligence, language, attention, perception, and executive functions. I was drawn into memory research by the idea that memory disorders might be extremely selective, because I felt that lesion studies should have considerable potential as means of exploring memory's neural bases. Third, it also became increasingly apparent that, although amnesic recall and recognition of pre- and post-morbidly acquired episodic and semantic memories was disrupted, other kinds of memory, such as that for motor skills, were not impaired (as had been noted anecdotally decades before by Claparede). In time, dissociations like this helped lead to the notion of multiple memory systems.

In relation to the first idea, it has long been clear that a connected system of structures plays a key role in episodic and semantic memory. Thus, it has become progressively clearer that damage to the MTLs, midline diencephalon, basal forebrain, or the fibre tracts that connect these regions, such as the fornix, can cause amnesia. This progress has depended not only on improved structural imaging of human amnesics (and on a handful of post-mortem studies), but also on animal studies. However, progress has not been smooth. Unfortunately, for years, MTL lesions in mammals did not produce the severe memory deficits that cases like HM suggested should be present. It was only when animal testing began to use memory tests that were more analogous to the ones on which human amnesics were impaired that the effects of MTL and other lesions in animals began to resemble more closely what was seen in human amnesics. With the development of analogues of object recognition memory testing, it became clear that large MTL lesions in monkeys and other animals consistently caused severe recognition memory deficits, similar to those seen in human amnesics (Mishkin 1978).

A central feature of human amnesia is impaired recall of episodic and semantic memories, but the development of acceptable animal analogues of recall has been a much slower process (although see Eacott et al. 2005). This has meant that progress has been very slow because accidental human lesions are rarely sufficiently focal, and, even if they are, current structural MRI is pushed to its limits in order to identify the damaged structure (e.g. nuclei and tracts within the thalamus). Furthermore, although the localization of animal lesions is much less of a problem, the absence, until recently, of recall tests has led to confusion. For example, monkey lesion studies have suggested that fornix and mammillary body lesions cause only transient recognition deficits (Zola-Morgan et al. 1989); this was interpreted as implying that damage to these structures played no part in amnesia. However, human studies are beginning to make clear that lesions to the fornix or mammillary bodies (to which the fornix projects) may minimally disrupt recognition, but still disrupt recall severely (see Mayes 2001). With colleagues, including John Aggleton and Daniela Montaldi, I have recently been able to confirm this pattern of memory impairment in a large group of patients with relatively selective fornix damage and accompanying mammillary body atrophy Tsivilis et al. (2008).

The second idea, that information can be normally processed and represented at input but that long-term memory for it still be disrupted following specific kinds of brain damage, is puzzling because it seems plausible that information is stored in the same neurones that represent it at input. If this is true, selective memory disorders should be found only when a region that modulates activity in other regions is damaged. Such damage might make storage-site function suboptimal, thereby affecting storage ability without noticeably influencing processing efficiency. But the MTLs are not viewed as modulating structures, although the basal forebrain may well modulate MTL and association neocortex activity. It is interesting that several researchers have recently argued that perirhinal cortex damage disrupts high-level visual object perception (Buckley et al. 2001; Bussey et al. 2002) and hippocampal damage disrupts high-level kinds of scene perception (Lee et al. 2005). These studies suggest that the key lesions have removed vital representation and storage sites for the same information. Nevertheless, even if confirmed, these perceptual deficits are subtle, and not incompatible with the preserved ability of a mixed group of amnesics to retrieve several kinds of information (e.g. object colour, object position, and object semantics) when tested immediately after presentation (Mayes et al. 1993). Furthermore, the putative relationship of perirhinal/hippocampal perceptual deficits to accompanying memory deficits remains to be established and, if the relationship turns out to be weak, the basic puzzle of how selective brain damage causes memory deficits without also disrupting processing at input and retrieval remains unexplained.

Despite these recent developments, theoretical accounts of amnesia have tended to focus on the idea that MTL, midline diencephalic, or basal forebrain lesions disrupt episodic and semantic memory not because they affect initial representation of information, or even some aspect of retrieval, but because they affect consolidation and possibly long-term maintenance of episodic and semantic memories. These possibilities were apparent from the early work on HM around 50 years ago, but there has not been a rapid movement towards a generally accepted storage theory of amnesia and, relatedly, of the neural bases of episodic and semantic memory, for several reasons.

One reason for slow progress is the difficulty of proving that a structure is implicated in storage of specific kinds of information and that damage to that structure disrupts storage so that some information is lost from storage. If removing a structure disrupts memory, this might be because the neural machinery essential for retrieval (and perhaps representation at input) is no longer functional, because the memories have been lost from storage, or for both of these reasons. Simple lesion effects cannot establish which of these possibilities applies. The use of a technique in which a lesion is followed by a stem-cell transplant procedure, which allows the lost tissue to regrow relatively normally, can, in principle, provide a partial answer. If memory is lost following the lesion, but returns once the transplant has grown, the damaged structure presumably forms a critical part of the retrieval machinery, but is not a storage site for the memory in question. Conversely, if the memory does not return once the transplant has grown, the site was presumably involved in storage of the lost memory (because the acquired synaptic connections will have been lost), although it may also separately form a critical part of the retrieval machinery. One hippocampal lesion study with monkeys that used this procedure found no evidence that the hippocampus was involved in storage (Virley *et al.* 1999). However, the lesion was confined to the CA1 field of the hippocampus, so a larger lesion may have produced a different result. In addition, animal research on long-term potentiation (LTP) over the past 30 years does suggest (although not yet conclusively) that the hippocampus is implicated in storage of the kinds of memory that hippocampal lesions disrupt. LTP has long been regarded as a model of the kind of synaptic change that mediates memory storage. It occurs prominently in the hippocampus, and evidence continues to grow that LTP-like changes in fields such as CA1 accompany the kinds of learning supported by the hippocampus (e.g. Whitlock *et al.* 2006). Nevertheless, there are still some researchers unconvinced that the hippocampus plays any direct role in the storage of episodic and semantic memory (e.g. Gray and McNaughton 2000).

Related to the idea of hierarchically arranged multiple memory systems, perhaps the most important reason why progress has been slow is that the organic amnesia syndrome probably comprises several distinct components, each with its distinctive lesion and pattern of functional breakdown, but these components have proved exceedingly hard to dissociate convincingly. For example, the extent to which anterograde and retrograde amnesia dissociate (with each occurring in relative isolation in different patients) and the factors that determine this are still unresolved. There has also been a long running dispute (at least 30 years) about the factors that determine whether retrograde amnesia relatively spares older premorbid memories or whether it affects them equally, regardless of how far back in the past they were formed. Indeed, there is a major dispute between two positions that assume the two kinds of amnesia have a common neural and functional cause, at least when amnesia results from MTL lesions. The standard view holds that MTL lesions disrupt the initial consolidation of episodes and facts, but that they also disrupt the interaction between the MTL and the association neocortex that would gradually develop stable neocortical storage, which makes the MTLs unnecessary for episodic and semantic memory (e.g. Squire and Alvarez 1995). This view predicts temporally graded retrograde amnesia for both episodic and semantic memories. The main rival hypothesis also postulates the same mechanism for semantic memory and therefore also predicts that older premorbid semantic memories are preserved in amnesia. It has, after all, been known for over a hundred years that very well established semantic memories are not affected in organic amnesia, only in dementias, such as the more recently characterized semantic dementia where neocortical damage is more extensive. However, this view differs in postulating that certain aspects of episodic memory remain dependent on the MTLs, gradually becoming more redundantly represented in this region so that only very large MTL lesions cause temporarily ungraded retrograde amnesia for episodic memories (Nadel and Moscovitch 1997).

Resolution of this dispute depends on determining precisely which MTL lesions cause retrograde amnesia, what kinds of memory are affected, and which factors control the duration and severity of the memory loss. It has proved surprisingly difficult to specify both the neural and the psychological factors involved. Good *in vivo* assessment of the size, location, and functional effects of lesions became available only in the 1990s, so that, assuming that lesion extent and location are the major determinants of the features of the retrograde amnesia, it is not surprising that progress has been slow. Further, animal studies began only around 1990 (e.g. Zola-Morgan and Squire 1990) and, because it was hard to execute studies of retrograde amnesia in animal model systems, progress has again been very slow despite the greater control of lesion extent and location, and of factors such as timing of learning. Useful animal models of episodic and semantic memory recall are only now being developed.

Another reason for slow theoretical progress is that it has proved very difficult to define the boundaries of which kinds of memory are preserved and which are impaired in organic amnesics. This has been particularly difficult in the case of priming, a form of memory that is usually regarded as non-declarative and contrasted with episodic and semantic memory. Priming is revealed by a change in the way that studied information is subsequently processed; such information may be identified more quickly or more accurately. For example, a sentence may be easier to hear in white noise if it has been heard previously than if it has not. Considerable evidence suggests that this memory-related increased processing efficiency occurs whether or not the participant is aware of previously encountering the prime. In other words, effective priming does not require any conscious memory for the remembered information. If, as many people believe, priming is preserved in amnesia, because the same kinds of information that can act as primes (e.g. words, sentences, faces, and objects) can also be recalled and recognized, this suggests that organic amnesia may not disrupt episodic and semantic storage, but rather the process that gives rise to feelings of memory. It is, therefore, crucial to establish (a) whether not merely some, but all, forms of priming are preserved after MTL, midline diencephalic, or basal forebrain lesions, and (b) whether priming and recognition/recall really are for the same information. Over 25 years of research have not fully resolved these two issues. For example, it is still unclear whether certain kinds of priming for novel items and associations are impaired in amnesia (e.g. Gooding *et al.* 2000). It has to be admitted that the area is a minefield because it abounds with tricky control problems. Thus, even in normal subjects, priming effects tend to be weak and performance is variable so that statistical power is low. Conversely there is always a risk that normal subjects may use recall or recognition in an intentional or unintentional way to boost their 'priming' scores inappropriately.

Relevance of more recent developments

As we have seen, techniques introduced or elaborated in recent decades now allow much more precise structural and functional measures of the brain to be made in life in humans, and also in animals. As a result, a wider range of evidence from animals as well as humans can be brought to bear on the central theoretical issues related to amnesia and the neural bases of episodic and semantic memory. So, although there is not complete agreement about whether the MTL is a storage site (and, even if it is, only for a while, according to the standard view), it is now very clear from a variety of sources that processed sensory, motor, and semantic information converges on the MTLs where some kind of binding occurs (e.g. Teyler and Discenna 1986). This reflects a fundamental property of episodic and semantic memories: they are associative combinations of more basic components. It is in the MTLs that associative binding occurs. It still needs to be elaborated how this binding relates to the connected regions where lesions also cause amnesia. Thus, although the basal forebrain modulates activity in the MTLs and in several neocortical regions, its precise role in memory is not established. Similarly, the role of midline diencephalic structures remains unclear. The problem is partly that these structures almost certainly have different roles, but they work very closely together with the MTLs as a system in order to mediate episodic and semantic memory.

Identification of this system has been facilitated by functional neuroimaging since the early 1990s, first with PET and later with fMRI. This established that a wide range of neocortical structures, including parts of the parietal, temporal, and frontal lobes, are activated during encoding and retrieval of episodic and factual information. It has actually proved easier to find activations in these regions initially than in the MTLs, midline diencephalon, and basal forebrain. One effect of these neuroimaging findings is to encourage researchers to check whether parietal and various frontal lesions cause the disruptions that a simple interpretation of the findings would suggest. Although the existence of some kind of frontal role in episodic and semantic memory (involving the elaboration of encoding, retrieval, and possibly other processes) has been proposed for some time, the effects of lesions in those parietal regions activated in memory neuroimaging studies is only now beginning to be explored (e.g. Simons *et al.* 2008).

Improved structural and functional techniques are now allowing the exploration of smaller subregions of the brain. This can be illustrated by work on the MTLs over the past decade. Realization that the individual regions of the MTLs, although highly interconnected, may play slightly different roles has been gradually emerging. In the 1980s, human studies did not differentiate the mnemonic role of the hippocampus, perirhinal cortex, entorhinal cortex, and parahippocampal cortex, although it was clear that larger MTL lesions produced more severe amnesia and monkey studies showed that rhinal cortex lesions produced very severe recognition impairments (see Zola-Morgan and Squire 1993). In humans, large MTL lesions led to very severe impairments in the ability rapidly to acquire episodic and semantic memories, whether these memories were tapped by recall or by recognition. However, studies of patients with MRI-confirmed lesions relatively confined to the hippocampus later showed that some of these patients had anterograde amnesias in which item recall and the form of cued recall, known as recollection, were badly impaired, but recognition was relatively intact (e.g. Mayes *et al.* 2002). Furthermore, familiarity, in which a feeling of memory for previously presented items that is unaccompanied by any recall, was intact in these patients (e.g. Holdstock *et al.* 2002). Consistent with this, Aggleton and Brown (1999) have argued that the hippocampus is not involved in familiarity (which is mediated by the perirhinal cortex and other structures), whereas it is critical for recollection (which, like familiarity, plays a role in recognition) and recall.

Interestingly, there are other patients with relatively selective hippocampal lesions who show much more severe item recognition deficits and impaired familiarity, as well as recollection (for a review see Mayes *et al.* 2007). The reason for the discrepancy is currently unexplained. Nevertheless, evidence is accumulating for a division of function between the hippocampus and perirhinal cortex. First, we have found that familiarity feelings for studied objects modulate the activity of the perirhinal cortex, but not that of the hippocampus, as a function of their strengths (Montaldi *et al.* 2006). Similar fMRI findings have been reported by other groups. Second, if familiarity and recollection really are mediated by distinct parts of the MTL and other brain regions, then perirhinal (and perhaps other lesions) should disrupt familiarity, but not recollection. Unfortunately, relatively selective perirhinal cortex lesions are virtually unknown in humans, and, even if this cortex does not mediate recollection directly, it was uncertain what effect lesions would have because the structure projects important inputs to the hippocampus. However, a recent study has shown that a very rare patient, who had undergone resection of part of the left perirhinal cortex, but not the hippocampus, in the treatment of intractable epilepsy, showed intact recollection, but impaired familiarity when familiarity was measured in three different ways (Bowles *et al.* 2007).

These fMRI and lesion studies support the view that different parts of the MTLs mediate qualitatively different kinds of memory. This view is also supported by a neural network model, which proposes that the hippocampus and perirhinal cortex represent information very differently in memory (Norman and O'Reilly 2003). These two MTL regions have different neural architectures, and the model argues that the hippocampus rapidly and automatically represents even similar inputs in a distinctive way (it pattern-separates), which suits it for pattern completion or recalling memories from partial cues (recollection). In contrast, the perirhinal cortex represents its inputs by identifying common features between even fairly different inputs, which, with rapid learning, suits it best for familiarity memory, but very poorly for recollection.

Since 2000 the emerging picture is that the MTLs are convergence zones for the kinds of information that constitute episodic and semantic memories. This information converges on different MTL structures, some of which also have different neural architectures. Not only is it likely that different MTL regions bind different kinds of information, but it is also likely that, in some cases, they do this in qualitatively different ways. The details are still unresolved, and several views are current. The one that I favour (Mayes *et al.* 2007) is that after one or two learning exposures the perirhinal cortex binds components into items (e.g. objects, faces, or words), but also binds similar items (e.g. two faces) together without creating new items so as to create a memory representation that mainly supports familiarity. The hippocampus binds any set of components together to make flexible representations that support recollection and recall. In particular, it binds associations between different kinds of information (e.g. faces and voices) that do not converge in other parts of the MTL. As the parahippocampal cortex has a similar structure to the perirhinal cortex, but receives different inputs, one might predict that it will show rapid learning by binding familiarity-supporting representations for whatever informational components converge within it. It has been suggested that these components might fall under the heading of 'context' (Eichenbaum *et al.* 2007).

It should not be forgotten that the MTLs mediate episodic and semantic memory by working not only with basal forebrain and midline diencephalon, but also with parts of the frontal, parietal, temporal, and occipital lobes. We are still a long way from having a fully developed theory of how this happens, and similar problems face all the memory systems that have been postulated.

Conclusion

I have argued that the major changes in research on the neuropsychology of human memory have been developments of research techniques, particularly those that enable exploration in life of brain structure and function. Application of these techniques has led to an extraordinary expansion of detailed knowledge of brain changes related to memory. For example, we now have a much more detailed knowledge about the biochemical, physiological, and structural changes that underlie storage at the neuronal level. If anything, we are less sure than we were decades ago about which psychological functions are unaffected By MTL lesions. Thus, on the basis of new detailed knowledge, some researchers believe that MTL lesions disrupt certain forms of working memory, high-level perceptual processing, and priming. So these functions may not be completely preserved. But, apart from ideas about multiple memory systems, general theoretical thinking about the kind of processing machinery that is needed to support memory has revealed only relatively minor elaborations on ideas that were around 50 years ago. However, this is beginning to change as the constraints that can be applied to neural network models of memory increase. The rich armamentarium of techniques that continues to grow in sophistication will deepen our understanding of the processing machinery at an increasing rate as our knowledge of structure, connections, biochemistry, and the learning rules followed by memory-related brain structures grows. With any luck, the next 50 years should prove to be a very exciting time in research on the neural bases of memory.

References

Aggleton, J. P. and Brown, M. W. (1999). Episodic memory, amnesia, and the hippocampal–anterior thalamus axis. *Behavioral Brain Sciences* 22: 425–89.

Bowles, B., Crupi, C., Mirsattari, S. M., *et al.* (2007). Impaired familiary with preserved recollection after anterior temporal-lobe removal that spares the hippocampus. *Proceedings of the National Academy of Sciences of the USA* 104: 16382–7.

Buckley, M. J., Booth, M. C. A., Rolls, E. T., and Gaffan, D. (2001). Selective perceptual impairments after perirhinal cortex ablation. *Journal of Neuroscience* 21: 9824–36.

Bussey, T. J., Saksida, L. M., and Murray, E. A. (2002). Perirhinal cortex resolves feature ambiguity in complex visual discriminations. *European Journal of Neuroscience* 15: 365–74.

Eacott, M. J., Easton, A., and Zinkivskay, A. (2005). Recollection in an episodic-like task in the rat. *Learning and Memory* 12: 221–3.

Eichenbaum, H., Yonelinas, A. P., and Ranganath, C. (2007). The medial temporal lobes and recognition memory. *Annual Review of Neuroscience* 30: 123–52.

Foster, J. K. and Jelicic, M. (ed.) (1999). *Memory: structure, function or process.* Oxford: Oxford University Press.

Gooding, P. A., Mayes, A. R., and van Eijk, R. (2000), A meta-analysis of indirect memory tests for novel material in organic amnesics. *Neuropsychologia* 38: 666–76.

Gray, J. A. and McNaughton, N. (2000). *The neuropsychology of anxiety* (2nd edn). Oxford: Oxford University Press.

Hebb, D. O. (1949). *The organization of behavior.* Chichester: John Wiley.

Holdstock, J. S., Mayes, A. R., Roberts, N., *et al.* (2002) Under what conditions is recognition spared relative to recall following selective hippocampal lesions in humans? *Hippocampus* 12: 341–51.

Lee, A. C. H., Buckley, M. J., Pegman, S. J., *et al.* (2005). Specialisation in the medial temporal lobe for processing of objects and scenes. *Hippocampus* 15: 782–97.

Mayes, A. R. (2001). Effects on memory of Papez circuit lesions. In: L. S. Cermak (ed.) *Handbook of neuropsychology* (2nd edn), vol. 4: *Memory and its disorders,* pp. 111–32. Amsterdam: Elsevier Science.

Mayes, A. R., Downes, J. J., Shoqeirat, M., Hall, C., and Sagar, H. J. (1993). Encoding ability is preserved in amnesia: evidence from a direct test of encoding. *Neuropsychologia* 31: 745–59.

Mayes, A. R., Holdstock, J. S., Isaac, C. L., Hunkin, N. M., and Roberts, N. (2002). Relative sparing of item recognition memory in a patient with adult-onset damage limited to the hippocampus. *Hippocampus* 12: 325–40.

Mayes, A. R., Meudell, P. R., Pickering, A., and Mann, D. (1988). Locations of lesions in Korsakoff syndrome: neuropsychological and neuropathological data on two patients. *Cortex* 24: 1–22.

Mayes, A. R., Montaldi, D., and Migo, E. (2007). Association memory and the medial temporal lobes. *Trends in Cognitive Sciences* 11: 126–35.

Mishkin, M. (1978). Memory in monkeys severely impaired by combined but not separate removal of amygdala and hippocampus. *Nature* 273: 297–8.

Montaldi, D., Spencer, T. J., Roberts, N., and Mayes, A. R. (2006). The neural system that mediates familiarity memory. *Hippocampus* 16: 504–20.

Nadel, L. and Moscovitch, M. (1997). Memory consolidation, retrograde amnesia and the hippocampal complex. *Current Opinion in Neurobiology* 7: 217–27.

Norman, K. A. and O'Reilly, R. C. (2003). Modeling hippocampal and neocortical contributions to recognition memory: a complementary-learning systems approach. *Psychological Review* 110: 611–46.

Rumelhart, D. E., McClelland, J. L., and the PDP Research Group (ed.) (1986). *Parallel distributed processing: explorations in the microstructure of cognition.* Cambridge, MA: MIT Press.

Scoville, W. B. and Milner, B. (1957). Loss of recent memory after bilateral hippocampal lesions. *Journal of Neurology, Neurosurgery and Psychiatry* 20: 11–21.

Simons, J. S., Pears, P. V., Hwang, D. Y., Ally, B. A., Fletcher, P. C., and Budson, A. E. (2008). Is the parietal lobe necessary for recollection in humans. *Neuropsychologia* 46: 1185–91.

Squire, L. R. and Alvarez, P. (1995). Retrograde amnesia and memory consolidation: a neurobiological perspective. *Current Opinion in Neurobiology* 5: 169–77.

Teyler, T. and Discenna, P. (1986). The hippocampal memory indexing theory. *Behavioral Neuroscience* 100: 147–54.

Tsivilis, D., Vann, S. D., Denby, C., Roberts, N., Mayes, A. R., Montaldi, D. and Aggleton, J. P. (2008). A disproportionate role for the formix and mammillary bodies in recall versus recognition memory. *Nature Neuroscience* 11: 834–842.

Virley, D., Ridley, R. M., Sinden, J. D., *et al.* (1999). Primary CA1 and conditionally immortal MHP36 cell grafts restore conditional discrimination learning and recall in marmosets after excitotoxic lesions of the hippocampal CA1 field. *Brain* 122: 2321–35.

Whitlock, J. R., Heynen, A. J., Shuler, M. G., and Bear, M. F. (2006). Learning induces long-term potentiation in the hippocampus. *Science* 313: 1093–7.

Zola-Morgan, S. and Squire, L. R. (1990). The primate hippocampal formation: evidence of a time-limited role in memory storage. *Science* 250: 547–63.

Zola-Morgan, S. and Squire, L. R. (1993). Neuroanatomy of memory. *Annual Review of Neurosciences* 16: 547–63.

Zola-Morgan *et al.* (1989).

15

Mental chronometry: long past, bright future

Michael I. Posner

In his *History of Experimental Psychology*, E. G. Boring (1950) labelled the late nineteenth century as the 'period of mental chronometry'. However, Boring argued that the subtractive method (Donders 1868) for measuring mental operations never worked. He believed that reaction times were too unreliable and their differences even more so. Moreover, he agreed with Kulpe (1985), who argued that total processes are not compounded of elements with separate times but rather were due to differential preparation between the tasks.

Despite Boring's prestige as professor of psychology at Harvard, his view turned out to be far off the mark. From the middle of the twentieth century to the present day, mental chronometry, originally based on reaction time and its derivatives and later incorporating the measurement of electrical activity and haemodynamic changes, has been developed as a means of tracing information flow in the human nervous system. This chapter first discusses the use of purely behavioural methods designed to partition overall response time into component processes, and then turns to measurement of brain activity, finally discussing the use of all these methods in combination as a current and future research direction.

Reaction time and its derivatives

Shannon and Weaver (1949) developed a general mathematical theory for the measurement of information. In subsequent years these ideas were widely applied to psychology (Attneave 1959) and they helped to revive the use of mental chronometry. It was found that the time to respond to a stimulus was a function of the amount of information transmitted from the stimulus to the response. This finding showed that reaction time (RT) was not dependent on the physical stimulus alone, but was influenced by what might have occurred, or, roughly speaking, of the person's expectation. Information transmitted allowed psychologists to combine the number of possible stimuli, their probabilities, and the error rate in a single correlation that sometimes accounted for more than 90% of the variance in particular laboratory tasks (Hick 1948; Hyman 1953). The Hick–Hyman Law was a major contribution to chronometric measurement. However, the slope of the function relating RT to information transmitted could vary widely depending on the compatibility between stimulus and response. When the fingers rested on vibrating keys and the person pressed the vibrator (Mowbray and Rhoades 1959), or when a vocal response to a written word was required, the slope was zero. When the response was highly compatible with the stimulus so that no conflict resulted, it appeared that response time did depend on the physical stimulus and not on the number of possibilities (Posner 1966). In most novel situations in which the stimulus to response mapping was unfamiliar, the person transmitted no more than 20–30 bits per second. Statistical models with a criterion for the occurrence of a response and a random walk based on the strength of the stimulus response combination were able to account for most of the data (Stone 1960). However, it was clear that people could concentrate their attention on one S-R association and modify the rate of information accumulation. Thus, both top-down and bottom-up factors influenced the RT.

Fitts' Law (Fitts 1954) related the time to move from a home button to a target (movement time) to the amount of information generated by the movement. This law continues to be applied in industrial situations. In some situations the Hick–Hyman and Fitts laws could account quite well for the time to begin and end a movement to a target. The amount of information that an aircraft instrument generates proved to be a good predictor of how long the pilot will spend examining it (Senders 1964). Despite these empirical successes, the idea of an infinite capacity to transmit information implied by a zero slope between information and reaction time led Neisser (1967) to declare that the era of information theory was dead. Mental chronometry would need more than a single mathematical tool that summarized input–output relations in order to describe the processing capacity of humans.

In a paper published in *Science*, Saul Sternberg (1966) showed that it took about 30 milliseconds (ms) per item to scan a list of digits in memory. Posner and Mitchell (1967) published a *Psychological Review* article using a version of Donders' subtractive method to show that it took about 80 ms to derive the name of a letter from its visual form. Both of these measurements were reliable and neither depended upon comparing separate tasks for which people could differentially prepare. Rather, they both embedded the measurement within a single random block of trials, so that predictions about what would occur were impossible.

At a meeting in honour of Donders' centenary, Sternberg (1969) presented the general additive factors method. His idea was to assume that overall RT in a task was the sum of a set of independent processing stages that summed to the total time. If this is true, he showed that the effect of any independent variable could be located within the sequence of processing stages by looking for a pattern of additivity and interaction between the unknown variable and variables chosen to influence particular stages. It was a very important contribution that greatly generalized the utility of Donders' approach, and has since been exploited in a wide number of experimental investigations (Sanders 1998).

A natural objection to Sternberg's method is to suppose that many processes can occur in parallel. For example, one can try to name the ink colour of the word **RED** and, while attempting to do so, also to acquire the word meaning in parallel (MacLeod 1991). In fact, brain processes are often carried out in parallel. However, it is rather easy to design tasks in which one stage must be completed before any useful information is available for the next state, and in such serial tasks the additive factors method remains a very useful tool.

Even if two processes occur in parallel it is still possible to demonstrate that they maintain their independence by showing that one independent variable can influence the time for stage X without affecting the time for stage Y, whereas another variable may influence the time for Y but not for X. In the book *Chronometric Explorations of Mind* (Posner 1978), this method was applied to the separation of visual and name codes of a single letter. Differences in colour and brightness between stimuli influenced the time for visual matches but not for name matches, whereas rhyming and other auditory changes influenced name matches but not visual ones. [See the section on Haemodynamic imaging and Sternberg (2004) for the same method used with functional magnetic resonance imaging (fMRI).]

Another chronometric approach is to separate those processes that occur in serial order from those that can be carried out in parallel (Sigman and Dehaene 2005). This model assumes that sensory and motor processes can be carried out in parallel, but that a central workspace constitutes a bottleneck, such as has been studied by the psychological refractory period. The serial processes are fixed in time while the parallel processes vary in the time required for integration of input. In a simple arithmetic task, determining whether an input digit is above or below 5, the major variance in times is attributed to numerical distance from 5, whereas the other processes contribute little variance and can be carried out in parallel with a secondary task. In a further study (Sigman and Dehaene 2006), it was shown that even the central stage cannot be an entirely passive bottleneck but can be employed strategically, based on features of the task (see also Meyer and Kieras 1997).

The link between speed and accuracy for rapid responses is a very close one. A given person may be slow and accurate or fast with lowered accuracy. This fact has been used to develop a method for tracing the time course of information processing based on error probability (Meyer *et al.* 1988). Subjects are given a task (e.g. 'Was the word DOG in a recent study list?'). They are then required to respond even before they are ready. One method is to train them to respond in synchrony with a tone. Sometimes the tone comes well before the person has any idea of the correct answer, and their response may be at chance levels. The accuracy (often measured as d', as taken from signal detection theory) is plotted as a function of time between the target and response signal. The resultant function shows the time to go from chance to perfect performance, and indicates that the time course of processing can be measured in terms of error rate. As RT and accuracy are both fundamental measures of performance the speed accuracy function provides a very fundamental way of linking them.

Chronometric methods have been used to test general models of cognitive processes. Major connectionist (Rumelhart and McClelland 1986) and symbolic (Meyer and Kieras 1997; Newell 1990) models of cognition have used RT and its derivatives to provide precise tests of models of human performance.

Although most of mental chronometry has involved the analysis of aspects of performance common to everyone, an important application has been to individual and group differences (Posner and Rueda 2002). Differences in RT in normal development and in a wide variety of mental disorders have been examined with the goal of developing diagnostic methods for the disorder or designing rehabilitative strategies. Although much of the work has used changes in overall RT as a measure, some studies have tried to locate the particular stage that might be damaged using additive factors methods. Recently it has also been possible to examine the genetic influences on these individual differences. For example, a number of dopamine and serotonin genes (Posner *et al.* 2007) have been shown to be related to a central executive control system measured by the degree of conflict in the Attention Network Task (Fan *et al.* 2002) that presumably involves some or all of the same anatomy discussed above as being related to the central bottleneck in dual-task performance (e.g. Sigman and Dehaene 2005).

Electrical potentials

In 1965, Samuel Sutton and colleagues (1965) reported a large positive wave in the scalp recorded event-related potential (ERP) at about 300 ms after input that they called the P300, which was elicited by low probability or surprising events. This raised the possibility of using scalp electrodes as a physical basis for tracing information processes in the brain.

Over the ensuing years a number of components of the event-related cortical potential were shown to reflect psychological functions. With auditory stimuli it was possible to record components that proved to come from brainstem and thalamic generators (Mokotoff *et al.* 1977) as well as cortical potentials related to events that abruptly mismatched prior input (Naatanen *et al.* 1978). In the case of brainstem potentials, these influences could be well validated because they could be recorded from implanted electrodes in animals. The brainstem and cortical mismatch negativity can be used to examine auditory and language processing in infants and non-verbal organisms, making it possible to examine hearing and language very early in life.

When a visual stimulus is presented the first cortical potentials occur from striate areas at 50 ms after input and from pre-striate areas at 90 ms after input. When attention was drawn to the location of these stimuli within the visual field the electrical potentials were increased in size, suggesting that attention influenced visual or components at least by 80–90 ms after input. While striate potentials can also be influenced by attention, this appears to arise due to feedback from pre-striate areas (Martinez *et al.* 2001). These findings raised a difficulty for some serial models of RT because they showed clearly that attentional influence could change the amplitude of the ERP of early cortical potentials. Although the influence of attention was early in time, determination of the anatomy of these effects depended upon methods that could provide a better link with the anatomy (see below).

Another important development from electroencephalography (EEG) that influenced mental chronometry was the recording of ERPs linked to the motor response (Coles *et al.* 1995). The lateralized readiness potential (LRP) was recorded as a DC shift on the side of the brain opposite the responding hand. Recordings of the LRP allowed the researcher to trace the time course of the build-up of information about the response well before any motor output. One of the important findings was that often the conflict between multiple responses could be seen by a build-up of information on the wrong side that was replaced by the correct response. It was also possible to show that many psychological tasks involved the start of motor output in the LRP a long time before the sensory processing was over, and thus provided some support for a continuous transfer of information to output rather than a transfer only after the sensory stage was over.

Electrical recording was also able to trace brain activity associated with an error in responding. Within about 70 ms after an error, there was increased negativity recorded above the frontal midline in comparison with the same response when correct (Bechtereva *et al.* 1990; Gehring *et al.* 1993). It was reported in the 1960s that people slowed following an error trial when they had either detected the error or received feedback that they had made an error (Rabbitt 1968). Rabbitt argued that error detection was computed at about the same time as the correct response. The EEG sign was confirmation of the rapid detection of error, and the finding that this influenced the next trial showed how important this self-monitoring was to human performance. The error negativity was one of the first components to be localized to a particular brain structure, the anterior cingulate gyrus, first by the use of algorithms that sought the best fitting generator (Dehaene *et al.* 1994) and also by experiments that used fMRI to localize the error effect (van Veen and Carter 2002). The linking of ERPs and haemodynamic imaging is discussed further in the final section of this chapter.

Haemodynamic imaging

In 1988 haemodynamic imaging became a tool for the localization of mental processes in brain tissue (Petersen *et al.* 1988). The use, first of positron emission tomography (PET) and later of fMRI, provided ample evidence that even in high-level cognitive tasks, such as word association, there was common localization of mental operations so that the activations could be averaged across subjects. Most of these studies were consistent with the view that cognitive and emotional tasks involve a small set of often widely scattered areas of activity, which must be brought together to perform the task.

The subtractive method of Donders, additive factors method of Sternberg, and independent manipulability methods discussed above in conjunction with RT have all had their counterparts in studies of imaging. The subtractive method applied to imaging is of special interest; although it depends on an assumption of linearity, it moves beyond RT both because one can make subtractions in both directions and because the effects of many different brain areas can be assayed. In most cases more complex activity brings in areas of activation in addition to the ones found for the simple control task. However, if the tasks are not well chosen, they may have quite different areas of activity. The ability to design a control task that includes most but not all of the components of the experimental task is difficult, because people may apply different strategies based on small changes between tasks. Despite these problems and the assumptions involved, the subtractive method has yielded relatively consistent results in many domains. The convergence between imaging, behavioural, and lesion methods suggests that, although many of the criticisms of the subtractive method are correct the use of imaging can greatly enrich our understanding.

The findings of imaging in many different task domains are consistent with the idea that networks of specific neural areas underlie human abilities. Imaging methods have been developed to image the structural and functional connectivity between these brain areas. Diffusion tensor imaging is a method for viewing white matter connections between neural areas. Effective connectivity uses the correlations in activity among areas to establish the flow of information between them. Causal modelling can provide good hypotheses about the relative direction of information flow between active areas (Posner *et al.* 2006).

The time course of haemodynamic change is rather slow, lagging several seconds behind the neuronal activity whose activation it reflects. Methods have been developed to examine the time course of activity in these areas in the range of several tens or hundreds of milliseconds. Although this level of temporal resolution may not be sufficient for many cognitive tasks that differ by 100 ms or less, it has had important applications. When tasks are relatively slow it is possible to obtain a good account of the order of the various modules involved and for how long each of the modules is active (Formisano and Goebel 2003).

Combining methods

The network idea that stems originally from Hebb (for a discussion of this history see Posner and Rothbart 2007) calls for a chronometric account of the sequences of anatomical operations and their functions in accomplishing a cognitive task. At present this requires a combination of behavioural, electrical, and haemodynamic methods (Bledowski *et al.* 2006). The behavioural methods provide a task analysis in terms of the component operations involved and their timing; the haemodynamic images show which brain areas are involved and can suggest an order and direction of information flow; the EEG methods provide a detailed time course and can also test the temporal frequency of synchronization of the different neural area involved in performing the task.

Several methods have been designed to relate scalp signatures based on electrical recording to the underlying generators as found in fMRI studies (Pascualmarqui *et al.* 1994; Scherg and Picton 1991). In simple tasks, such as processing a click or flash, that involve only one or a very small number of generators, considerable validation of these algorithms has already taken place (Martinez *et al.* 2001). In their studies, Hillyard and colleagues have systematically moved stimuli to various locations in the visual field and shown how the ERP and fMRI generators converge on similar areas of the primary visual cortex (Martinez *et al.* 2001). They found that the earliest primary visual cortex activation is not influenced by attention but that, later, attention does modify primary visual cortex activity via feedback from pre-striate regions. For more complex tasks the algorithms seemed to work when the subtraction used allows for only one or a very small number of widely separated generators to be active at any one time. When, for example, RT for reading a visual word aloud is subtracted from generating the use of the word, it has been possible to show that frontal (area 47) activity occurs about 200 ms after input and that Wernicke's area is active at about 500 ms, whereas the overt response does not occur until about 1100 ms (Abdullaev and Posner 1998) and coherence analysis using EEG suggests transfer of information from the frontal to posterior areas at about 450 ms (Nikolaev *et al.* 2001).

Many cognitive tasks involve extensive re-entry into a particular anatomical area at different temporal periods after input. To be able to tell how many times and when in the sequence a particular area is active can be important for interpreting the performance of the network (Bledowski *et al.* 2006; Debener *et al.* 2006; Posner *et al.* 2006). For tasks such as generating the use of a word, the long time taken to produce an answer provides ample opportunity for extensive re-entrant processes, illustrating how important temporal information is in understanding network function. Finding activity in the visual system for an auditory task may mean that there are direct connections between audition and vision that were not expected, or it may mean that higher centres act on the visual system by attention or by developing a visual image. In order to determine what is the case, one needs to know the order and timing of the anatomical modules involved. Thus, mental chronometry has gone beyond the measurement of RT to play an important role in understanding the neural networks that underlie human performance.

In the years ahead we may expect further application of mental chronometry to the analysis of neural networks. The degree of synthesis so far possible between behavioural, electrical–magnetic, and haemodynamic measures suggests that each will play an important role in this task. Moreover, it would be foolish to suppose that there will be no new methods at all levels of analysis. Improved links between human and animal models will also allow the chronometric paradigm to be pushed into more precise analysis, as cellular activity like EEG can be a source of precise temporal information (Pouget *et al.* 2005). The range of new methods and questions makes the achievements and future of mental chronometry even brighter than many of us would have thought half a century ago.

References

Abdullaev, Y. G. and Posner, M. I. (1998). Event-related brain potential imaging of semantic encoding during processing single words. *Neuroimage* 7: 1–13.

Attneave, F. (1959). *Applications of information theory to psychology*. New York: Holt.

Bechtereva, N. P., Kropotov, J. D., Ponomarev, V. A., and Etlinger, S. C. (1990). In search of cerebral error detectors. *International Journal of Psychophysiology* 8(3): 261–73.

Bledowski, C., Kadosh, K. C., Wibral, M., *et al.* (2006). Mental chronometry of working memory retrieval: a combined functional magnetic resonance imaging and event-related potentials approach. *Journal of Neuroscience* 26: 821–9.

Boring, E. G. (1950). *A history of experimental psychology*. New York: Appleton Century Crofts.

Coles, M. G. H., Smid, H. G. O. M., Scheffers, M. K., and Otten, L. J. (1995). Mental chronometry and the study of human information processing. In: M. D. Rugg and M. G. H. Coles (ed.) *Electrophysiology of mind*, pp. vii–ix. New York: Oxford University Press.

Debener, S., Ullspeerger, M., Siegel, M., and Engle, A. K. (2006). Single trial EEG-fMRI reveals the dynamics of cognitive function. *Trends in Cognitive Science* 10: 558–63.

Dehaene, S., Posner, M. I., and Tucker, D. M. (1994). Localization of a neural system for error detection and compensation. *Psychological Science* 5: 303–5.

Donders, F. C. (1868/1969). On the speed of mental processes. *Acta Psychologica* 30: 412–31.

Fan, J., McCandliss, B. D., Sommer, T., Raz, M., and Posner, M. I. (2002). Testing the efficiency and independence of attentional networks. *Journal of Cognitive Neuroscience* 3(14): 340–7.

Fitts, P. M. (1954). The information capacity of the human nervous system in controlling movement. *Journal of Experimental Psychology* 47: 381–91.

Formisano, E. and Goebel, R. (2003). Tracking cognitive processes using fMRI mental chronometry. *Current Opinion in Neurobiology* 13: 174–81.

Gehring, W. J., Goss, B., Coles, M. G. H., Meyer, D. E., and Donchin, E. (1993). A neural system for error detection and compensation. *Psychological Science* 4: 385–90.

Hick, W. E. (1948). On the rate of gain of information. *Quarterly Journal of Experimental Psychology* 4: 11–26.

Hyman, R. (1953). Stimulus information as a determinant of reaction time. *Journal of Experimental Psychology* 45: 188–96.

Kulpe, O. (1985). *Outlines of psychology* (trans. E. B. Titchener). New York: Macmillan.

MacLeod, C. M. (1991). Half a century of research on the Stroop effect—an integrative review. *Psychological Bulletin* 109: 163–203.

Martinez, A., DiRusso, F., Anllo-Vento, L., Sereno, M., Buxton, R., and Hillyard, S. (2001). Putting spatial attention on the map: timing and localization of stimulus selection processing striate and extrastriate visual areas. *Vision Research* 41: 1437–57.

Meyer, D. E. and Kieras, D. E. (1997). A computational theory of executive cognitive processes and multiple-task performance, Part 1. Basic mechanisms. *Psychological Review* 104(1): 3–65.

Meyer, D. E., Osman, A. M., Irwin, D. E., and Yantis, S. (1988). Modern mental chronometry. *Biological Psychology* 26: 3–67.

Mokotoff, B., Schulman, G., Galambos, C., and Galambos, R. (1977). Brain-stem auditory evoked-responses in children. *Archives of Otolaryngology—Head & Neck Surgery* 103(1): 38–43.

Mowbray, G. H. and Rhoades, M. U. (1959). On the reduction of choice reaction times with practice. *Quarterly Journal of Experimental Psychology* 11: 16–23.

Naatanen, R., Gaillard, A.W. K., and Mantysalo, S. (1978). Early selective attention effect on evoked potential reinterpreted. *Acta Psychologica* 42: 313–29.

Neisser, U. (1967). *Cognitive psychology*. Englewood Cliffs, NJ: Prentice Hall.

Newell, A. (1990). *Unified theories of cognition*. Cambridge, MA: Harvard University Press.

Nikolaev, A. R., Ivanitsky, G. A., Ivanitsky, A. M., Abdullaev, Y. G., and Posner, M. I. (2001). Short-term correlation between frontal and Wernicke's areas in word association. *Neuroscience Letters* 298: 107–10.

Pascualmarqui, R. D., Michel, C. M., and Lehmann, D. (1994). Low-resolution electromagnetic tomography: a new method for localizing electrical activity in the brain. *International Journal of Psychophysiology* 18(1): 49–65.

Petersen, S. E., Fox, P. T., Posner, M. I., Mintun, M., and Raichle, M. E. (1988). Positron emission tomographic studies of the cortical anatomy of single word processing. *Nature* 331: 585–9.

Posner, M. I. (1966). Components of skilled performance. *Science* 152: 1712–18.

Posner, M. I. (1978). *Chronometric explorations of mind*. Hillsdale, NJ: Lawrence Erlbaum Associates.

Posner, M. I. and Mitchell, R. F. (1967). Chronometric analysis of classification. *Psychological Review* 74: 392–409.

Posner, M. I. and Rothbart, M. K. (2007). *Educating the human brain*. Washington, DC: APA Books.

Posner, M. I. and Rueda, M. R. (2002). Mental chronometry in the study of individual and group differences. *Journal of Clinical and Experimental Neuropsychology* 24: 968–76.

Posner, M. I., Sheese, B., Odludas, Y., and Tang, Y. (2006). Analyzing and shaping neural networks of attention. *Neural Networks* 19: 1422–9.

Posner, M. I., Rothbart, M. K., and Sheese, B. E. (2007). Attention genes. *Developmental Science* 10(1): 24–9.

Pouget, P., Emeric, E. E., Stuphorn, V., Reis, K., and Schall, J. D. (2005). Chronometry of visual responses in frontal eye field, supplementary eye field and anterior cingulate cortex. *Journal of Neurophysiology* 94: 2086–92.

Rabbitt, P. M. A. (1968). Two kinds of error signaling in a serial choice task. *Quarterly Journal of Experimental Psychology* 20: 179–88.

Rumelhart, D. E. and McClelland, J. L. (1986). *Parallel distributed processing*. Cambridge, MA: MIT Press.

Sanders, A. F. (1998). *Elements of human performance*. Mahwah, NJ: Erlbaum.

Scherg, M. and Picton, T. W. (1991). Separation and identification of event-related potential components by brain electric source analysis. *Electroencephalography and Clinical Neurophysiology. Supplement* 42: 24–37.

Senders, J. (1964). The human operator as a monitor and controller of multi-degree of freedom systems. *IEEE Transactions on Human Factors in Electronics* HFE-5: 2–6.

Shannon, C. E. and Weaver, W. (1949). *The mathematical theory of communication.* Urbana, IL: University of Illinois Press.

Sigman, M. and Dehaene, S. (2005). Parsing a cognitive task: a characterization of the mind's bottleneck. *Public Library of Science* 3: e37.

Sigman, M. and Dehaene, S. (2006). Dynamics of the central bottleneck: dual-task and task uncertainty. *Public Library of Science* 4: e220.

Sternberg, S. (1966). High speed scanning in human memory. *Science* 153: 652–4.

Sternberg, S. (1969). The discovery of processing stages. *Acta Psychologica* 30: 276–315.

Sternberg, S. (2004). Separate modifiability and the search for processing modules. In: N. Kanwisher and J. Duncan (ed.) *Attention and performance XX: Functional brain imaging of visual cognition.* Oxford: Oxford University Press.

Stone, M. (1960). Models for choice reaction time. *Psychometrika* 25: 251–60.

Sutton, S., Braren, M., Zubin, J., and John, E. R. (1965). Evoked potential correlates of stimulus uncertainty. *Science* 150: 1436–9.

van Veen, V. and Carter, C. S. (2002). The timing of action-monitoring processes in the anterior cingulate cortex. *Journal of Cognitive Neuroscience* 14: 593–602.

16

A life in grey areas: cognitive gerontology from 1957 to 2007

Pat Rabbitt

The history of science is written about, and sometimes by, remarkable people who have radically changed our understanding of the world, but the footnotes of pedestrian scientists can tell how it felt to live through these major transformations without temptations to structure chaos or edit muddle into prescience.

During 1956–1957 the psychology department at Cambridge University was a uniquely good place to observe the transformation of a subject that could be taught, and perhaps even understood in its entirety, by any one of its practitioners into mutually incomprehensible specializations. After taking Part 1 of a degree in almost any other subject one could graduate, after a single further year, allegedly equipped to begin research in any branch of 'psychology'. Oliver Zangwill had recently succeeded Sir Frederick Bartlett as Head and, with the newly appointed Larry Weiskrantz, had begun to shift the ethos of the department from Bartlettian, behaviour-based. human experimental psychology to physiological psychology and neuropsychology. But Zangwill not only taught the neuropsychology of Henry Head enlivened with descriptions of patients he saw at the National Hospital in Queen's Square, he also gave us some of the little Social Psychology we got. Most junior staff had been appointed by Bartlett, and his genial signed photograph hung on almost all of their office walls. The other Zeitpoltergeist haunting grubby beige corridors was Bartlett's charismatic and untimely deceased protégé, Kenneth Craik, who had been appointed by Bartlett as first director of the Medical Research Council's Applied Psychology Research Unit (MRC APRU). Applications of psychology were key to Bartlett's legacy. He is currently most famous for his contributions to the theory of memory and of social psychology, but it was leadership in military applications, both on submarine hydrophone detection systems during World War I and again as a national coordinator of applied psychological research in World War II, that won recognition from practitioners of the established sciences, credibility with government, and representation on committees of UK funding agencies. The wartime colleagues he appointed to lectureships exemplified the Cambridge ethos that, at a pinch, a competent scientist could teach all of his or her subject—and perhaps much of any other. So William Hick, a practising psychiatrist, gave disturbing seminars illustrated by scratchy tape—recordings of confrontations with cowed patients protesting that they really had seen Red Indians in suburban Cambridge—and also intimidating lectures on applications to psychology of Shannon and Weaver's (1947) information-processing theory, to which he had made a seminal personal contribution (Hick 1952). Derek Russell Davis, another psychiatrist, had worked with Kenneth Craik on a primitive aircraft simulator, the 'Cambridge Cockpit', providing some of the first contributions to understanding the effects of fatigue on pilot performance and of the effects of life stress on human errors in driving and mines. His clinical lectures and case demonstrations were tranquil. Richard Gregory's humour, brilliance, track record of applied research in submarines, and remarkable contributions to Vision Science are evident from his chapter in this book (see Chapter 9). His lectures were, in effect, notes for the famous *Eye and Brain*, now in its fifth edition (Gregory 1997).

"C." Grindley, who had begun his research career as a physicist, was a paradigmatic example of the Cambridge idea of universal academic deployment. While working in Bristol as a colleague of Paul Dirac, he had also given lectures in psychology to prisoners in Dartmoor. His career in the Cambridge Cavendish Laboratory was curtailed abruptly by Ernest Rutherford with the advice: 'Grindley, if I were you I should take up Psychology'. Obediently he crossed Downing Street to work with Lord Adrian, in Physiology, on human detection thresholds for rates of changes in tactual pressure and, perhaps as a sequel, to mutual mapping of the sensitivity of the entire human male skin surface with Oliver Zangwill (allegedly) to the alarm and distress of an intruding cleaning lady. He had also anticipated Skinner's work on operant conditioning by training a guinea-pig to turn its head appropriately for rewards of carrot. During the war he had introduced effective reforms of haphazard processes of aircrew selection. His colleagues maintained that the hospitality of RAF messes launched his career as an irredeemable, gentle, and charming alcoholic whose lectures on Animal Behaviour were interrupted by strange entrapments, such as failures to break out of physical demonstrations of how Ant Lions delve their burrows by persistent circling and by problems in distinguishing between cigarettes and sticks of chalk. In spite of these difficulties, with the support of Valerie Townsend he continued to publish, well regarded papers throughout the 1960s (e.g. Grindley and Townsend 1966, 1968), and before his retirement he published the first demonstration that humans can control attentional sensitivity in their visual fields without making eye movements, a ground-breaking study that inspired elegant work by Mike Posner and many others (Grindley and Townsend 1970—then known as the Big G and T paper).

My time as a research student from 1957 to 1961 was made more tolerable by long afternoons in his company following his solitary lunches in the Castle pub on Regent Street. This was an education in the exhilaration of playful scientific speculation, in how formidable cleverness can be coupled with extreme sweetness and gentleness of nature, and in the grace and gaiety of his self-mockery and disdain for vanity, self-regard, or pomposity.

Graduating in 1957, I was certain that psychology was the only thing that I wanted to do but, with a mediocre second-class degree, this seemed impossible. Anne Taylor, now Anne Treisman, then aptly nicknamed 'needle' by Richard Gregory, gained her predicted outstanding First and went to a research studentship in Oxford. I mooched around Cambridge sandpapering trucks for painting at Marshall's Airport, swallowing chagrin and wondering what next. As on very many occasions in my career, John Morton rescued me from depression. Oliver Zangwill had recognized his undergraduate brilliance and negotiated a Department of Scientific and Industrial (DSIR) research studentship to keep him at Cambridge. However, because he was otherwise occupied producing review sketches, his degree class did not allow him to take this up. Zangwill rapidly found him alternative support with Margaret Vernon at Reading, puzzled to find another candidate, discovered that I was still hanging around and made the offer. I eagerly accepted and was told that I would be supervised by Donald Broadbent, who had been my sole undergraduate tutor, and set the 24 weekly essays that completely summarized my pawky knowledge of Psychology. Oliver's encouragement that I 'obviously got on well' with Donald was a pleasant surprise. Brilliant mentors can be exhilarating, but also baffling and sometimes painfully abrasive. A whine that I would like to work on schizophrenia with the gentler and vaguer Derek Russell-Davis was ignored.

I was luckier than I could then understand. During 1957–1958, Donald was completing his masterpiece, *Perception and Communication* (Broadbent 1958), running an exciting personal research programme, directing applied work for the RAF, and assuming directorship of the MRC APRU. Consequently our encounters during my first research year were few, brief, and decisive. At the first he gave me a research project based on recent demonstrations that people can recognize words as members of particular semantic categories (typically as 'obscene' or 'threatening'), even when they are too briefly presented to be identified as individual words, such as 'fellatio' or 'pain'. Donald suggested that people might be taught to make categorical discriminations between emotionally neutral items, such as letters and digits below the item recognition threshold. This required a tachistoscope, but none was available. Richard Gregory thought up a splendidly unfeasible device synchronizing a gravity-driven shutter and a variable-sized empty sector in a rotating aluminium disc. My second and third meetings with Donald were brief because I could only report that the contraption did not yet work. At the fourth I reported that it now sometimes worked but that my results made no point. Donald threatened to terminate my scholarship. Thus braced, I abandoned the machine and reversed the problem by timing people as they sorted visiting cards marked with digits and capital letters of the alphabet into randomly assigned categories. The number of items in each of two categories made no difference to sorting times, but with four or more categories times slowed as a multiplicative function of category number and size. At our fifth meeting Donald remarked that I was 'getting along like a house on fire'. The idiom was alarmingly unfamiliar, but proved to be a reprieve. Reassuringly the results were publishable (Rabbitt 1959), and Donald and I contentedly avoided each other for two years until he rang to ask whether I had yet written a thesis and, if so, what its title might be.

My career in the study of 'Reaction Times', had begun, but so, insidiously, had another in Cognitive Gerontology. I ran out of young adult acquaintances who would tolerate my dull experiments and began to solicit affable, late middle-aged porters around the Downing Street Science site. I was unsurprised that they were slower than young adults, but distressed that they were never indifferent to category size (Rabbitt 1965). I was saved by Alan Welford—a very different personality and intellectual influence. Possibly because of his second job as Chaplain of St John's College, his lectures were, for that department at that time, uniquely well prepared and tightly organized, but also somnolently sonorous. With kindness, intelligence and patience he taught me to be intrigued rather than dismayed that there were marked individual differences in performance that were entirely neglected by current models for decision processes. Oriented by this advice and by the appearance of *Ageing and Human Skill*, his account of work of the Nuffield Age Research Unit that he had directed (Welford 1958), I began to be impressed—by individual differences and by the extreme variability of human cognitive performance.

In 1962 I was hired by Reuben Conrad as staff member at the MRC APRU, and during my first year spent eight hours a day teaching postmen (higher grade) to use a ten-finger keyboard intended for letter-sorting machines. As many of these were middle aged and some, unfortunately, could not be trained because they had fewer than ten fingers, resources and time were available for modest work on age comparisons and human variability.

This supported further conversations with Alan Welford and with his sabbatical visitor Jim Birren, who kindly offered me a temporary post-doctoral position for 1963–1964 in his age research unit at the National Institutes of Health (NIH), Bethesda, Maryland. There I encountered a much richer gerontological tradition.

The agenda of Welford's Nuffield Unit had been to improve the efficiency of the British workforce by exploring how, and if at all possible why, even those skills that people have brought to remarkable levels during their working lifetimes deteriorate as they age. The focus on applications echoed the wartime work of Bartlett and his colleagues, and its current extensions at the MRC APRU. In the 1950s, without computers, it was impossible adequately to simulate the tasks and systems studied by the simple laboratory paradigms on which the limited models then current in academic human experimental psychology had been based. The obligation to find some ways in which to help humans to cope with complicated equipment and scenarios undermined credulity in the disingenuously simple academic 'models' of human performance of that time, but usually left investigators only with specific recommendations for improvement of particular systems but with no idea how these could generalize to plausible descriptions of human mental processes. Like Broadbent's (1958) contemporary masterpiece, *Perception and Communication*, Welford's (1958) *Ageing and Human Skill* describes how he and his many talented associates used problems posed by complex tasks to transcend the limitations of the current psychology by inventing an entire new language for modelling human performance. For example, E. R. F. W. (Ted) Crossman was the first to suggest 'neural random noise' as an explanation for age-related slowing of decisions. Although he did not work in Welford's unit, Richard Gregory extended this idea to ageing sensory systems. Harry Kay produced seminal work on age and motor skills. Jacek Szafran moved to the USA where he continued applied work with ageing aircrew. The MRC recognized the success of the unit as an engine for useful research and a school for scientific talent, and offered to fund its continuation in Cambridge with Welford as director. Zangwill declined to house it. Welford declined to leave Cambridge to direct it elsewhere. The MRC funded two units to research the effects of age on workforce effectiveness and mobility, directed by Alaistair Heron in Liverpool and by Huwell Murrell in Bristol. In 1966 Welford did at length leave Cambridge for Adelaide, South Australia, where he built up a successful department with a much wider research agenda than cognitive gerontology.

Jim Birren's research was driven by broader concerns than industrial or military applications. Influenced by the psychophysical tradition of 'Smitty' Stevens he saw sensory psychophysics (Birren 1959) and the investigation of putatively 'elementary' processes such as times to make simple choices (reaction times; RTs) as tools to understand age-related changes in neural processing (Birren 1956, 1965). During 1963–1964 his lab supported work on ageing rats as well as his personal work on human hand tremor, heart rate, psychophysical judgements, and, increasingly, on RTs, with past and current collaborators such as Jack Botwinnick, Joseph Brinley, and Joe Robbins. In particular Brinley (1965) has the distinction of a clever insight that thoroughly confused discussions of age and information processing for the next forty years. He found that, independently of task difficulty, mean RT for groups of older people can be accurately estimated by multiplying means of groups of younger adults by a simple constant (from 1.1 to 1.5 depending on the difference in group ages). Birren was eager to regard this 'general slowing' across tasks as evidence that RTs provided a unique insight into the effects of age on the central nervous system, and it became his obsession from the 1960s (Birren 1965) to the early 1980s (Birren 1979; Birren *et al.* 1980). A brilliant meta-analysis by John Cerella (1985) validated, extended, and formalized Brinley's discovery, and Tim Salthouse made much deeper new experiments showing that even on memory tasks, in which decision speed is neither measured nor constrained, part of the variance between individuals that is associated with differences in their ages disappears, or is greatly attenuated, when individual variance in their decision times is also taken into account. Tim concluded that slowing of information processing in the ageing brain directly causes all observed effects of age on mental abilities (Salthouse 1985, 1991, 1996).

Salthouse's 'general slowing' theory was the first attempt at an overall theory of cognitive ageing. It was a necessary and timely provocation because it exposed the major weakness of research in the psychology of ageing: thoughtlessly atheoretical use of each newly emerging experimental paradigm of 'mainstream' cognitive psychology to compare older and younger groups. However, the suggestion that 'general slowing' may not just be one aspect of changes in mental abilities but actually *the* common functional *cause* of *all* age-related changes in mental abilities seemed to leave nothing left to explain and to block further research. In some it caused irritable apathy for a variety of logical and empirical reasons tediously rehearsed elsewhere (Rabbitt 1996, 1999, 2002). Others found more constructive responses. Gus Craik and his associates quietly continued investigating aspects of cognitive functions for which general slowing can have no explanatory value, such as the nature and relative efficiency of different kinds of memory representation and encoding process (see Chapter 6 of this volume). A more direct challenge was doggedly to seek exceptions to the annoyingly ubiquitous 'Brinley–Cerella plot'

(Myerson and Adams 1998; Myerson *et al.* 1990, 1992). Another was to seek alternative models for the functional basis of age differences in decision speeds. Hasher and Zacks and their associates proposed that differences in decision times between young and older adults could be better understood in terms of qualitative rather than quantitative differences between highly prac-tised 'automatic' and novice or 'controlled' processing (Hasher and Zacks 1979), to which Shiffrin and Schneider (e.g. 1984) had first drawn attention. A different move was to try to find tasks on which age differences were greater than 'general slowing' might predict. Hasher, Zacks, and their associates, intrigued by accumulating evidence that age affects frontal and temporal cortex earlier than other areas of the brain (Albert 1993; Gur *et al.* 1987; Haug and Eggers 1991), began to speculate, like later authors such as West (1996), that age might affect performance on 'frontal and executive' tasks earlier than on others. Hasher, Zacks, and associates were chiefly concerned with 'inhibi-tion' of unwanted information in perception and memory as a key example of executive control dependent on frontal lobe integrity (e.g. Hasher and Zacks 1988; Hasher *et al.* 1997, 1991; Kane *et al.* 1994).

On the whole, results of age comparisons on 'frontal' tasks have been mixed, although more recent work, requiring complex and sensitive statistical analy-ses, suggests that while age indeed may affect frontal tasks more than others, differences are very small and the amount of age-related variance accounted for by general slowing is at least an order of magnitude greater than that asso-ciated with changes in frontal or executive function (e.g. Verhaegen and Barsak 2005). A more direct strategy was to question the statistical validity of analyses using 'Brinley functions' (e.g. Ratcliff *et al.* 2000) and to develop and test more rigorous models for analysing decision processes (Ratcliffe *et al.* 1999). A further strategy was to illustrate that differences in mean decision times are only part of what has to be explained because increases in RT means can be largely accounted for in terms of increasing moment to moment vari-ability (Hultsch *et al.* 2000, 2002; Rabbitt *et al.* 2001b).

These various endeavours eroded confidence in 'general slowing theory' but, although it was clearly logically unsatisfactory, the theory could not be disproved by behavioural evidence alone. As with all powerful scientific para-digms, comfortable disbelief required new kinds of data.

Throughout the twentieth century a reckless, but necessary and sustaining, optimism for human experimental psychologists was that models based entirely on behavioural comparisons would eventually provide useful guides to neural functions supporting cognition. Brain imaging has abruptly brought about the changes that other authors in this book have termed 'the neuropsy-chological revolution' and, inevitably, show up the naivety of late twentieth century models. The careful work of Salthouse and his colleagues convincingly showed that behavioural data alone do not disassociate the effects of age from slowing of information-processing speed on most cognitive tasks. But recent work has shown that gross brain changes such reduced cerebral blood flow, age-associated atrophy, and white matter lesions account for all of the differences in speed between people that is associated with differences in their ages; they account for little or no differences in intelligence or in performance on frontal tasks (e.g. Rabbitt *et al.* 2008c).

Birren's preoccupation with RTs was moderated by his location in the NIH, then possibly the largest medical research centre in the world. This exposed him to discussions of how biological factors, health, and demographics determine 'successful' old age (crf. Birren *et al.* 1963). Birren's extraordinary warmth, congeniality, and energy won him collaborations across many disciplines. His resulting broad interests are evident from the editorial work that he has sustained over his lifetime, particularly the *Handbooks of Human Ageing*, which tracked and shaped directions of work in the field. His medical and epidemiological interests followed his friend and mentor, Nathan Shock, who had, in Baltimore, initiated the first, and now the longest, longitudinal study of age-related changes, with a main emphasis on the collection of data on pathological and physiological changes. During the 1960s and 1970s the methodology of longitudinal studies was markedly improved by a series of theoretical contributions by Paul Baltes, John Nesselroade, and Werner Schaie (e.g. Baltes 1968; Baltes and Nesselroade 1970; Baltes *et al.* 1979; Schaie 1965; Schaie and Baltes 1975), and by the steady output of analyses from Schaie's Seattle study (Schaie 1983) and from many other large and well -conducted medically oriented studies. Growing interest in these studies as a way of obtaining information about ways to cope with the surge in the proportions of elderly in the populations of industrialized nations revived the interest of funding agencies in the UK in ageing research.

During the late 1960s, the UK MRC had become disappointed with the Liverpool Age Research Unit, in spite of Alastair Heron and Sheila Chown's (1967) large, excellent, but short longitudinal study based on volunteers from Merseyside industries. The MRC closed the Liverpool and Bristol Units, and funding for cognitive ageing became hard to obtain. In 1968 I moved to Oxford, where I could only find support for work on RTs and selective attention in young adults until 1979 when a revival of public interest in the looming problems of ageing populations allowed a successful bid to begin a longitudinal study. A brief start in Oxford was curtailed by a move to Durham in 1982, but funding continued there for a study based in Newcastle with a parallel cohort in Manchester when I moved there in 1984 to direct the Age and

Cognitive Performance Research Centre. This study extended until 2004, supported by a patchwork of grants by the UK Economic and Social Research Council (ESRC), MRC, European Commission, Wellcome Trust, Unilever plc, and the University of Manchester.

Perhaps the broadest questions about cognitive changes that longitudinal data can answer are: When do changes first appear? How fast do they then proceed? Do all cognitive abilities change at the same rates or do some decline earlier than others? Do individuals show different rates of cognitive changes? Do individuals show different patterns of cognitive changes? Can we identify factors that accelerate or slow rates of cognitive change or that produce some patterns of changes rather than others? During the 1980s and 1990s it became clear that none of these questions could be approached without development of new statistical methodologies. For example, in the 1960s Baltes and Schaie had noted, as an inconvenient theoretical possibility, that if participants take the same or similar cognitive tests, even at long intervals, improvements with practice may disguise declines of performance with age. Ways of separating these practice effects from age-related declines were not then available, so, like all my colleagues, I was glad to argue that they must be negligible if tests were re-administered at intervals as long as four years. Our accumulating data confuted this expedient optimism and further suggested that older and less able individuals might gain less from practice and so appear to decline faster than the young and more able. We could confidently publish only cross-sectional analyses, comparing people of different ages, until Peter Diggle came to our aid (Rabbitt *et al.* 2001a, 2004). Mary Lunn showed us how to confirm our guesses that improvements with practice were smaller in the old and less able (Rabbitt *et al.* 2008a), and also that true rates of decline with age, or with the onset of pathology, cannot be correctly estimated unless dropouts and deaths are also taken into consideration (Rabbitt *et al.* 2005). It becomes clear that rates of decline accelerate during the eight years preceding death or dropout, and that healthier individuals show very slight changes even during their eighth decade (Rabbitt *et al.* 2008b).

This general picture is consistent with experiments by investigators adopting the 'medical model', that most of the variance in amounts of decline in individuals can be attributed to differences in general health, and in the burdens of pathologies that accumulate with age (e.g. Houx 1991; Knottmerus and Jolles 1998; van Boxtel *et al.* 1998). Recent improvements in brain imaging now show both how patterned age-related changes in brain mass and structure are correlated with cognitive changes and, even more interestingly, how age appears to affect the number and kinds of brain area involved in different, particular kinds of task (Raz 2000; Raz *et al.* 1998) The aetiology of these changes can be related to the increasing general burden of pathologies and to specific effects of particular conditions. It now seems no longer worthwhile to carry out large and prolonged longitudinal studies that collect only behavioural data. Studies are useful only when they include neurophysiological and neuropsychological data, particularly imaging data, detailed information about health and the number, kinds, and progress of pathologies, and focused batteries of cognitive tests. Such studies need involve only small numbers of carefully selected and thoroughly documented individuals over relatively short periods of time—five rather than twenty years or longer. After spending half a working lifetime on a large behavioural study, I am delighted that my younger colleagues will not have to go through all that again.

References

Albert, M. (1993). Neuropsychological and neurophysiological changes in healthy adult humans across the age range. *Neurobiology of Aging* 14: 623.

Baltes, P. B. (1968). Longitudinal and cross-sectional sequences in the study of age and generation effects. *Human Development* 11: 145–71.

Baltes, P. B. and Nesselroade, J. (1970). Multivariate longitudinal and cross-sectional sequences for analysing ontogenetic and generational change: a methodological note. *Developmental Psychology* 2: 163–8.

Baltes, P. B., Cornelius, S. W., and Nesselroade, J. R. (1979). Cohort effects in developmental psychology. In: J. R. Nesselroade and P. B. Baltes (ed.) *Longitudinal research in the study of behaviour and development*, pp. 142–156 New York, Academic Press.

Birren, J. E. (1956). The significance of age-changes in speed of perception and psychomotor skills. In: J. E. Anderson (ed.) *Psychological aspects of aging*, pp. 97–104. Washington, DC: American Psychological Association.

Birren, J. E. (1959). Sensation, perception and the modification of behaviour in relation to aging. In: J. E. Birren, H. A. Imus, and W. F. Windle (ed.) *The process of aging in the central nervous system*, pp. 143–65. Springfield, IL: Charles C. Thomas.

Birren, J. E. (1965). Age changes in speed of behaviour; its central nature and physiological correlates. In: A. T. Welford and J. E. Birren (ed.) *Behaviour, aging and the nervous system*, pp. 142-165. Springfield, IL: Charles C. Thomas.

Birren, J. E. (1979). Tutorial review of changes in choice reaction time with advancing age. In: H. Baumeister (ed.) *Bayer Symposium No. 6*, pp. 232–47. Bonn: Springer.

Birren, J. E., Butler, R. N., Greenhouse, S. W., Sokoloff, L., and Yarrow, M. R. (1963). Human aging. Washington, DC: US Government Printing Office.

Birren, J. E., Woods, A. M., and Williams, M. V. (1980). Behavioural slowing with age. In: L. W. Poon (ed.) *Aging in the 1980s: psychological issues*, pp. 293–308. Washington, DC: American Psychological Association.

Brinley, J. F. (1965). Cognitive sets, speed and accuracy of performance in the elderly. In: A. T. Welford and J. E. Birren (ed.) *Behaviour, aging and the nervous system*, pp. 114–49. Springfield, IL: Charles C. Thomas.

Broadbent, D. E. (1958). *Perception and communication*. Oxford: Pergamon Press.

Cerella, J. (1985). Information processing rates in the elderly. *Psychological Bulletin* 98: 67–83.

Gregory, R. L. (1997). *Eye and brain; the psychology of seeing* (5th edn). Princeton, NJ: Princeton Science Library.

Grindley, G. C. and Townsend, V. (1966). Further experiments on movements masking. *Quarterly Journal of Experimental Psychology* 18: 319–26.

Grindley, G. C. and Townsend, V. (1968). Voluntary attention in peripheral vision and its effects on acuity and differential thresholds. *Quarterly Journal of Experimental Psychology* 20: 11–19.

Grindley, G. C. and Townsend, V. (1970).Visual search without eye-movement. *Quarterly Journal of Experimental Psychology* 22: 62–7.

Gur, R. C., Gur, R. E., Orbist, W. D., Skolnick, B. E., and Reivich, M. (1987). Age and regional cerebral blood flow at rest and during cognitive activity. *Archives of General Psychiatry* 44: 617–21.

Hasher, L. and Zacks, R. T. (1979). Automatic and effortful processes in memory. *Journal of Experimental Psychology, General* 108: 356–88.

Hasher, L. and Zacks, R. T. (1988). Working memory, comprehension and aging: a review and a new view. In: G. K. Bower (ed.) *The psychology of learning and motivation*, vol. 22, pp. 193–225. San Diego, CA: Academic Press.

Hasher, L., Quig, M. B., and May, C. P. (1997). Inhibitory control over no-longer relevant information: adult age differences. *Memory and Cognition* 25(3): 286–95.

Hasher, L., Stoltzfus, E. R., Zacks, R. T., and Rympa, B. (1991). Age and inhibition. *Journal of Experimental Psychology: Learning, Memory and Cognition* 17: 163–9.

Haug, H. and Eggers, R. (1991). Morphometry of the human cortex cerebri and cortex striatum during aging. *Neurobiology of Aging* 12: 336–8.

Heron, A. and Chown, S. (1967). *Age and function*. London: Churchill.

Hick, W. E. (1952). On the rate of information gain. *Quarterly Journal of Experimental Psychology* 4: 11–26.

Houx, P. J. (1991). Rigorous health screening reduces age effects on a memory scanning task. *Brain and Cognition* 15: 246–60.

Hultsch, D. F., MacDonald, S. W. S., Hunter, M. A., Levy-Bencheton, J., and Strauss, E. (2000). Intraindividual variability in cognitive performance in older adults: comparison of adults with mild dementia, adults with arthritis, and healthy adults. *Neuropsychology* 14(4): 588–98.

Hultsch, D. F., MacDonald, S. W. S., and Dixon, R. A. (2002). Variability in reaction time performance of younger and older adults. *Journals of Gerontology* 57B(2): P101–15.

Kane, M. J., Hasher, L., Stoltzfus, E. R., Zacks, R. T. and Connelly, S. L. (1994). Inhibitory attentional mechanisms and aging. *Psychology and Aging* 9: 103–12.

Knottmerus, A. and Jolles, J. (1998). The relation between morbidity and cognitive performance in a normal aging population. *Journals of Gerontology, Series A, Biological Sciences and Medical Sciences* 55(A): M147–54.

Myerson, J. and Adams, D. R. (1998). Mathematical and connectionist models of individual differences in processing speed. *Abstracts of the Psychonomic Society* 3: 49.

Myerson, J., Hale, S., Wagstaff, D., Poon, L., and Smith, G. A. (1990). The information loss model: a mathematical theory of age-related cognitive slowing. *Psychological Review* 97: 475–87.

Myerson, J., Ferraro, F. R., Hale, S., and Lima, S. D. (1992). General slowing in semantic priming and word recognition. *Psychology and Aging* 7: 257–70.

Rabbitt, P. M. A. (1959). Effects of independent variations in stimulus and response probability. *Nature* 183: 1212.

Rabbitt, P. M. A. (1965). An age decrement in the ability to ignore irrelevant information. *Journals of Gerontology* 20: 233–7.

Rabbitt, P. M. A. (1996). Intelligence is not just mental speed. *Journal of Biosocial Science* 28: 425–49.

Rabbitt, P. M. A. (1999). Measurement indices, functional characteristics and psychometric constructs in cognitive ageing. In: T. J. Perfect and E. A. Maylor (ed.) *Models of cognitive aging*, Ch. 6, pp. 160–187. Oxford: Oxford University Press.

Rabbitt, P. (2002). Aging and cognition. In: J. Wixtead and H. Pashler (ed.) *Stevens' handbook of experimental psychology* (3rd edn), vol. 3, pp. 793–860. New York: Wiley.

Rabbitt, P., Diggle, P., Smith, D., Holland, F., and McInnes, L. (2001a). Identifying and separating the effects of practice and of cognitive ageing during a large longitudinal study of elderly community residents. *Neuropsychologia* 39: 532–43.

Rabbitt, P., Osman, P., Moore, B., and Stollery, B. (2001b). There are stable individual differences in performance variability, both from moment to moment and from day to day. *Quarterly Journal of Experimental Psychology, A* 54(4): 981–1003.

Rabbitt, P., Diggle, P., Holland, F., and McInnes, L. (2004). Practice and drop-out effect during a 17-year longitudinal study of cognitive aging. *Journals of Gerontology, Series B, Psychological Sciences and Social Sciences* 59: 84–97.

Rabbitt, P., Lunn, M., and Wong, D. (2005). Neglect of dropout underestimates effects of death in longitudinal studies. *Journals of Gerontology, Series B, Psychological Sciences and Social Sciences* 60: 106–9.

Rabbitt, P. M., Lunn, M., and Wong, D. (2008a). Death, dropout and cognitive change in old age. *Journals of Gerontology, Series B, Psychological Sciences and Social Sciences* (in press).

Rabbitt, P., Lunn, M., and Wong, D. (2008b). Practice, age and ability in longitudinal studies of cognition. *Journals of Gerontology, Series B, Psychological Sciences and Social Sciences* (in press).

Rabbitt, P. Lunn, M. and Wong, D., (2008c). Intelligence reduces risks of increasing frailty and death in old age, *Journals of Gerontology, Series B*. in press.

Ratcliff, R., Van Zandt, T., and McKoon, G. (1999). Connectionist and diffusion models of reaction time. *Psychological Review* 106: 261–300.

Ratcliff, R., Spieler, D., and McKoon, G. (2000). Explicitly modelling the effects of age on reaction times. *Psychonomic Bulletin and Review* 7: 1–25.

Raz, N. (2000). Aging of the brain and its impact on cognitive performance: integration of structural and behavioural findings. In: F. I. M. Craik and T. Salthouse (ed.) *Handbook of aging and cognition* (2nd edn), pp. 1–90. Mahwah, NJ, Lawrence Erlbaum.

Raz, N., Gunning-Dixon, F. M., Head, D. P., Dupuis, J. H., and Acker, J. D. (1998). Neuroanatomical correlates of cognitive aging: evidence from structural MRI. *Neuropsychology* 12: 95–114.

Salthouse, T. A. (1985). Speed of behavior and its implications for cognition. In:
J. E. Birren and K. W. Schaie (ed.) *Handbook of the psychology of aging* (2nd edn),
pp. 400–426. New York: Van Nostrand Reinhold.

Salthouse, T. A. (1991). Mediation of adult age differences in cognition by reductions in
working memory and speed of processing. *Psychological Science* 2(3): 179–83.

Salthouse, T. A. (1992). Influence of processing speed on adult age differences in working
memory. *Acta Psychologica* 79(2): 155–70.

Salthouse, T. A. (1994a). The aging of working memory. *Neuropsychology* 8(4): 535–43.

Salthouse, T. A. (1994b). The nature of the influence of speed on adult age differences in
cognition. *Developmental Psychology* 30(2): 240–59.

Salthouse, T. A. (1996). The processing speed theory of adult age differences in cognition.
Psychological Review 103(3): 403–28.

Schaie, K. W. (1965). A general model for the study of developmental problems.
Psychological Bulletin 64: 92–107.

Schaie, K. W. (1983) The Seattle Longitudinal Study: a 21 year exploration of psychometric
intelligence in adulthood. In: K. W. Schaie (ed.) *Longitudinal studies of adult
psychological development*, pp. 64–135. New York: Guilford Press.

Schaie, K. W. and Baltes, P. B. (1975). On sequential strategies in developmental research.
Description or explanation? *Human Development* 18: 384–90.

Shannon, C. E. and Weaver, W. (1949). *The mathematical theory of communication.*
Urbana, IL: University of Illinois Press.

Shiffrin, R. M. and Schneider, W. (1984). Automatic and controlled processing revisited.
Psychological Review 91: 269–76.

van Boxtel, M. P. J., Buntink, F., Houx, P. J., Metsemakers, J. F. M., Knottmerus, A., and
Jolles, J. (1998). The relation between morbidity and cognitive performance in a
normal aging population. *Journals of Gerontology, Series A, Biological Sciences and
Medical Sciences* 55(A): M147–54.

Verhaegen, P. and Barsak, C. (2005). Ageing and switching of the focus of attention in
working memory. Results from a modified N-back task. *Quarterly Journal of
Experimental Psychology* Special Issue (P. Rabbitt, ed.): 134–54.

Welford, A. T. (1958). *Ageing and human skill.* Oxford: Oxford University Press.

West, R. L. (1996). An application of prefrontal cortex function theory to cognitive aging.
Psychological Bulletin 120(2): 272–92.

17

From little slips to big disasters: an error quest

Jim Reason

A bizarre beginning

One afternoon in the early 1970s I was making tea in our kitchen when the cat arrived clamouring to be fed. I opened a tin of cat food and flicked a large spoonful into the teapot. I laughed it off, blamed the cat, and washed out the teapot. But on reflection, I saw that this slip had interesting properties. Both making tea and feeding the cat were routine activities performed in a familiar environment. My attention, hitherto occupied with unrelated matters, had been captured by the cat's pleading just at the moment when I was about to spoon tea-leaves into the pot; the act of dolloping cat food into some receptor-like object had migrated into the tea-making sequence. Even the spooning actions were appropriate for the substance: sticky cat food requires a flick to separate it from the spoon; dry tea-leaves do not. Local object-related control mechanisms were at work.

Although bizarre, it was evident that there was nothing random or potentially inexplicable about this action-not-as-planned. Both behavioural sequences were largely automatic. Both competed for my limited attention and effectors simultaneously, and an element from the higher priority cat-feeding task had intruded into the tea-making sequence at a time when spoon use was appropriate, and the teapot, like the cat's dish, afforded containment.

Little did I realize at the time that these and related issues would occupy me for the next thirty-odd years. This largely naturalistic mode of enquiry suited me well as I had little talent for or interest in laboratory experiments, particularly in cognitive psychology.

The scope of the chapter

When my error quest began, its focus was quite narrow and strictly cognitive in flavour. Any adequate theory of human skill must account for coherent action sequences that deviate from current intentions, particularly when they take relatively few recurrent forms. Everyday absent-minded actions occupied the early years, the data being collected by either diaries or self-report questionnaires.

In the mid-1980s, largely due to analyses of the Chernobyl disaster (Reason 1987), it was clear that a distinction needed to be made between unintended errors and intentional deviations from standard procedures.

In the late 1970s and 1980s, a number of nasty disaster scenarios—Tenerife, Three Mile Island, *Challenger*, King's Cross, Zeebrugge, Clapham Junction, and the like—called for an even broader disciplinary spectrum. We need to distinguish between slips and mistakes (rule-based and knowledge-based), and between active failures (errors and violations) and latent factors—poor working conditions, fallible managerial decisions, cultural deficiencies, and regulatory and economic influences.

In the late 1980s and 1990s, my goal was to find a conceptual framework that could be applied to all such organizational accidents, regardless of domain: the so-called 'Swiss cheese' model. This went through a number of versions, but common to all of them was the central importance of systemic defences, taking many different forms, that prevented local hazards from coming into damaging contact with people, assets, and the environment.

Slips and lapses: the diary studies

Between the mid-1970s and early 1980s, we carried out a number of diary studies of everyday absent-minded slips of action (Reason and Mycielska, 1982) to clarify what goes absent in absent-mindedness, and to establish what circumstances are most likely to provoke unintended departures of action from intention. We also hoped to develop a classification of what appeared to be a limited number of recurrent error types.

As expected, absent-minded slips were most likely to occur in highly familiar and relatively unchanging surroundings—kitchens, bathrooms, bedrooms, offices, and the like—and while carrying out well practised tasks that diarists rated as being recently and frequently performed, and largely automatic in their execution.

Another factor was the inappropriate deployment of the limited attentional resources at some critical choice-point in the action sequence. For the most part this involved attentional capture by external distraction or internal preoccupation. But there were occasions when too much attention was directed at some largely automatic action sequence. This usually involved a 'Where am I?' query following an interruption. Two wrong answers could ensue: either that the person was not as far along as they actually were—resulting in a repetition—or that they were further along—resulting in an omission.

Approximately 40% of all absent-minded slips, by far the largest single category of error, involved strong habit intrusions. Here actions are diverted from their intended route by the lure of some other well-trodden pathway. More specifically, they take the form of intact, well-organized sequences that are judged as recognizably belonging to some activity other than that currently intended. This other activity was consistently rated as being recently and frequently engaged in, and as sharing similar locations, movements, and objects with the intended actions.

Two further classes of action slip could be identified from our error corpus: place-losing errors, mostly involving omissions and repetitions, and interference errors, involving the blending of inappropriate routines, or the transposition of items within an action sequence.

Place-losing errors arise under a variety of circumstances. First, when a person makes a conscious check on the progress of a largely automatic sequence of actions, and comes up with the wrong answer—what we termed the 'nosy supervisor' syndrome. Second, when a habitual task is interrupted by the need to carry out another routine that was not planned. (For example: 'I walked to my bookcase to find the dictionary. In taking it off the shelf other books fell on to the floor. I put them back then returned to my desk without the dictionary.') Third, when a series of tasks is planned to run sequentially, and the individual moves to the next task before the current one is complete— the 'premature exit'. And then there is the forgetting of previous actions when the person has no recollection of successfully completed routines. (For example: 'While showering I could not remember whether I had washed my hair or not. If I had, then the evidence had been washed away.')

Interference errors, on the other hand, result from 'cross-talk' between two currently active tasks (blends and spoonerisms), or between elements of the same task (reversals or spoonerisms). A typical blend is when elements from the previous task carry over into the next. (For example: 'I had just finished talking on the phone when my secretary ushered in some visitors. I got up from behind the desk and walked to greet them with my hand outstretched saying "Smith speaking".') A reversal is when the actions are correct, but the objects for which they were intended get transposed.

Slips and lapses: questionnaire studies

In the 1980s, research groups in Oxford and Manchester used self-report questionnaires to examine individual differences in proneness to absent-minded action slips and memory lapses (Broadbent *et al.* 1982; Reason 1989, 1993; Reason and Lucas 1984). In general, these questionnaires described a wide range of minor slips and lapses, and asked people to indicate along some ordinal scale how often a particular kind of error cropped up in their daily lives.

Although the specific forms of these questionnaires and the types of people to whom they were given differed from one research group to another, the results from these various studies showed a surprising degree of agreement—surprising, that is, for this kind of psychological research. The main findings are summarized below.

- There is strong evidence to indicate that people do, in fact, differ widely in their proneness to absent-minded errors. Proof that this is not simply a question of how they would like to present themselves is their spouses' agreement with their self-assessments. Moreover, responses suggested that a characteristic liability to error is a fairly enduring feature of the individual, at least over a period of 16 months or more.

- Liability to minor cognitive failures spans a wide range of mental activities and does not appear to be specific to any one domain such as memory, action control, and so forth. Thus, individuals who acknowledge that they experience more than their fair share of memory lapses also report making a relatively large number of errors resulting from failures of attention and recognition, and conversely. It would seem, therefore, that susceptibility is determined by the characteristic way in which some universal mental control process—a limited attentional resource perhaps—is deployed. This appears to operate relatively independently of the particular parts of the cognitive system in which it could show itself.

Attention control in a nutshell

Conscious concerns, whether internally or externally generated, consume the major part of the limited attentional resource during waking hours. In addition to continual moment-to-moment variations in the total amount of this resource that is available, the quantity drained off by these conscious concerns differs according to their nature and intensity. All mental and physical activities, no matter how automatic they may appear, make some demands on attention. The more habitual the activity, and the more invariant the environment in which it occurs, the smaller is this demand. But it is always present in some degree.

One difficult to dispute feature of absent-minded errors, as the term itself suggests, is that most slips and lapses occur when a large part of this resource has been 'captured' by something other than the task in hand. Now, if our highly routine actions depart from intention because the limited resource is being employed elsewhere, the obvious conclusion is that, on those particular occasions, a greater degree of attentional involvement is necessary to ensure the desired outcome. I am not suggesting that a fixed amount of attentional resources is required throughout. But there are occasions, particularly at critical choice-points at which a familiar sequence branches into a variety of well-trodden paths, when a larger attentional investment is necessary.

As schemata (knowledge structures in long-term memory) appear capable of being activated independently of current intentions—by needs, emotions, context, associations with other schemata, and the frequency and recency of past use—some part of the attentional resource is always being deployed to restrain those activated schemata not required for our current plans. The more highly activated these unwanted schemata are, the more of the attentional resource will be consumed in inhibiting them. Execution of any activity requires the correct sequencing of several necessary schemata, and, as each of these transitions between schemata might potentially lead in many directions, some attentional supervision is needed to keep them on the right track. To do this it is necessary not only to select, but also to suppress, those pre-programmed action sequences that seek to usurp control at transitions.

If schemata were merely passive entities, like computer programs, which acted only on orders from above, this problem would not arise. But schemata behave in an energetic and highly competitive fashion to try to grab a piece of the action. Our evidence suggests that when the attention resource is largely claimed by something other than the immediate activity, it is this suppressive function that is most likely to fail. In short, this appears to be what goes absent in absent-mindedness.

Mistakes

If we define error as the failure of planned actions to achieve the actor's desired outcome (Norman 1981; Reason 1977), then there are two ways in which this can occur. Either the plan may be adequate, but the actions do not go as planned—these are the slips, lapses, trips, and fumbles that have been discussed above. Or the actions conform to the plan but the plan is inadequate to achieve its goal. Here, the failures reside at a higher level—with the mental processes involved in assessing the available information, planning, formulating intentions, and judging the likely consequences of the planned actions. These are termed *mistakes* and have been further subdivided into two categories according to the performance levels at which they occur (see Rasmussen 1983): *rule-based mistakes* and *knowledge-based mistakes*.

Mistakes generally occur when we have to stop and think; that is, when we are faced with a problem or the need to make a decision or formulate a changed plan of action. Expertise in any field is based in large part on the possession of stored production rules of the kind *if X then do Y*, or *if X has the features A, B, C, then it is a Y*. Human beings are furious pattern-matchers. When confronted with an unplanned-for situation we are strongly disposed to identify a familiar pattern and, where necessary, apply a problem-solving rule that is part of our stock of expertise. But these pattern-matching and rule-applying processes can be in error. Rule-based mistakes take three basic forms.

- We can misapply a normally good rule because we fail to spot the contraindications. (Example: A general practitioner fails to identify that a child with a fever in a flu epidemic has meningitis.)

- We can apply a bad rule. (Example: The technician involved in rewiring a signal box just prior to the Clapham rail disaster had acquired the habit of bending back the old wires rather than removing them.)

- We can fail to apply a good rule. Standard operating procedures (SOPs) usually embody good rules. Failing to comply with SOPs can be both an error and a violation. We will discuss violations shortly.

Knowledge-based mistakes occur in entirely novel situations when we have run out of pre-packaged problem-solving rules and have to find a solution 'on the hoof'. These are highly error-provoking conditions; indeed, it is usually only trial-and-error learning that leads us eventually to an answer. The errors act like runway markers to mark out the scope of allowable forward progress.

The under-specification hypothesis

Is there a general rule that could be applied to all categories of error? Here is my attempt at one:

> When the mental processes necessary to ensure correct performance are under-specified—by any of a number of means: inattention, forgetting, incomplete knowledge, noisy sensory data, and the like—the cognitive system tends to 'default' to a response that is frequent, familiar, and hitherto useful in that particular context.

This may lead to error but it is none the less a highly adaptive process. For example, when asked who said, '*The lamps are going out all over Europe; and we shall not see them lit again in our lifetime*' most people (more than 90% in British audiences) respond with Winston Churchill. It was actually said by Sir Edward Grey, the Foreign Secretary, in 1914. The Churchill answer was wrong but it followed a sensible pathway. The quotation suggests that an English-speaking statesperson said it on the verge of something cataclysmic—the

Second World War. Who was the gabbiest statesman of that time? Winston Churchill. If we can predict an error with a high degree of confidence, we begin to understand the processes that give rise to it.

Widening the scope

Until the mid to late1980s, my primary concern had been the cognitive mechanisms of error and the light that they could throw on the largely covert processes by which we control our routine everyday thoughts and actions. To this end, I sought to provoke predictable errors in captive lecture audiences. But the real world of hazardous industries was making itself increasingly felt, even in the ivory tower; most particularly this involved aviation, nuclear power generation, road transport, mining, oil and gas exploration, chemical process plants, railways and maritime operations. Gradually my focus shifted away from absent-minded people in familiar surroundings to the unsafe acts of those on the front line of complex, well-defended systems, as well as their teams, workplaces, and the organizational processes that shaped their behaviour. The detailed reports of catastrophic events proved to be a rich source of material regarding real-life mistakes and violations.

Violations

Violations—deliberate but usually non-malevolent deviations from safety rules and procedures—fall into three categories: routine, optimizing, and necessary violations. In each case, the decision not to abide by SOPs is shaped by individual, social, and organizational factors, though the balance of these influences varies from one type of violation to another.

+ Routine violations typically involve corner-cutting at the skill-based level of performance (see Rasmussen 1983)—that is, taking the path of least effort between two task-related points. These shortcuts readily become a part of the person's behavioural repertoire, particularly when the work environment is one that rarely sanctions violations or rewards compliance. Routine violations are also promoted by 'clumsy' procedures that direct action along what seems to be a longer-than-necessary pathway.

+ Optimizing violations, or violating for the thrill of it, reflect the fact that human actions serve a variety of motivational goals, and that some of these are quite unrelated to the functional aspects of the task. Thus, a driver's functional goal is to get from A to B but, in the process, he or she (usually he) can optimize the joy of speed or indulge aggressive instincts. Optimizing tendencies are characteristic of certain demographic groups, particularly young males.

- Whereas routine and optimizing violations are clearly linked to the attainment of personal goals—that is, least effort and thrills—necessary violations have their origins in particular work situations. Here, non-compliance is seen as essential in order to get the job done. Necessary violations are commonly provoked by systemic deficiencies with regard to the site, tools, and equipment. They can also provide an easier way of working. The combined effect of these two factors often leads to these violations becoming routine rather than exceptional.

Organizational accidents and Swiss cheese

What distinguishes organizational accidents from other types of bad event is the presence within the system of diverse and redundant barriers, controls, and safeguards—defences-in-depth. Some of these defences are engineered: alarms, containments, physical barriers, automatic shutdowns, and the like. Others rely on people: pilots, ship's watch-keepers, surgeons, train drivers, and control room operators. Yet others depend on procedures, regulations, safety management systems, and administrative controls. Their collective function is to protect potential victims and assets from the operational hazards. Most of the time they do this very effectively, but there are always gaps and weaknesses.

In an ideal world, each defensive layer would be intact. But in reality they are more like slices of Swiss cheese, having many holes—though, unlike the cheese, these holes are continually opening and shutting, and shifting their location. The presence of holes in any one layer does not normally cause a bad outcome. Usually, this can happen only when the holes in many 'slices' line up momentarily to permit a trajectory of accident opportunity, bringing hazards into harmful contact with victims, assets, or the environment.

The holes in the defences arise for two reasons: active failures and latent conditions. Most organizational accidents involve a combination of these two factors.

- Active failures are the unsafe acts committed by people at the 'sharp end', the front-liners at the human–system interface. They take a variety of forms: slips, lapses, mistakes, and procedural violations. Active failures have an immediate but usually short-lived impact on the integrity of the defences. Followers of the person approach often look no further for the causes of an accident once they have identified these proximal unsafe acts. But, as mentioned above, nearly all such acts have causal contributions that extend back in time and up through the levels of the organization.

- Latent conditions and latent failures are the ubiquitous 'resident pathogens' within the organization. All systems have them regardless of whether they have been involved in an accident or not. They arise from decisions made by designers, builders, procedure writers, maintainers, and senior management. These may have been mistaken, but they need not be. All such strategic decisions have the potential for introducing pathogens into the system. Latent conditions have two kinds of adverse effect: they can translate into error-provoking conditions within the local workplace (for example: understaffing, time pressure, inadequate tools and equipment, poor training, inexperience, and the like), and they can create long-lasting holes or weaknesses in the defences (untrustworthy alarms and indicators, unworkable procedures, weakened barriers, design and construction deficiencies, etc.). As the term suggests, latent conditions can lie dormant within the system for many years before they interact with local triggers and active failures to create an accident opportunity. This is when the holes in the cheese line up to create a pathway (often of very brief duration), allowing the hazards to cause harm and loss. Unlike active failures, whose specific forms are hard to foresee, latent conditions can be identified and remedied before an adverse event occurs. Understanding this leads to proactive rather than reactive safety management.

Current concerns

From the mid-1990s until the present, my main concern has been the problem of patient safety in medical care. This is a huge problem and exists everywhere. Around 10% of hospital patients are harmed, and sometimes killed, by medical and institutional errors. Healthcare professionals are not unusually fallible, but the conditions under which they work are highly error provoking: a huge diversity in tasks and equipment, little sharing of the lessons learned from adverse events, great uncertainty and limited knowledge, vulnerable patients, a one-to-one (or few-to-one) delivery of care, and a culture that equates error with incompetence.

A number of high-level reports (Donaldson 2000; Kohn *et al.* 2000) have strongly endorsed a systemic, as opposed to a person-oriented, approach to medical error. This is good, but it does little for the front-line professionals in the short term. They cannot easily change the system. Rather, they need 'mental skills' that will help them identify and step back from error-prone situations. We are developing tools to deliver this 'error wisdom' at the present time.

End piece

For me, there have been three main conclusions to emerge from this error quest. First, the same situations keep on producing the same errors in different people—the problem lies mainly with error-provoking situations rather than error-prone people. Second, fallibility is part of the human condition. It is here to stay. We may tweak it, but we cannot change it. We can, however, change the conditions under which people work to make them less provocative and more forgiving. Third, error *per se* is very banal, even boring: it is like breathing or dying. What is truly interesting, however, is not the 'human-as-hazard' aspect, but the notion of the 'human-as-hero', that is, the adaptations, adjustments, compensations, and recoveries that front-line people make on a daily basis to keep imperfect systems working and mostly safe. These will occupy me for the next thirty years.

References

Broadbent, D. E., Cooper, P. J., Fitzgerald, P. F., and Parkes, K. R. (1982). The Cognitive Failures Questionnaire (CFQ) and its correlates. *British Journal of Clinical Psychology* 21: 1–16.

Donaldson, L. (2000). *An organisation with a memory*. London: Department of Health.

Kohn, L. T., Corrigan, J. M., and Donaldson, M. S. (ed.) (2000). *To err is human: building a safer health system*. Institute of Medicine. Washington, DC: National Academy Press.

Norman, D. (1981). Categorization of action slips. *Psychological Review* 88: 1–15.

Rasmussen, J. (1983). Skills, rules, knowledge: signals, signs and symbols and other distinctions in human performance models. *IEEE Transactions: Systems, Man & Cybernetics* SMC-13: 257–67.

Reason, J. (1977). Skill and error in everyday life. In: M. Howe (ed.) *Adult learning: psychological research and applications*, pp. 21–44. London: Wiley.

Reason, J. (1987). The Chernobyl errors. *Bulletin of the British Psychological Society* 40: 201–6.

Reason, J. (1989). Stress and cognitive failure. In: S. Fisher and J. Reason (ed.) *Handbook of life stress, cognition and health*, pp. 405–21. Chichester: Wiley.

Reason, J. (1990). *Human error*. New York, Cambridge University Press.

Reason, J. (1993). Self-report questionnaires in psychology: Have they delivered the goods? In: A. Baddeley and L. Weiskrantz (ed.) *Attention, selection, awareness and control: a tribute to Donald Broadbent*, pp. 406–423. Oxford: Clarendon Press.

Reason, J. (1997). *Managing the risks of organizational accidents*. Aldershot: Ashgate.

Reason, J. and Mycielska, K. (1982). *Absent-minded? The psychology of mental lapses and everyday errors*. Englewood Cliffs, NJ: Prentice-Hall.

Reason, J. and Lucas, D. (1984). Absent-mindedness in shops: its correlates and consequences. *British Journal of Clinical Psychology* 23: 121–31.

18

Visual Perception 1950–2000

John Ross

This chapter tells a tale of the study of visual perception during the second half of the twentieth century as seen by a somewhat peripheral observer, who came to perception late in his scientific career. It ignores or touches only lightly on many topics, including adaptation, attention, the perception of faces, and the mysteries of colour.

Back then

Behaviourism had a strong grip on psychology in 1950. This began to loosen only in about 1956, but the field of perception was spared its most stultifying effects because it is difficult to take the subjective out of perception. By 1956 a great deal of the phenomenology of vision was known (Helmholtz having single-handedly contributed much of it, and the Gestaltists adding a lot more); most of the now standard visual illusions had been discovered, and colour theory, though described as a 'jungle' in the 1950 *Annual Review of Psychology*, had developed to a level daunting to all but its adepts. Wartime work on what came to be called 'human factors' in the USA and the 'human engineering' in the UK had revealed much about perceptual strengths and weaknesses. It usefulness in war and subsequently in the design of instruments such as radar screens had added even more respectability to the study of perception.

The laws of colour mixture were well established, as was the fact that cones were effectively filters for wavelength, but there was deep controversy about the explanation of the appearance of colour. The trichromatic theory, championed by Helmholtz, explained it by the filtering properties of three types of cone (S, M, and L); the opponent process theory, first proposed by Hering, instead appealed to three opponent processes: black *vs* white, red *vs* green, and blue *vs* yellow, but no physiological basis had yet been proposed for opponent processes. Colour matching was better explained by the trichromatic theory, perceived colour differences better by opponent processes. The opponent process theory, which had languished somewhat, received a boost from work published in the 1950s (Hurvich and Jameson 1957). A true (if possibly not final) reconciliation between the two, with a plausible physiological basis for opponent processes, was not achieved until the brink of the twenty-first century, with the discovery that ganglion cells within the retina added and subtracted signals from the cones. For a summary see (Kandel *et al.* 2000).

New ideas

In the early 1950s it was still possible for vision scientists to believe (as some philosophers still do) that a perceiver had direct contact with the external world, that the brain was 'idempotent' (had no neuroanatomical centres specialized for particular tasks) and that the functional neuropsychology of perception required little more work than to invert the upside-down images from the eyes and combine them. J. J. Gibson (1950) proposed that there was a direct 'pick-up' of invariants in the flow of images on the retina. There was no structural or functional map of the visual system, no hint of its hierarchical organization, and no understanding of information processing. No information-processing devices (as distinct from information-transmitting devices such as telephones) were known, or could provide analogies for the function of the brain. It was not at all clear what neurones were needed for.

Some new ideas that emerged during, or shortly before, the 1950s shaped the course of research into visual perception over the rest of the century, and made belief in unmediated perception untenable for vision scientists. Pre-eminent in influence was Claude Shannon's idea that information could be quantified. His theory of information enabled it to be quantified in 'bits' on the assumption that signals registered by a receiver reduced uncertainty about the content of a message being sent. (One bit is the reduction in uncertainty reduction when a signal decides the choice of one of two equally probable alternatives.) Within the community of vision scientists, the assumption that information reduced uncertainty resonated with Helmholtz's doctrine of unconscious inference, which carried with it the implication that the perceiver, like the receiver in information theory, has preconceptions about what might possibly be the case and uses visual information to resolve his or her uncertainty. It also paved the way for accepting the possibility of Bayesian inference as a guiding principle for visual analysis. Like Shannon's information theory, the Bayesian framework assumes the existence of a set of prior probabilities that guide perceptual processing. Surprisingly it was not until the middle 1950s that Richard Gregory put the proposition that percepts are literally hypotheses about the world, to be abandoned if they fail further testing. It was even later that Bayesian framework began to be applied formally to perception.

Information theory introduced another theme that powerfully shaped subsequent research on visual perception: the theme of coding. Shannon's theory permits not only the measurement of the amount of information that may be transmitted but also the measurement of the efficiency with which transmission is effected. If more than the minimum necessary number of symbols is used the message includes redundancy that can be removed by efficient recoding. It was not long before the vision community learnt to ask how the eye encoded information to send it to the brain, how efficient this encoding was and how the brain decoded the messages it received. As early as 1959 Horace Barlow (1959) suggested that redundancy reduction resulting in sparse coding is an overriding organizing principle for visual perception and he was (is?) still actively and fruitfully pursuing the theme more than forty years later.

Ideas about how machines might process information began to emerge. Work on both sides of the Atlantic led to the development of what we now know as computers and, along with it, what we now know as computer science. Ideas about how the brain might undertake computations began to burgeon; in 1958, John von Neumann published a book comparing computers and brains. But explaining how the visual system might engage in computations was one thing; showing how it could do the computations necessary to locate edges, to identify figures and segregate them from ground, or to resolve ambiguities and organize scenes was another, and proved more difficult than anyone initially had imagined.

New techniques and big discoveries

As these ideas began to influence thinking about visual perception, a quiet, almost unnoticed, methodological shift began. Research in visual perception began to make increasing use of measurement techniques developed for the study of psychophysics, and to adapt these for its own purposes. (Psychophysics is the somewhat arcane, and so far never successful, pursuit of the laws connecting objective and subjective, like light intensity and brightness, or sound intensity and loudness.) Psychophysical techniques have provided visual science with something that is rare in psychology: measurements that are precise and replicable, on ratio scales such as area or time, and even on dimensionless scales such as contrast and sensitivity. Because these measures are precise and replicable, and because, when they are applied, individual differences between observers tend to be small, papers reporting careful measurements on a few individuals or even a single person are now perhaps more the rule than the exception, in the perception literature. Such measurements freed vision scientist from the inconvenience of having to use large numbers of subjects and from the necessity to assess effect sizes in terms of individual variation. The use of precise models to explain or, even better, quantitatively predict the results of experiments became common. As these methods became more widely used and trusted, the term psychophysics lost its original meaning, coming to mean 'the experimental study of perception by recording verbal reports and behavioural reponses'or 'the direct, quantitative study of sensory performance'.

After the 1960s neurophysiological techniques for recording the responses of individual cells in the visual cortex became more widely used, and in the 1990s it became possible both to record from specific brain loci in awake animals and to image neural activity in humans and animals while they were exposed to visual stimuli. The new technique, functional magnetic resonance imaging (fMRI), measures blood oxygen level in the brain to index neural activity at given locations. The use of fMRI increased as knowledge of and questions about the functions performed at different sites increased,. Toward the end of the twentieth century, studies combining psychophysics, electrophyiological recording, and brain imaging became increasingly common.

Two discoveries in the late 1950s and early 1960s had already entirely changed the field of discourse. They were originally independent, and at one time regarded as antagonistic, but later linked. One was that visual neurones had structured receptive fields enabling them to detect features or even events. Such receptive fields had originally been suggested by Hartline, and confirmed by Kuffler in the USA and Barlow in the UK for ganglion cells in the retina, showing that they detect and report to the brain the presence of or change in spots of light or dark. Thus it became clear that the retina analysed the images that it received and did not simply send copies of them to the brain. This discovery was extended in studies of frogs by Lettvin, Matturana, McCulloch, and Pitts, who, in a 1959 paper entitled 'What the frog's eye tells the frog's brain', dramatized the fact that the eye transmitted coded messages about features of retinal images after first subjecting them to a local analysis. They identified four operations that the eye performed and reported upon: sustained contrast detection, net convexity detection, moving edge detection, and net dimming detection. They argued that each of these identified a feature of the frog's environment useful to the frog in surviving and in catching prey; for example, a moving edge might indicate a predatory bird or an insect that might be eaten. The idea of a 'moving edge' detector was a precursor to the later idea of spatiotemporal receptive fields (Burr and Ross 1986).

The concept of what a receptive field might be developed greatly in complexity. Hubel and Wiesel (1968), in work that later earned them the Nobel Prize, showed that cells in the striate visual cortex responded not to spots of light, but to lines of a particular orientation. Some (simple) cells required lines to be in a particular position within their receptive fields, others (complex cells) did not; some required lines to be moving and others did not. Hubel and Wiesel's work revealed a highly regular, orientation-based, columnar organization of cells at the first stage of the visual system and thereafter a hierarchical arrangement seemingly abstracting progressively more complex information from visual images as signals from them ascended the visual system. Later discoveries unearthed cells at higher levels with receptive fields for detecting global pattern, and even paths of global motion. Speculation began as to whether there existed a 'grandmother cell', a cell that responds to the observer's grandmother. No such cell has been found, but there is a recent report of cells that fire only when the faces of Jennifer Aniston (!) or Bill Clinton (neither of them a grandmother) enter their respective receptive fields (Quiroga *et al.* 2005).

The other idea, emerging originally from the psychophysical studies of Campbell and Robson (1968), was that images were analysed by functionally independent spatial-frequency channels, with the controversial suggestion that the brain performed some kind of Fourier analysis of visual images. The implication of Hubel and Wiesel's discoveries had seemed to be that visual analysis broke down the image into local features, like lines. The implication of Campbell and Robson's work seemed to be that visual analysis started by describing the image in terms of global Fourier-like components. In some places, most notably on the Berkeley campus of the University of California, tensions ran high between those who favoured local lines and those who favoured global waves as the components of visual images.

Campbell and Robson, citing an early paper by Hubel, had already pointed out in their original paper that '*receptive fields of ganglion cells might provide a physiological basis for the frequency-selective channels suggested by the psychophysical results*' (1968, p. 565). Tension was eased by a gradual shift to the idea that images were analysed in local patches at different scales and in different orientations (wavelet rather than Fourier analysis). A link between the two developments was made possible by the recognition that different receptive fields operated at different orientation and different scales. The effect of the linkage was to alter radically ideas about the information available in an image, the processes by which information was extracted, and how visual perception could and should be studied.

In addition, vision scientists began better to understand and control visual stimuli. Fourier analysis provided an alternative description of stimuli, useful in calculating how visual mechanisms would respond to them. As computers became more available, affordable, and tractable, they allowed the construction of high-precision stimuli of great complexity and sophistication, like the random-dot stereograms that Julesz introduced in 1959. Computers enabled not only the construction of such stimuli, but also analyses such as two-dimensional Fourier analysis and the processing of images to restrict the information that they could provide. This capacity proved invaluable in dealing with natural images sampled from a wide variety of environments to determine how visual mechanisms may have evolved to extract information from them efficiently.

By common agreement, the most dazzling book of the half-century was Bela Julesz's *Foundations of Cyclopean Perception* (Julesz 1971), but the most influential was David Marr's *Vision: A Computational Investigation into the Human Representation and Processing of Visual Information*, published in 1980 after his early death.

Julesz was a Hungarian, trained as an engineer, who disdained precise psychophysical measurements. He preferred razzle-dazzle—stunning demonstrations that produced, as he described them, '57 dB effects'. He worked at the then richly funded Bell Laboratories, and boasted that he had the funds and equipment to do experiments for which no other vision scientist could find resources. His greatest coup was the random-dot stereogram (used by the even more flamboyant Salvador Dali in one of his paintings), which demonstrated that the visual system could extract a startlingly vivid pattern in depth from a pair of images, neither of which conveyed any indication of pattern or depth. Some, who still clung to the belief that stereo vision depended upon matching features in the two images formed by the eyes, were outraged, to the point of denying (by refusing to look, in some cases) that they saw what was plain to everyone else.

Marr was a Cambridge mathematician, who early decided to pursue a career in neuroscience. His book *Vision* (Marr 1982), published after his untimely death in 1980 at the age of 35 years, articulated a theme, earlier suggested by Kenneth Craik—who died in 1945 even younger than Marr—that the visual brain built itself an internal model of reality (Craik 1966). Marr called this reality a representation, and set out to show in detail how such a representation could be computed by the brain given the mechanisms it was known to possess, and given the indeterminacies in going from 2D images to 3D representations. Marr's work set the agenda for much that was to follow in the field of computational vision, as well as in experimental studies. Marr himself (Marr and Poggio 1979) proposed a model for stereopsis to explain how the brain computed pattern-in-depth from Julesz's random-dot stereograms.

Specialized and distributed processing

By the end of the twentieth century it was almost universally agreed that the brain analysed different aspects of visual stimuli, such as colour, form, and motion, separately, and formed different maps, not all aligned, to assign the results of its multiple analyses. This seemed to follow from what neurones in different parts of the brain responded to, and led to the so-called 'binding problem'—how information about different aspects of stimuli was pulled together in our percepts. No plausible solutions have been proposed, and doubts have been expressed both that the visual system is organized quite as hierarchically as is commonly accepted and that the binding problem exists (Lennie 1998).

During the 1980s it began to be widely, but not universally, accepted that there were two distinct pathways in the visual system, anatomically separate and functionally independent: a ventral, parvocellular pathway and a dorsal, magnocellular pathway. Broadly speaking the parvocellular is thought to handle form and colour, the magnocellular spatial relationships and motion. This hypothesis is consistent with a mass of anatomical, electrophysiological, psychophysical, clinical, and brain imaging evidence. Textbooks now present the existence of these two pathways and their functional independence as fact, dubbing them the 'what' and 'where' pathways; but as early as 1993 Merigan and Maunsell warned that the description of the two pathways as parallel and independent was likely to be only a rough approximation to the truth. In the same year, Goodale and Milner (1992) suggested that the ventral pathway was responsible for (conscious) perception and the dorsal for action, which could be guided by vision unconsciously, as happens in 'blindsight' (Sanders *et al.* 1974).

Discovery of even greater specialization was in store. Two areas within the dorsal (magnocellular) pathway (known as MT and MST in the monkey brain) were found to combine information from local motion detectors in order to compute the direction and speed of motion over large distances, and to respond to the optic flow, described much earlier by Gibson, that results from motion of an observer walking, driving, or flying through the environment. In area V4 of the ventral pathway, neurones were found that responded only to particular types of global pattern—concentric circles or a fan of radial lines, for example. These can be considered as static analogues of optic flow detectors and there is some evidence to suggest that, despite the supposed independence of the ventral and dorsal pathways, they participate in the analysis of optic flow. In the early 1980s neurones were discovered in the temporal cortex of monkeys that responded selectively to faces (Perrett *et al.* 1982), and, as mentioned above, in 2005 it was claimed, on the basis of electrophysiological studies of epileptics, that some neurones in humans respond selectively to particular well-known faces (Quiroga *et al.* 2005).

How far have we got?

By 2000, the study of visual perception had moved toward the centre of mainstream science with papers being accepted by general science journals such as *Nature* and *Science*, and in more specialized but still broad journals such as *Current Biology*, *Neuron*, the *Journal of Neuroscience*, and *Nature Neuroscience*. This trend accompanied a growth after 1960 in the number of good-quality international journals devoted specifically to visual perception, such as *Perception*, *Vision Research*, *Spatial Vision*, and (the electronic) *Journal of Vision*.

Vastly more was known about the visual system in 2000, anatomically and functionally, than was known in 1950. Vision scientists had tools, experimental, analytical, and theoretical, that had developed greatly in range of application and precision over the half-century. No stimulus was too complex to consider constructing, no variation in timing, contrast, texture, or colour too difficult to manage, and no aspect of perception too subtle to be measured. The number of people working on visual perception, and their level of skill, increased greatly.

And yet large gaps in our understanding remained, and still remain: How do we keep the perceptual world stable, despite the continual darting about of our eyes? Why does the world look so vividly complete, given the paucity of the information about it that the visual system contains (Sperling 1960) and given our blindness to change (O'Regan *et al.* 1999)? Why have visual prosthetics, the spectacles and contact lenses we wear, remained much the same as when first invented, and why have optometrists continued to use the Snellen chart to measure visual acuity? Why have improvements in the quality of television, and in animation techniques, been made with such little influence from the findings of late-twentieth-century vision scientists? Why has the age-old moon illusion, along with old warhorses such as the Mueller–Lyer and the Poggendorf illusions, so stubbornly resisted explanation?

The explanatory gap between the brain activities set in train by visual stimulation and our visual experience of the world yawns as wide as ever, perhaps wider. It is not just that qualia seem so out of reach: it is the sheer externality of the world, the richness with which we see it, and its compelling reality that seem so far from what we understand about the calculations the brain makes and the hypotheses, representations, or models it constructs.

References

Alhazen, I. (1083/1959). Book of optics. In: A. I. Sabra (ed.) *The optics of Ibn al-Haytham.* London: Warburg Institute, 1989.

Barlow, H. B. (1959). Possible principles underlying the transformations of sensory messages. In: W. A. Rosenblith (ed.) *Sensory communication*, pp. 217–234. Cambridge, MA: MIT Press.

Burr, D. C. and Ross, J. (1986). Visual processing of motion. *Trends in Neurosciences* 9: 304–6.

Campbell, F. W. and Robson, J. G. (1968). On the application of Fourier analysis to the visibility of gratings. *Journal of Physiology (London)* 197: 551–6.

Craik, K. (1966). *The nature of psychology.*, Cambridge: Cambridge University Press.

Gibson, J. J. (1950). *The perception of the visual world.*, Boston: Houghton Mifflin.

Goodale, M. A. and Milner, A. D. (1992). Separate pathways for perception and action. *Trends in Neurosciences* 15: 20–5.

Hubel, D. H. and Wiesel, T. N. (1968). Receptive fields and functional architecture of monkey striate cortex. *Journal of Physiology (London)* 195: 215–43.

Hurvich, L. M. and Jameson, D. (1957). An opponent-process theory of color vision. *Psychological Review* 64: 384–404.

Julesz, B. (1971). *Foundations of cyclopean perception*, Chicago: University of Chicago Press.

Kandel, E. R., Schwartz, J. H., and Jessell, T. M. (2000). *Principles of neural science*, New York: McGraw-Hill Health Professions Division.

Lennie, P. (1998). Single units and visual cortical organization. *Perception* 27: 889–935.

Lettvin *et al.* (1959). What the frog's eye tells the frog's brain.

Marr, D. (1982). *Vision.* San Francisco: Freeman.

Marr, D. and Poggio, T. (1979). A computational theory of human stereo vision. *Proceedings of the Royal Society (London) B* 204: 301–28.

Merigan, W. H. and Maunsell, J. H. (1993). How parallel are the primate visual pathways? *Annual Review of Neuroscience* 16: 369–402.

Neumann, J. V. (1958). *The computer and the brain*, New Haven: Yale University Press.

Newton, S. I. (1730/1952) *Opticks.* New York: Dover Publications.

O'Regan, J. K., Rensink, R. A., and Clark, J. J. (1999). Change-blindness as a result of 'mudsplashes'. *Nature* 398: 34.

Perrett, D. I., Rolls, E. T., and Caan, W. (1982). Visual neurones responsive to faces in the monkey temporal cortex. *Experimental Brain Research* 47: 329–42.

Quiroga, R. Q., Reddy, L., Kreiman, G., Koch, C., and Fried, I. (2005). Invariant visual representation by single neurons in the human brain. *Nature* 435: 1102–7.

Sanders, M. D., Warrington, E. K., Marshall, J., and Wieskrantz, L. (1974). 'Blindsight': vision in a field defect. *Lancet* 1: 707–8.

Sperling, G. (1960). The information available in brief visual presentations. *Psychological Monographs: General and Applied* 74: 1–29.

19

Human performance: from then to now

Andries F. Sanders

Then

I was a young Psychology graduate and my employer, the Institute for Perception at Soesterberg, allowed me to attend the Brussels 1957 International Congress of Psychology. I was thrilled by my first scientific meeting ever but rapidly became miserable because I failed to comprehend almost anything that I heard. I was not yet aware that, aside from the difficulties imposed by the typically poor presentation skills of most academic speakers, a thorough background knowledge of a topic is required to understand and appreciate an oral presentation. Moreover, I suffered from a language problem. However, in retrospect, two symposia on the final day of the Congress shaped my interests. One was on Applications of Information Theory and the other was entitled 'Too busy or too bored'. Both were mainly inspired by researchers from the Applied Psychology Research Unit in Cambridge.

The central message of the first was that processes in between input and output are controlled by the information contained in the input rather than by the input itself. The prime concern shifted from S-R associations to 'information processing' between stimulus and response. The information metaphor was primitive—a fixed and limited-capacity telecommunication channel, which replaced the equally primitive Behaviourist metaphor of an associative telephone exchange. The related research was eloquently summarized in Broadbent's (1958) influential *Perception and Communication*, which argued that previously neglected topics of research could be unified by the guiding principle of the telecommunication metaphor preceded by a selective filter and a preselective short-term memory system to safeguard the system against temporary overload.

It was striking how quickly this new set of concepts and interests replaced the earlier Behaviourist ones—no more than 15 years after the publication of

Hull's (1943) *Principles of Behavior*. After the mid-1950s Behaviourist theorizing and results were almost totally neglected. Incidental attempts to stress communalities (e.g. Berlyne 1957) were effectively ignored. It may well be a characteristic of a paradigm shift that previous work is viewed as obsolete. Central themes of Behaviourism—learning and motor behaviour—were undervalued, and animal laboratories rapidly disappeared from psychology departments. Though renewal is necessary, this carries the cost of loss of appreciation of earlier accomplishments. As an illustration, effects of long-term work had been studied extensively in the context of effects of massed versus spaced practice on performance in tracking and in serial reaction tasks. The usual finding was a negligible practice gain during a massed session followed by a marked improvement at the beginning of the next massed session—contrasting with continuous gains during spaced practice with brief rest intervals between trials. The obvious conclusion was that the absence of practice effects in the massed condition was not due to poor learning (i.e. deficient habit formation), but to a suboptimal drive state, referred to by the term 'reactive inhibition'. Such research is highly relevant to the interpretation of studies on sustained attention and vigilance. Yet, references to reactive inhibition are rare.

Another consequence of the paradigm shift was that relations between Psychology and Physiology were largely disconnected—perhaps with the exception of the study of evoked potentials and galvanic skin responses, The guiding metaphors of information theory—as well as of its successors—were not inspired by Physiology but by Technology and Computer Science. I remember a remark by a leading American psychologist during the early seventies that Physiology had done nothing but carry Psychology on wrong tracks—with clear reference to Behaviourism. Nobody took issue.

The second symposium in Brussels included a discussion of two applied research themes: perceptual-motor load and vigilance, springing from applied problems during World War II. They launched much research on reaction processes, selective attention, visual search, performing under adverse conditions, and short-term memory, topics that had been neglected by Behaviourists. These were main themes at the first Attention and Performance conference (Sanders 1967), at which Human Performance was defined as the combined basic and applied analysis of human skills.

It is relevant that most applied work is commissioned by non-academic bodies and so is described in reports rather than in the open literature At Soesterberg I was involved in applied research, concerned with semi-automatic systems of the 1960s, such as perceptual-motor load, air-traffic control, guiding aircraft in airports, ship manoeuvres in harbours or in shallow waters, industrial quality control, the relative merits of paced versus self-paced work, display design, human signal detection in radar and sonar, and a variety of issues related to traffic safety. Some questions had simple solutions, such as. a licence plate number that can be easily encoded and retained. Others, such as a new ship-traffic control system for the Rotterdam harbour system or optimal visual search strategies during driving, were much more complex, requiring extensive research and collaboration. However, the boundaries between process-oriented and task-oriented research (Schmidt 1987) were weak, transient, and viewed as mutually dependent and inspiring.

Signal detection

The popularity of Information Theory was short-lived because it had no provision for feedback and learning, and could not account for strategic interaction between an individual and their environment. Moreover, some main predictions were falsified. For instance, the linear relation between choice reaction time (RT) and amount of stimulus information, suggesting an information-based constant processing rate, was hard to reconcile with the marked effects of practice and S-R compatibility. In addition, the effect of information load was confounded with the effect of the probability of stimulus repetition between successive trials. When repetition probability was held constant, the relation of RT to information load simply vanished (Kornblum 1969). The demise of the information metaphor was the first step from 'then' to 'now'. It was followed by numerous new technology-based models and a considerable theoretical diversification (see Chapter 15).

Some of the new models aspired to the status of unifying principles, whereas others aimed at covering a smaller domain. Control theory, concerned as it was with manual tracking, originally belonged to the latter category; yet subsequent optimal control theory had the wider claim of modelling supervisory as well as manual control (Sheridan 1987), thus also pretending to be a general Human Performance model. I remember heated discussions with engineers, interested in performance, who did not see the necessity of testing the optimal control model. It was only a matter of parameter estimation; the model itself represented an engineering truth. Signal Detection Theory—with its measures of sensitivity and response bias—was the major unifying principle of Broadbent's (1971) second main book, *Decision and Stress*. Decision-related notions were fostered by merging signal detection theory and Bayesian revision of opinion. In 1964, I was introduced to all of this while undertaking post-doctoral work at the Michigan Human Performance Center, where Paul Fitts (ergonomics, reaction processes), Ward Edwards (decision-making), and

Arthur Melton (memory) were the main investigators. Edwards (1966) proposed a Bayesian model of two-choice reaction time, whereas decision-type models for recognition memory were under way. Many RT models were proposed, based upon various decision rules (Luce 1986) that were inspired more by mathematical convenience than by psychological reality. Consequently most were short lived, with the notable exception of Ratcliff's (1978, 1988) stochastic diffusion model which, in line with the mainstream, proposed a continuous signal-detection process feeding into an equally continuous random-walk decision process. This model appears to cover a wide domain of data on RT in traditional choice reactions, in target classification, and in same–different responses.

Limited capacity

The notion of limited capacity survived the fall of the Information metaphor and remained popular for two further decades. It simply shifted from a telecommunication device to a small-capacity digital computer. Practice effects were accounted for by 'more efficient programming' and strategic factors by 'allocation policy'. There were differences between views—fixed computer capacity (Norman and Bobrow 1975), energetic 'effort' capacity with a variable limit (Kahneman 1973), and scarce fixed economical resources (Navon and Gopher 1979)—but all shared the common assumption that performance required some portion of the same general and undifferentiated processing capacity. The conceptual framework was particularly useful for researching perceptual-motor load in multiple task performance. Indeed, capacity theories reflected the applied interest in task load—or lack of task load—arising from rapidly developing industrial automatization. Operators were freed from boring repetitive work, but faced with equally boring supervisory control. A combination of different tasks might provide optimal operator load (e.g. Moray 1979).

I was never charmed by the capacity concept. It seemed to me void of psychological content, because, although in different amounts, all mental processes were supposed to consume the same general capacity. As computers became more powerful, the limited-capacity metaphor faded (Navon 1984; Neumann 1987). A new conceptualization of parallel-distributed neural nets had obvious references to Neurophysiology, and stressed the enormous brain capacity and the prevalence of in-parallel distributed processes. Again, behavioural evidence accumulated that time-sharing of different tasks is widely possible. There remain instances, though, in which a combination of seemingly simple decision processes creates a serious bottleneck. In a thoughtful analysis, Neumann (1987) argued that limits are met as soon as even simple task demands conflict with respect to appropriate action. Response conflict evokes widespread inhibition so that appropriate responses can be selected and errors prevented. But this is far removed from the limited-capacity view.

Linear stages and choice reactions

Linear stage theory had roots in Donders (1868)—just as capacity theory had in Külpe (1905)—and was revived by Sternberg (1969) in his influential paper to the Donders Centenary at Eindhoven. A reaction process would consist of a number of successively operating processing stages, the outcome of a stage serving as input for the next one. Sternberg's method of inferring these stages from patterns of additive and interactive effects of experimental variables was called the Additive Factors Method (AFM). The method has little to say about the sequence of stages and about processes occurring within a stage, each stage needing its own processing model.

A main difference between stage and capacity theory is probably that the first suggests a modular and the second a holistic organization of perform-ance, a contrast that also has classical roots (e.g. Goldstein 1938; Lashley 1929; see also Chapter 8). I vividly remember a 1980 stay with Daniel Gopher at the Technion, Haifa, Israel, and our intense discussions about the relative merits of either approach, including the possibility of multiple resources as potential bridge (Gopher and Sanders 1984). The AFM evoked considerable debate, which I reviewed in my *Elements of Human Performance* (Sanders 1998). The objections mainly concerned the credibility of some of Sternberg's original axioms, such as the unidimensional and serial nature of the stage sequence and the absence of feedback and feedforward processes. Some of these proved to be less compelling than they seemed at first sight. Thus, evidence from computer simulation suggested that the AFM still holds in most models of continuous flow between stages (McClelland 1979). As a result, the issue of discrete versus continuous processing evoked considerable research (e.g. Sanders 1990). The work of Miller (1988, 1993) and of Meyer and collab-orators (1988) deserves mention, because of their methodological power in developing critical tests and conditions.

Parallel processing within stages poses no problem for the AFM, but stages operating in parallel are clearly problematic and would lead to inconsistent patterns of interactions and additivities of variables. A preponderance of par-allel routes, of strategic manipulation, and of feedforward/feedback loops would entail chaotic outcomes of relations between experimental variables, and this would entirely discount the AFM. Most of my research during the 1970s and 1980s investigated the prospects of a stage structure in traditional choice reactions (Sanders 1980, 1990), suggesting a pattern of some six stages.

Stage robustness was illustrated by replicated findings that unusual conditions—such as sleep loss, long-term work, sedatives, and stimulants—left the stage structure intact and specifically affected some, but not other, stages. A one-dimensional processing flow was usually sufficient to account for the results; nevertheless, evidence for a second dimension occurred, under coherent conditions of highly arousing stimuli (Sanders 1983), thus setting a limit to the AFM. The AFM also encountered a limit in the case of separable multidimensional stimuli, confirming the widespread evidence for parallel processing of separate stimulus dimensions, and inspiring Miller (1982) to his view of asynchronous discrete processing. Given its powerful role in other areas of performance research, the lack of evidence for feedback/feedforward processes in choice reaction times may be most surprising, Yet loops within stages would not pose a problem for the AFM, whereas traditional choice processes may be too fast for larger loops to affect RT. It remains to be seen whether evidence for feedback/feedforward would arise in conditions of longer RTs, exceeding, say, two seconds.

In my view, the AFM has been instrumental in building cumulative evidence in favour of a modular processing flow in choice reactions. However, as I argued in *Elements of Human Performance* (Sanders 1998), the AFM never claimed to be a general unifying principle for all cognitive performance. It has a limited domain of application, and the obvious question is how far this stretches. Perhaps the question of domain extent is more useful than an endless quest for general unifying principles. Too small a domain, though, would of course limit the relevance of the AFM. It could well be that choice reaction tasks force subjects to one-dimensional processing, which, in turn, might have little bearing with regard to real-life tasks. I will return to this point in the next section.

There is evidence that the AFM domain exceeds elementary choice reaction tasks. In a large range of studies (Sanders 1998, pp. 196–213), I found that shifting the eyes from one stimulus to a another, presented at the right side of the first stimulus, is triggered when the identification stage of that first stimulus is completed. This conclusion derived from findings that effects on choice reaction time of variables, affecting stages up to and including the identification stage, did recur fully in the fixation time of the first stimulus, whereas the effects of variables affecting later stages did not.

Simple paradigms and real-life tasks

For nostalgic reasons I have spent much space discussing stages. Now, I will turn to the critical issue of generality. It used to be assumed that results on simple experimental paradigms (choice reactions, short-term memory, tracking, etc.) were reliable reflections of real-life tasks, such as manual tracking to driving, and choice reactions as a prototype for interaction with certain environments. From the 1970s, Ergonomics became concerned with much more complex human–machine systems, raising doubts about the validity of simple paradigms (e.g. Flach 1990). Many felt that total task simulation would offer much better prospects, and increasingly sophisticated simulators of, say, flying an aircraft, driving a car, or manoeuvring a ship, found their way to the applied laboratories, whereas basic research was gradually abandoned. My Soesterberg Institute was no exception. Along the same lines, Allport (1980) expressed the gloomy view that common laboratory paradigms were artificial and irrelevant to real life and system design.

I addressed the dilemma in Attention and Performance X (Sanders 1984): simple paradigms are experimentally manageable and easy to analyse, but potentially artefactual and perhaps hardly valid ecologically; in contrast, full simulations, approaching the 'richness of reality', may be of direct applied significance but are too complex to enable detailed analysis or to choose between theoretical views. A caveat regarding the negative validity of a simulator is that a slight deviation from actual reality may render it counterproductive, as illustrated by some studies on the transfer of training from simulation to real driving (Moraal and Poll 1979). This does not imply that the relevance of simulation should be underrated (e.g. Sanders 1991). On the contrary, Performance Theory has always been interested in the description of complex everyday skills such as typing, driving, flying, human–computer interaction, and monitoring. In all of these cases simulations are obviously relevant.

As a way out, Gopher and I (1984) proposed a back-to-back strategy to test how far findings from simple paradigms can be applied to increasingly complex simulations. This can establish the domains of validity of models based on simple paradigms. It is recognized that a particular model or conceptual approach is never all-encompassing and must somewhere reach its limits. If findings in an elementary paradigm fail to hold in a more complex setting, the question arises as to how the situation has changed—perhaps in interesting ways.

The back-to-back idea concerned tests of the validity of results in artificial simple situations to increasingly closer approximations of the real world. This was actually a major research proposal but, to my regret, has not been followed up seriously. Instead, the last decades have shown a pronounced decline in common interests between Cognitive Psychology and Ergonomics, perhaps due to another major development, to which I will now turn.

The biological revolution

Some readers may consider all that has been said so far as belonging to 'then'; for these, 'now' is what is commonly called the Biological Revolution, the consequence of developments in brain imaging techniques—positron emission tomography (PET), functional magnetic resonance imaging (fMRI), and magnetic electroencephalography (MEG)—during the last 10–15 years. These techniques allow more precise and extensive measurements of brain correlates during performance of simple paradigms. PET and fMRI recordings suggest that the dream of establishing the anatomical and physiological basis of mental processes may be coming true. Two main features of the previous paradigm shift from Behaviourism to Cognitive Psychology were a new conceptual framework and a neglect of older work. Now behavioural, or technological, notions are being replaced by brain terminology. I first encountered this during Donald Broadbent's retirement Festschrift in 1993, where Mike Posner— an early and important leader in this field—reported PET studies in relation to his three components of attention: alertness, conscious attention, and orienting. Increased blood flow in the frontal lobe appeared to be related to alertness (e.g. maintaining sustained attention), and conscious attention (i.e. investing effort) had connected active brain structures centred around the anterior cingulate gyrus, whereas orienting had a prime site at the posterior parietal lobe (Posner 1993). Posner and his collaborators were careful to relate their brain imaging measures to performance on well-researched elementary paradigms, but clearly their terminology shifted from behavioural to neuroscientific concepts (i.e. 'anterior and posterior' attention systems).

I would be the last to underrate the relevance of the new brain imaging techniques to theoretical descriptions of mental processes and human performance. Uncovering brain areas involved in the various types of mental activity obviously involves more than correlating brain structures to behaviour. It adds to theory and enables control of intervening variables that have, so far, been hard to trace. Aside from extreme statements like 'I am my brain'—which raise considerable philosophical problems—I am convinced that the biological approach will enable rapid progress in relating brain function to behaviour. It would be disappointing, though, to see a rupture with the past, as happened during the 1950s. This may not occur as long as the new movement sticks to the experimental rigour that characterized behavioural experimentation during the last decades. The problem could arise that the fascination with brain images leads to neglect of rigorous behavioural experimentation, which is crucial to render the pictures meaningful. There are many experimental studies in which the cognitive tradition of the last fifty years has been enriched rather than abandoned. I was pleased to read Posner's plea (see Chapter 15) for combinations of behavioural, electrical, and haemodynamic methods. This will not be easy, but is not impossible. Not surprisingly, I was also pleased with Dehaene's (1996) work on the AFM, showing converging evidence from brain and behavioural measures. Stages were laid out in separate brain areas, supporting a modular nature of information processing.

These new studies are hopeful signs of a gradual incorporation of the 'then' into the 'now'. Time will tell whether this will happen or whether 'then' will be abandoned in favour of a new 'now'. This latter move is not uncommon in science and may be useful so long as the antithesis, evoked by a paradigm shift, is eventually followed by a higher-order synthesis.

I end by expressing the hope that, in the course of events, psychologists will not be too fascinated by the new intellectual climate of Cognitive Neuroscience so as to continue neglecting human factors and leaving that field completely to engineers. The point is that I do not envisage combined fMRI–simulator research. Thus, the Soesterberg Institute has chosen to ignore Neuroscience and to concentrate solely on applicable behavioural research. That is where their money comes from. I am not convinced, therefore, by the term Neuroergonomics as a weak attempt to link human factors to the high tide of the biological revolution.

References

Allport, A. (1980). The state of cognitive psychology: a critical note of W. G. Chase: visual information processing. *Quarterly Journal of Experimental Psychology* 31: 141–52.

Berlyne, D. E. (1957). Uncertainty and conflict: a point of contact between information theory and behavior theory concepts. *Psychological Review* 64: 329–39.

Broadbent, D. E. (1958). *Perception and communication*. London: Pergamon.

Broadbent, D. E. (1971). *Decision and stress*. London: Academic Press.

Dehaene, S. (1996). The organisation of brain activations in number comparison: event-related potentials and the additive factors method. *Journal of Cognitive Neuroscience* 8: 47–68.

Donders, F. C. (1868). Over de snelheid van psychische processen. Onderzoekingen gedaan in het physiologisch laboratorium van de Utrechtse Hoogeschool. *Tweede Reeks* 11: 92–130.

Edwards, W. (1966). Optimal strategies for seeking information: models for statistics, choice reaction times and human information processing. *Journal of Mathematical Psychology* 2: 312–29.

Flach, J. M. (1990). The ecology of human–machine systems. I: Introduction. *Ecological Psychology* 2: 191–205.

Goldstein, K. (1938). *The organism*. New York: American Book Company.

Gopher, D. and Sanders, A. F. (1984). S-Oh-R: Oh stages! Oh resources! In: W. Prinz and A. F. Sanders (ed.) *Cognition and motor behavior*, pp. 231–254. Heidelberg: Springer.

Hull, C. L. (1943). *Principles of behavior.* New York: Appleton Century.

Kahneman, D. (1973). *Attention and effort.* Englewood Cliffs, NJ: Prentice Hall.

Kornblum, S. (1969). Sequential determinants of information processing in serial and discrete choice reaction time. *Psychological Review* 76: 13–131.

Külpe, O. (1905). *Outlines of psychology.* New York: Macmillan.

Lashley, K. S. (1929). *Brain mechanisms and intelligence.* Chicago: University of Chicago Press.

Luce, D. (1986). *Response times.* New York: Oxford University Press.

McClelland, J. L. (1979). On the time relations of mental processes: an examination of systems of processes in cascade. *Psychological Review* 86: 287–330.

Meyer, D., Osman, A. M., Irwin, D. E., and Yantis, S. (1988). The dynamics of cognition and action: mental processes inferred from speed-accuracy decomposition. *Psychological Review* 95: 183–257.

Miller, J. (1982). Discrete versus continuous stage models of human information processing: in search of partial output. *Journal of Experimental Psychology: Human Perception and Performance* 8: 273–96.

Miller, J. (1988). Discrete and continuous models of human information processing: theoretical distinctions and empirical results. *Acta Psychologica* 67: 191–257.

Miller, J. (1993). A queue-series model for reaction time with discrete stage and continuous flow models as special cases. *Psychological Review* 100: 702–15.

Moraal, J. and Poll, K. J. (1979). *De Links-Miles rijsimulator voor pantservoertuigen: verslag van een veldonderzoek.* IZF Report 1979–23. Soesterberg, Netherlands: TNO.

Moray, N. (ed.) (1979). *Mental workload: its theory and measurement.* New York: Plenum.

Navon, D. (1984). Resources: a theoretical soupstone. *Psychological Review* 91: 216–34.

Navon, D. and Gopher, D. (1979). On the economy of processing systems. *Psychological Review* 86: 214–55.

Neumann, O. (1987). Beyond capacity: a functional view of attention. In: H. Heuer and A. F. Sanders (ed.) *Perspectives on perception and action*, pp. 361–394. Hillsdale, NJ: Erlbaum.

Norman, D. A. and Bobrow, D. G. (1975). On data-limited and resource-limited processes. *Cognitive Psychology* 7: 44–64.

Posner, M. I. (1993). Interaction of arousal and selection in the posterior attention network. In: A. Baddeley and L. Weiskrantz (ed.) *Attention: selection, awareness and control. A tribute to Donald Broadbent*, pp. 390–405. Oxford: Clarendon Press.

Ratcliff, R. (1978). A theory of memory retrieval. *Psychological Review* 85: 59–108.

Ratcliff, R. (1988). Continuous versus discrete information processing: modelling accumulation of partial information. *Psychological Review* 95: 238–55.

Sanders, A. F. (ed.) (1967) Attention and Performance I. *Acta Psychologica* 27.

Sanders, A. F. (1980). Stage analysis of reaction processes. In: G. E. Stelmach and J. Requin (ed.) *Tutorials in motor behavior*, pp. 331–354. Amsterdam: North Holland.

Sanders, A. F. (1983). Towards a model of stress and human performance. *Acta Psychologica* 53: 61–97.

Sanders, A. F. (1984). Ten symposia on Attention and Performance: some issues and trends. In: H. Bouma and D. Bouwhuis (ed.) *Attention and Performance*, 10, 1–10. Hillsdale, NJ: Erlbaum.

Sanders, A. F. (1990). Issues and trends in the debate on discrete vs. continuous processing of information. *Acta Psychologica* 74: 1–45.

Sanders, A. F. (1991). Simulation as a tool in the measurement of human performance. *Ergonomics* 34: 995–1025.

Sanders, A. F. (1998). *Elements of human performance.* Mahwah, NJ: Erlbaum.

Schmidt, R. A. (1987). *Motor control and learning; a behavioral emphasis.* Champaign, IL: Human Kinetics.

Sheridan, T. B. (1987). Supervisory control. In: G. Salvendy (ed.) *Handbook of human factors*, pp. 1243–68. New York: Wiley.

Sternberg, S. (1969). The discovery of processing stages: extensions of Donders' method. *Acta Psychologica* 30: 276–315.

20

The perception of time

John Wearden

In this chapter, I will discuss what seem to me some highlights from the study of time perception, concentrating principally on developments since the 1960s, and mostly on ones that are much more recent. The reader unfamiliar with the field is warned that the material discussed here represents only a small sample of the potential research available and reflects my personal choices, and sometimes personal involvements. For example, an important distinction in contemporary timing research is that between *prospective* and *retrospective* timing. The former involves situations where people are alerted in advance that timing is important (e.g. 'Hold down this button for one second'). The latter involves situations where unexpected questions about time are asked (e.g. 'How much time has passed since you started reading this chapter?'). Most modern opinion regards these two types of timing as being distinct, with prospective timing involving some sort of internal timer, and retrospective time judgements being based on the quantity of something non-temporal (e.g. the amount of information processing, or 'contextual change') that has occurred during the time period judged. The vast majority of both classical and recent research has concentrated on prospective timing, and this area will be my sole concern here. For a discussion of some issues in retrospective timing, see Wearden (2005).

In successive sections I first provide some background to contemporary timing research by discussing a small amount of historical work, then proceed, successively, to sections on the rise of internal clock models in the 1960s and 1970s, the resurgence of research on human time perception in the 1990s, and work on the neural basis of timing, dating from the 1980s onwards, before a brief conclusion.

In the beginning: 1864–1960

The study of time perception, at least in its commonest form, that of the judgement of the duration of stimuli or events, has a long history. Lejeune and Wearden (submitted for publication) identified Höring (1864) as the first publication on the subject, and this was closely followed by the extraordinary book *Der Zeitsinn nach Versuchen* ('The Experimental Study of the Time-sense') by Höring's teacher, Vierordt, in 1868. In the later nineteenth century, interest in time perception was keen, with many studies focusing on the potential existence of an 'indifference point', a duration that was neither over- nor under-estimated, considered by some to be a basic psychological unit of time. Nichols (1891) and Woodrow (1930) reviewed much of this early research.

In spite of its venerability, the study of time perception since the nineteenth century has often teetered on the brink of virtual extinction, sometimes occupying only a tiny number of active workers. Before the 1960s, where the story of this chapter properly begins, notable highlights were the work of François and Hoagland on body temperature and time judgements (for a modern review see Wearden and Penton-Voak 1995), and the studies by Goldstone and colleagues on judgements of the duration of auditory and visual stimuli (see Wearden *et al.* 1998). A figure who deserves particular mention is Paul Fraisse, not only a specialist in time perception (see his magisterial book from 1964), but also probably France's best-known experimental psychologist in any domain for many years. His prestige helped to keep the fragile flame of time perception alive in French-speaking countries during periods when Anglophone psychologists had little or no interest in the subject.

An exception to the general neglect of time perception in the USA and UK was work on timing in animals, deriving mainly from research by Skinner (1938), which by the end of the 1950s had resulted in an enormous body of experimental results (for just some of them see Ferster and Skinner 1957). However, for reasons connected with the ideological basis of Skinnerian psychology, this work was divorced from the study of time perception itself (Lejeune *et al.* (2006) discuss the history of Skinnerian research in the timing field), and was not connected with it until much later, as will be seen below.

Internal clocks: 1960–1990

The idea that people and animals perform some sorts of time judgement by using an internal clock-like device, a sort of 'organ' for the perception of duration, can be traced back at least to the 1920s (Wearden and Penton-Voak 1995), but the years between 1960 and 1990 saw its principal flowering. In 1963, Michel Treisman produced what everyone would agree is a landmark in the development of internal clock theory. Treisman (p. 18) modestly writes that his model '*derives from suggestions which have been made before ... and attempts to put them together in not too arbitrary a fashion ...*', but in fact his model was so sophisticated and advanced for its time that it was only equalled, but perhaps not surpassed, by a rather similar proposal of Gibbon, Church, and Meck (1984), which still dominates many studies of time perception.

In Treisman's model, the raw material for time judgements comes from an arousal-sensitive pacemaker, which sends pulses to a counter. The pulses are assumed to be periodic. As well as the pacemaker and counter, the model also involves a store of 'reference' durations (e.g. temporal standards or other values needed for the timing task in hand), and a comparator mechanism. Comparison of values in the counter and the store determines behavioural output, or time judgements.

Treisman's model contains the basic mechanism of a pacemaker–accumulator clock, which was later used by Gibbon *et al.* (1984), but also shows that in order to generate any kind of timing judgements more than the basic clock mechanism is needed, with both some kind of store of reference times and, most importantly, some comparison mechanism also intervening to produce behaviour. Treisman's work thus situates a simple clock mechanism within the framework of a more complex cognitive system involving both memory (store) and decision (comparator) mechanisms.

An enduring mystery is why publication of Treisman's article failed to produce an immediate upsurge of interest in time perception. The work was published as a monograph supplement to *Journal of Experimental Psychology*, a premier outlet for experimental research, so was presumably highly visible, and, although the work had some mathematical aspects, it was not particularly obscure or difficult to understand, particularly by the standards of the psychophysics of the period. However, the neglect of Treisman's achievement began almost from the date of its first appearance. It was not referred to in Cohen's (1964) popularization of research on Time Psychology published in *Scientific American* just after the appearance of his article, nor was it referenced for further reading. On the other hand, Treisman's own account of his model in a 'popular science' publication (Treisman 1965) cited Cohen (1964), but this article did not appear to lead to widespread interest in Treisman's own work.

A model very similar to that of Treisman was developed by Gibbon and colleagues in 1984—their *scalar expectancy theory* (SET). This model also had a pacemaker–accumulator clock as its basis, as well as reference and working memory stores and decision processes. The main difference between the models lay in their application: Treisman was concerned to account for data from studies of time perception in humans (of which there was little that he could use), whereas Gibbon *et al.* were interested in explaining data from studies of animal timing, vast amounts of which had accumulated since the 1930s—see Lejeune *et al.* (2006) for a review of some early work by Skinner and others;

this article also discusses some competitors to SET in the domain of animal timing.

Animal psychology furnished innumerable experimental studies, usually with very orderly data, that could be used to evaluate Gibbon *et al.*'s model. In addition, a characteristic of SET-based research in the 1980s was a marked physiological flavour. A particular highlight is psychopharmacological research by Meck (1983, 1996), which used drug effects to dissociate the different parts of the SET system. For example, data suggested that the rate of the pacemaker of the clock was affected by dopamine levels ('ticking' faster when dopamine levels were higher), whereas the reference memory store (where animals stored 'important' times, such as those associated with reinforcement) was manipulable by changing acetylcholine levels. I shall return later to attempts to understand the neural basis of timing. Another feature of SET, and one that it shared with Treisman's original work, was a concern with exact quantitative modelling of data, using mathematical analyses or computer simulation.

Much research with animals established that their timing behaviour frequently conformed to the 'scalar properties' of time (for a review see Lejeune and Wearden 2006). The first scalar property is *mean accuracy*, the requirement that the internal 'estimate' of some real time, t, is on average exactly equal to t. The second is the *scalar property of variance*, the requirement that the standard deviation of time 'estimates' varies linearly with their mean, a form of Weber's Law. Lejeune and Wearden (2006) illustrate how these properties are measured in data from animals, and they also identify some situations in which the scalar properties are violated. Given the success of SET as an account of animal timing, it seemed only natural to attempt to apply this model to human time perception. Although the possibility of scalar (i.e. Weberian) timing in humans had been discussed much earlier (even in the nineteenth century), the application of ideas related to SET started only towards the end of the 1980s.

Human time perception: 1990–present

In 1988, Wearden and McShane published an article reporting data from humans who produced time intervals ranging from 0.5 to 1.3 s without counting. The behaviour obtained was in almost perfect accord with the two scalar properties of time: the mean time produced tracked the time requirement almost perfectly, and the standard deviation was an almost constant fraction (about 0.13) of the mean. This was followed in 1991 and 1992 by four articles (Allan and Gibbon 1991; Wearden 1991a,b, 1992) more explicitly employing the theoretical apparatus of SET (i.e. the clock, memory, and decision processes) to account for human performance on tasks of bisection and temporal generalization, both methods that are analogues of procedures previously used with animals (e.g. Church and DeLuty 1977; Church and Gibbon 1982). An advantage of these analogue methods is that they necessarily ask participants what seem to be very simple questions about time judgements. In bisection, people receive examples of 'short' and 'long' standards (e.g. tones 200 and 800 ms long, respectively) and then have to decide to which standard subsequently presented comparison durations are more similar. In temporal generalization, a single standard (e.g. a tone of 400 ms) is presented, and the participant must then judge whether subsequently presented comparisons are, or are not, the standard. These procedures can be used with slight variations to study timing in children, and data from both provide measures that can be used to evaluate conformity to the scalar properties of time (Wearden and Lejeune 2008).

Allan (1998) and Wearden (2003) provide general reviews of the application of SET to human time perception. Although constraints of space preclude me from entering into the details here, I will select what seem to me a few highlights of this work.

Firstly, the application of SET breathed new life into the old idea that humans possess a pacemaker–accumulator internal clock, and some studies have demonstrated that the putative pacemaker can be made to run faster (Penton-Voak et al. 1996; Treisman et al. 1990) or more slowly (Wearden 2008). Differential pacemaker speed has also been used as a potential explanation of the venerable auditory/visual differences in duration judgements ('tones are judged longer than lights'—Goldstone and Lhamon 1974; see Wearden et al. 1998), as well as the 'filled duration illusion', the finding that empty intervals (e.g. starting and ending with clicks) are judged as shorter than 'filled' ones (e.g. continuous tones) (see Wearden et al. 2007).

As well as the study of internal clock processes, the success of SET has stimulated research on the roles of memory and decision processes in timing (e.g. Jones and Wearden 2003, 2004; Wearden and Grindrod 2003) and, in general, has encouraged the view that a full explanation of timing behaviour requires the internal clock mechanism to be situated in a more elaborate cognitive structure, involving attention, memory, and decisions (e.g. Wearden 2004); this is basically an elaboration of the position taken by Treisman in 1963.

The quantitative modelling often associated with SET's explanation of animal performance also translated into studies with humans, and has led to the development of models of performance on many different timing tasks (e.g. Wearden 1992, 1995; for a review see Wearden 2004). These models enable us to decompose performance into its underlying psychological components, so permitting differences between groups and conditions to be attributed with some confidence to differences in underlying mechanisms, and this has been exploited in another important development, the study of timing in different participant populations.

Perhaps the clearest progress in this area has come from studies comparing children of different ages, and adults, also sometimes of different ages. Droit-Volet (2003a) reviewed much of this work and illustrated how the use of SET enables researchers to draw stronger conclusions than just that younger children are poorer at timing than older children and adults. For example, several studies have shown that, rather than children having fundamentally different decision processes from adults, the variability of time representations decreases with age. In addition, some work suggests that the youngest children may systematically misremember standard durations as being shorter than they are (see Droit-Volet *et al.* 2001; McCormack *et al.* 1999), but that this tendency disappears from about 8 years of age. In addition, other work has implicated difficulties in paying attention to the timing task in younger children as being an important determinant of their performance (e.g. Droit-Volet 2003b; Droit-Volet and Wearden 2001).

At the other end of the developmental scale, some studies have used ideas from SET, or similar ones, to account for data from older adults (e.g. McCormack *et al.* 1999; Wearden *et al.* 1997). In Wearden *et al.*'s (1997) study, for example, modelling based on the principles of SET revealed that, at least in some cases, the variability of time representations increased systematically with increasing age and decreasing IQ. In general, however, effects of ageing on prospective timing are rather small, with older people generally exhibiting the same pattern of behaviour as younger ones, albeit with more performance variability. The common complaint of older persons that 'time seems to pass more quickly' with increasing age is difficult to explain simply in terms of the processes used to account for prospective timing, and the understanding of this 'distortion' of subjective time seems to need some alternative explanation, as well as novel sorts of research (Wearden 2005).

Time and the brain: 1990–present

Concern for the neural basis of time perception is not new, and speculation about brain mechanisms that subserve timing processes can be found as early as Hoagland (1933). Research in the early 1980s with animals, conducted mostly by Meck and colleagues, gave renewed impetus to the search for the physiological basis of timing mechanisms (e.g. Meck 1983). Compared with researchers seeking the physiological basis of auditory and visual perception, those interested in time perception are disadvantaged by the absence of an 'organ' that provides the obvious starting point of the perceptual process both psychologically and, perhaps more importantly, neurophysiologically, thus allowing connections to be traced from the external organ to the brain, and permitting good first guesses as to the brain areas involved in the process. One reaction to this difficulty was to take the clock-memory-decision structure of SET literally and to try to map this on to brain structures.

Meck (1996) discusses an attempt to do this, with the *substantia nigra pars compacta* providing dopaminergically sensitive pacemaker neurones, whose output was collected by regions of the basal ganglia, with other areas of the brain providing memory and decision mechanisms. Although this attempt to 'physiologize' SET accounted for much data, more recent research has taken different directions, largely because of the alleged physiological implausibility of the pacemaker–accumulator mechanism that is the basis of SET (e.g. Matell and Meck 2004).

Interest in the neurological basis of time perception has produced a considerable increase of activity in the time perception field but, unfortunately, a simple summary of definite progress remains difficult to provide at the time of writing. However, a single article that summarizes some of the main ideas is that of Buhusi and Meck (2005). Some studies have used scanning techniques to identify the brain areas that appear to be involved in timing, but an obvious problem, alas without any obvious solution, is what control conditions should be used. For example, if certain brain areas are activated during a timing task, do these relate to timing *per se*, or to memory and decision processes that might be common to judgements of other types of stimuli? Various control procedures, of different degrees of subtlety and ingenuity, have been proposed (e.g. Macar *et al.* 2004; Nenadic *et al.* 2003), and it is true that certain brain regions (e.g. parts of the basal ganglia, the supplementary motor area of the cortex) appear as 'usual suspects' in many, but not all, timing tasks. However, the function of these activated areas is unclear, and some work using scanning or electrophysiological measures appears little more than a reaffirmation of materialism, the idea that brain processes underlie psychological processes, in some way that is currently difficult to specify.

Other studies have looked at timing in patients with various sorts of brain damage or brain degeneration, such as people with Parkinson's disease. Here, performance differences between patients and controls are sometimes (Harrington *et al.* 1998), although not always (Spencer and Ivry 2005), found, but even when between-group differences appear marked, as in Malapani *et al.* (1998), it is not always clear how they can be explained. Obviously a persistent problem when comparing patient groups with controls is that any difference in performance on timing tasks may be due to differences in factors other than those relating to time perception *per se*, such as memory and attentional changes, or differences in motor performance.

An important theoretical shift linked to neuroscience-based considerations has been the general abandonment of the pacemaker–accumulator clock as a basic mechanism of timing, in spite of the fact that psychological models embodying such a process make many novel and accurate predictions about behaviour (e.g. see Wearden and Jones 2007), and its replacement either by nothing definite (i.e. research without any quantitative theoretical modelling, or any theoretical basis at all) or by some sort of oscillator-based process. Once again, constraints of space preclude discussion of the details of this sort of model, but the general idea is that the representation of time intervals is accomplished not by the accumulation of 'ticks' from a pacemaker, but in terms of vectors of oscillator states (Church and Broadbent 1990), or 'coincidences' of oscillator firing patterns (e.g. Matell and Meck 2004). Such models enable the timing of durations that are very long compared with the rate of firing of neurones (with periods of milliseconds), and avoid the problem of 'unbounded accumulation', that is, the problem of how the timing of long intervals (in animal experiments sometimes many minutes long) can be accomplished by neurone-like units that fire thousands of times in the interval to be judged.

Oscillator-based models essentially represent different durations by different patterns of neural activity, not by more neural activity for longer durations (as in an accumulator process), and this qualitative representation can cause problems (e.g. see Wearden and Doherty, 1995, for a discussion of the Church–Broadbent model). For example, two time intervals that are very different in real time may have very similar pattern representations, and the model may have no way, without 'add-ons' that specifically perform the function, of producing ordinal judgements (i.e. deciding whether one duration is longer or shorter than another as opposed to just different from it), although such judgements appear very easy for people to make, perhaps even easier than judgements of the equality of two event durations.

In general, then, research on the neural basis of timing has not yet uncovered the mechanism by which duration judgements are generated, in spite of considerable, and expensive, experimental effort and theoretical speculation.

Concluding remarks

This chapter is intended to give the reader a brief overview of what seem to its author the most interesting developments in the study of time perception since the 1960s. As mentioned above, the choice of topics is a personal one, but I hope that researchers in the field would agree that at least some of the most important trends have been discussed here. Work on the experimental study of time perception in humans has made significant progress since the 1980s, with the possibility of the development of comprehensive quantitative models, based on SET and developments thereof, which may account not only for performance on standard timing tasks, but also for differences between different participant populations, as well as providing a bridge between modern theory and classical findings known since the nineteenth century (Wearden and Lejeune 2008). What the neural mechanisms of time perception are remains, at the time of writing, a very open question, with data suggesting the involvement of many areas of the brain, whose exact function in the timing process is currently unknown. However, in spite of many outstanding problems, the last 20 or 30 years have probably seen more progress in our understanding of time perception than in the previous 100, and the properties of what the early German experimenters called *Der Zeitsinn*, have been explored more extensively than the pioneers of the subject, such as Vierordt, could probably ever have imagined.

References

Allan, L. G. (1998). The influence of the scalar timing model on human timing research. *Behavioural Processes* 44: 101–17.

Allan, L. G. and Gibbon, J. (1991). Human bisection at the geometric mean. *Learning and Motivation* 22: 39–58.

Buhusi, C. V. and Meck, W. H. (2005). What makes us tick? Functional and neural mechanisms of interval timing. *Nature Neuroscience* 6: 755–65.

Church, R. M. and Broadbent, H. (1990). Alternative representations of time, number, and rate. *Cognition* 37: 55–81.

Church, R. M. and DeLuty, M. Z. (1977). Bisection of temporal intervals. *Journal of Experimental Psychology: Animal Behavior Processes* 3: 216–28.

Church, R. M. and Gibbon, J. (1982). Temporal generalization. *Journal of the Experimental Analysis of Behavior: Animal Behavior Processes* 8: 165–86.

Cohen, J. (1964). Psychological time. *Scientific American* 211: 116–224.

Droit-Volet, S. (2003a). Temporal experience and timing in children. In: W. Meck (ed.) *Functional and neural mechanisms of interval timing*, pp. 183–208. Washington, DC: CRC Press.

Droit-Volet, S. (2003b). Alerting attention and time perception in children. *Journal of Experimental Child Psychology* 85: 372–84.

Droit-Volet, S. and Wearden, J. H. (2001). Temporal bisection in children. *Journal of Experimental Child Psychology* 80: 142–59.

Droit-Volet, S., Clément, A., and Wearden, J. H. (2001). Temporal generalization in 3- to 8-year-old children. *Journal of Experimental Child Psychology* 80: 271–88.

Ferster, C. B. and Skinner, B. F. (1957). *Schedules of reinforcement.* New York: Appleton Century Crofts.

Fraisse, P. (1964). *The psychology of time.* London: Eyre and Spottiswoode.

Gibbon, J., Church, R. M., and Meck, W. H. (1984). Scalar timing in memory. *Annals of the New York Academy of Sciences* 423: 52–77.

Goldstone, S. and Lhamon, W. T. (1974). Studies of auditory–visual differences in human time judgment: 1. Sounds are judged longer than lights. *Perceptual and Motor Skills* 39: 63–82.

Harrington, D. L., Haaland, K. Y., and Hermanowicz, D. L. (1998). Temporal processing in the basal ganglia. *Neuropsychology* 23: 3–12.

Hoagland, H. (1933). The physiological control of judgements of duration: evidence for a chemical clock. *Journal of General Psychology* 9: 267–87.

Höring, A. (1864). *Versuche über das Unterscheidungsvermögen des Hörsinnes für die Zeitgrössen.* Dissertation, Tübingen University.

Ivry, R. B. and Spencer, R. M. C. (2004). The neural representation of time. *Current Opinion in Neurobiology* 14: 225–32.

Jones, L. A. and Wearden, J. H. (2003). More is not necessarily better: examining the nature of the temporal reference memory component in timing. *Quarterly Journal of Experimental Psychology* 56: 321–43.

Jones, L. A. and Wearden, J. H. (2004). Double standards: memory loading in temporal reference memory. *Quarterly Journal of Experimental Psychology* 57B: 55–77.

Lejeune, H. and Wearden, J. H. (2006). Scalar properties in animal timing: conformity and violations. *Quarterly Journal of Experimental Psychology* 59: 1875–908.

Lejeune, H. and Wearden, J. H. (submitted). The beginnings of Time Psychology: Vierordt's 'The Experimental Study of the Time Sense'. *European Journal of Cognitive Psychology*

Lejeune, H., Richelle, M., and Wearden, J. H. (2006). About Skinner and time: behavior-analytic contributions to research on animal timing. *Journal of the Experimental Analysis of Behavior* 85: 125–42.

McCormack, T., Brown, G. D. A., Maylor, E. A., Darby, A., and Green, D. (1999). Developmental changes in time estimation: comparing childhood and old age. *Developmental Psychology* 35: 1143–55.

Macar, F., Anton, J.-L., Bonnet, M., and Vidal, F. (2004). Timing functions of the supplementary motor area: an event-related fMRI study. *Cognitive Brain Research* 21: 206–15.

Malapani, C., Rakitin, B., Meck, W. H., Deweer, B., Dubois, B., and Gibbon, J. (1998). Coupled temporal memories in Parkinson's disease: a dopamine-related dysfunction. *Journal of Cognitive Neuroscience* 10: 316–31.

Matell, M. S. and Meck, W. H. (2004). Cortico-striatal circuits and interval timing: coincidence detection of oscillatory processes. *Cognitive Brain Research* 21: 139–70.

Meck, W. H. (1983). Selective adjustment of the speed of internal clock and memory processes. *Journal of Experimental Psychology: Animal Behavior Processes* 9: 171–201.

Meck, W. H. (1996). Neuropharmacology of timing and time perception. *Cognitive Brain Research* 3: 227–42.

Nenadic, I., Glaser, C., Volz, H.-P., Rammsayer, T., Hager, F., and Sauer, H. (2003). Processing of temporal information and the basal ganglia: new evidence from fMRI. *Experimental Brain Research* 148: 238–46.

Nichols, H. (1891). The psychology of time. *American Journal of Psychology* 3: 453–529.

Penton-Voak, E. P., Edwards, H., Percival, A., and Wearden, J. H. (1996). Speeding up an internal clock in humans? Effects of click trains on subjective duration. *Journal of Experimental Psychology: Animal Behavior Processes* 22: 307–20.

Skinner, B. F. (1938). *The behavior of organisms: an experimental analysis.* New York: Appleton Century Crofts.

Spencer, R. M. C. and Ivry, R. B. (2005). Comparison of patients with Parkinson's disease or cerebellar lesions in the production of periodic movements involving event-based or emergent timing. *Brain and Cognition* 58: 84–93.

Treisman, M. (1963). Temporal discrimination and the indifference interval: implications for a model of the 'internal clock'. *Psychological Monographs* 77 [whole issue 576].

Treisman, M. (1965). The psychology of time. *Discovery* October 1965.

Treisman, M., Faulkner, A., Naish, P. L. N., and Brogan, D. (1990). The internal clock: evidence for a temporal oscillator underlying time perception with some estimates of its characteristic frequency. *Perception* 19: 705–48.

Vierordt, K. (1868). *Der Zeitsinn nach Versuchen.* Tübingen: Laupp.

Wearden, J. H. (1991a). Do humans possess an internal clock with scalar timing properties? *Learning and Motivation* 22: 59–83.

Wearden, J. H. (1991b). Human performance on an analogue of an interval bisection task. *Quarterly Journal of Experimental Psychology* 43B: 59–81.

Wearden, J. H. (1992). Temporal generalization in humans. *Journal of Experimental Psychology: Animal Behavior Processes* 18: 134–44.

Wearden, J. H. (1995). Categorical scaling of stimulus duration by humans. *Journal of Experimental Psychology: Animal Behavior Processes* 21: 318–30.

Wearden, J. H. (2003). Applying the scalar timing model to human time psychology: progress and challenges. In: H. Helfrich (ed.) *Time and mind II: information-processing perspectives,* pp. 21–39. Gottingen: Hogrefe & Huber.

Wearden, J. H. (2004). Decision processes in models of timing. *Acta Neurobiologiae Experimentalis* 64: 303–17.

Wearden, J. H. (2005). The wrong tree: time perception and time experience in the elderly. In: J. Duncan, L. Phillips, and P. McLeod (ed.) *Measuring the mind: speed, age, and control,* pp. 137–58. Oxford: Oxford University Press.

Wearden, J. H. (2008). Slowing down an internal clock: Implications for accounts of performance on four timing tasks. *Quarterly Journal of Experimental Psychology* 61: 263–74.

Wearden, J. H. and Doherty, M. F. (1995). Exploring and developing a connectionist model of animal timing: peak procedure and fixed-interval simulations. *Journal of Experimental Psychology: Animal Behavior Processes* 21: 99–115.

Wearden, J. H. and Grindrod, R. (2003). Manipulating decision processes in the human scalar timing system. *Behavioural Processes* 61: 47–56.

Wearden, J. H. and Jones, L. A. (2007). Is the growth of subjective time in humans a linear or nonlinear function of real time? *Quarterly Journal of Experimental Psychology* 60: 1289–302.

Wearden, J. H. and Lejeune, H. (2008). Scalar properties in human timing: conformity and violations. *Quarterly Journal of Experimental Psychology* 61: 569–587.

Wearden, J. H. and Penton-Voak, I. S. (1995). Feeling the heat: body temperature and the rate of subjective time, revisited. *Quarterly Journal of Experimental Psychology* 48B: 129–41.

Wearden, J. H., Wearden, A. J., and Rabbitt, P. (1997). Age and IQ effects on stimulus and response timing. *Journal of Experimental Psychology: Human Perception and Performance* 23: 962–79.

Wearden, J. H., Edwards, H., Fakhri, M., and Percival, A. (1998). Why 'sounds are judged longer than lights': application of a model of the internal clock in humans. *Quarterly Journal of Experimental Psychology* 51B: 97–120.

Wearden, J. H., Norton, R., Martin, S., and Montford-Bebb, O. (2007). Internal clock processes and the filled-duration illusion. *Journal of Experimental Psychology: Human Perception and Performance* 33: 716–29.

Woodrow, H. (1930). The reproduction of temporal intervals. *Journal of Experimental Psychology* 13: 473–99.

21

From effects to systems in neuropsychology

Lawrence Weiskrantz

Tracing changes is a complex matter—analysis of behavioural change is difficult enough, let alone conceptual change. Neuropsychology today is in many ways strikingly different from when I entered the field, but in other ways (at least for the visual system) many of the issues are not all that different from the days of William James or David Ferrier or Luigi Luciani or Hermann Munk. My entrée into neuropsychology was in some ways an accident. I started my undergraduate studies at Swarthmore College as a Physics major, but was drafted into the army in my third year, in 1944. When I returned from overseas service, and bolstered by the 'GI Bill' (which covered tuition and other fees of veterans), I thought a broader education would be welcome and actually possible. Swarthmore at the time had a very strong and interesting psychology department—Wolfgang Köhler, Solomon Asch, David Krech, Hans Wallach, among others—and I had a roommate, Mike, who was a son of Max Wertheimer and whose sister, Lise, was also a student there. I became a family friend of both of them. And so, after some dithering, I started afresh and decided to read Psychology, but, given the history of the war and other horrors, such as the Holocaust and the widespread racial prejudice, I thought Social Psychology would be the most useful and challenging. For graduate work (after a gratuitous MSc stint at Oxford) I took the tough road for my PhD to the Department of Experimental Psychology at Harvard, because I wanted to get a solid base in experimental method before going to the socially complex domain.

The career accident occurred when I was suddenly invited to teach a course in physiological psychology at Tufts University. Their lecturer had become ill and they appealed to the Harvard Department for an instant replacement for a course already in progress. As I had taken that course at Harvard, they recommended me. I managed to stay ahead of the class by a page or two of Morgan's textbook, but became deeply engrossed in the subject and never looked back. My PhD with Karl Pribram and collaborations with him and colleagues, especially Mort Mishkin, more or less sealed the matter. My translation to the UK came when, out of the blue, a post-doctoral fellowship was awarded me by the US National Academy—I had not applied for it, and had not even known of its existence. I choose to go to Oxford for a year to learn about silver staining, a difficult but important method then in neuronal tracing, with Paul Glees in the Oxford Physiology Department. From there, various unanticipated invitations and appointments arose.

My PhD thesis was typical of what neuropsychologists (except that then we were called physiological psychologists) would do at that time. It was *the study of an effect*. In my case it was the effect of a lesion of the amygdala in the monkey and, a bit later, the effects of occipital, inferotemporal, and frontal lesions, in both monkeys and people. Effects were surprising and eventful stuff back then. Karl Lashley was the dominant figure in the field, and his theories of mass action and equipotentiality were much to the fore. He allowed some specialization in the brain for sensory-receiving and motor areas, but the rest was a non-specialized conglomerate in which the size of the lesion was all that mattered. As it happens, I attended his graduate seminar courses at Harvard, and it was hard not to be overwhelmed by his incredible erudition and charisma—was there nothing he did not know!—and not to be floored by the sheer mass of his weekly reading assignments. This lanky, ectomophic figure clearly did not like his trips to the North from Orange Park in Florida; he appeared in the department in Memorial Hall buried in a heavy fur-lined coat, emitting dark and persistently clinging smoke from an obscure brand of Turkish cigarette. It is a bit ironic that the evidence from the Pribram Lab, perhaps more than any other, first put the nail in his theoretical coffin—ironic because Pribram was an admirer and had been influenced deeply by Lashley. Pribram had been practising as a clinical neurosurgeon and recounted his surprise to learn that Lashley was still alive, and so went to Orange Park to work with him. Lashley had tried to localize the memory trace, but had failed, and suggested memory was subserved by the mass of cortical tissue that was not specialized for sensory or motor function. But it was discovered by Pribram and Mishkin, amongst other things, that lesions of the inferotemporal cortex in the monkey would interfere specifically with visual learning and memory, and with nothing else, and that parietal lesions would similarly effect tactile tasks. I happened to be in the lab when Lashley visited it and was told about the inferotemporal lesion evidence, which he suggested—a bit weakly—might just be a diminution of visual attention. Lashley was a great man; he was wrong about some important theoretical issues, but he was gloriously wrong in the sense that he was one of the first to tell us how and what to find out, and he was an unforgettable teacher.

Later, from several labs, the evidence for specific lesion effects mounted—it emerged that hippocampal lesions would have a devastating effect on what later became called episodic memory, and that frontal lobe lesions would interfere with short-term memory, or what later became called working memory, basal ganglion lesions on motor skills, etc. 'Raw' effects were turning up both in the animal work and in the human clinic. Indeed, in the clinic the effects were used as diagnostic tools—for example, visual prototype deficits point to parietal lobe lesions, memory problems to medial temporal lobe lesions, and so forth. This was before the days of good CT scanning or ERP recordings and long before the days of MRI, and the neuropsychological evidence was clinically valuable. But no line of historical demarcation can be absolute. Even in those early days of 'effect studies' there was talk of the 'Papez Circuit' for the control of emotion.

Given the robustness of the evidence for specific lesion *effects*, questions of interpretation and inferences came to the fore. It was widely agreed that the function being interfered with by a lesion was not simply its complementary. As Richard Gregory pointed out forcefully, a transistor that made a radio squeak when removed was not simply inhibiting a squeak function. On the other hand, when double dissociation was obtained (if task A but not task B was affected by lesion I, and task B but not task A was affected by lesion II) reasonable grounds were available for an inference of the two underlying systems being independent. Closer argument led to the conclusion that double dissociation of lesion effects was a necessary but not a sufficient basis for inferences of independence.

But the study of effects became even more interesting when they turned out to be incomplete. For example, it emerged that patients with devastating memory deficits, associated with hippocampal damage or the severe alcoholic toxic effects in Korsakoff's disease, could actually show good storage and retention of material when tested with priming or other methods, although they insisted that they could not remember anything about the material (or the investigator, for that matter). From this came the birth of implicit memory. Lesions of the occipital lobe in the monkey turned out to be less devastating than was thought possible given the apparent blindness that ensued, and in human patients the residual visual function and capability became known as blindsight. Similar phenomena were turning up across the whole spectrum of neuropsychological effects: aphasic patients could show both semantic and syntactic processing, neglect patients could respond to events in their left fields, prosopagnosic patients could show autonomic effects to familiar faces, and so forth (Weiskrantz, 1997). In all cases, the residual function occurred without the awareness by the patients (Weiskrantz, 1991), who hence became candidates for the study of neural bases of conscious awareness. Of course, as with all counterintuitive phenomena, a host of counter-suggestions were advanced, for example that the 'implicit' or 'unconscious' phenomena were merely weaker versions of the explicit or conscious, qualitatively unchanged. Or that subjects' criteria, in signal detection terms, had become more conservative or, in the case of blindsight, that the cortical lesions in the clinical cases were patchy and incompletely, or that there was stray light sneaking into the intact visual field from the hemi-anopically blind one. After much work, the implicit phenomena remain intact. Meanwhile, the study of similar effects in animals has opened up, with evidence, for example, of blindsight in monkeys and also in the construction of tasks that reflect an explicit memory system.

Effects are still being pursued, for instance in the use of transcranial magnetic stimulation (TMS) to attempt to simulate the effects of cortical damage but in a reversible manner (anticipated many years earlier by demonstrations that pulsed electrical stimulation of the frontal cortex could reliably and reveribly simulate the effects of lesions on delayed response tasks (Weiskrantz et al., 1960)), and anodal changes in resting cortical potential could reversibly simulate the effect of visual cortical lesions (Ward and Weiskrantz, 1969), and, of course, in the domain of psychopharmacology where treatments with transmitters are used to counter known effects of specific brain damage, as in Parkinson's disease. But the 'raw' spectrum of effects of early neuropsychology is now more or less complete, at least for the cerebral cortex, and treatment effects such as TMS are now cast in a specific search for an answer to specific experimental questions, such as whether stimulating a particular region before or after stimulation of another region can throw light on a processing sequence. There remains, of course, a whole host of effects to be pursued for subcortical loci that are opening up with the study of deep brain stimulation in the treatment of clinical conditions, the pathology of which is rooted in deeper structures. (William James had speculated whether the consciousness of the 'lower optical centres' could mix with that which accompanies cortical activity—perhaps we may be able to make a start on that question.) But today the major focus has turned to the study of systems.

There are many reasons for the shift. Firstly, the brain imaging methodology more or less imposes an interest in activity in and across several loci. Secondly, the results of original study of effects themselves stimulate analysis in terms of systems. For example, blindsight evidence highlights the importance of parallel visual pathways for visual processing, especially the midbrain extra-striate pathways. Similarly, effects of occipital damage yielded a strong interest in an early version of 'two visual systems'. The effects of parietal versus temporal lobe damage, together with the study of agnosia, led to the contrast between the dorsal versus ventral visual systems. Multiple memory systems have emerged from the study of dissociable memory deficits, raising questions, for example, of whether there is a frontal system that is important for working memory, the hippocampus and adjoining structures for explicit memory. Thirdly, the cognitive horizons themselves have expanded, and box-and-arrow conceptual diagrams in information-processing terms coincided with the onset of the study of lesion effects. The evidence from neuropsychological cases could directly affect the validity of such diagrams; for example, it could not be that short-term memory flowed into long-term memory in a serial fashion, because they could be doubly dissociated neuropsychologically.

I would have been bold, when I started my career more than 50 years ago, to admit to an interest in the neurology of conscious awareness. Indeed, when during my MSc stint as a graduate student in Oxford, Oliver Zangwill submitted a paper for me to the *Quarterly Journal of Experimental Psychology* (in my name—perhaps he was the bold one, not I) reporting surprising visual after-effects of fixation of 'imaginary' visual stimuli, the Journal's editor called me aside a few weeks later and reported that, as Zangwill liked the paper, he would of course accept it, but somewhat archly recommended that I should think carefully about my future career. (I asked him to publish and he did, in 1950.) Not only the study of implicit processing in neuropsychology, but also the interests of philosophers, physicists, neurologists, cognitive psychologists, and others in a possible scientific basis for consciousness, have made an active entrée into the domain of systems analysis and discussion. The effect of graduation from effects to systems is exciting because completely new frontiers and methods are emerging, ever in flux. The challenges are much greater than the reporting of effects, as great as these were, because we now have an infinite number of degrees of freedom, and we are still not at the stage of theorizing such that imaging results can be crucial for disconfirmation. But the empirical advances have been stimulating; it has become possible, for example, in blind-sight cases to conduct fMRI measurements of the brain structures that are active when the subjects are visually aware; these can be contrasted directly, and with performance matched, with those that are active when they report no awareness (Sahraie *et al.* 1997). Knowledge of the structures that are implicated for explicit versus implicit domains, combined with increasing knowledge of the anatomical network within which they are enmeshed, holds promise for advancing both the neural and the theoretical basis of classical issues that once were thought to be intractable to scientific enquiry.

References

Sahraie, A., Weiskrantz, L., Barbur, J. L., Simmons, A., Williams, S. C. R., Brammer. M. J. (1997). Pattern of neuronal activity associated with conscious and unconscious processing of visual signals. *Proc. Natl. Acad. Sci. USA* 94: 9406–9411.

Ward, R. and Weiskrantz, L. (1969). Impaired discrimination following polarisation of the striate cortex. *Expt. Brain Res.* 9: 346–356.

Weiskrantz, L., Mihailovic, L., and Gross, C.G. (1960). Stimulation of frontal cortex and delayed alternation performance in the monkey. *Science* 131: 1143–1444.

Weiskrantz, L. (1991). Disconnected awareness for detecting, processing, and remembering in neurological patients. The Hughlings Jackson Lecture. *J. Roy. Soc. Med.*, 84: 466–470.

Weiskrantz, L. (1997). *Consciousness lost and found*. A neuropsychological exploration. Oxford: Oxford University Press.

22

Experimental psychopathology and psychological treatment

J. Mark G. Williams

The behaviour therapy revolution

Since the first emergence of psychology as an experimental science in the late nineteenth and early twentieth century, its application to psychological disorders had been a prominent goal (McDougall 1944). The story is complex, and only some of its themes can be explored here, but it is convenient to take as a starting point two major developments that took place during the 1950s: the publication of Eysenck's (1952) review of the efficacy of psychological treatment and Wolpe's (1958) book on the use of systematic desensitization in psychotherapy.

Seen in context, these were revolutionary developments. Earlier in the century, psychological understanding and treatment of psychological problems had been dominated by psychoanalysis and its theory that neuroses arose from unconscious conflicts. This was despite the fact that a great deal of laboratory work had been done on fear conditioning and extinction, building on Pavlov's seminal work on classical conditioning and Skinner's work on operant conditioning. In particular, there had been a number of experimental demonstrations of Pavlovian fear conditioning in humans, for example the famous case of Little Albert, whose relationship with harmless white rats was severely disrupted by the pairing of exposure to such a rat with a loud and startling noise. The implications seemed clear enough: neurotic (fearful) behaviour is caused by conditioned reflexes. Neutral stimuli that just happen to be present at the time (the bell in Pavlov's original experiment, the white rat in Watson's experiment) become 'conditioned stimuli' through contiguity. Anxiety was seen as a learned response, occurring in reaction to signals that predict (i.e. have in the past been followed by) injury or pain (unconditioned stimuli). The resultant fear acts effectively as a motivator of behaviour: any behaviour that brings about a state of relief, safety, or security (reduction of fear) will be strengthened (Mowrer 1939). Yet, despite these advances,

most 'application' to clinical problems consisted of studies of verbal conditioning and the re-statement of dynamic principles and paradigms in learning
theory terminology (Dollard and Miller 1950). Such mapping between an old
and a new field had little impact on clinical practice.

So why the change in the 1950s? The first reason was the blistering attack on
the prevailing psychodynamic orthodoxy, both theory and practice,
by Eysenck (1952). He pointed out that there was no evidence that psychodynamic treatments produced outcomes that were any better than spontaneous
remission. Eysenck pointed, by contrast, to early outcome studies of behaviour
therapy that showed a large percentage of patients had sustained improvement—a larger proportion than those who would have improved spontaneously. He argued that, in as much as the dynamic formulations were
testable, they were wrong—but mostly their formulations were untestable.
Eysenck's attack on current clinical practice had far-reaching effects. It put *evidence of efficacy* as the central tenet of what the field of psychotherapy should
be concerned with, an approach that now seems wholly justified in the light of
the subsequent success of behavioural and cognitive therapies (Roth and
Fonagy 2004).

The 1950s had thus already seen an increased interest in the use of behaviour therapy when, in 1958, Stanford University Press published *Psychotherapy
by Reciprocal Inhibition* by Joseph Wolpe. Experiments on cats had shown
that conditioned fear of certain locations could be gradually overcome by
feeding them closer and closer to the original location (eating being incompatible with fear—hence 'reciprocal inhibition'). Wolpe suggested that
fear conditioning in humans could be similarly counter-conditioned through
reciprocal inhibition and, furthermore, that such reciprocal inhibition was
the main basis of psychotherapy's effects. In humans with fears and
phobias, imagination of gradually more fearful phobic objects or situations
under conditions of an incompatible state (deep muscle relaxation) would
lead to large reduction in the symptoms of fear. Wolpe's results showed
that the majority of patients responded very well to this approach, and the
popularity of experimentally based behavioural work gained ground with
dramatic speed.

By the end of the 1960s many empirical studies showed compelling evidence
for the efficacy of behaviour therapy (Rachman 1971). An example is the
successful treatment of the severe and intractable problem of obsessional-
compulsive neurosis using exposure (Hodgson *et al.* 1972), an approach
derived specifically from response prevention theories in animals. The dominance of behaviour therapy in the field of clinical psychiatry and psychology
seemed complete.

Meanwhile, however, it was becoming clear that not all the components that were thought essential for behaviour therapy to work were either necessary or sufficient. Rachman (1977) cited six factors that showed the conditioning theory of fear acquisition to be incomplete. (1) Many people fail to acquire fears in what are undoubtedly fear-evoking situations (e.g. air raids). (2) It is often difficult to produce conditioned fear reactions in humans, even under controlled laboratory conditions (Hallam and Rachman 1976). (3) Not everything is as easy to condition to an unpleasant unconditioned stimulus as everything else, so the equipotentiality premise is clearly untenable (Seligman and Hager 1972). Rachman was able to cite some old and some new experiments. First, Valentine (1946) had succeeded in producing a fear of a caterpillar in an 8-year-old child, but failed to make her fear a pair of opera glasses. More recently Ohman and colleagues (1975) had carried out fear conditioning experiments and had found it easy to establish pictures of snakes as conditioned stimuli, but not pictures of houses. Consistent with these laboratory findings (4) the distribution of fears in normal and neurotic populations is difficult to reconcile with the conditioning theory; epidemiological studies find more fear of spiders and snakes that fear of dentists in Western populations, for whom exposure to pain in the dental clinic was far more prevalent than pain associated with meeting spiders and snakes. (5) The clinical reports of phobic patients do not report large traumatic events at the origin of their phobia. (6) Fears can be reduced by vicarious and cognitive processes, so it seemed likely that they might be acquired by similar processes of modelling and by simple verbal instruction or warning.

Cognitive processes in anxiety disorders

This reference to cognitive influence in the origin and reduction of fear picked up a growing theme in the anxiety literature (Mathews 1990). Meichenbaum, Gilmore, and Fedoravicius (1971) had shown that speech anxiety could be reduced by getting participants to make explicit their 'self-talk', without exposing participants to the feared situation. Yet, despite the growing doubts about the sufficiency of older fear conditioning models, the clear demonstrations that a cognitive approach to anxiety might improve outcomes beyond those achieved by behaviour therapy did not happen until the 1980s when, influenced by Beck's cognitive approach to depression (see below), a number of young experimental psychopathology researchers began to look at hitherto intractable psychological fear responses and to use the cognitive approach in their analysis of what maintained the disorder and what, therefore, might alleviate it.

Prominent among these was David M. Clark. He had noticed that one of his patients with panic disorder was hyperventilating, and hypothesized that such hyperventilation would, through its physiological effects, including a decrease in carbon dioxide in the blood, be responsible for some of the cardinal panic symptoms such as dizziness and faintness. Clark tried hyperventilating himself and noticed many of the symptoms that his panic patients reported. However, he did not have a panic attack. Why not? He reasoned that it was not the dizziness itself that was important but the catastrophic *interpretations* that patients made of these symptoms which produced the belief that something physically catastrophic was about to happen, such as a stroke or heart attack. This cognitive theory of panic disorders (Clark 1986) became a hugely influential model. It led to therapies in which patients were actively encouraged to reproduce the symptoms in the clinic as a way of testing the extent to which these indicated serious physical illness or merely the misinterpretation of innocuous body sensations.

However, Clark and his colleague, Paul Salkovskis, noticed that in some cases even patients' exposure to and then control of their own symptoms did not produce the desired change. For example, they had taught patients to control their breathing as an alternative to hyperventilation. Salkovskis (1991) suggested that such controlled breathing may, for some patients, represent a *safety signal*. That is, that patients believed (a) that something catastrophic was about to happen and (b) that the catastrophic event had been prevented by them controlling their breathing. The patients' dysfunctional beliefs about the meaning of the bodily symptoms was thus maintained: 'If I had not sat down quietly and breathed slowly I would have had a heart attack'. The challenge for the cognitive therapist was to find ways in which people could identify the safety behaviours and then do precisely the opposite. So if 'safety' is sitting down quietly, they are encouraged to do vigorous exercise. This shift in therapy, to identify safety behaviours and challenge them, assisted the development of a number of effective treatments for a range of conditions: hypochondriasis (Warwick *et al.* 1996), social phobia (Clark and Wells 1995; see Butler and Hackmann 2004), post-traumatic stress disorder (PTSD) (Ehlers and Clark 2000; see also Foa *et al.* 1995), and generalized anxiety disorder (Borkovec and Newman 1999). Recent laboratory work has confirmed the causal status of cognitive biases (Hirsch and Mathews 2000; Mathews and MacLeod 2002) and the way in which cognitive processes have different impacts on psychopathology (Holmes and Hackmann 2004; Wegner *et al.* 1987) that are often transdiagnostic (Harvey *et al.* 2004). Cognitive treatments for anxiety have continued to make use of these laboratory findings (see Bennett-Levy *et al.* 2004; Craske and Barlowe 2001).

Psychological models and treatment of depression

In the 1950s and 1960s behavioural psychologists had concerned themselves largely with anxiety-based disorders. They had seen depression as being outside their range of relevance because the cardinal features of the disorder were not behavioural, but seemed biological (eating disturbance, sleep disturbance, inability to concentrate, loss of energy, agitation, and retardation). The behavioural aspects (loss of interest in activities) seemed secondary to the biological syndrome and the other symptoms (guilt, suicidal ideation) were more 'subjective' and therefore thought less open to behavioural treatments. However, this did not prevent some psychologists, in the late 1960s and early 1970s, from formulating depression in behavioural terms: as a low rate of response-contingent positive reinforcement (Ferster 1973; Lewinsohn 1974; for a review see Williams 1992).

A. T. Beck had been writing about a cognitive formulation of depression for some time, but little attention was paid to his theory. It seemed obvious to many psychologists that negative thinking was a predominant feature of depression, but this was seen as a *symptom* of depression rather than part of the causal pathway. Intriguingly, it was probably not Beck's writings that aroused the interest in cognitive models of depression, but Seligman's 'learned helplessness' theory (Seligman 1975), derived from his work with animals. Seligman argued that the emotional, cognitive, and behavioural components of depression were due to the perception of response-reinforcement independence that would lead to an expectation of future helplessness—a *cognitive* theory.

Seligman's model provided a coherent, plausible, and testable account of the onset of depression, but the treatment implications of the model were very sketchy: giving patients experiences that would 'reverse helplessness'. The result was that, in the mid-1970s, a cohort of experimental and clinical psychologists had a coherent cognitive theory, but no equivalent coherent therapy to accompany it. It is perhaps no surprise that the publication of Beck's successful cognitive therapy trial for clinical depression (Rush *et al.* 1977), followed soon after by the manual (Beck *et al.* 1979), should arouse immediate interest.

Beck proposed that the *cognitive* aspects of depression—negative thoughts about the self ('I'm a failure'), the world ('Everyone is against me'), and the future ('Nothing will ever improve')—were a critical aspect of both what *caused* depression in the first place, and then *maintained* the depression. Beck's approach was to encourage patients to 'catch' their negative thoughts and ideas, to write them down and treat them as hypotheses to be tested against the evidence. He worked collaboratively with patients to set up behavioural experiments to test out the validity of the negative thoughts.

In parallel with these clinical developments, laboratory research was demonstrating the validity of the underlying theory, using new information-processing paradigms to demonstrate links between severity of depressed mood and memory bias (Teasdale *et al.* 1980), and showing that interrupting negative thoughts could indeed alleviate depressed mood (Teasdale and Fennell 1982). The 1970s saw a burgeoning of interest in laboratory studies on depression, and ended with the overwhelming conclusion that depressed mood could have an enormous effect on negative thinking, interpretations, and memory; that the negative thinking of depressed people was characterized by stable and global attributions for events (Abramson *et al.* 1978); and that self-referent negative thinking was the hallmark of depression and would need to be challenged if depression was to be treated psychologically (Beck *et al.* 1979). A number of randomized controlled trials (RCTs) substantiated the claim that challenging negative thoughts could alleviate depression and prevent recurrence over at least two years (for a review of early studies see Williams 1992), and subsequent trials have borne out this optimism (DeRubeis *et al.* 2005; Hollon *et al.* 2005).

Understanding and treating the process: the third wave of behavioural cognitive psychotherapy

Most cognitive theorists assumed that the important mediator of change in therapy was changing the patients' degree of belief in their negative thinking. For example, in panic disorder somebody might believe, 'I'm about to have a heart attack'; in depression somebody might believe, 'I'm not good enough'. But evidence began to emerge from the treatment of depression that would show that the theory on which it is based was, in some respects, insufficient.

We have seen already the remarkable success of cognitive therapy for depression. Many studies have found that it is as effective as antidepressant medication in reducing depression. More importantly, the effects of cognitive therapy last. By contrast, when people are taken off their antidepressant medication the depression tend to recur within one to two years. But this is a paradox because studies have found that the *degree of belief* in dysfunctional attitudes and negative thoughts changes equally during both pharmacological and psychological treatment. The successful mediator of change in cognitive therapy cannot therefore be the change in degree of belief. DeRubeis had argued that during cognitive therapy the patient learns a raft of compensatory strategies to use when mood starts to be disturbed. But what is it that these compensatory strategies do?

Safran and Segal (1990) had suggested that the critical change process was 'decentring': the ability to observe one's thoughts and feelings as temporary, objective events in the mind, as opposed to reflections of the self and necessarily true. From this decentred perspective '*the reality of the moment is not absolute, immutable, or unalterable*' (p. 117). Similarly, John Teasdale (1988) had argued that in depression an important process that maintained the disorder was 'depression about depression'. The person interprets their mood as meaning that they are inadequate in some way. Notice how this represents a shift in perspective from the idea that it is degree of belief in thoughts that maintains a disorder to the way a person *reacts* to their own thoughts and feelings. If this was so, then either cognitive *or* behavioural treatments might be equally effective in bringing about this changed perspective (Dimidjian et al., 2006; Jacobsen and Martell 2001). The scene was set for the development of what has become known as the 'third wave' of behavioural/cognitive treatments that share the perspective (cf. Acceptance and Commitment Therapy—ACT) that change in the form or frequency of negative thoughts was not the mediator of change (see Hayes *et al.* 2005). For example, Teasdale, Segal and Williams (1995) had suggested that individual differences in vulnerability to depression would depend on differential reactivity to sad mood, differences in the tendency to react by adopting a ruminative and avoidant mode of mind (cf. Wegner *et al.* 1987). This mode of mind is toxic because it assumes thoughts to be a true reflection of reality, striving to close perceived discrepancies between actual and ideal representation of the self through the use of memory and by checking against future images of what might happen (Segal *et al.* 2002). So training depressed patients while in remission to *recognize* the activity of this mode of mind, and instead to *disengage* from it and *switch* to a more adaptive mindful mode, would reduce subsequent vulnerability to relapse. On the basis of both this theory and the clinical evidence from Kabat-Zinn's work using mindfulness training for patients with chronic pain, and Linehan's use of mindfulness as part of dialectical behaviour therapy for patients with a diagnosis of borderline personality disorder, they tested the impact of mindfulness-based cognitive therapy (MBCT) in two RCTs, showing that this approach halved the risk of relapse for patients with a history of three or more previous episodes (Ma and Teasdale 2004; Teasdale *et al.* 2000).

Concluding remarks

From the early days of behaviour therapy, theoretical and clinical developments have gone hand in hand. The maxim that theories not only have to be true, they also have to be useful, is no more borne out than in this field. We have identified three stages in the development of theory and practice: behavioural, cognitive, and the recent third-wave approaches such as MBCT and ACT. Importantly, these latter approaches do not seek to replace behavioural and cognitive approaches, but to exist alongside them, testing out which strategies are most effective and what the essential moderators and mediators of change are. This combination of investigating underlying theory and improving practice in the light of both laboratory and clinical research is the hallmark of psychological treatment development over the last fifty years, and the hundreds of thousands of patients who have benefited over the years are a testimony to its success.

References

Abramson, L. Y., Seligman, M. E., and Teasdale J. D. (1978). Learned helplessness in humans: critique and reformulation. *Journal of Abnormal Psychology* 87: 49–74.

Beck, A. T., Rush, A. J., Shaw, B. F., and Emery, G. (1979). *Cognitive therapy of depression*. New York: Guilford Press,.

Bellack and M. Hersen (series ed.), and P. Salkovskis (volume ed.) *Comprehensive clinical psychology*. vol. 6: *Adults: clinical formulation and treatment*, pp. 439–59. Oxford: Elsevier Science.

Bennett-Levy, J., Butler, G., Fennell, M. J. V., Hackmann, A., Mueller, M., and Westbrook, D. (2004). *Oxford guide to behavioural experiments in cognitive therapy*. Oxford: Oxford University Press.

Borkovec, T. D. and Newman, M. G. (1999). Worry and generalized anxiety disorder. In: A. S.

Butler, G. and Hackmann, A. (2004). Social anxiety. In: J. Bennett-Levy, G. Butler, M. J. V. Fennell, A. Hackmann, M. Mueller, and D. Westbrook (ed.) *Oxford guide to behavioural experiments in cognitive therapy*, pp. 141–160. Oxford: Oxford University Press.

Clark, D. M. (1986). A cognitive approach to panic. *Behaviour Research and Therapy* 24: 461–70.

Clark, D. M. and Wells, A. (1995). A cognitive model of social phobia. In: R. G. Heinberg, M. R. Leibowitz, D. A. Hope, and I. Schneier (ed.) *Social phobia: diagnosis, assessment and treatment*, pp 69–93. New York: Guilford Press.

Craske, M. G. and Barlow, D. H. (2001). Panic disorder and agoraphobia. In: D.H. Barlow (ed.) *Clinical handbook of psychological disorders* (3rd edn), pp. 1–64. New York: Guilford Press.

DeRubeis, R. J., Hollon, S. D., Amsterdam, J. D., *et al*. (2005). Cognitive therapy vs. medications in the treatment of moderate to severe depression. *Archives of General Psychiatry* 62: 409–16.

Dimidjian, S., Hollon, S. D., Dobson, K. S., Schmaling, K. B., and Kohlenberg, R. J. (2005). Behavioral activation, cognitive therapy, and antidepressant medication in the acute treatment of major depression. *Journal of Consulting and Clinical Psychology* 74: 658–70.

Dollard, J. and Miller, N. E. (1950). *Personality and psychotherapy*. New York: McGraw-Hill.

Ehlers, A. and Clark, D. M. (2000). A cognitive model of post-traumatic stress disorder. *Behavior Research and Therapy* 38: 319–45.

Eysenck, H. J. (1952). The effects of psychotherapy: an evaluation. *Journal of Consulting Psychology* 16: 319–24.

Ferster, C. B. (1973). A functional analysis of depression. *American Psychologist* 28: 857–70.

Foa, E. B., Hearst-Ikeda, D. E., and Perry, K. J. (1995). Evaluation of a brief cognitive-behavioral program for the prevention of chronic PTSD in recent assault victims. *Journal of Consulting and Clinical Psychology* 63: 948–55.

Hallam, R. S. and Rachman, S. (1976). Current status of aversion therapy. In: M. Hersen, R. Eisler, and P. Miller (ed.) *Progress in behavior modification*, vol. Ii, pp. 179–222. New York: Academic Press.

Harvey, A. H, Watkins, E., Mansell, W., and Shafran, R. (2004). *Cognitive behavioural processes across psychological disorders: a transdiagnostic perspective to research and treatment.* Oxford: Oxford University Press.

Hayes, S., Follette, V., and Linehan, M. M. (ed.) (2005). *Mindfulness and acceptance: the new behavior therapies.* New York: Guilford Press.

Hirsch, C. and Mathews, A. (2000). Impaired positive inferential bias in social phobia. *Journal of Abnormal Psychology* 109: 705–12.

Hodgson, R., Rachman, S., and Marks, I. M. (1972). The treatment of chronic obsessive-compulsive neurosis: follow-up and further findings. *Behaviour Research and Therapy* 10: 181–9.

Hollon, S. D., DeRubeis, R. J., Shelton, R. C., *et al.* (2005). Prevention of relapse following cognitive therapy versus medications in moderate to severe depression. *Archives of General Psychiatry* 62: 417–22.

Holmes, E. A. and Hackmann, A. (ed.) (2004). Mental imagery and memory in psychopathology. *Memory* 12(4).

Jacobsen N. and Martell, C. (2001). Behavioural activation treatment for depression: returning to contextual roots. *Clinical Psychology: Science and Practice* 8: 255–70.

Lewinsohn, P. M. (1974). A behavioural approach to depression. In: R. M. Friedman and M. M. Katz (ed.) *The psychology of depression: contemporary theory and research,* pp. 157–85. New York: Wiley.

Ma, H. and Teasdale, J. T. (2004). Mindfulness-based cognitive therapy for depression: replication and exploration of differential relapse prevention effects. *Journal of Consulting and Clinical Psychology* 72: 31–40.

Mathews, A. (1990). Why worry? The cognitive function of anxiety. *Behaviour Research and Therapy* 28: 455–68.

Mathews, A. and MacLeod, C. (2002). Induced processing biases have causal effects on anxiety. *Cognition & Emotion* 16: 331–54.

McDougall, W. (1944). *An outline of abnormal psychology.* London: Methuen.

Meichenbaum, D. H., Gilmore, J. B., and Fedoravicius, A. (1971). Group insight versus group desensitization in treating speech anxiety. *Journal of Consulting and Clinical Psychology* 36: 410–21.

Mowrer, O. H. (1939). A stimulus–response analysis of anxiety and its role as a reinforcing agent. *Psychological Review* 46: 553–65.

Ohman, A., Erixon, G., and Lofberg, I. (1975). Phobias and preparedness: phobic versus neutral pictures as conditioned stimuli for human autonomic responses. *Journal of Abnormal Psychology* 84: 41–5.

Rachman, S. (1971). *The effects of psychotherapy.* London: Pergamon Press.

Rachman, S. (1977). The conditioning theory of fear-acquisition: a critical examination. *Behaviour Research and Therapy* 15: 375–87.

Roth, A. and Fonagy, P. (2004). *What works for whom: a critical review of psychotherapy research* (2nd edn). New York: Guilford Press.

Rush, A. J., Beck, A. T., Kovacs, M., and Hollon, S. (1977). Comparative efficacy of cognitive therapy and pharmacotherapy in the treatment of depressed out-patients. *Cognitive Therapy and Research* 1: 17–37.

Safran, J. D. and Segal, Z. V. (1990). *Interpersonal process in cognitive therapy*. New York: Basic Books.

Salkovskis, P. M. (1991). The importance of behaviour in the maintenance of anxiety and panic: a cognitive account. *Behavioural Psychotherapy* 19: 6–19.

Segal, Z. V., Williams, J. M. G., and Teasdale, J. D. (2002). *Mindfulness-based cognitive therapy for depression: a new approach to preventing relapse*. New York: Guilford Press.

Seligman, M. (1975). *Helplessness: on depression, development and death*. San Francisco: Freeman.

Seligman, M. and Hager, J. (ed.) (1972). *Biological boundaries of learning*. New York: Appleton Century Crofts.

Teasdale, J. D. (1988). Cognitive vulnerability to persistent depression. *Cognition and Emotion* 2: 247–74.

Teasdale, J. D. and Fennell, M. J. V. (1982). Immediate effects on depression of cognitive therapy interventions. *Cognitive Therapy and Research* 6: 343–51.

Teasdale, J. D., Taylor, R., and Fogarty, S. J. (1980). Effects of induced elation-depression on the accessibility of memories of happy and unhappy experiences. *Behaviour Research and Therapy* 18: 339–46.

Teasdale, J. D., Segal, Z. V., and Williams, J. M. G. (1995). How does cognitive therapy prevent depressive relapse and why should attentional control (mindfulness) training help? An information processing analysis. *Behaviour Research and Therapy* 33: 25–39.

Teasdale, J. D., Segal, Z. V., Williams, J. M. G., Ridgeway, V., Lau, M., and Soulsby, J. (2000). Reducing risk of recurrence of major depression using mindfulness-based cognitive therapy. *Journal of Consulting and Clinical Psychology* 68: 615–23.

Valentine, C. W. (1946). *The psychology of early childhood* (3rd edn). London: Methuen.

Warwick, H. N. C., Clark, D. M., Cobb, A. M., and Salkovskis, P. M. (1996). A controlled trial of cognitive behavioural treatment of hypochondriasis. *British Journal of Psychiatry* 169: 189–95.

Wegner, T. M., Schneider, D. J., Carter, S. R., and White, T. L. (1987). Paradoxical effects of thought suppression. *Journal of Personality and Social Psychology* 53: 5–13.

Williams, J. M. G. (1992). *The psychological treatment of depression: a guide to the theory and practice of cognitive-behaviour therapy* (2nd edn). London: Routledge.

Wolpe, J. (1958). *Psychotherapy by reciprocal inhibition*. Stanford, CA: Stanford University Press.

Index